Books by Arthur Stratton

THE GREAT RED ISLAND

ONE MAN'S ISLAND

LORD LOVE US (a novel)

THE GREAT RED ISLAND

THE
GREAT RED
ISLAND

by Arthur Stratton

CHARLES SCRIBNER'S SONS · *New York*

PICTURE CREDITS

Documentation Française, Section Afrique et Outre-Mer: 1, 2, 3, 4, 44; French
Embassy Press and Information Division: 43; New York Public Library, Prints
Division: 42; United Nations: 46; Wide World Photos: 45; all other photos by
the author.

MAP BY SAMUEL H. BRYANT

for DIONYSUS

Contents

Contents

Illustrations

xi

List of Illustrations

THE GREAT RED ISLAND

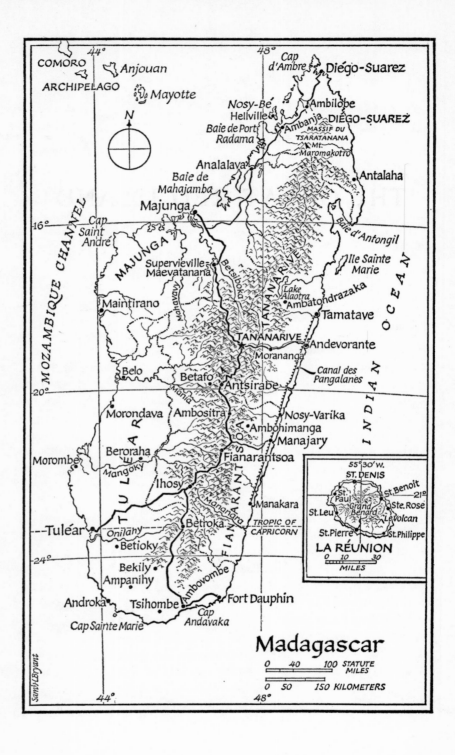

COMORO
ARCHIPELAGO
Anjouan
Mayotte

Cap
d'Ambre
Diégo-Suarez
Nosy-Bé
Hellville
Ambilobe
Ambanja
DIÉGO-SUAREZ
Baie de Port
Radama
MASSIF DU
TSARATANANA
Mt.
Maromakotro
Analalava
Antalaha
Baie de
Mahajamba
Majunga

16°
Cap
Saint
André
MAJUNGA
Supervieville
Maevatanana
Baie
d'Antongil
Ile Sainte
Marie
TANANARIVE
Lake
Alaotra
Ambatondrazaka
Maintirano
Tamatave
TANANARIVE
Andevorante
Morananga
Canal des
Pangalanes
Belo
Betafo
Antsirabe
20°
Morondava
Ambositra
Nosy-Varika
Ambohimanga
Manajary
Beroraha
Fianarantsoa
Morombe
Ihosy
Manakara
Betroka
TROPIC OF
CAPRICORN
Tuléar
Onilahy
Betioky
24°
Bekily
Ampanihy
Androka
Tsihombe
Fort Dauphin
Cap Sainte Marie
Cap
Andavaka

MOZAMBIQUE CHANNEL

INDIAN OCEAN

TULÉAR

FIANARANTSOA

Besiboka

Mahavavy

Mania

Mangoky

Mananara

Ambovombe

55°30'W.
ST. DENIS
St.
Paul
St. Benoit
Ste. Rose
St. Leu
Grand
Bénard
Le Volcan
St. Pierre
St. Philippe
LA RÉUNION
0   10   30
MILES

21°

Madagascar

0   40   100 STATUTE
MILES
0   50   150 KILOMETERS

Sam L. Bryant

Antalaha: In Vanilla I

THE BEAN

MADAGASCAR, a great island of red lateritic soil, lies in the blue water of the Indian Ocean across the Mozambique Channel from southeast Africa, of which it once was part. Geologists inform us that the mountainous independent island, now called the Malagasy Republic, is still moving a fraction of an inch a year towards the other Polynesian islands out to sea. If so, since the beginning, Madagascar has traveled 250 miles, wherever it is bound.

From the air, this great land fragment looks like an experimental continent undertaken and then abandoned before it took final shape. Light-struck, raw-surfaced, Madagascar gives the bleak effect of failure. Even so, its unfinished immensity makes clear what the mature mind of the Creator, having learned in trial and error what dry land should be, brought about when the time was ripe. Then, in an outpouring of genius, the soil and the rocks, the rivers, the lakes, the hills and the mountains, the plains, the green fields, and the forests of the earth formed as we know them in our own climates.

Indeed, if Madagascar's endless mile after mile of empty wastes look like a first attempt to create a land fit to live in, so in fact it is. The Malagasy rocks and sands are among the oldest under the sun. The island is a fragment of Gondwana, a great dry land mass, the first to rise above the surface of the waters covering the cooling and solidifying planet, the Earth. Gondwana broke up; bits of it are embedded in the Deccan, Australia, Africa below the bulge, northern South America,

1

Antarctica, and a scattering of archipelagoes and South Sea Islands. In the Paleozoic and Mesozoic eras, the uneasy surface of the crusting globe did not lie still; tides rushed in the ocean troughs; mountain chains arose; volcanoes erupted; the earth quaked. Now Western Europe, it is said, and France in particular, has the best climate in the world for human life; the good Lord knows the land is beautiful. But something went wrong with Madagascar, the vitality leached out of it. The rocks and the lateritic subsoil never grew a skin of loam.

Few things rooted there—or, rather, a collection of endemic oddities grew up and took on outrageous shapes, like fans, like plumes, like lace, like branching coral growths, like swords; others swelled up and bloated as though diseased; others put out green fur instead of leaves to hide their long, sharp thorns. The first explorers swore they found a vegetable octopus, tentacled and muscular, a bloodthirsty constrictor, a hungry tree rooted in the xerophytic, xenophobic forests, a man-eater. Likewise, the mushrooms of Madagascar are very strange.

It is no wonder that the animals then abandoned the mainstream of development to specialize themselves in peculiar attributes. A queer bird was the aepyornis, the largest of the flightless struthious birds—of all birds, for that matter, ratite or not. It laid an egg as big as a professional football, bigger—two-and-a-half-gallon size. The last clutch hatched perhaps a thousand years ago. The brood grew until the chick was taller than a man; an adult stood up eight to ten feet tall.

By then mankind had found this once desert island, first the mysterious Vazimba, who were, perhaps, black, possibly Pygmies, and, probably, from Africa; much later, Negroes crossed the Mozambique Channel, bringing with them malaria, an African disease, in their black blood. But in between arrived the Malagasy ancestors, immigrants forced out of Polynesia; they brought their culture with them, and they came by chance, carried in their seaworthy out-rigger canoes along the ocean currents, their sails filled by the prevailing winds, to land on empty shores only two or three thousand years ago. The east coast, in truth, is green with rain forests, and under the escarpment, the littoral is fertile.

Up in the highlands where the Vazimba and the aepyornis lived, the climate changed, perhaps as the forests were burnt down and the swamps dried up. And so, having lived too long set in their ways,

2

neither the giant birds nor the Pygmies could bring themselves to change their nature; both are extinct. A drumstick would have fed a tribe—and perhaps did.

Of lemurs, Madagascar has almost the monopoly; this charming primate family branched off the main stem of the tree too soon—before the monkeys, before the apes, before the *Hominidae.* They had the island to themselves, and peacefully, they made a dead end of it. The giant among them (small man-sized) is now extinct; the others among the 39 varieties and species are doomed to be preserved in reservations, in museums, and in foreign zoos.

Archeologists and anthropologists have yet to come upon the traces of any sort of prehistoric man in Madagascar, although across in Africa lie troves of chipped and polished bones and stones made to fit the early hand of man. Yet no artifact, no painted cave, no tooth, no jawbone of any sort of human ancestor has come to light in Madagascar in modern times. The modern times are French.

On May Day, in 1958, the fifty thousand, more or less, French men, women and children then resident in Madagascar—the colonials, the businessmen, the functionaries, the servicemen, and the *évolués* and the *assimilés,* who are the Malagasy, or the Chinese or the Indians, of Madagascar sufficiently cultivated and civilized in the French manner to be given French citizenship by French authorities—made it worthwhile for the florists of Tananarive, the Malagasy capital, with the assistance of Air France and the air arm of the Messageries Maritimes, TAI, both of which great private companies are underwritten and partly owned by the French government of France, to fly down from Paris tubs full of fresh lily-of-the-valley, roots and all, lifted from the black loam of the vernal woods and spring gardens of France— 5,460 air miles and 24 hours elapsed time away (by Super-Constellation, half that time by Caravelle)—to sell in Madagascar in the Austral fall, at 250 francs CFA (*Colonies françaises africaines*), or at 500 old French francs (5 new), the *brin*—and that word means the root, the tender leaves, the stem, the opened white flower bells, and the unopened green buds, perhaps a dozen blooms in all—of the fragrant, delicate, heart-stirring muguet that will not grow in Madagascar, not in the cool highlands, nor in the hot coastal lowlands, neither out of doors nor in fresh greenhouses.

The Great Red Island

The CFA franc then currency in Madagascar was misnamed from the start (in 1948), for the great offshore African island with its Polynesian culture was by then no longer a French colony; and ten years later, on the first of May, 1958, the island had but eighteen more days in its half-life as a territory of Overseas France. When the lily-of-the-valley was offered for sale, the CFA franc was worth 210 to the American dollar. Thus the individual, uprooted plant cost $1.19. It is the habit of the French, who cannot conceive of a way of life different from their own, to present one another with a nosegay of muguet on the first of May, for good luck. Good luck is something the French in Madagascar have never had, nor, except possibly in the eight years from 1897 to 1905, under General Governor-General Joseph Gallieni, good management. Madagascar is the fourth largest of the islands of the world (after Greenland, New Guinea, and Borneo).

The chances are that few Americans will ever go to Madagascar, but their old clothes may well make the trip. Given to charity, sold at church bazaars, the cast-off summer suits and dresses are sold to be steamed, baled, and sent to Mr. Bernard Spira, of Tananarive, the importer and wholesaler, a displaced person. They then are distributed to be sold in many-colored piles in the open markets of the island, nine hundred and ninety-nine miles long, where the clothes, no matter what their style, are bargains. But although they keep an untold number of the five and a half million Malayo-Polynesian-Melanesian-African Malagasy men and women warm and decent at a price considerably less than the cost of a suit-length or a dress-length of imported French dry goods, this charity *friperie* does great disservice to the brown-skinned people—especially to the girls of sixteen or so, once famous for the beauty of their South Sea Island breasts. The Malagasy of the eighteen tribes, in particular, the wild ones, are a great deal handsomer when they go naked, or nearly so. The women all used to wear sarongs, the men wore loincloths. Both wore the *lamba*, a kind of shawl—it served as blanket and as shroud—woven of wild silk or cotton. Today the *lamba* is a symbol of independence.

On my way to Madagascar, decently clothed in drip-dry, I fastened my seat belt well in advance of my descent, via Air France, to land. Some like to fly, not I. Psychologists belatedly inform us that flying is by no means the ideal means of travel for statesmen, diplomats, and

4

high negotiants. It is, in fact, a shock to the human nervous system. The hurtled voyager cannot keep up with himself in the air. He needs time and peace to pull himself together at the end of the flight. I am glad for this scientific, authoritative, dispassionate observation from the psychologists, but, as for me, I have known it all along.

As usual, I have not thought it wise to speak up—because I thought it was my fault. I know that I am a good traveler; I do not get seasick nor airsick. I always get my visas stamped into my passport, I get my shots, I work out my itinerary, and I buy my tickets. I arrange my letters of credit and I carry the right, restricted sums of foreign currencies, and I have taught myself how to pack my bags. Well beforehand, I check my flight, and always show up early at the airport to go through the formalities. Yet, invariably, once I've walked, but not run, to climb the ramp to bend my head to step into the hands of God and His angelic hostesses, and, having belted myself in, once airborne, I find that I have done it again—left an item of my luggage behind me on the ground. It is my right mind.

It catches up with me after a slight delay of twenty-four—or at most forty-eight—hours. But in the meantime in the air, lacking the equipment for thought, I ought not to try to talk, for I am struck dumb. I know so, yet sometimes I cannot help myself. In common courtesy, I am made to respond. And that is how I got into vanilla.

Just before take-off from Orly, a New York export-import merchant "in vanilla," as he said, a man of my own age, sat down next to me in the aisle seat. He talked, I recall, all the way to Madagascar—for twenty-two flying hours, not counting the one on the ground in Khartum, and the other in Nairobi. And so, as we unbuckled our seat belts in Madagascar at the end of the flight, throughout which, speechless and helpless, I had been a truly captive audience, I heard him tell me that I had a rare gift—I was a good listener—and that he had enjoyed my conversation. Then he added that he was sorry we could not continue it. He regretted that we parted company in Tànanarive. Therefore, I cannot see why he was taken aback when I heard myself saying that I'd be delighted to accompany him on his business trip into the vanilla country of Antalaha down on the hot and humid northeast shore. But even he was silent when, at 4:30 in the dark morning of the next day, we left on the local flight of Air Mad, which is the short name for the island airline officially called Air Madagascar, and such is its nature.

A great deal more than I had thought possible of the New York merchant's conversation had sunk in en route. (And by the way, as in his nature he was a merchant, let Merchant serve as his name. He was, in life, a complex human being, compounded of much more good than ill, both in principle and in effect—a distinguished and a successful man, a thoughtful and a responsible American—according to his name and his nature, but in the pages of this book, let him be faceless.) It was his contention that the Malagasy vanilla industry, the major supplier of the commodity to the world, was in peril; it needed a thorough reorganization from the ground up to the extract. Vanilla is one of the island's best cash crops, and it is bought and sold in Yankee dollars. For years, Mr. Merchant's company had imported the cured bean, a perishable, sophisticated seed pod, bought and sold, sold and bought, in a wildly speculative market, and hell to handle, not only because the graded commodity can go bad in the holds of the ships on the way to the consumer, or overnight upon arrival unpacked in the New York warehouses, but also because no merchant, baker, or candy-maker can count its cost at any time, nor on the date of delivery. Mr. Merchant's plan to reorganize vanilla was simplicity itself, but it called for revolutionary changes. He wanted to stabilize and standardize the commodity by means of sound business practices. It was a matter of bringing common sense to the market. First he planned to organize the growers, the curers, and the carriers, the packers, the merchants, the handlers, the bankers, and the brokers in a cooperative enterprise, so that they work together for their mutual benefit; next he hoped to increase the annual crop, then fixed at about 500 tons, by means of the basic law of supply and demand, so to tie it to the birth rate of the States. The children of America could easily absorb a crop of 5,000 tons a year. Thus a vanilla cooperative in Antalaha would benefit not only the Malagasy economy, but also, by extension, the whole world of free enterprise.

Once he had convinced the local men in vanilla, Mr. Merchant planned to return to New York, there to "service the commodity" sent him by the cooperative. He would introduce modern merchandizing techniques, and, by means of good public relations, project a healthy image of the wholesome trade. Today vanilla is bought and sold in a market not unlike a battlefield of total warfare, where ulcers, heart-attacks, and strokes are ordinary wounds. Vanilla is sold and bought in a heavy atmosphere of anger and uncertainty; there is no good will or good faith apparent. To service the commodity would be to restore peace across the board between Antalaha and New York, to bring order out of chaos.

Malagasy vanilla is called Bourbon vanilla because the original commercial crop of cured seed pods from the *Vanilla planifolia* vines was grown in the early nineteenth century, on the neighboring island of Réunion. The plant is a climbing terrestrial orchid native to Mexico. Réunion, short for La Réunion des Patriotes, used to be called the Ile de Bourbon. This once desert island of the Mascarenes has been a French possession since the seventeenth century; it used to be a way station on the route to India in Cardinal Richelieu's and Colbert's mercantile French Empire, in the days of Louis XIV. The French Revolution dethroned the Bourbon king, and changed the island's name to Réunion; the Restoration, following Napoleon's downfall, restored the Bourbons and the island's name. The Revolution of 1848 changed it back again—and Réunion it has remained until today—an overseas department of the French Fifth Republic.

The Aztecs of undiscovered Mexico first cured the natural vanilla bean. I cannot imagine how they stumbled on the process. They used the flavoring in chocolate—another of the "cruel" Aztecs' contributions to a world of mild delights. The cultivated, not to say overcivilized, discovery of artificial fecundation was made in the experimental garden of a French museum, in Paris (according to one story). Three parent vines of Mexican *Vanilla planifolia* orchids in the eighteenth century were brought from the New World and planted under glass in the then Jardin du Roi by some forgotten Frenchman with an inquiring, collector's mind; they survived until the hard winter of 1944–45, when, after liberation, none of the curators could find fuel to heat their scientific hothouses. Vanilla orchids cannot survive a chill of 50° Fahrenheit.

But back in 1820 (or perhaps it was 1837), a young French botanist named Charles Moreau, in Mexico near Vera Cruz, watched a melipoma bee at work, and went back to Paris to experiment in the gardens of the Museum of Natural History. He hit upon the thorn, and thus became the father of vanilla as a commodity in commerce. Or, if Moreau did not, then, according to another story, Joseph, a Malagasy slave, the property of Mr. Edmond Albius, a planter of Réunion (then again called Bourbon), did the trick. Albius had imported cuttings from the three vines in the Paris museum for his experimental garden of rich, well watered, well drained volcanic soil. It is known that in 1841, Albius had his slave Joseph demonstrate the hand-pollination of the tricky orchid to a group of other Créole plantation owners. So Bourbon vanilla spread from Réunion to Madagascar in the 1880s, and to Tahiti, to the Antilles, and back to Mexico.

Before the First World War and the 1929 Depression, most of the vanilla of Antalaha was produced on great plantations owned by French or Créole colonists, and worked by indentured Malagasy hands supplied on contract by the administration of the island. The French abolished slavery in 1896—it was one of their first acts after their conquest of Madagascar. But to raise taxes, they were forced to adapt and continue the system of forced labor used by the nineteenth-century kings and queens of Madagascar. Thus the vanilla workers were drafted or conscripted, as for military service; good or bad, the system worked. At that time, Madagascar produced 80 per cent of the world supply— perhaps a thousand tons. Today the crop is half the amount.

But as Pax Britannica and the Colonial system broke up, so did the great and stable plantations. Today 90 per cent of the reduced commodity is grown on small family holdings of the Betsimisaraka tribal people of Madagascar. Pronounced "Bay-tsee-mee-shark," and meaning "the Inseparable Many," their land includes Antalaha, Tamatave, and the northeast shores and slopes of the escarpment. The second in number of the eighteen Malagasy tribes, there are about 775,000 Betsimisaraka. They are melanic people, a mixture of Polynesian and Negro bloods.

To grow, harvest, cure, manipulate, and pack a kilogram of vanilla for the market costs (or did in 1958) 810 francs CFA. I can, if I must, analyze this figure, and account for it, franc by franc, but what is the use? Let it stand, if only as an arbitrary point of departure. Nor shall I transpose the CFA francs into U.S.A. dollars, for the conversion involves shifting rates of exchange, variable bank rates, uncertain climatic conditions, and at least two black markets, the one of Paris and the other of Hong Kong. The point is that when this same kilogram of vanilla beans is sold for 3,500 francs CFA, the man who then owns, and thus sells, the commodity appears to make a profit, roughly, of some 320 per cent. That seems to be an excessive profit even in the old-fashioned and classic Colonial-Imperial form of capitalistic economy—in fact, it seems to be almost a proof of Karl Marx's and Lenin's contentions. Yet the fact of the matter is not so. In the first place, vanilla prices are never fixed; they fluctuate enormously, sometimes dipping to below cost price. Then, there are other factors to consider. Out of the profit, the planter or the merchant must subtract the money to pay off the banker, who has advanced the money to finance the seasonal "campaign"—the word used to denote the work and the time needed to bring the vanilla bean from the flowering through the growing, harvesting, curing, and selling periods, and even longer, for it must include the care of the plants and the cultivation of the soil during the period of rest between the picking of the beans in July, and the opening of the first bloom in September.

The planter-merchant must likewise pay the interest on the banker's loan. The rate of interest is not fixed by any sort of law regulation. Although Madagascar is the fourth largest of the world's islands, it is a small human community. Business there is conducted on highly personal and individual lines. Therefore a banker—and he is a Frenchman whose bank is a branch of, or closely connected with, one of the French banks of France—perhaps working on the theory that the punishment should fit the criminal, if not the expected crime, fixes his rate of interest on the loan according to the known character of the borrower (or worse, perhaps according to the amount of his cut, or investment, or bribe). Thus the rate of interest varies, in the same community for the same season's campaign, from 5 to 8 per cent per year, or even as high as 1 per cent per month.

Until this payment has been made, the bankers can direct and control all sales at any time throughout the growing or the curing periods, and, at the end of the harvest of one crop, they can refuse to finance the next campaign unless they are pleased with the way that the borrower has handled the sales of the previous season's cured beans. Thus the overlapping seasons allow the bankers to pile up the financing as in a vanilla-flavored layer cake.

And, because it would be foolish of him to sell his beans as soon as they are cured, when the market is at its lowest, he must store them until the price goes up, which is to say as long as he can hold out—from January until July, if he has strong nerves, a tight warehouse, great courage, good luck, and cooperative bankers—and if he has cured his beans in the sun.

The cost of labor in Madagascar still is cheap. In 1958, the legal rate was 21 francs CFA an hour for a forty-hour week. However, by law, the planter was called upon to supply his hands with free medical attention, including the salary and expenses of a resident doctor if the plantation was large enough and far enough removed from any other hospital or medical officer of the government health service.

Even so, the planter runs an even greater risk in labor relations—one that can make or break him if a crisis takes place in the fecundating or harvest seasons. Despite the fact that most of the Malagasy are what in America we would call unemployed, or out of work, there is no pool of labor in the island, and in Antalaha, workers are always in short supply. Thus the planter must know how to please his workmen and their families. He must know how to encourage them, instruct them, and convince them of the need to work for a living so to keep them on the job during the essential periods of the vanilla campaign and cure.

The Betsimisaraka tribal men and women are very free men and women, indeed. The Malagasy laborer has none of his European or American counterpart's inducements to work for fixed wages during certain hours of the day or the night, and regular days of the week, throughout the year—not even with a paid holiday in summer. The Malagasy's needs are simple and his wants are easily satisfied. He is not concerned with climbing any sort of social, spiritual, or economic ladder to get within reach of any real or illusory goal on top. His concept of success does not goad him along to "improve" himself, to keep up with the Joneses, or to buy himself some status symbols like a Cadillac or a mink coat. In short, most of the Malagasy see no virtue in work as such. They have no drive to occupy their minds or their hands; they like to do nothing serious at all; they have no sort of compulsion to steady occupation; they do not live from payday to payday. A Malagasy man and his family can get by very happily with highly irregular working hours amounting to no more than three or four wage-earning months of the year. The rest of the time they spend in resting up after enjoying themselves. Thus there is a chronic labor shortage in Madagascar the while there is also a chronic unemployment. And also thus, despite the apparently outrageously high percentage of profit in vanilla, the industry is falling off, the volume of trade is decreasing, and the quantity and quality of the unserviced commodity is diminishing and declining, the while the volume of the demand increases in direct proportion with the world's increasing vital statistics.

The Malagasy don't care. It seems then that the "underprivileged" people of this "undeveloped" island—here the quotation marks apply, for the words do not necessarily reflect the Malagasy laborer's attitudes —do not want to take advantage of the vanilla industry in order to bring in the privileges of intense economic development. It may be that they do not understand modern economics. It is certain that the Malagasy men and women who work the vanilla plantations, who turn the soil, plant the vines, pollinate the orchids, tend the brooms as the seed pods ripen, harvest the beans, and then cure them, are not consumers of their product. Vanilla is to them a needless and a meaningless commodity. Their work, as such, does not make sense to them in terms of any immediate need. They do not use the vanilla they supply to the world, which is not their world at all. Candy, ice cream, and cake make up no part of their daily or holiday diet. They never entertain at birthday parties for themselves or their children. Indeed, most of them, including the first elected President of the Malagasy Republic, do not know the date of their birth, neither the day nor the month nor the year. Our time is not their time. And their most efficient labor-saving device is not a washing machine, nor a vacuum cleaner, nor a power lawn-mower, nor a suburban ranch wagon. It is not to work at all. When a backwoods Betsimisaraka tribesman wants to save his labor, he quits work and he lies down. So he enjoys life. It is his life.

Antalaha: In Vanilla II

THE FRENCH

ON our way in the early morning flying into the dawn, the Air Mad plane landed on, and took off from, several open fields—at Tamatave, the island's chief port, on the clove island of Sainte-Marie, at Maroant-setra in the Bay of Antongil (the annual rainfall there is like the Flood itself). At last we got ourselves ready for the descent upon Antalaha (pronounced "Ahnt-ta-la," I forget what it means). Half of the seats of the DC-3 had been removed to make room for roped and crated cargo: a Frigidaire, tires, spare parts—springs, a rear axle, a radiator; boxes of rapidly wilting lettuces and fresh vegetables from the highlands (they will not grow in the heat of the coast); cans of film for the local cinemas. Some of the freight was alive; an insecurely covered basket of fresh crabs had overturned at one point in an air pocket; we all scrambled to help round them up as they scuttled, claws uplifted, underfoot and underseat. Some of the passengers had on wash-and-wear, others were nearly naked.

Unannounced but not unobserved (most of the small airfields have no radios), we came in for a landing on what seemed to be a green meadow beside a glittering lagoon. The pilot set us down very well indeed alongside the skeletal fuselage of a cannibalized Junker. Our plane taxied to a standstill by a corrugated iron shed, in front of which were parked two or three random automobiles and trucks. As we got out into the hot, thick, wet air, I felt the sweat break out all over me and trickle down my grooves and hollows. My drip-dry clothes could not absorb my effluence. So it must feel to be eroded, I thought as Mr. Merchant and I stepped out of the sun into the shade of the sheltering wing.

From the vari-colored crowd of three or four dozen men and women waiting against a background of thick green vegetation, a white man of our age, perhaps a bit older, detached himself and came to shake our hands. Thin, erect, but not so tall as we, dressed in what certainly had been fresh khaki cotton shirt and slacks an hour earlier that morning, he was sweat-stained, but obviously used to it. And as clearly, he was a Frenchman in authority. His face, informed with the intelligence peculiar to the French, was shaped and marked by the mind at work in the matter of flesh. He looked at us and he saw us. He smiled and spoke the formulas—in good English—that the French long ago worked out in civil courtesy. This was a cultivated man. He was our host, Mr. Merchant's associate in vanilla, who had flown down from Tananarive ahead of us in his own private airplane. Merchant's insurance policy prevented him from taking any but a scheduled flight. That was all right with me.

But his associate used his own plane as readily as he drove his automobile, and in greater comfort, as I soon found out. This Frenchman was a pioneer, and that is to say he was himself an anachronism, an obsolescent form of human life on earth. The word "pioneer" has in its meaning both a fixed time and a limited place. The noun is defined in a serviceable dictionary as "one of those who first enter or settle a region, thus opening it for occupation and development by others," and as "a plant or animal which successfully invades and becomes established in a bare area." A pioneer, then, can have a life-span of but a single generation in his prime; he makes place and gives way to his own get—who are not pioneers.

This man, in his sixties, was a trail blazer, and for convenience I shall call him Blaze-Trail, or just Mr. Blaze. His own name is a compound of aristocratic geography linked by particules. That is as it should be, for he was born on the neighboring Indian Ocean island of Mauritius, of a French Créole father and a French mother from France. Among his paternal ancestors were nobles found guilty of heredity, and, indeed, of environment, at the beginning of the French Revolution; these lucky few were exiled, as to a devil's island, from France;

thus they escaped the Terror and the guillotine. They kept their heads and they did their best to preserve their way of life.

All islands, and especially the once-desert islands, faraway places, seem to be dangerous natural habitats; they tend to isolate the forms of life that they support. So René Blaze at sixty-five, after a lifetime of pioneering, found himself to be a sort of living fossil, at home only in the past. With his characteristic critical French mind, he recognized the fact. There can be little comfort in the knowledge. This distinguished man had voluntarily left Mauritius, the British Crown Colony since the Napoleonic Wars and the Congress of Vienna, formerly the biggest and the best of the French Mascarenes, and he had gone to settle Madagascar, but time encircled him. Perhaps he served his purpose.

Once the dodo had Mauritius to itself before Mauritius had a name (it was named after a seventeenth-century Dutch stadholder), and before the *Didus ineptus,* a silly, flightless, and extinct bird of the pigeon family, as big as a goose but inedible, was reclassified in human knowledge as *Raphus cucullatus,* and written off. After the dodo, the pure-white, aristocratic French Créoles owned the island (the Indians now are taking over from them); they kept themselves to themselves, and preserved themselves in sugar—they are very rich. Ignoring the changes of the outside world, they achieved stability. But Mr. Blaze rejected both dodo and Créole extinction; he settled in Madagascar, in the waters around which enormous island swims a stupendous fish, free of time.

The steel-blue coelacanth is armored in rough and heavy scales, yet he is flexible enough to have survived 60- or 75,000,000 years, at which date latter-day ichthyologists wrote him off in their books. But unaware of scientific knowledge, and apparently even of natural laws, the formidable, gat-toothed coelacanth—six feet long, 150 pounds in weight —went on swimming in ignorance among coral reefs. Refound alive in 1938, the coelacanth, like man himself, is the only one surviving member of his own order (the *Hominidae,* for one, the *Latimeriidae* for the other). "Of all living creatures," notes the *Encyclopaedia Britannica* of 1960, "the coelacanth has lived the longest with the least change of form." (Pronounce it "sell-a-canth.") It is to be said of and for scientists that they like to be proved wrong.

And I should like to think that this incredible fish has been preserved in Davy Jones's locker, like the sperm of selected bulls and men kept in a deep freeze, for future generations, so that, if we go on with our nuclear fissioning, evolution can go back, if need be, to start the life cycle of the world once again, as it was in the beginning—say, 350,000,000 years ago, as best we know.

At that calculated time, the coelacanth's remote ancestors—and they were ours, too—the rhipidistians, somewhat similar fish (but with the difference that they *are* extinct, except for what each one of us retains of them in our anatomy), emerged from the seawater, and walked or crawled through the salt marshes out onto the stony earth. These joint progenitors were the original pioneers, they blazed the trail for all the existing vertebrate armies of the land, and of the air, and of the sea. They laid down our lives for us, and died.

The rhipidistians were revolutionaries, they invented the backbone and they grew skeletons. To be sure, their bones were soft and mostly cartilaginous, but they served. Their next step was to turn four of their appropriate fins into legs. As legs go, they were rudimentary—not very good legs if we can judge from their own fossils, and from their closest surviving kin, the coelacanths. On these legs, they walked out of the water to invade a new world, a vegetable and a mineral kingdom— save, it may be, for some viruses, amoebae, worms, and bugs. They made way for the reptiles, the birds, the mammals, possibly for the angels, and certainly for the coelacanth, although he was written off before his time.

Then in 1938, unaware of what it was doing, a coelacanth swam into the net of a South African trawler working the mouth of the Chalumna River. When the fishermen hauled it on deck, they saw they had caught something strange, not good to eat. (In fact, unknown to science, the islanders of Anjouan in the Comoro Archipelago have been catching and eating coelacanths for, I suppose, two or three thousand years—before which time there were no Comorians. I have not tried this ancient, oily flesh, but I am told, on the good authority of the French scientists of the rue Buffon, in Paris, that it must taste like soap.) The South African trawlers did not toss the trash fish overboard, but, as per agreement, turned their curious find over to Miss Marjorie Courtenay-Latimer, librarian and curator of the East African

Museum, of East London. She called in Professor J. L. B. Smith, an ichthyologist, who, in amazement and delight, identified the decomposing prize, and named it *Latimeria chalumna*, of the *Latimeriidae*. The curator and the professor both seem to be of English descent.

I had my first look at a coelacanth, the living being that most closely resembles our common ancestor, gutted and pickled, floating in a glass tank of preservative in Tananarive; and the coelacanth, in effect, looked out at me. Perhaps I saw myself mirrored in the smelly tank; if so, this was not the old Adam that I have been led to believe I knew. At that, we are, at best, but remote and collateral cousins. The coelacanth decided 290,000,000 years ago, in round numbers, that it did not like it there on earth, and so it went, slipping and sliding, back where it came from, back into deep water, leaving the pioneering rhipidistian to carry evolution on its back—or in its backbone.

So Mr. Blaze, another pioneer, left Mauritius, but never to return. First he went to France. Older than the twentieth century, he was 18 in 1914. So he joined the French Army, and then the French Air Force; he survived. Demobilized, he struck out for Madagascar.

Perhaps because of his war record of his good connections, he got a place in one of the great French Colonial commercial monopolies, such as the Compagnie Lyonnaise de Madagascar, or the Compagnie Marseillaise, or the Compagnie Bordelaise, or the Compagnie Havraise, all equally and likewise de Madagascar, but with headquarters in the French cities that their names incorporate. They are owned partly by private investors in France and in Madagascar, and partly by banks and holding companies—which may, in turn, be partly owned by the French government, which certainly guarantees and supports their activities, and them. Thus by regulating, directing, controlling, and warranting these Malagasy monopolies, the French government has had an almost lethal effect upon free enterprise in the island. In such conditions, perhaps stagnation was inevitable, given the fact that the French authorities passed laws to exclude all foreign competition from the colony—in order to make the island self-supporting in the empire. Under state protection and regulation, the businessmen in the monopolies became prisoners of the state.

Yet the system worked; the Lyonnaise, the Marseillaise, et cetera, still dominate the island's business and commercial life. They are into everything. From the Colonial ministry they got huge land grants to develop plantations of coffee, tobacco, rice, vanilla, sisal, sugar cane, cotton, and other crops to sell to France. They got land concessions as pasture for herds of cattle as part of the attempt to establish a meat packing and canning industry, and for hides. Thus Madagascar provided *"singe"*—monkey meat—which is what the *poilus* called canned corned beef in two world wars. (In fact, the first time I ever heard of Madagascar, I read the name on a can of *singe* at Bir Hakim, in Libya, in May of 1942. The Free French from Madagascar there described their island to me. Somehow I got the picture of an endless highland plain of tall grass through which great herds of humped and lyre-horned cattle stampeded north, and then stampeded south, under a luminous, clear blue sky. At that, I found the reality not to be far off the fantasy—except for the stampedes.) However, the meat packing business has not prospered; the Malagasy business priced itself out of existence, after the last war. Shipping costs, labor costs, the world's far distant markets, the cost of the imported cans and the machinery mounted up to put an end to it. Zebu beef is not high grade, not very good to eat, except for the filet mignon. Only the sharks that gathered to feed on the offal thrown into the sea beside the last factory miss the industry; and they got over it.

The big monopolies got the mineral rights to exploit the subsoil of their concessions. Their surveys show that Madagascar has some of almost all the minerals, but not enough for profitable exploitation. There are samples, but few loads or deposits of great size. The list is long: gold (but not silver), iron, nickel, beryllium, graphite, mica, asbestos, coal (of poor quality), and radioactive ores, quantities of semi-precious stones—garnet, tourmaline, aquamarine, pink beryl, amethyst, citrine, jasper, agate, and the finest piezo-electric quartz crystals in the world; but no diamonds, no emeralds, no sapphires, no rubies—although there are quantities of corundum. There are lakes of pitch; there may be petroleum, but nothing like the oil of the Sahara.

The Lyonnaise, the Marseillaise—all the monopolies make money, or have in the past. It is hard to tell how much; they do not make statistics public. At their headquarters in the various cities of France, they do not welcome inquiries from strangers. In the field, the various exclusive rights and grants to import finished goods from France, and to export raw materials to France, are equally apportioned among them; they get along very well together, working along parallel lines in well worn ruts. To be sure, some customers prefer Vittel to Vichy; therefore, there is a certain mild pursuit of customers for bottled water from the French mineral springs. But little new blood coursed through the hardening arteries of trade.

I do not know why René Blaze left his secure employment in the monopoly early in the 1920s to strike out for himself. To do so, he literally had to go about his business on foot, walking the paths from town to town; there were no roads. The Malagasy never got around to inventing the wheel in principle or on vehicles. Sometimes he sat in that uncomfortable chair attached to poles shouldered by two or four or eight native porters. The Malagasy version is called the *filanzana*, and it is still in use in the remote back woods. Mr. Blaze told me that he used to enjoy the company of his porters. As he made his journeys across the arid south, the Mahafaly or the Antandröy tribesmen used to bring him up to date on all the news and gossip. They carried on a continuous conversation with the man they carried in the chair in a sort of running commentary of the features of the landscape and the people—in particular on the qualities of the girls. And the girls were always beautiful and naked then, and smiling, amiable, sharp of tongue, and quick of wit. Old or young, or middle-aged, they all enjoyed a joke.

The Malagasy are great walkers; they don't think twice about setting out to hike from one end of the huge island to the other. They cover ground at a steady pace, packing down the paths with the hard soles of their bare feet. Mr. Blaze dealt in hides, zebu and crocodile; to get from town to town, once he knew his territory, he bought a bicycle, and later a motorcycle. To be sure, the going was rough, and the wheels frightened the people and their animals. As he told me about it, he put his hand to his thick hair—one evening as he approached a village, a watchdog had sprung to attack the wheeled invader. Blaze had flown over the handlebars onto his head. Dogs were introduced to Madagascar long ago.

From his spill, Blaze picked himself up and went off to buy his first airplane. By then he had an automobile, indeed, a pleasure car limited to city streets or an excursion in the dry season on the gravel roads of the highlands. In the early 1930s, a small airplane was the most practical means of covering the great island; it still is. Although he had learned to fly the hard way in the First World War in France, Madagascar enlarged his experience. The rolling high pastures are easy to take off from and to come down onto, but in the desert south all that grows bears thorns as hard as nails, and sharper, and in the western wastelands termites build nests taller than a man and harder than concrete. Among these obstacles, Blaze learned to make running repairs on his downed airplane with shoelaces and strips of cloth torn from his shirt.

In 1958, a long way from Wichita, he sold the four-seater model for about $10,000; it had a range of 800 flying hours. Then his trained mechanics replaced the original engine with the spare (included in the purchase price), and sent the old one off to be overhauled in Kansas. To be sure, Blaze owned and operated a garage and workshop to sell spare parts and replacements, and to service and repair the airplanes, the heavy equipment, and the cars he sold. So, after he returned to Madagascar from his war years in Canada and the United States, he built up a big business, American style.

He brought back with him a powerful intangible asset—the concept of American teamwork, something the individual, independent French have never bothered to put to use. Back in business with his grown sons and other young French and Créole men, he taught them to work together for the general good. Each was assigned to handle and service a separate commodity—one, say, had the Caterpillar account, another Chevrolet trucks. But they all worked together as a team—the Trail-Blazers. He was captain, he was coach, he was the boss.

In 1958, the Blaze company controlled or supplied a quarter of the Malagasy market in automobiles, trucks, tractors, bulldozers, and agricultural machinery. Thus Blaze contributed one quarter of the figures recorded in the *United Nations Statistical Yearbook 1958*. In 1957, 15,000 passenger cars and 15,600 commercial vehicles drove over the 20,000 miles of highway in Madagascar, of which 870 miles then were asphalted, and about 5,000 were described as passable in all weathers. In a tropical climate of cyclones and flash floods, 20,000 miles of roads seem very little for an accidented island of 228,600 square miles of desert, escarpment, highland, mountain, steppe, bush, forest, and jungle, but the French built every inch of whatever sort of road under almost impossible conditions. And even so, the highway network is bigger and better than the roads of East Africa, the Congo, and independent Ethiopia. Thus Mr. Blaze materially contributed to the opening up of Madagascar, and the development of the Malagasy.

He was, in 1958, a well-to-do man; indeed, in Madagascar, he was rich. In Tananarive, he and his family live in a charming red brick house under the Queen's Palace in the high town; it is small but it is historic. Jean Laborde, "the Grand Frenchman," a pioneer of the first three quarters of the nineteenth century, built it. Léon Superbie, a French gold prospector of the 1880s, lived in it when he held and worked the unrewarding mineral rights to a concession, from the last Merina queen, of three or four million acres of Sakalava tribal territory. Mrs. Blaze has made it comfortable. She remarked that the attic under the tile and corrugated iron roof, being both hot and dry, was ideal for the aging and maturing of Malagasy coffee beans. In a copper pot in the living room, she liked to make her favorite flower arrangement—fifty dozen flame-red carnations (not big blooms; they cost about $5.00, and that included the tip for the old Malagasy woman who grew them, and who sold them on Friday in the Zoma flower market). The living room is ample, but not palatial.

An hour's flight from Tananarive, the Blazes own and operate a model dairy and experimental breeding farm, stocked with imported cattle and selected zebu strains, on the reclaimed shores of Lake Alaotra; the concession amounts to a thousand acres, with another thousand of improved pasturage. Mrs. Blaze is trying to cross the breeds to establish a line of animals that will thrive under the harsh Malagasy conditions and resist the ticks, the steers to put on a weight of beef, the cows to give ample milk of high butterfat, the race to breed true.

Shortly before independence, the family built a weekend cottage in the reforested watershed of Lake Mantasoa, the reservoir supplying Tananarive twenty-five miles by good road away. The house in the contemporary manner is built of fieldstone, of plate glass, and of pallisander, ebony, and rosewood. There the young Blaze men water ski, sail out of the yacht club, and fish for large-mouth black bass, introduced from the United States in 1951. Lacking natural enemies and competition, they grow to enormous size; the smaller ones make better eating.

In Canada and in New York, during the war years, Blaze learned by doing the American ways of influencing public opinion—for France. Back in Madagascar, after the unexpected Rebellion of 1947, the first of the French Colonial uprisings following the Second World War, Blaze found himself, as a Franco-American-Malagasy businessman, inevitably drawn into politics and propaganda—and not just to protect his own private investment in the island. By then, although pioneering in a new enterprise, he had become, along the lines of classic French development, a conservative man. His critical French mind informed him that he could not stop the break-up of empire, but he believed that Madagascar could be saved for France—and by extension, for the Malagasy themselves, as well as for democracy—by being brought to the attention of French as well as foreign investors. He trusted the methods that had brought him success; he set out to advertise the island, thus to make it prosper under the French Union, which, in 1946, replaced the Colonial empire, and which, in 1959, was in turn replaced by the French Community—both the creations of General de Gaulle.

He expanded the Blaze enterprises to enter the fields of journalism, commercial and political propaganda, information, and public relations. He backed a weekly newspaper, a quarterly magazine, and a political party for sound, conservative men to rally around in Madagascar—for those who believed in the *Présence Française*.

And what is the *Présence Française?* Much more than the French Presence, it is a troublesome idea to get hold of, let alone to translate. Those who understand it and make use of it leave the words in French. As a slogan and a symbol, the sense varies with geography and experience. In Algeria recently, the Secret Army—the terrible O.A.S.—was a *Présence Française*, which, bleated from French horns, turned into *Algérie Française*. In Mauritius, the *Présence Française* is a fantasy of the sugar-cured Ancien Régime, a reaction of race purity and innate supremacy. In Europe when it thrived at its most powerful, in the eighteenth-century courts of the Germanies, of Poland, and of Russia, the *Présence Française* meant the use of the French language as the vehicle of French thought, French civilization, and

21

French culture in rich and educated polite society and in diplomacy, along with French taste in good manners, and French elegance in dress and interior decoration. The *Présence Française*, then, is inseparable from the French emprise—the French quest for glory and grandeur.

I myself believe that the French of all the peoples (or races, or nations, or historic entities, or ethnic groups, or tribes, or clans, or families, or varieties of human beings) of the world have utilized the human substance—which is to say the whole gift, the total potentiality: the mind, the intellect, the body and the senses in the flesh, the soul and the spirit—to the fullest human capability. God and the rest of us know how difficult and damnable the French can be, and yet what human individual is more beautiful? What city surpasses Paris? What language has greater clarity?

The French faults are salient, and that is essential in the balance, for the French virtues are unmatched. None on earth, since the fifth-century Athenians, have so clearly revealed mankind to man in the values of his nature. The French revealed what a civilized, cultivated, complete man and woman, in time, may make of themselves if (*Deus vult*) evolution is given the chance. So the Frenchman stands as a milestone carved with a pointing hand on the road. It may be that we have gone by the French-marked moment in the new territory of time/space. Even so, time cannot darken their untouchable accomplishment; every broken fragment of their moment shines with grandeur and with glory. None now stands high enough to belittle their achievement. Such is the *Présence Française*.

But on a lesser plane, and as applied to the former French colonies, the phrase in propaganda means the continuing dominance of French economic, cultural, and political ideas and practices—of the continuing ties to France. At its most abstract, the *Présence Française* translates as the principle of French guiding influence—the civilizing mission still at work among the "unenlightened," the "underdeveloped," the "underprivileged," and the uncivilized regions of the former French world. At its mildest, the phrase translates vaguely as "the French Way of Life."

"The French Way of Life," "the American Way of Life"—they are offensive and defensive phrases, designed to be evocative, all things to all (French or American) men—and their enemies. Their appeal is less to the mind than to the emotions. Thin-skinned and rubbery, they are inflatable—with hot air, with poisonous gases, and with the water of life, or the wine. They are explosive. And yet there is virtue in them.

The French way of life—the *Présence Française* in France—is a matter of opinion; French opinions are classic, recognizable, and fixed. The French way is a web of measurements, of value-judgments, of useful standards. Its medium is conversation; the French talk and think their way through life. At their worst, the talk and the thought are as hard as bricks that bricklayers build into walls. At their best, the French, having taken thought, talk the way architects design and construct houses for human habitation, and the monuments. At its best, the French way of life is a logical and reasonable order imposed upon nature—such are the cities and the landscapes of France.

In Madagascar, the transported French way of life has not survived unchanged to grow in the new climate; transplanted, it does not flower and fruit as in France. I had a conversation there with a chic and well born, lovely and well married young French woman. She told me why. She had gone down to Madagascar with her brilliant husband, brought in to prepare the ground for a French university of Madagascar. She wore on the ring-finger of one narrow hand—I recall it vividly—a large, round, surely ancestral diamond of great fire and watery limpidity. She formed a circle with her thumb and index finger, a closed circle, and she said, "*Madagascar, c'est zéro!*" There is nothing here, nothing—no intellect, no thought, no art, no theater, no architecture, no culture, no civilization, no society, no conversation. There is nothing to do in Madagascar. Soon she went back to Paris, France, where there are things to be done. There was no time to build the foundations, let alone to open the university before independence. French culture, French lilies-of-the-valley, cannot take root in such barren ground.

In another conversation in the French language in the immense island—of great spaces, enormous distances, wide horizons, brilliant sunlight, and blazing sunsets—I found the effect of Madagascar upon at least one member of the French present there in April, 1958. I spoke with a well made French Colonial businessman in his thirties, a handsome man, a hard worker, a success. He had arrived from France by way of the Indo-Chinese wars in which he had been wounded, ten years earlier. He had found his opportunity as well as his wife in the French community of Tananarive; he had settled in. He talked of the aftereffects of independence, then coming fast. He said that he hoped he would not have to leave the Malagasy Republic, for the life of the island suited him. One thing he was sure of: if he had to go, he would not return to his birthplace in Champagne. He had gone home on his honeymoon. He had found that none of his family or friends showed the slightest interest in his life in Madagascar, or in Madagascar—"the forgotten island." Nor in his bride, except as an exotic addition to the family, a charming creature— and she was neither Malagasy, nor *métisse*, nor Créole, she was *French*. Nor, indeed, in him except as a son, a brother, a schoolmate—someone who had been away from home for years. It startled him to see how he had grown far away from France; it shocked him to realize how little France had changed. In the small city of his birth, he found himself shut out from the enclosed, familiar places, and, worse, he saw his friends and relatives as conniving, plotting, deviously searching for ways to get around the laws—and to get away with it. He missed the spacious emptiness, the sunlight, and the freedom of those far Malagasy horizons. He had no intention, if he was forced to leave Madagascar, of returning to the petty, venal, stingy, greedy, dismal life of France. So, he thought of South America—Brazil, Chile—where, indeed, there are some few elements of the old *Présence Française*, as there are no longer in North America.

Mr. Blaze's ventures in, if not the American way of life as adapted to Madagascar, at least in the American way of advertising and public relations, did not thrive. There may be hidden persuaders in the island, but there are no supermarkets, no economy of plenty, no planned—but instead, an awful, tropically induced—obsolescence. There was, in short, no Malagasy demand for his conservative views, nor for his political party, nor for Madagascar in the outside world.

A practicing Roman Catholic, a big businessman, and a colonial, he stands far right in politics. What else could he be but a reactionary, having begun the action of his life as a pioneer in an unopened out-of-the-way island inhabited by black, brown, and tan primitives? He blames "Paris" for all the trouble in Madagascar, and he refers to the liberal Colonial administrators, to the meddlesome do-gooders, to the yellow journalists, and to the malicious intellectuals (for instance, François Mauriac, and, to be sure, Sartre).

"The white man is committing hara-kiri," said Blaze, once a pioneer in the land, in the waters, and in the air of Madagascar. He brought himself to the island; he is, himself, a representative of Western culture. That is to say, of what, notwithstanding all its errors, outrages, and mistakes, is the highest achievement in civilization of the human race. No other of the known cultures of the past has climbed so high or gone so deep in Europe, in Africa, in Asia, in the Americas, and in the islands. Hara-kiri, an honorable form of self-denial and self-destruction, if a messy business, was once the ultimate rejection of evolution, the last resort of an aristocratic way of life, the *Présence Samouraie.*

Blaze is right when he says, wearily, that the Malagasy of the island that he knows incomparably well are not yet ready to take on the responsibilities of self-rule and self-government in our world. Yet who was the Tunisian—an *évolué* and a witty French *assimilé,* to be sure—who wondered, when something of the same was said of the Tunisians of Tunisia, whether the French of France were yet ready, willing, and able to assume the terrible responsibilities of self-government and self-rule, in liberty, equality, and fraternity?

The coelacanth goes on swimming as it always—or as good as always—has in its deep waters around Madagascar.

Antalaha: In Vanilla III

THE CHINESE AND THE INDIANS

BE that as it may, fact or fancy, there was nothing actively prehistoric about Blaze when he met us at the airfield outside Antalaha. Having greeted us with French courtesy, he saw to it that our bags were put into his small Peugeot. He then introduced us to a fellow passenger, who had come in our plane. He was giving her a lift to town. She was a neat and self-contained Chinese wearing a European summer frock, and she too was seriously courteous. We all got in; Blaze drove along rutted, pot-holed, mud-puddled dirt road—*the* road, a bad one, neither banked nor hard-surfaced in any season, impossible to maintain throughout the summer rains, then dwindling to end. But the road was a road, and it ran straight along the almost level shoreland between the hot Indian Ocean and the tropical forests of the rising hills.

I sat beside our passenger in the back seat. Having nothing to say, she said nothing in the Chinese way. Perhaps she was twenty, perhaps she was forty—whatever her age, she was used to it; she took up little place. Her name was Mme. Lock Hang Leck Lo Nug, or Mrs. Lo Nug. She neither smiled, nor frowned, nor spoke—I do believe she did not budge during the rough ten miles to town. When Mr. Blaze drew up and stooped in front of a long, thin, wood-and-corrugated-iron building, her husband's warehouse and office, she got out and so did we. She stood on her feet and let the men talk. Her husband was in vanilla as a curer, packer, and exporter; he was a small and thin Chinese man, wearing sun-tan cotton shirt and slacks.

Still suffering from mindlessness, and jolted by the ride, I did not join the vanilla shop-talk, but took refuge from the sun on the dark verandah of the one-story warehouse among the wooden crates, and I smelled something strange.

I have been told that, of all the five or six senses through which a man perceives the world, the sense of smell is the most powerful and the least biddable in its evocations. Tunes are for the whistling; images return in dreams; but perfumes and stenches cannot be conjured up in absentia from the source. French perfume composers build their fortune on this fact, and they use the scent of vanilla. Since that moment on the verandah in Antalaha, when I uncork a bottle of extract, I get a whiff of danger not usually associated with a dish of ice cream and cake.

There in the shadowy hot reaches of Lo Nug's warehouse, I flaired disaster in vanilla; it took the unprepossessing shape of a plump and bland Overseas Chinese, a chunky man in an ice-blue nylon shirt, tan cotton pants, and the ugly plastic sandals that seem to be France's most popular gift to the hot and former colonies. They are a system of molded straps of dead grey-white, and they are silent. The man came out of the inner recesses of the dark and fragrant shed; he hesitated for a moment in the glaring sunlight; then he made an abrupt volte-face, as though to take shelter in the sweet recesses of his friend's dark place of business. However, he turned to look back, and he happened to catch Mr. Blaze's eye. He seemed to take courage.

Then Blaze called out to him to greet him with more than business cordiality in his calm French voice. I looked on in a fragrance of vanilla, reflecting that Chinese hair does not adapt itself to Occidental barbering; black and straight, it stands up when it should lie down. Under his unruly hair, the man's round, yellow countenance did not reveal that he had just been declared bankrupt—in debt for 25,000,000 francs CFA (about $125,000). Such is the nature of the wildly speculative vanilla market.

Having said good-by and having shaken hands all around in the French manner, we got back into the Peugeot and drove off. Blaze explained that earlier in the season, the plump bankrupt Chinese, a vanilla broker named Lin Sing Lo Luk, in vanilla for years, had gambled and had lost. But, as with a debt of honor, he had fulfilled his bad bargain with New York; it wiped him out. In bankruptcy—in utter ruin—he had likewise agreed to pay his creditors $75,000 over a period of the next three years. He delivered the beans to New York; he assumed the debt; Lo Luk proved himself to be an honorable Chinese and an honest broker. So Mr. Blaze had made a point of greeting him with more than the ordinary respect and cordiality. Even so, it seemed to me that there was more to the story than met the eye—or the ear, or, indeed, the nose. It turned out to be a story of solidarity.

The Chinese of Madagascar, as is the choice of the Overseas Chinese elsewhere, maintain their separate racial identity—they choose to be what they are; they are Chinese. Assimilation into other communities requires as a first step a rejection of their past, and, indeed, of their present nature. The Chinese have neither cause nor reason to reject themselves; always in China they have absorbed their conquerors and their minorities—even a community of Jews vanished among them leaving only one or two high noses behind.

The Malagasy Overseas Chinese have never lived in Chinatown. Most of them are not urban. Usually they are rural shopkeepers in the back woods of the eastern half of the island (the Overseas Indians work the western territory), where in the villages they establish general stores. Buying and selling at a profit in the wholesale-retail trade is a foreign concept. Perhaps because they never got around to inventing money, the Malagasy had no commerce, no credit, no cash and carry, and nothing on the installment plan—before they were discovered. Today, the French, the Créoles from Réunion, the Chinese, the Indians, and the Merina highlanders dominate in business in Madagascar.

As businessmen, the Chinese are known for their integrity—which is to say, they are as honest as good businessmen can be. The Malagasy like to deal with them, and, on the other hand, so do the French. The Malagasy like the Chinese because, when they came into Madagascar, they chose to live among the Malagasy on the same footing—or *standing*, to use a French word meaning status. The French like the Chinese because both people come from comparably ancient and refined cultures, recognizably civilized. In Madagascar, the Overseas Chinese are *with* both the primitive Malagasy and the sophisticated French, but, on either hand, they are agreeably different *from* them.

Thus, neither superiors nor inferiors, the Chinese meet the Malagasy and the French as equals.

Even so, they keep themselves to themselves, and, operating on a different time sense, patiently consider themselves to be not immigrants but voluntary exiles, temporarily abroad, and sensible about the whole thing. They are, to us, timeless and changeless—eternally Chinese. They understand survival. They brought with them a thorough understanding of money, mathematics, and the fine art of double-entry bookkeeping, none of which applied abstract sciences did the Malagasy of the Betsimisaraka tribe then possess. This lack gave the young Chinese men, the first to come, their opportunity. Alone, each one of them, carrying his goods packed on his back, walked out into the back-woods villages of native huts, and set up shop. He learned the Malagasy language. He lived on the level of the local people. He even produced a few mixed children, which the Malagasy, being tolerant and understanding sex, did not at all mind; the children, to be sure, were Malagasy, not Chinese, not sad half-breeds. They belonged to their mothers. Then when the Chinese shopkeeper had saved up enough hard cash in French currency or perhaps in gold, he sent off to China, to his native village or town, and ordered himself a mail-order bride. His old mother, or an aunt perhaps, picked out a suitable virgin for him, and sent her off to share his life and work beside him in the country store. They prospered.

According to the census, on 31 December 1958, there were 8,039 Overseas Chinese in residence in Madagascar. However, these official statistics, being Franco-Malagasy, were compiled under difficulties in troubled times, and are, I gather, somewhat less than accurate. No two lists ever quite agree. My hunch is that the Chinese like it that way; for although they are neither inscrutable nor unaccountable, they prefer not to be counted. They are likewise careful not to be remarkable as they go about their business. A certain confusion suits their purpose, which is to be let alone to work hard and to make money hand over fist. They enjoy both anonymity and statistical flexibility, if not downright inaccuracy, in the bookkeeping department.

A few of the Chinese have applied for, and been granted, French citizenship papers along with French passports in perfect order. There cannot be many of these assimilated Chinese, although both

Mr. and Mme. Lock Hang Leck Lo Nug, of the vanilla business, have made the change; and in doing so, they have sacrificed neither face, nor *amour propre*, nor the respect of the French, the Créole, the Malagasy, or the Overseas Chinese communities (what the Indians think about them does not matter).

Both the French and the Chinese, having been civilized and cultivated for centuries, understand full well the nature and the usages of the truth. To tell the truth is admirable and, indeed, essential—but never to be indulged in indiscriminately. Like Sunday clothing, the truth is too valuable to be put to daily wear and tear. And both the Chinese and the French know that it is the common human experience not to be able to be honest at all times; thus they are tolerant of one another, and admire one another. Many a French colonial has returned to France from what used to be French Indo-China with a chic and charming, and above all intelligent, Chinese *wife*.

In historical fact, although the Chinese have known the general whereabouts of Madagascar from the days of the Yuan (1280–1364) and the Ming (1368–1644) emperors—bits of celadon and blue-and-white porcelain have been found in Vohémar—no Chinese went down to settle in the island until after the French took over in the nineteenth century. Since then, they have never caused trouble.

However, there is one major difference between the Oriental and the European Overseas businessmen; the Chinese have a special knowledge, or knack, that the French lack. They know how to cheat the Malagasy back-woods man, the major grower of vanilla, and make him like it.

The transaction of buying and selling the green bean goes on throughout the year. It ends, at harvest time, with the Chinese country storekeepers owning 80 per cent of the crop, of which 90 per cent is grown on individual Malagasy small holdings. It is a fleecing that the Betsimisaraka tribesmen and their wives seem thoroughly to enjoy; it goes on slowly, bit by bit, never all at once. It is a protracted pleasure for both sides. The Malagasy farmers and villagers have simple needs, but what they want they buy from the Chinese general store, which is equipped to satisfy all of them. One day they may want a pint or two of kerosene for the lamp, another day it is a box of matches, some sugar, some rum. So it goes. The well-to-do now buy a nylon shirt, a pair of cotton shorts, a length of flannel to make into a *lamba*, a pair of plastic sandals, a comb, a looking glass, the pot, the pan, the knife, the fork, the dish, the glass—all the necessities and the luxuries of life as lived in a rectangular cabin with walls made of the spines of raffia-palm fronds grooved vertically together and lashed to a scaffolding of bamboo or eucalyptus poles, and thatched with banana leaves.

The Chinese shop is the best built-edifice in the community, for purposes of safe shopkeeping, not out of ostentation. It may be built of stone, brick, timber, or corrugated iron, or a construction that combines all of these with woven mats and thatch. It is a social meeting place, not unlike the supermarket. The Malagasy goes to shop; he takes his time. Nobody hurries him or tries to pitch him a hard sell. All he may want to buy is a box of matches, a purchase good for an hour or two of sedate fun. From the start, both buyer and seller know that the transaction will take the form of barter. No currency changes hands. For money, they use the green vanilla beans still growing on the vine; each gets what he wants, which is, I suppose, the feel of life, the sensation of reality.

For, when the Malagasy have gone to sleep, the Chinese shopkeeper and his wife pull the shutters to, lock the doors, and light the discreet kerosene lamp. They then begin to do the homework for tomorrow's reasonable, placid, matter-of-fact, steady, unemotional chicanery. They load the dice; they stack the deck. Standing at the counter cleared for action, they bring up the boxes of safety matches, and, one by one, empty out the matchsticks. They then refill them, having first put in the two at the bottom lying one on top of the other to make a cross like an X. The others go in evenly and regularly, except for the five or six left over, which are reserved to fill a new and empty box the same way.

Then, having fixed the matches, the Chinese and his wife, and later on his sons and daughters-in-law, for it is a family enterprise, haul out the sacks of sugar. Each one is carefully emptied onto sheets of brown paper spread upon the floor. From this hill of sweetening, a local product, not excessively refined, still pale tan in color—sand color —irregularly granulated, he takes out 10 per cent by weight, no more, on scales he understands precisely. He then mixes into the remaining pile of sugar an exactly corresponding weight of sand—sand of a fine quality, calculated never to grit in the teeth. When he has finished stirring it, he scoops the nine-to-one mixture back into the sugar sack; nine times later, he fills up a tenth sack, kept for the purpose. Then he sweeps the floor.

Next to hand comes the new consignment of rum put up in bottles of a liter each; it is the very strongest kind of rum—raw, newly distilled, cheap, the color of human urine. You understand. He adds some pepper to the adulterant; his customers like a fiery drink. Or so I was told. I know all this only at second hand. I did not see the additives go in with my own eyes. But, true or false, a fact or only anti-Chinese propaganda in underhand economic warfare, it is worth noting, to fill in the vanilla picture.

What can be proved is the obvious fact that at the end of the local fiscal year, the Chinese shopkeeper owns 80 per cent of the vanilla crop. And with the green beans in hand, the Chinese owner sends word to his brother or his cousin in Antalaha, or possibly a relative in vanilla in Vohémar, Sambava, or Andapa, which are the lesser centers of the trade, that he has so many kilos of green beans to sell outright, or to be cured on shares. Such a man is M. Lo Nug, of Antalaha, whose wife had ridden into town with us from the airport. He bought, cured, and sold the finished product.

Thus he was fairly certain to come out ahead of the game each year. His friend, Lo Luk, being a broker, a middle man who bought and sold, ran greater risks. He *had* to speculate in vanilla futures. Thus when he won, he won both ways; and when he failed, he got it coming and going.

It is likely that Lo Luk closed his disastrous contract with New York before he had bought a single kilo of vanilla; perhaps he had taken options on a tonnage of green beans then coming into the possession of the Chinese shopkeepers, or in the early stages of the curing process. That was in late August and early September. But between then and November, when he set out to buy the 42 tons of cured beans, the price had gone up to $15.50 per kilo. He then had the choice of breaking his signed contract with New York, or of buying beans at $15.50 to sell at $12.50. He could either lose his honorable business reputation, or the sum of $125,000. The fact is that he chose to keep his honor and go bankrupt. He delivered the disastrous beans. He could have welshed, as in fact the senior Mukra, an Indian vanilla exporter of the company S. V. Mukra et Fils, when confronted by a similar choice, decided to do. Why did Lo Luk go through with it?

He did so apparently because the Chinese community, acting in solidarity, told him to do so. Lo Luk's failure was well publicized. Everybody in vanilla was made to understand all aspects of Lo Luk's disaster. It looked as though the Overseas Chinese community of Madagascar had made a special production of the case of Lo Luk, the honorable Chinese broker. As a consequence, whether intentional or not, it began to look as though Lo Luk's honor, specifically assessed at $125,000, was more valuable to the Chinese as a whole than the equivalent hard currency. Like everything else about Madagascar, this singularly bad bargain cannot be considered by itself as a bad, but simple, business transaction; it cannot be taken out of the context of current events.

The place was the vanilla market of Antalaha; the time was the season of 1957–58. The price of the commodity was already dangerously inflated; Mukra, the defaulting Indian, had already raised the tensions in Antalaha and the tempers of the New York buyers, who, it began to emerge, were caught short. (The senior Mukra, by the way, perhaps with the money he had saved by losing face, had found it prudent to take off on an unexpected business trip to Paris—he was a naturalized French citizen. He left his son in charge of business in Antalaha.) Not only was the market taut, but outside, in the rest of Madagascar, the political tensions had begun to rise, affected by the death throes of the paralyzed Fourth Republic, which died ingloriously that May. The Overseas Chinese community began to think things out in terms of over-all survival, and not in terms of Lo Luk's vanilla beans. They had a lot more to lose than Lo Luk's lost $125,000 —a loss which more than likely the whole community absorbed. They had to think of staying on in business under the rulers of whatever government the free people of independent Madagascar chose to set up. They knew that the French, most likely, would pull up stakes and go home to France—or elsewhere. They knew that the Malagasy hated the Créoles, and had little respect for the Indians. They did not want to have to go home to Taiwan or the mainland. The Chinese

33

like it there on Madagascar; they have a lot to lose. Nobody knows how rich they are.

Another incident that winter—that is to say, Austral summer—cast a small but revealing light on their collective state of mind, and that was the theft of our friend Mme. Lo Nug's jewelry along with the unbanked receipts for the day's vanilla business in her husband's office, to the value of a million francs CFA in gold, pearls, jade, pink beryls—the best of the semi-precious gem stones found on the island—and possibly some fine-quality red tourmalines—it being hard to say because Mme. Lo Nug never wore her jewelry outside the house—and 700,000 francs CFA in cash. With the CFA franc then worth (in the official rate of exchange, but not in Hong Kong or on the black markets) 175 to the dollar, the loss amounted to \$5,714.28 plus \$4,000, a prosperous sum.

Is was also grand larceny. Everyone agrees that the Malagasy are gentle, mild, and honest people in their natural, unevolved, and unassimilated state. Crimes of passion may take place, but theft of negotiable valuables, rarely. Yet it came out that reliable witnesses had seen unmistakably Malagasy young men, wearing European shirts and shorts, stealthily climbing out a broken window and its forced open shutters at the scene of the crime. They took to their heels and disappeared into the rain forests and, as a matter of fact, vanished. They were as though swallowed up and obliterated; they never were caught and brought to stand trial. It was assumed that because the theft took place just before the gift-giving season of Christmas celebrations, and because the young men were dressed in assimilating, civilized clothing, they were Protestant Christian converts who wanted to make impressive gifts to their girl friends, and to offer suitable donations to their adopted church—or temple, as the French Roman Catholics say. The Chinese are not Christians; and the Lo Nugs are French assimilated citizens. The pressures of civilization have fragmented the Malagasy tribal codes until who knows who does wrong? The Lo Nug family did not force the issue of justice; they wrote off the loss and hushed it up.

For years, the Chinese of Madagascar, at any rate in vanilla, have been falsifying their business account books—as well as, when need be, such essential but on the whole unimportant and bothersome things as their residence-permits, their birth certificates, their passports and visas, their work-permits, and all the so-called necessary papers, records, and other documents. Known to be lightning calculators with an abacus in hand, they also have an innate sense of double-entry bookkeeping—in fact, triple-entry. In Madagascar, it is said that the Chinese businessmen keep three sets of books, as a sort of defense in depth. The first, written out in French, is kept out in the open for the benefit of the income tax assessor and the other interested government officials; it is known to be falsified, but it is a useful convenience. The second, also kept in French, is likewise false; but the figures come closer to the truth. They thus are reasonable and acceptable if, as has happened, the figures of the first books are contested in court action. The third accounting is kept in Chinese characters, and in code; it is exact and accurate to the last centime. This set of books is kept for the eyes of the family alone, and thus it cannot be falsified. It is hidden away in a place of safekeeping much more reliable than Lo Nug's till, or Mme. Lo Nug's jewel box.

S. V. Mukra and his son are Indians, which is to say they come of Gujerati stock from Bombay. Both father and son were born on Madagascar. The father is a practicing Moslem; the son told me that he is not. They own and operate an important export-import house in Tamatave, the only properly equipped port of the island, with branches in Tananarive and Majunga, and associated companies in Paris and New York. They deal in spices, essential oils, rice, cement, cloth, hides, and anything else that brings them in profit.

When Lo Luk made his bad bargain with New York, Mukra made a similar one, and this time we have the name of the buyer—Ogilvy & Company, of Pearl Street, well known vanilla brokers. It is a fact that Antalaha knows every one of the vanilla dealers in the United States, the addresses of their offices, the names and natures of their personnel, their strengths and weaknesses, the volume of their annual business, the almost hourly state of their credit rating; nothing can be hidden halfway round the world—neither their tastes in sexual pleasures, nor the condition of their ulcers. So everybody in Antalaha anticipated the events as they developed in the breaking of the Mukra-Ogilvy contract.

It seems that Ogilvy and Mukra had signed a contract early in

October by the terms of which Mukra was to deliver thirty tons of vanilla in January at the price of $12.50 the kilo—it was the price Lo Luk fixed in his disaster. However, early in December, the Antalaha market price went up to $14.00 per kilo, perhaps as a result of Lo Luk's desperate and well publicized (or possibly calculated and unconcealed) search for enough beans to fulfill his bargain. Then Ogilvy, sitting in his skyscraper office on the other side of the world in Pearl Street, got frightened. That is to say, he had to have vanilla to satisfy his customers. So, anticipating Mukra, whose personality and reputation were familiar to him, and speculating that once the Antalaha market had begun to climb, the price per kilo would shoot up, Ogilvy decided to take action. He covered himself by buying his required thirty tons—which, according to the classic pattern, he had already sold at the going rate plus 2 per cent commission, although he had none of the commodity on hand. He paid $14.00 per kilo; thus his purchases not only raised, but also established and confirmed, the world-wide price of vanilla for December, 1957.

It was while he set the market whirling in a spiral motion that he received the notification from S. V. Mukra & Son that they were unable to deliver according to the terms of the October contract, and thus defaulted, broke their contract, and acted in bad faith. All the other merchants of Antalaha were well aware of the Mukra family character and business reputation. To the Indians, and, secretly, to almost all the others, the contract was, after all, but a scrap of paper, not worth a $45,000 loss. However, because Ogilvy acted before the date of shipment specified in the contract, and thus before the written agreement with the Mukras had expired, New York got the full blame for the breach of contract, and for the out-of-contract purchase that had bulled the market. By breaking the Mukra contract, which the local merchants knew very well that the Indians had no intention of honoring, Ogilvy insulted the entire community in vanilla, questioned their collective integrity, demonstrated New York's ill will and lack of faith—and incidentally brought them all a nice fat profit on future sales. Thus Antalaha had it both ways.

For, although the other vanilla merchants had no respect for Mukra, and decided to freeze him out of the market for the remainder of the season, they also decided to work together to punish New York for showing them that the American dealers in vanilla were in short supply—a valuable fact that they badly wanted to find out. Thus they raised the asking price by fifty cents a kilo, and sat back to wait for more orders from New York, at which time they would raise the price another notch. Such is the united front in Antalaha; but as with other allies, they come together to present a united front only in the face of an immediate enemy, such as New York.

It was a cold warfare in a hot climate. The Antalaha merchants first agreed upon a series of skirmishes in psychological warfare to harass the buyers. They did so by arranging to have false orders cabled from their associates in New York, one to each of the major houses. With each false sale, the actual market price went up, usually in steps of half a dollar each. And this strategy succeeded! How? How can a set of rigged and counterfeit sales that put no shipments of the actual commodity into the hold of the freighters out of Tamatave bring about a rise in price for actual transactions? New York is not stupid; there the community of importers of this specialized commodity is very small. Every member comes to know the other fellow's business, and so can estimate sales, and draw surprisingly accurate conclusions as to individual profits and the volume of business. Perhaps the distance lends enchantment. Whatever it is, such is the nature of the fantastically speculative vanilla market that even apparently hard-headed Wall Street men can ever trust themselves, let alone one another, in dealings with Antalaha.

Perhaps the explanation lies in the nature of the buyer and the seller; both are salesmen, and so are minted, heads and tails, in the same coin. Ring heads and tails tolls. The supersalesman of his nature must be liable to being supersold. The sales pitch is a siren song, and, in listening to what he says, the salesman eats his own words. He gets drunk on what comes out of his own mouth; he bites on his own hook —in this instance, baited with a vanilla bean. A good salesman practices his own pitch in front of a long looking glass. I suspect that he never quite believes himself.

Thus, when confronted with the sudden flurry of rigged orders cabled from New York, and nervous about being caught short, the New York buyers lost their precarious equilibrium. They began to suspect some of their fellow-countrymen and rivals—that is to say, each began to suspect the others of doing what he found it natural to do in similar circumstances. They all began to suspect that some genuine orders were coming under cover of the false ones. Thus the buyers' united front, essential in a coalition to stop inflation, cracked, shattered, and broke. Suddenly each broker and each house began to make small token purchases to scout the market, to test the enemy's armament, and "to protect" themselves. They actually inflated the vanilla market to keep it from collapsing from punctured inflation.

So in Antalaha, these cold but emotional, compulsive gamblers and salesmen, speculating with their own commodity, began to believe what they, themselves, proclaimed in the false cables that they had written out and cabled to New York to have returned to them. Each began to wonder if the other house's cables were not camouflage for real orders. Not all this volume of traffic could be false. It is human nature to have faith. It takes a merchant in vanilla to catch a merchant in vanilla. So, in the manner of the Indian rope trick, the Antalaha merchants tossed a price up into the air, and made it stick. It hung there for all the world to see without any visible means of support. Then each merchant climbed up the trick rope and perched on a platform built on top, like so many Simeon Stylites, or possibly Shipwreck Kellys, supported by a kind of mass hypnosis brought on by the close study of imaginary sales. Is this what is meant when a man—a businessman —is said to have lifted himself by his own bootstraps?

Indeed, it contained elements of the miraculous, this unbelievable display of financial parthenogenesis, by which these merchants, by no means otherwise virginal, created a real and solid market price without the aid of active competition.

I turned in at the hotel where we had put up, and climbed the steps to join my friends, the American and the French businessmen, at the far corner of the outer verandah fronting on the beach; they were sitting at an oilcloth-covered table made in France in the Second Empire's version of the Louis XV style; its veneers were disintegrating in the hot and humid climate. Merchant had his notebook open on the table, and his ballpoint pen in hand; he was jotting down the facts of the vanilla timetable as Blaze answered his questions as to the growth, the estimated yield, the harvest, the cure, and the shipment of the commodity. They spoke in English because Mr. Merchant does not understand French; and, because he is a merchant who believes what he says about the need to be honest, straightforward, sincere, and above-board, he was speaking, on the verandah in Antalaha, in his customary clear, taut, high-pitched, and nervous tone of voice.

It was tea time, and there in Antalaha of all places we sat drinking hot tea like a lot of Britishers, whose theory is that it cools the body in the tropics. Maybe so; but we drank hot tea in deference to Mr. Blaze's blood-pressure. For along with teamwork, public relations, and bulldozers, Blaze had imported a by-product, a side-effect of the American way of life and work: tension. Besides that, he had encountered most of the tropical diseases—malaria, typhoid fever, infectious jaundice-hepatitis, and the various dysenteries.

He went on talking, answering specific questions about the vanilla business, while Merchant took notes. It seemed to me that Blaze spoke with increasing reluctance, as though he did not like to see his figures and his conclusions noted down—recorded. Perhaps Merchant sensed it, too, for the American raised his voice and spoke in carrying tones; and that had the odd effect of causing the Frenchman to lower his voice and, as he replied, to twist his neck to look around him and behind him, as though to be sure he was not being overheard.

I looked and saw a young man standing by the bar. Clearly he was an Indian; and almost as clearly, he was reconnoitering, although he was dressed in spotless white cotton shirt, shorts, socks, and shoes, as though for tennis. He even carried a racket under one arm. He ordered a bottle of beer. I had had enough of tea, and I was frankly curious. So I left the two businessmen talking quietly, and went to sit on a tall bar stool. Tennis, anyone? He spoke American English. I gathered that he had done his homework. If so, he must have known the answers to the questions he then asked me; they were about my business—who I was, where I came from, what was I doing in Antalaha? I took a drink of beer and looked at him.

He was a tall, thin young man with light brown skin and a pale complexion. He wore his thick, straight black hair trimmed and carefully combed; but for some reason, he had apparently neglected to shave for several days, or, considering the long but scattered growth, perhaps for several weeks. The effect was to disfigure a set of delicate Oriental features. He spoke good English, although he had not got rid

39

of the sing-song intonational accent of most Indians. And he addressed me—I guess because he wanted to establish his absolute equality—in a way that was both surly and servile, in effect both arrogant and vulnerable. Come to think about it, I don't know exactly how he did it with only the ordinary assortment of not bad human features at his disposal. It threw me off; hell, I wasn't about to hit him.

Without answering I asked him who he was, where he came from, and what he was doing in Antalaha. Then, because there is no use in being offensive, I said I came from New York, and that my name was Stratton. He told me that he knew New York well, and identified himself as the young Mr. Mukra. I'm afraid I did a double take. So this immaculate—aside from the skimpy beard—young man was the notorious scion of the unreliable Maison Mukra, who, by defaulting his contract with Ogilvy & Company, had set the spiral rising in vanilla prices. He told me that he had come from Tamatave to keep an eye on the unsteady market while his father, the head of the house, was in Paris, where he'd been called on sudden business. I already knew that both father and son had been frozen out; and so I wondered what, in fact, had brought young Mr. Mukra to Antalaha. Whom did he find to play tennis with? But I did not ask that question; instead I asked how he liked New York. He said he wouldn't live there if you gave him the place, but it was a good town for a visit. It turned out that he had studied at the Harvard School of Business, in 1954–1955. He was, he informed me, a French citizen, and had been educated in France. Yet as he told me so, his tone of voice and his attitude seemed to me to disparage and belittle his acquired nationality and, by implication, his adopted country and all the French.

Having made that clear, apparently he decided that I had asked enough questions; so he made a point of asking me once again why I had come all the way from New York to Madagascar, and what I was doing at the moment in Antalaha. He was insistent. He spoke with a nagging, nervous, shy effrontery, at once offensive and discouraged. I automatically parried his interrogation, and was very grateful to Mr. Blaze, who had come up to us, and at that moment took over the conversation. Merchant had gone to his room to fetch some papers. Blaze smiled, greeted the son of the house of Mukra with just efficient courtesy, and explained that I had accompanied Merchant, who had stopped off in Madagascar on a business trip to Australia. But he made no mention of the wholly obvious reason that brought any foreigner in Antalaha, which was to buy vanilla.

It was a lesson to me in proper business comportment. Mr. Blaze then addressed me with his usual cheerful civility to ask me how I had enjoyed my visit to the vanilla plantation, and, although he made no visible gesture, he cut me free of Mukra's company and steered me away from the bar, back to our corner of the verandah. He did nothing to detain the young Indian, who, left alone, stood irresolute for a moment, inviting the pleasure of our further company, which he did not receive. Soon he passed by our table, carrying his tennis racket as though it were a shield, or possibly a sword—proof that he was, indeed, a citizen of the larger outside world, the equal of anybody in Antalaha. He went into his room, the end one in the row of six that gave onto the verandah. Carefully he pulled the double wooden shutters to—doors that closed out the light but let the sea breeze blow through. It was distressingly easy to imagine him standing just inside, his ear to the louvers, breathing gently as he listened for our comments about him. The Indians have been coming into Madagascar for a thousand years or more, although at first, like the Arabs from Muscat and Oman, they did not come to stay. They sailed down, running before the monsoon winds, in trading vessels loaded with finished products—cloth, jewelry, brassware, weapons, and utensils, for instance, made in India and what is now West Pakistan. They landed at Majunga or some other port on the northwest shore, and they usually stayed six months to sell their goods and buy up cargoes to take back with them. Then, when the trade winds began to blow up from the south, they got back into their ships, loaded with hides, rice, slaves, and whatever else they knew would sell easily at home in the bazaars, and ran before the wind back to Bombay and Karachi, or wherever they had come from. Some few stayed behind. But since the 1880s when the French first began to "protect" the Sakalava and the other northern and western tribes against the armies of the highland Merina kings and queens, more and more Indians have come to stay. However, there is no Indian "problem"—as in South Africa, Kenya, Tanganyika, or Mauritius. The requirements to be demonstrated and the guarantees of ready cash necessary to have in hand before any foreigner—or even French national—can get permission to settle in Madagascar permanently, have kept out the influx of Indians that British colonies or territories cannot exclude.

But once they got into Madagascar, they, too, elected to stay out of the melting pot. There were 13,353 of them in 1958. They still refuse assimilation with the other ethnic groups, except in casual and infrequent bastardy. The men for the most part have changed their clothes to put aside Oriental dress, turbans, fezzes, and all. They wear the ubiquitous nylon shirt and tan cotton trousers, although some few prefer to keep the more comfortable striped pajama suit. The women have chosen to keep their bright saris, or long tunics worn over "harem" pants. At that, in Tananarive, I did see one slim beauty in a blouse and tight slacks doing her daily marketing among the rows of lovely flowers and bright fruits and vegetables in the patterned shade of the great white parasols of the Zoma; she had cut and curled her hair, too.

But most of the women let their long, thick, oiled and perfumed black hair hang down their backs in braids. They paint their mouths with lipstick of the latest shades, and ring their eyes with kohl. Some paint their toenails and fingernails. What little feet and slim hands they have! And how the prosperous ones do pile on the gold chains, bangles, brooches, earrings, anklets, filigree, hairpins, and even nose studs. Alas, the slim girls run to flesh as soon as they have married. They get fat while they are young and keep it up into middle age. The old ones seem to lose it all. The children though, and especially the skinny little great-eyed girls with their oval faces, are not dressed in an Oriental style. They wear clean, pale, frilly, prim Victorian frocks, beribboned and beruffled to their knobby knees, with white socks and white or patent leather, one-strapped, round-toed shoes. Their mothers like either French high heels, or gold-embroidered, spangled scarlet slippers.

Altogether, they are as brilliant as a flight of parrots, macaws, and cockatoos; and as noisy. Circumspect and well behaved in public (except while struggling to board a bus, a train, or a plane), at home —behind the shutters or the woven screens—the women and children of the Indian community laugh, shout, call out, talk, scream, and cry noisily, the while the radio blares Indian and Moslem music, the while an indeterminately sexed singer with a nasal wail strains and gasps among the quarter tones, and, for all I know, the eighth tones too. The men keep quiet.

But they are a slippery and an unpopular lot. They are supposed to suffer from both the sadist and the masochist complaints that overcome each one of them in on-again-off-again, fair-weather-foul-weather attacks. In their relations with the other islanders, the Indians never present the bland and steady personality of the Chinese. How they behave depends upon the other fellow. They seem to react, and never to act. Always on the defensive, they are always offensive. Thus, in dealing with an Indian merchant, for instance, in vanilla, if the French— or any other—merchant is reasonable, the Indian goes wild. If he is courteous, the Indian is insulting; but if he attacks, the Indian backs down. Indeed, the clue is to be aggressive with the Indians. They are unreliable. Any contract that specifies the fixed amount, quality, time of delivery, and terms of payment serves only as a point of departure for the Indian. Kindness and consideration are to the Indian of Madagascar sure signs of weakness.

Thus to work with an Indian, I was told that a man must be ready to use force—even to the extent of closing his fist and threatening to hit the bastard in the nose. Shouts, insults, and displays of anger are all part of the business of dealing with the Indians. As Mark Twain said about another kind, I was told that the only good Madagascan Indian was a dead Indian.

With all this background information fresh in my mind, I paid careful attention to young Mr. Mukra, in Antalaha, who, it must be said, although he spoke French, English, Malagasy, and Gujerati, at no time in my hearing shouted or raised his voice. Nothing he said was unusual, or even very interesting. He criticized the French, but there's nothing new in that; and what he said about them was banal. The French have said it all themselves, much better. Therefore, it must have been his tone of voice, or his own attitude toward the words he voiced. Something about him emerged from him; it might have been a smell. Its effect was of one of those damned transistor radios tuned in to an announcer saying, "This man is not to be trusted." He even walked in a friendless way. I cannot imagine a background that would open up to receive him. This young man was an island; he was an enclave. I find him very disagreeable to think about, and hard to write about. I cannot think who played tennis with him.

Antalaha: In Vanilla IV

THE CRÉOLES

In the middle of the heavy afternoon, the sun went under, and a strong wind blew in to rattle the coco-palm fronds—it's a dry noise in a wet world. Dark clouds rolled across the sky from over the Indian Ocean, and it began to rain. It rains on 260 days of the year in Antalaha, a town of perhaps ten thousand people, only five or six hundred of whom actually handle the vanilla as curers, packers, traders, and so on. For the past five or six years they have enjoyed the convenience of electricity; and in 1960 they got water piped in from deep-drilled artesian wells. As the capital of the Bourbon vanilla business, it is the wealthiest town per capita in Madagascar.

We had retired to the Hôtel des Orchidées, where each of us had a separate room. That was good luck, for the Hôtel des Orchidées has but half a dozen bedchambers to let. Each has a wash basin fixed to the wall, of which one of the taps was never installed, and the other gives down with a trickle of running water. When we were there, it was cold rain water, or, rather, lukewarm rain water, none too clean for it had been collected in barrels from the gutters of the sloping corrugated-iron roof. Otherwise, the rooms are hard to describe, and harder still to account for. That is, the room I had was square, without a ceiling between me and the corrugated iron, but with windows, a door onto the verandah, a bed, a table, a chair or two, and a wardrobe standing against the inner wall. There was also a strong, peculiar smell. What could have gone on in that room in the recent past, I wonder. Not vanilla.

Once when a guest had made a fuss—not one of us!—by complaining to the proprietress, Mme. Blondin, a pale-tan colored, wavy black haired Créole, way beyond her first youth and well into her forties, she had not minded at all. He had pointed to the filthy and stained wash basin; to the limp, dank smelly towel; to the rusty clothes hooks; to the mildewed and scaling walls; to the lumpy, deformed, and dubious bed with its spotted, stained, frayed, torn, damp, and stinking mosquito net; and to the fat rolls of slut's wool wafting about under the bed among the dead moths and beetles—some of the two-inch-long cockroaches, lying on their backs, were still twitching, albeit feebly, their DDT-poisoned legs when, in all innocence, I had bent down to look under there. To the irate guest, Mme. Blondin replied, without rancor, and without lifting her antenna-like, plucked and penciled eyebrows, "If you do not like it here, you have only to go elsewhere."

In Antalaha, there is no elsewhere to go to. It must be said in her defense that if Mme. Blondin is a poor housekeeper, with easily satisfied, or low, or non-existent standards of cookery, cleanliness, comfort, and convenience, she did not choose to take on the job of running the Hôtel des Orchidées. If she had her way, she'd turn the key in the front door and walk off. She runs the place only as a favor to the vanilla community. Her husband, a local grocer, got the hotel as part payment on a bad debt. The previous owner had drunk himself out of business—and charged his groceries and beverages at the Blondin store. Therefore, saddled with it, the Blondin family moved in and opened it up, but they had no sense of gracious hospitality. The dirty room I slept in cost about $3.00 a night; breakfast was 35 cents; lunch and dinner cost about $1.20 each, without wine or coffee, which were extra; with 10 per cent for service. Thus this stay did not come high. In fact, the Blondins ran their place as a sort of public service.

There is no *bourse*, no special market, no exchange to house the vanilla business. Because all foreign and local buyers who have to go to Antalaha, if only to test the market, must put up at, and with, the Hôtel des Orchidées, and because there is no other restaurant or café in town, the hotel and its verandahs serve as the point of arrival and departure, the focus of the trade. The merchant sleeps there, eats there, gets up and goes out to make his social and business calls at the offices and warehouses in town, and returns there to unwind, to sort things out, and to plan his strategy. No wonder it is festooned with cobwebs and spider webs. The Blondins could afford to be indifferent to such small details as their guests' comfort. They had a monopoly. Their bad debt of a bad hotel was for them a sideline. They shunted their frustrations onto it, and let them roll. The Blondins are Créoles, and nobody loves them.

Their dumping ground of the emotions was a sprawling wooden bungalow in need of paint insecurely settled on its piles six feet above a wasteland of a sandy garden across the road from a strip of tough grass, a narrow beach, and the hot Indian Ocean. A solitary, melancholy, hump-backed cow, tethered on the grass, chewed a bitter cud and bellowed, looking out to sea. Under the hotel where the breezes were supposed to blow, an accumulation of unhinged shutters, empty crates, broken furniture, stove-in-barrels, and nameless things had piled up to give the muscular young cocks and hens a jungle gym for unnecessary exercise. A broad flight of rotting and unpainted steps, edged by a shaky railing, led onto the outer verandah where the tables for lunch and dinner were set up, and onto the inner verandah which served in place of public rooms and corridor to the chambers. The core of the hotel was the bar, behind which stood the display of shelved offerings of all the bottled drinks of Western Europe, or so I think, crowding a magnificent radio-phonograph. The old fox terrier on the trademark must long ago have gone deaf in the service; but he still cocked his ear to the loud voice of his master.

The hotel had once had a bathroom; a bush shower, which is to say a patented five gallon bucket with a perforated bottom and a spring-hinged shut-off device operated by standing under it and pulling on a hanging rope, was still attached by hooks and pulleys to the roof above a tub. But, perhaps from lack of use, the shower room had been converted to a bedroom for the Blondins well fed, seventeen-year-old son, who slept late behind his curtains in the morning. So there was a choice between a sticky dip in the hot salt sea, or, as it occurred to me in the night, going out to rinse off in the rain.

On that first night I woke up when the rain fell. I shoved aside the dank mosquito net, got up, pushed the bed out of the way of the trickle from the worst of the leaks in the roof, got back into my cage, tore the netting as I tucked it back under the flabby mattress, and lay down. I had it in mind to go back to sleep. But one does not go back to sleep in a booming room under a corroded corrugated-iron roof in a tropical downpour. When I was much too young, I went to see Jeanne Eagles in *Rain*; so I should have known about the shock of water falling straight down hard on the beat-up iron overhead; and on its side-effects. Where can that fall of water come from?

It was not a question of *la vache qui pisse*. There are not that many cows in Madagascar, not even when helped out by bulls and calves, although by conservative count they all add up to 6,500,000 head, and tail. This rain fell harder than it is possible to imagine. I listened and heard the wet drumming roar rise and increase in bels and decibels as *more rain fell* in greater volume and at greater speed. It came down hard upon my iron drum. I thought of solid geometry, but that didn't do any good. In an attempt to latch onto the power of positive thinking, I thought to put this downpour to good use, and to go out into it with a cake of soap. But I had learned the hard way not to go out into a flattening barrage.

The hotel had no inside toilet, no water closet and no cesspool. Its one facility was a chemical can, without the chemicals, housed in a shed in the back yard. To get there, I had to go, or not go, out of my room, across the two verandahs, down the treacherous front steps, around to the right, down the twisting path among the scratchy vegetation, and to the rear—and then back in a round trip to retrace the labyrinth in order to get the key that unlocked the flimsy wooden door. The key, a long and weighty piece of iron, hung on a rusty nail at one end of the bar. Why was this dark, disgusting, and unemptied can, with its broken wooden seat upon it, kept locked up? Not to keep out the swarms of large, soft-bodied, and loud flies, but to exclude the Malagasy patrons of the "black bar," which is to say the other, segregated bar hidden away at the back of the hotel and reserved for the use of the autochthonous peoples—or for all those thirsty paying customers who did not then qualify as *évolués, assimilés*, Indians, Chinese, Créoles, or Europeans. Thus this privy, although it was barely functional as such, had come to serve a higher purpose, that of a status symbol for the superior, the exclusive, the imported white man's burden, a part of which is drunkenness.

The Malagasy at this black bar, and the others like it on their island, have learned to like the strong red wine of Algeria, and the cheap rum distilled from the sugar of Réunion and Madagascar. The more advanced among them have also acquired a more civilized taste for the wonderful wines of France, for cognac, for Pernod, for chartreuse, framboise, and mirabelle, and some go so far as to like Holland gin and Scotch whisky, with or without Perrier water. It is a sign of culture and an educated palate.

In back of the Hôtel des Orchidées beside the can arose a growing pile of empty bottles. The labels had washed off, but the glass kept the old, familiar shapes. Green, brown, and transparent, they glittered in the early morning sun; it was a big heap, a mound, a tumulus taller than I standing beside it. What to do with a pile of empties so far away from France? Some had broken. It was a most depressing sight.

I turned away, and found a partial answer to my question as I walked back, key in hand, through the neglected garden. I saw that someone, probably not Mme. Blondin, but some predecessor, a French proprietress I concluded as I discovered the formal patterns of *parterres* and sanded paths strangled by the jungle growth, had found a use for some of the empties. What French woman can bring herself to throw away an empty bottle? So it must have been a French hand that, in times gone by, selected all the handsome, round, ten-pin-shaped green Perrier water bottles—the big ones, not the demis—and thrust them neck down, one after the other, into the pinkish sandy soil, to put an edging round the borders, and to separate the flower-beds from the interlacing paths.

Clearly, Mme. Blondin, who was born in Madagascar, did not bother with the garden, or let it bother her. Anyhow, she was careful to stay out of the sun, for the sun would tan her, and the suntan would darken her pale skin. She was very light-skinned for a colored woman. Her husband and her son are darker, but she is beige. It is a handsome color said to go with anything; her complexion, unlike even the most expensive holiday suntan, does not fade, for it does not lie close to the surface in patches; it goes deep.

To judge from what she did to her face, Mme. Blondin did not much like her skin tone. She made herself up a great deal; or, to be correct, she made herself down. I tried to work out the various steps in this construction of a face, and came to the conclusion that first she spread on a firm foundation. Next she paid close attention to the shading of her handsome caramel-colored eyes, and to the beading of the lashes. Then somewhere along the line she painted on an inadequate little Mae Murray mouth. To begin with, I guess she first shaved off her own eyebrows, for the ones she rerouted in black pencil had nothing to do with hair. I cannot understand why she should have thought it enhanced her appearance to draw on thin lines remarkably like the antennae of those giant cockroaches. She must have spent hours seated at the dressing table. What she carried out into the open on her face was a hard mask as abstract as any Greek persona. But although it had its dramatic effect, I couldn't figure out whether it was supposed to be tragic or comic. Yet I got the point, which was that Mme. Blondin hoped to tell the world that she was French, and not what indeed she was, which is a Créole from Réunion.

What is a Créole? All the lexicons agree that a Créole is a person of French stock born overseas, outside France, in a colony like Madagascar, or a former colony like Louisiana or Mauritius, that is usually a hot country in a latitude inhabited by dark-skinned natives, black, brown, or red. A Créole, then, is an overseas Frenchman. The Créoles of Réunion, since 1946 an island overseas department of France, thus qualify, for they are French-born too. But according to the dictionary definition, they are also born willy-nilly liars; it is in their mixed blood for them "to lie as naturally as they breathe"—which is what is said of them in Antalaha. Almost none of the Réunionnais-Reunionese can be called white. The name of their island has taken on an apt and an ironic meaning. It is a place of reunion for all the races of the earth. It started out from scratch; the island was an empty place before 1642. There are no islands like it left on earth.

There are stories that sound to me like fables told by the white French colonists of two Créole brothers from the same Réunion marriage bed, the one born as white as day, and blond to boot, the other as black as night with wooly Negro hair; the one as white as the driven snow, of which a few flakes sometimes fall on the Piton des Neiges, the other black as sin, of which perhaps there is a good deal, the island being a Roman Catholic stronghold, without any sort of birth control, but with decided definitions of right and wrong, and not

49

enough work even for the devil to find for their idle hands. But the white brother and the black brother make a combination of Créole siblings of which the possibility all geneticists now deny. A man can be as light or as dark as the total of the united genes from the sperm cell and the ovum; and none of the Réunionese is a strict half-and-half breed. The genetic pattern of a Créole, if worked out and charted, must look like an empty crossword puzzle.

Almost all of them have come down from a shadowy but known ancestry colored in the seventeenth century by the blood of Malagasy and Negro slave women. George Washington, Thomas Jefferson, and Alexander Hamilton as young men all knew the reason why.

Most of the facts of life are known about the Créoles of Réunion, where proximity and distance merged to overpopulate the once lovely South Sea Island, desert and green before the French colonists and slaves went in. So the Créole, a by-blow of time, place, and nature, was produced as a side-effect of modern life. To be sure, he was not crossbred as carefully as are dogs, cats, horses, prize cattle, and test-tube babies; but he is an artificial breed. If the anthropologists reason right, he is the projection in little of what the future man in large will look like—a sort of preview of coming attractions after the American melting pot has simmered long enough. So maybe it is a good idea to take a look at him.

Créole history begins in 1642 when Richelieu's and Colbert's mercantile French Empire took over Réunion as a stop on the way to India. The French East India Company established a group of first-class young French male colonists there, supplied with African and Malagasy slaves to do the heavy work. Then came a cargo or two of carefully chosen orphan brides, healthy girls sent out from France at the request of the serious young men. There followed sailors, explorers, pirates, castaways, more colonists, French nobles exiled before the Terror, and even one American from New York State—a Welshman whose clipper ship was impounded by the British Navy in the Napoleonic Wars, of which our own War of 1812 was an extension. The British took the island in 1810, but returned it to the restored Bourbon kings at the Congress of Vienna. They kept the American ship, but the man stayed on, married, and settled down. After 1945, when required to establish his French citizenship, one of this American's descendants in the fifth or sixth generation had trouble authenticating himself as a Réunionnais for proper French documentation. The Créoles had not needed papers before that; and none of us did before the First World War, except the diplomats and travelers into Czarist Russia and Imperial China.

In the nineteenth century, the established Créole planters—today mocha coffee, Bourbon vanilla, sugar cane, and perfume plants like sweet geranium and vetiver are the chief exports—brought in fresh lots of slaves until 1848, on which date slavery was abolished. After that the planters imported coolies from China, and Tamils from Coromandel as cheap labor. All these have blended in. In 1665, there were 12 inhabitants; in 1717, there were 1,200, of whom 1,000 were Malagasy and Kaffir slaves. In 1848, there were 60,000 slaves and 43,000 free men and women.

The island now has about 275,000 inhabitants; it is 140 miles around and has 970 square miles of surface, most of it unworkable, with one of its peaks 10,000 feet high, and with a difficult cyclonic climate. Its density of population works out at 283½ inhabitants per square mile, but that figure gives no idea of the way the people live crowded along the shore, for two-thirds of the island is uncultivable, it being steep volcanic mountainside or sterile heath.

Consequently, living in chronic unemployment without natural enemies, the islanders have not always had enough to eat. Thus the Créoles as a race, not yet established solidly enough to breed true, are apt to be undersized—around five feet tall—but durable, as tough and sinewy as mountain goats, and as tenacious of life. There are too many Créoles for the island of Réunion to support.

After 1945, a few thousand Créoles crossed over into Madagascar, one of the few remaining underpopulated terrains left with suitable land for pioneering, and settled them in a highland river bottom where the soil is rich and the climate agreeable. But the Malagasy hate the Créoles and reject them. In the Rebellion of 1947, the tribesmen did their best to kill or drive out all they could. So the migration dwindled and dried up. Twice before, in 1840 and again in 1885, the dates of two moves France made to take over Madagascar, some few Créoles managed to establish themselves on the big neighboring island. At the second try, the French Navy established a workable protectorate from their island of Nosy-Bé around the northern tip with Diégo-Suarez Bay, down the east coast and the vanilla country to their other offshore island of Ste.-Marie. So the Créoles got a bridgehead there as French colonists.

At first, preference had been given to the French from France; but it was soon found that the hot, wet climate along the wild northern shores of Madagascar did not suit the newcomers from France, who could not put up with the conditions, although these otherwise carefully screened and well instructed *"petits blancs"* did their best to follow out the latest scientific advice for their good hygiene. They did what they were told and put on the working clothes that they had been advised to bring out with them: long woolen underwear, long woolen trousers, and woolen tunics buttoned tight up to the choker collar at the throat. To protect their heads from the sun they put on pith helmets; to protect their feet from the damp, they laced up their stout high leather boots. Even today a few of the very old-timers wear a modified version of these clothes made out of tan cotton drill; they persist in wearing the pith helmet that the young men today have discarded. The uniform today is shorts and bush jacket, or just plain shorts, with sandals on their bare feet, although in town the businessmen wear formal light-weight suits.

The logic behind the theory of the woolen underwear and outer wear, which surely a good many of them had on when they were buried, seems to have been that if wool in several layers covering the body kept out the cold and warded off the chill of winter winds, so wool in similar layers would keep out the heat and insulate the body from the ill effects of tropical fevers. Even so, the small white Colonial settler found that he could not do the work he had set out from France to do. He felt ill, and if he did not seek a change of air, he often died. In those days, nobody knew much about malaria; they just came down with it and had it in their bloodstreams and their enlarged spleens all their lives.

And that explains how the Créoles came to be brought in and given preference. Perhaps they had, indeed, developed, if not an immunity, at any rate a resistance to the African disease. Suddenly their few remaining drops of "black" blood, their touch or two of the tarbrush, hitherto a somewhat shameful drawback, no worse among the tolerant

French than a hanged horse-thief uncle out West, became a valuable asset, like a hereditary predisposition to survival, or higher mathematics. It was thought that their blood's admixture caused the Réunion Créoles to acclimate themselves rapidly, and to thrive along the rich vanilla shores. At that, there might be something in supposition. I am informed that the Negro's dark skin, which does absorb more of the sun's rays than a white skin, has lying under it a greater network of capillaries. Thus the more he sweats and the greater the evaporation, the cooler his blood. Perhaps the Créole inherited this built-in cooling system.

But as time passed and new French colonists came in, the Créoles found that their survival had become their shame. It became a cause for jealousy, envy, and spite; and it was attributed to their native birth and called attention to the black blood of their slave ancestresses, albeit much diluted in the course of three centuries. As a result, the French, and in particular the French women, made it fashionable to be unwell. Malarial blood and Colonial livers became chic status symbols and true marks of recognition, like the red rosettes of the Legion of Honor. The Créole soon was forced to be ashamed for being healthy, when all proper Frenchmen were not. The fact that he survived kept him out of the planters' club where the sick man was a snob, and it was bad taste to be well.

There thus arose an odd sort of barrier that was not a color bar but that was based on a side effect of color; the white Frenchmen of France, and thus necessarily superior men and women, failed in the lowlands, while French citizens from Réunion, Créoles of color, managed to hold out. They succeeded at least in staying alive, a fact that came to make them suspect. So, to fail was good and natural, and to succeed was bad and abnormal. What is worse, it was unreasonable. So, in the end, color and the Créole ancestry were forgotten, and the Réunionese character was made to take the blame.

For the cause of French failure as durable colonists—whether encased in heavy woolen clothing or in heavier prejudices, or not; and thus whether or not based on misconceptions cut out of the whole cloth of French "logic" and carefully stitched together with French "reason" of how to meet new and unfamiliar conditions—seems to be that the Frenchman can live and thrive only in France. Oh, the Frenchman of France is a weathercock, a chanticleer, perched, permanent and un-

53

changeable upon the towering peak of human attainment. It is his job to point out the direction of the changing wind. He is always himself, shapely, sharp-edged, outlined against the sky, steadfast in all weathers, transfixed by his own perfection as he faces into mankind's destiny. A Frenchman has no choice in all his freedom. He cannot get down from where he is, spiked to eternity, in France. It is his place. He has to leave it to the lesser breeds, and to his half-breeds, to populate the other regions of the earth. In any case, after the 1914–18 war, there were too few good Frenchmen left alive to export from France to Madagascar, or anywhere else, except into the history of the kind carved into war memorials. The Frenchman has nowhere to go but down.

In 1957, the *Service de Statistiques* of the Loi-Cadre government of Madagascar listed the number of Créoles among the French inhabitants of Madagascar as 20,755. It is perhaps significant that in 1959 this official service, part of the Ministry of Finance and Economics of the provisional government of the independent Malagasy Republic then taking shape, did not list the Créoles as a separate ethnic group, but added them in with the "French of metropolitan origin" to make a total of 52,047. The service did, however, separate the French citizens "of other origins"—meaning the French-assimilated and French-naturalized people of tribal Malagasy, Chinese, Indian, "other Asiatic," and, I guess, African and other European origin—16,383 all told. There were then 68,430 people with French citizenship papers living in Madagascar.

Of these, twenty-one or twenty-two thousand are Réunionese, some of them as firmly established as the well-to-do Palimore family of Antalaha, in vanilla; others operate hotels, or a small, precarious retail business; or they manage the minor provincial branches of the big French export-import companies; or they are the Air France and Air Madagascar agents in the towns and cities. Some work for the government as minor functionaries—school-teachers, clerks, customs officials. A fair number of the prettiest young women with the lightest complexions marry (or do not marry) the French bachelors who come out as civil servants or as employees in the Madagascar branches of French banks, engineering and construction companies, or shipping lines, sent out for a three-year tour of duty. At some time in their lives, usually when they are young, these pale young women cultivate anemia and bleach their hair. Only the most fortunate arrive in middle age without the thin-lipped hard mouths, disdainful voices, and coldly calculating regard—inherited from their predominant French ancestry. Mme. Blondin, perhaps by choice, made use of all these regrettable traits of national character.

After a bad dinner, Blaze's friend Mr. Guihenno joined us to talk shop. Plump and compact, the very type of displaced Frenchman, he sat at table with us drinking coffee and discoursing. He gave us to know why the price of vanilla had risen so dangerously high in the year of 1957–58. He spoke clearly, as though he were laying down the law, and not just expressing an opinion. I realized that in vanilla, as in politics, every man is a supreme authority, and what he says is right. Guihenno contended that New York, and not Antalaha, had set the inflation in motion; and what was more, he could put a date to it. It had happened on December the fifteenth. The day before, on 14 December 1957, he had cabled New York to offer one of his old customers—whose name, of course, he withheld—two tons of vanilla, at $14.75 the kilo; prime vanilla, he'd had his eye on it for a long time. On 15 December he had received a cable *in the clear* (I did not understand the significance of this phrase, which Mr. Guihenno stressed ominously, until later when Mr. Blaze explained it). This open cable in English accepted the offered two tons at $14.75, and bid for five more tons at "up to" $15.00! Mr. Guihenno paused to let the two-bit margin sink in.

To be sure, New York's intentions had been good; the old friend and customer had wanted to give Guihenno a little leeway. It was a generous thing to do, but hell is paved with good intentions, said Mr. Guihenno solemnly. Like all American generosity, it was naïve, ill-advised, and destructive in effect. In this particular instance, it had raised the price of vanilla from $14.75 to $15.00 per kilo. And as all the merchants in Antalaha had immediately learned the exact wording of this cable, the market rose, and rose again; once set in motion, it did not stop. Antalaha read into that two-bit generosity the meaning that New York was in desperate short supply. Other orders flowed in; they proved Antalaha's contention. Not only Ogilvy, but also X——, Y——, and Z—— (he named three respected and well known New York vanilla brokers) sent out exploratory offers for small amounts. The fact was that they had no more of the commodity in stock to satisfy their old customers.

Thus Antalaha, in a perfectly reasonable way, had set about consolidating their forces. The merchants agreed among themselves not to sell a kilo of vanilla for ten days—a short time for a sellers' strike, when you consider that Antalaha had waited nearly ten years to get their revenge for 1946. Perhaps the most notable part of the agreement was the fact that all Antalaha had agreed to cooperate in this display of force. Ten days of a united front in vanilla—it was as formidable as the Maginot Line in 1939 in France. And it had the same effect; for all the merchants sitting snug and smug behind it made use of the time to penetrate one another's secrets. Mr. Guihenno stopped talking. I wondered if he had said all he had to say. I wanted to ask him how the merchants learned one another's secrets, and what they were; but I held my peace. And that was good, for Mr. Guihenno was timing his last lines, which, as though casually, he threw away. "Palimore broke first. He filled an order from X—— for fifty tons at $16.25." Palimore is the biggest merchant in Antalaha, a Créole, whom we were scheduled to visit first thing in the morning tomorrow—just to pay our respects.

Then, speaking English, Mr. Blaze told us about the local spy apparatus. One reserved the use of the telephone and telegraph service in Antalaha only for the gravest personal emergency, Mr. Blaze began; but he did not spell out the nature of such a crisis. I gathered that he had promised his wife that he would call or wire her if his blood-pressure rose alarmingly. Otherwise he had instructed his secretary, a young French woman, as well as his customers in New York, never to telephone or cable business matters, or even personal affairs to him while he was in the vanilla market town. The notorious PTT, I might add, which is the state owned and operated French Post, Telephone, and Telegraph Service, like French Radio and TV, is a government-run monopoly, and a stronghold of petty bureaucrats with a special mentality and sense of power.

The conversation then took on a somewhat philosophical coloring as Mr. Merchant began to comment on the state of the vanilla market. I did my best to translate. He said that a wildly fluctuating and speculative market broke down the absolutely essential balance between supply and demand, and profit and loss. Without these basic relationships between producer and consumer, seller and buyer, in normal operations, business cannot be good business, it can only be bad business. A merchant cannot perform his function in society, he cannot make his contribution to a free society, unless he has the public's good will and full confidence.

Already the youngsters of America have come to associate ice cream with the pleasant sound of jangling bells from the Good Humor man (one of Pavlov's disciples), and so, if things go on the way they are for much longer, the young idea in America will acquire a taste for artificial vanillin. They will grow up not knowing what they have missed; that will be too bad. But it will be much worse for the vanilla producers and the vanilla market of Antalaha; the real bean will perish on the vine. New York will not put up with another price war. Buyers' strikes and sellers' strikes destroy the public's faith not only in the market, but also in the merchant. Once the public anger is aroused, watch out. It is the public duty of the producers to service the commodity—with the help of the vanilla merchants in Antalaha and in New York. The time has come for a cooperative, for teamwork, not for total economic warfare. Another such battle as that of 1947–48 would write finis to real Bourbon vanilla.

In putting all this into French, I made a careful effort *not* to reproduce the New York merchant's passionately convinced tone of voice. But even so, perhaps as in music, his emotional sincerity communicated itself to old Mr. Guihenno—who, at a moment while I stopped to search for the right phrase in French, suddenly exploded. French words erupted from him. Abruptly I reversed gears, and did my best to put them into English for Mr. Merchant.

The gist of the matter was that in 1947 Guihenno's modest warehouse in Marseilles was—for the first time after the barren years of war and occupation and liberation—once again sweet-smelling with vanilla, brought to him from Antalaha and Tamatave in the holds of the troopships returning from the repatriation of Malagasy conscripts and workers. Guihenno had invested his future life in that Bourbon vanilla; each bean was chocolate brown, unctious, flexible, and frosted with crystals. It was as good as gold. There it lay; it would not move. "Then," said Mr. Guihenno—and his tone of voice conjured up an image of Satan himself—"Sonnheim paid me a visit."

Blaze interpolated that Sonnheim, then aged 81 or 82, and now dead, was a well known vanilla broker of New York, but originally of Hamburg, from which port city he had prudently withdrawn when

Hitler came to power in the early 1930s; then he had had the good sense to move to what had been the New York branch of his spice trade. It crossed my mind that possibly Mr. Guihenno may have, in the last years of the war, tried to work out a . . . oh, let's call it a *modus vivendi* with the Nazi occupying forces in the southern French port.

Sonnheim came in, looked around the Guihenno warehouse, took up a random bundle of vanilla, spread the beans like an open flower, and sniffed; his educated nose found no sign of the moth or of mold; he observed the exquisite frost crystals of real, true vanillin, and he put the packet back. In desperation, Guihenno offered him the lot at sixty cents American per pound. The old man's face twisted as he spoke to us about all this past history on the porch of the Hôtel des Orchidées, in March ten years later, and in another hemisphere. He gave us what I am sure were Sonnheim's exact words (in translation): "Sixty cents is too much for vanilla." Sonnheim had then turned away and walked out of the warehouse in Marseilles. In so doing, he had broken Guihenno. The old, bankrupt Frenchman spoke to us of this with an intensity of hatred that made clear one of the causes of the instability of the market in Antalaha.

I was sitting at table with my back to the verandah railing and the Indian Ocean; I faced the interior of the hotel. Something at the back of the bar moved, a ray of light caught my eye. I got a glimpse of Mme. Blondin's far-from-Greek profile as she let the curtains to her living quarters fall together. I told myself that she'd been listening to our conversation; and then I said to myself, Nonsense, what if she has? She has to amuse herself any way she can. And I'd been hearing too much about the spying in the market and the PTT. So I said nothing to the men whose business was not my business. I came into it only as an observer, and not as a participant—except to translate as needs be. I was, I told myself, like all neophytes entering upon unknown ground, beginning to flair danger everywhere. For me a spook lurked behind every bar and every tree in the jungle. I was trigger happy, I told myself. I had deer fever. I informed myself that I knew better. To be sure, Mme. Blondin had not been spying on us in the service of her Créole cousins, the Palimores. Her eavesdropping—if such it was— came about through plain old-fashioned nosiness, the pastime of a lonely, uneducated, under-entertained, tough, French concièrge-type hotelkeeper who never read a book, had little chance to get out to the twice-a-week movies, and was confined behind her bar when she had clients. Her prying into what was none of her business, I said to myself, was none of my business. But, indeed, it turned out to be part of the vanilla business. I, myself, did not then know that Merchant and Blaze were getting ready to buy ten tons.

Mr. Guihenno, then a bit calmer, soothed by Mr. Blaze's quiet and very tired voice, stood up, thanked us for our company, shook hands all around, and retired alone for the night. So did we.

I woke up next morning to the bellowed yearnings of the love-sick cow tethered across the road on her strip of grass beside the sea. I left my dank bed and went out—indeed, I stopped to dress—onto the verandah in search of fresher air and a little breakfast. A small, thin, brown manservant, dressed in sweaty shirt and shorts, left off polishing the floor with the flat side of half a dry coconut, husk and all (he stepped on the round end with one bare foot, put his weight on it, and scrubbed it back and forth, very effectively), and he went, as I asked him to, to fetch me a pot of tea. I sat down, and, looking at a cow tethered across the road, beside the sea, alone in the still and saturated air of the heavy early-morning heat, I gave way to fantasy.

I had read the night before that seacows used formerly to haul themselves up onto these beaches. It follows that if seacows did so, seabulls likewise did. Dugongs, they are called, and they are classed among the sirenians; for sirens they appeared to be to the wrought-up, far-gone sailors on those long Renaissance voyages of discovery. And—as who does not know in our informed, unbelieving age?—those lonely men turned these blubbery, aquatic mammals into mermaids: hallucinatory beings, anatomically impervious to air, to water, and to man. Dugongs make, or made, very stout mermaids.

It would have been better for these great fat sirens if they had taken off weight; for, had they reduced, the chances are that they would have survived, to haunt us all the better. Yet their blubber, not their beauty, in the end proved to be their undoing. They have long since vanished from the purlieus of Antalaha, having been hauled up, beached, cut up, and boiled down for oil. What is, or what was, the use of siren oil?

Mr. Blaze, mercifully and tactfully silent, then joined me at table, looking, I thought, weary. He sat down and called out "Boot!"—which Malagasy word is spelled *boto*, and means garçon, or manservant, or boy. Merchant then walked by, wearing swimming trunks; he hailed us, and headed for the beach of the bellowing brown cow. He looked tired, too. While I thought, nostalgically, of New York plumbing, Mr. Boulanger called out after him, "Be careful! Do not go out beyond your knees! There are sharks out here!" I wonder what mermaids ate. Dugongs are vegetarians. The sirens were maneaters.

As, indeed, are the sharks swimming through the deep Malagasy waters—the ferocious great white shark, thirty feet long and longer; the blue shark, shorter, half as long, but long enough; the fearful tiger shark; and the monster hammerhead. In these deep waters, there are sporting gamefish, too—sawfish and tarpon.

Mr. Blaze then remarked, speaking quietly, that we were going to pay a courtesy visit later in the morning to the House of Palimore, Créoles, the biggest and the richest producers and merchants in vanilla. He then said, most casually, that I might as well leave the interpreting and translating of Mr. Merchant's remarks to him. That is to say, perhaps it would be better if I permitted him to do the often tedious chore of translation.

I got the point. "Are the Palimores the sharks in vanilla?" I asked—and saw at once, from the expression of distaste on his face, that I had made a stupid gaff. I should not have spoken out loud.

"Not necessarily," he replied. "I believe no one overheard you." He then went on to explain that the Créoles speak a special language, difficult to interpret because it is, to unfamiliar ears, compounded of what Mr. Merchant, for example, might just take to be falsehoods—if not a great lot of downright lies. "But," he went on, "it is just their habit of speech, it means nothing once you get the hang of it. It does no harm. You will see, they make long faces and they speak in mournful tones. They will say that business is bad, very bad, and that the current crop of green beans on the vines was much damaged by the drought in October. We all know the contrary to be true. Next season we shall have at least 500 tons of cured beans to sell."

He then went on, speaking very quietly, to tell me that the present Head of the House—he named no names, but he spoke of Mr. Paul Palimore, a man well along in his sixties—appeared to be having trouble with his sons, the eldest of whom must be forty. Mr. Blaze explained that in Sambava, a town on the outskirts of the vanilla district, he had heard the other day a rumor that the family was putting pressure on the old man to retire. There was even some talk of a secret family conference. Neither the boys nor their mother, who held the purse strings, had minded the old man's girls. Throughout his fifties, the Head of the House had . . . so, he had liked young girls. But apparently all that was over now, and he had taken up another pastime—gambling. It is a cold passion. There is no end to it. Blaze stopped to think a moment. "It is a long way to Monte Carlo," he remarked. "The family does not like it; and nor do the rest of us. He is playing the vanilla market as the rest of us play poker. The Chinese, the Malagasy, and the Créoles—they are all born gamblers. But the Chinese are reasonable, and the Malagasy . . . it does not much matter what they do. When the old man plays, he does not care whether he wins or loses."

Merchant, dressed but unfreshed from his tepid dip, then joined us. As soon as he had breakfasted, he got out his notebook and began to hammer questions at Blaze, and to note down the answers. I got up and went for a walk in the incoherent town, false-fronted, as flimsy as an old-time Western setting, but lacking the goodies and the baddies and the high moral tone. Soon I returned to the hotel; and shortly we left to pay our courtesy call on the Créoles.

I have since learned a good deal more about the House of Palimore, in its third generation in vanilla. Paul Palimore's father, Anselm Palimore, began it; the House still owns and operates one of the few remaining great plantations, as well as numerous small holdings. They work vanilla from the start to the finish of the commodity; a son of Anselm, a younger brother of the present Head, manages the plantations, the growing and the harvesting of green beans. A third son, a still younger brother, and *his* oldest son alone know the secrets of the special Palimore curing process, which work they perform themselves at the crucial moments. A brother-in-law manages the warehouses. A cousin-german and his son, a first cousin once removed, manage the trucking and transport company affiliated with, and working for, the House.

Paul Palimore's oldest son is, of course, assistant general manager. Mrs. Palimore is the treasurer. A younger son is the local agent for . . . it is either for Air France or Air Madagascar, I forget; a very distant cousin, perhaps one of Mrs. Palimore's relatives, is the agent for the rival company, either Air Mad or Air France. The House uses both companies' services, impartially. And other members of the family work in Tamatave, in touch with the shipping agents and the customs officials; and in Tananarive, closely in cooperation with the bankers. And so on. I believe a daughter, married to a French official in the Colonial service, lives in Paris; and another (or perhaps she is a cousin) brought off a marriage to an importer in a San Francisco spice company. The point is that this close-knit family has always worked harmoniously and equably together; and each member of the House always knew where he stood in relation to all the others; and he knew that all the others knew what he was doing to promote the interests of the House. And the Old Man at the top began to gamble with the family assets. That shook the House to its foundations. Suddenly, each Palimore found that he stood alone. In this emergency, none cried aloud; all gathered, as some herds do, to face the common unknown danger. Bent on paying our courtesy visit, we happened to stop by at the moment of the crisis.

A minor cousin came to answer our knock at the front door; courteously, he escorted us into the office, and seated us in chairs back to the windows, facing the Head of the House, who sat alone behind his ordinary desk, as though busy doing the routine work of an ordinary morning. The cousin then excused himself, and left the room.

Mr. Paul Palimore greeted us. He saw at once that I was of no importance to him in any way; and so he gave his attention to Mr. Merchant and Mr. Blaze—and left me free to watch him. A big man and a tall man, he had the habit of authority. But time and the climate, plus, I suppose, his appetites, had melted him. His skull showed through his skin. The bulk of his weight had shifted from his shoulders to his belly; and he was all one color. Cotton shirt, cotton slacks, leather sandals, hands, wrists, arms, hair, and face—and so were his lips and his teeth, even his eyeballs—all were tan, except for the pupils of his eyes. These were black holes in iced-tea-colored irises. They seemed to pinpoint everything, as the eyes of the blind do. For all his presence, he seemed to me to be absent, detached, disengaged; and that puzzled me until I realized that, sitting tense and still behind his desk, he was wholly concentrated on listening—but not to us.

Then the other Palimores came in, one by one, all smiling, all tense, all cordial—and all tan. The Palimores are tall, big men. To this day, I have no idea how many of them came into the room. They filled it. I do know that they shared a strong family likeness heightened by what appeared to be a uniform taste in dress. Their skin was light golden brown; so were their cotton shirts and cotton trousers. At that, one or two of the younger men had on shorts and short-sleeved shirts, but cut out of the same bolt of cloth. Perhaps they had a cousin in the wholesale trade.

The Palimores took up their stations behind the desk, and to the right and the left, flanking the old man, the Head of the House. From their defense in depth, they faced us, smiling; but we were not the enemy, and they knew that. I found myself sitting on the edge of my hard chair.

I looked at the old man behind his desk. Gambling is a cold passion. It overtakes a man and frees him; it concentrates him. It is a clean concern that fortifies him; it lasts; it upholds him when all the lesser and the major bits and pieces of life fail him. Every other human beginning has its own implicit and explicit end. But any gambler knows that he can rely on luck—it comes in fast and strong; it runs out; but the law of chance is steadfast. A man can count upon it; it is real. A man wins or loses. Everything else is false. The game itself is trivial. To be sure, there must be rules—means to an end, conventions, not to be confused with ideas of order.

Card players in their hands of bridge believe their honor cards and counted winning tricks to be bits and pieces that fit together in the pattern of this play of social order; and chess is an exercise for cardinals and chiefs of state, who put the named pieces through their arbitrary feudal paces. These players do not look beyond their fan of cards or checkerboard. A gambler takes the next step. He confronts reality. Reality is chaos. Chance alone can flash a light through it. Those whose eyes see by means of chance's focused beam are the rare soldiers at moments in wars, the still fewer mathematicians, the astronomers, and possibly the physicists who climb up beyond their arrangements and rearrangements of the molecules to look back of the stars. And the true gambler who makes use of the cards as they fall like steps in a staircase spiraling out of time and space. That's the way Paul Palimore had rid himself of the Créole's cage.

For a dozen years past, after the old man had served his time as lover, husband, father, breadwinner, the male human being, Mother Nature's instrument, he had tried to break out of his split solitude by going after the girls, the young ones, the pretty girls as fresh and as fragrant as opening flowers. He had enjoyed himself then with the young girls as they came along, following the winding footpath among the trees, carrying their youth like jars of clear spring water balanced on their lovely heads, their shoulders back, their young bodies erect, their slim hips moving as they stepped forward, casually and easily, smiling, flashing their eyes and their white teeth. It was not so much their breasts that moved him as the pure line of the slim throat, the effortlessly straight back, the slim-fingered hands like birds on the wing, the long legs ending in high-arched feet, moving one in front of the other as certainly as time. Such was his joy; it lasted him ten years or a bit longer; then it ended. He remembered them with pleasure sometimes as he lay awake, hunting sleep. The lovely line of girls came stepping along towards him out of the forest.

His sons had not minded; his daughters had not. The slim and lovely girls had not bothered his wife. She had her books to keep, and her rubbers of bridge in the evening. It was a reasonable game, one he had never taken to. It was based upon man-made, or, indeed, woman-made, order. The name of the game—a span between here and there, thrown across a river or a chasm, something constructed to serve a purpose—it suited the play. Auction and contract—he had enough of them by day at work. It suited his wife. Hearts, diamonds, clubs, spades—these were her old, familiar implements, wrung out, dried out, made tolerable, made into deployable symbols. His wife enjoyed a game of bridge. She played for money, to be sure. She liked to win; so she won. But for him, winning was beside the point. So was losing. Sometimes he thought he knew how God felt, God of his early days, of his first communion, when "Let there be light!" God said. *And there was light!* He caught a flash of it when the right card fell.

Or so it seems to me as I remember old Mr. Palimore. I know a great deal more about him now, bits and pieces gathered together after the fact. I've been sorting them out, and trying to put myself in his place. Lord, how alone, how solitary, but how whole he seemed when we first entered the untidy office, his neglected room. I suppose our visit had interrupted the family conference in which all of his own brothers, sons, daughters, sons-in-law, nephews, and the cousins, and, to be sure, his wife had turned against him. They had given him their ultimatum, which was to step down from the position of authority, and to leave Antalaha. He must have realized that they, and not he, rode the run of luck just then.

All that good businessmen should be, they were, these golden Créoles, the young members of the House of Palimore, glossy with self-assurance, exuding the positive in their knowledge of standing on the right side, in full possession of themselves. They knew what they were doing. They were assuring the future; they were maintaining the continuity of the House. Much more than a year's harvest cured and stored in the well built warehouses ready and waiting to be sold —more than this wealth of vanilla was at stake. They stood up to preserve their way of life. I thought it was ironical that they had learned and inherited all their force and all they knew from the old man, who had, to be sure, got it from his father, the original Anselm Palimore. How they resembled one another. They might have been multiplied in a mirrored room. They looked alike, standing there vigorously at ease, each in a family stance. Most striking of all was their courtesy. How pleasantly they made us welcome. How politely they waited for us to say what we had come to say; and then to go.

We were cut off from contact with the old man by the closed circle of their joined will. We were excluded almost as visibly as though they had linked hands to make a human chain around him. They were there to pit their united strength against him so to keep him in order. We had happened to come along at the moment of crisis; therefore, they made use of us. It was to be a test of strength. They all knew that we—that is to say, Merchant and Blaze—were in the market for ten tons of first-quality vanilla. On any other day, after the usual back-and-forth of bargaining, they would have sold it to us; we would have bought it. But not then. The others looked at us, but the energy flowed out of those uniform, golden-brown Créoles to ring the old, solitary, silent Head of the House like a high-tension barrier. He paid them no attention, and gave very little to us.

He looked across his desk at us; and then he saw us, two foreigners in the company of an old acquaintance, a Frenchman, a long-time friendly adversary, like him an expert, a past-master at the vanilla game. He stirred himself; the tan fingers of his right hand closed around something on his desk—I think it was a paper knife. I saw that the loosened skin on the back of his hand was freckled with brown spots. Paul Palimore got down to business and he began to talk.

Yet, clearly, neither his mind nor his heart was in the game. Every one of us in that room knew that he had conceded defeat; he had thrown in his hand. None had moved; yet the tension went out of the air in that small, shabby, dusty office of the Head of the House of Palimore, in vanilla. I sat back in my chair. Too late, I realized that I was guilty of a discourteous act, for Mr. Paul Palimore held himself erect.

I listened in admiration, free to do so because I knew what the Palimores did not know. And that was that Mr. Merchant and Mr. Blaze had stopped off on the way to pay their courtesy visit, to do business with our old friend, the French-assimilated Overseas Chinese, Mr. Lock Hang Leck Lo Nug. They had bought from him ten tons of excellent vanilla at a good price ($17.00 the kilogram, or $170,000 worth of the fragrant commodity, F.O.B. Antalaha). Mr. Lo Nug was glad to sell because he wanted to empty his warehouse so that he and Mme. Lo Nug could leave on a projected business and pleasure trip. They were going "home"—to Paris, France.

I listened as one listens to music while Mr. Palimore explained, sadly, why he was being forced, against his will, to ask the outrageous price of $17.85 the kilogram for ten tons of vanilla of no better quality. It all had to do with a cabled order he had received in the clear that morning from New York.

Something distracted me; I caught myself just in time to keep from sniffing the air. Vanilla is a sweet commodity, based upon the natural aldehyde, a crystalline frost secreted by the enzymes in the seed-casing of a thorn-fecundated climbing terrestrial orchid flower, brought into Madagascar by way of Paris and Bourbon, from Mexico. Discovered by the Aztecs, developed by the French, grown by the Malagasy, handled by the Chinese and the Indians, cured by the Créoles, bought by New York, vanilla is a smelly business. Like the perfumes of Arabia and of France, it is compounded of a hundred essences. It takes a man with a "nose" for perfumes (it is like an ear for music) to sort them out.

The components are essential oils distilled from flowers, from fruits, from spices, from trees and plants—barks, roots, leaves, and saps; from animal secretions; and, to be sure, from chemicals—the synthetics. These all are blended; they are held together and made lasting by a fixative. The basic flower scents are wild orange blossom, ylang-ylang, attar of roses, lily, and jasmine; the fruits and spices are vanilla, clove, pepper, the aromatic herbs, and, I suppose, apple; the wood is sandalwood; the roots are vetiver and orris; the saps are frankincense and myrrh; the leaves are geranium and lemon verbena; musk and civet are the animal odors; one fixative is made from ambergris, which is a morbid substance of great price vomited forth by sperm whales; and, I am told another is the colorless, odorless distillate of human excreta. The perfumes in their pretty flacons have been given charming names.

Antalaha in vanilla smells of the sweet and edible frosted orchid seed pod, manipulated, touched by human hands; but the business smells of money palmed in a hot climate, and of sweaty armpits, and of murky, underhand, secret practices; it smells of history and of the tropical jungle. It smells of that old rot in the state of Denmark, a social odor. It is as gamy as . . . the game of life. It smells as high as the high cost of living—no higher. Deodorants are palliatives. Olfaction is a part of breathing in the air, but the nose is a bad judge of good and evil. Some like it as it is; some may not. But we get used to things.

I was glad to leave Antalaha early the next morning on the airplane for Diégo-Suarez. Mr. Blaze and Mr. Merchant took a later plane south to Tamatave. They had business to transact with the customs officials and the shipping lines in order to expedite their ten tons of vanilla to the customers awaiting it anxiously in New York—for, indeed, New York had allowed itself to be caught in short supply. Mr. Merchant had come to the conclusion that the moment in vanilla, and in Madagascar, was not favorable for the establishment of a cooperative. Even so, he went ahead to service the commodity as best he could, as far as he could go, alone.

Diégo-Suarez

Who discovered Madagascar?

A Portuguese ship captain and navigator did; his name was either Diégo Diaz or Diogo Dias. Rounding the Cape of Good Hope in stormy weather, he went astray, and when he sighted land, he took it to be Africa. When, on a clear winter day, 10 August 1500, he sailed his ship into a great bay to the north, Diégo Diaz came to the conclusion that he had discovered an enormous, hitherto unknown desert island. He claimed it for Portugal, and named it for the saint on whose day he had sailed into one of the safest harbors in the world. St. Lawrence, patron of the new possession, was an early Christian martyr, a Roman and a bishop. He was grilled over embers. When asked if he was ready to abjure, he said, "Turn me over." Madagascar looks like a fish fillet on the map grids. But Saint-Lawrence did not survive as a name for the new island, perhaps because the Portuguese did not settle there, as they did in Goa in India, and in Mozambique and Angola in Africa.

Even so, Diégo Diaz was a member of an august company of mariners: Prince Henry the Navigator (1394–1460), the royal patron; Bartholoméu Dias (c.1450–1500), the discoverer of the Cape of Good Hope, in 1488; Vasco da Gama (c.1469–1524), who went to India in 1497. These were the great men; Diégo Diaz's discovery of Madagascar has not got his curriculum vitae into the encyclopedias. Yet he made a great find; in that bay, in 1942, four hundred vessels of all the Allied forces gathered on their way to Egypt with troops, tanks, armaments, and airplanes to win the battle of El Alamein in October.

In 1506, the year Christopher Columbus died, a Portuguese named Suarez sailed into the unnamed bay, burned a few native villages, and took twenty-one male and female slaves back to exhibit in a fair in Lisbon. The eponymus Diégo Suarez, or Diogo Saoures, arrived in 1543. It is not clear why he gave his name to the bay. It is the best harbor in the Indian Ocean, and one of the most beautiful anywhere, with space enough, as the British newspapers said in 1942, to contain the combined navies of all the world, anchored in peace. In 1942, the British and the South Africans under the command of Rear Admiral E. Syfret began their invasion of Madagascar by taking Diégo-Suarez from the Vichy French.

After the French invasion of Madagascar in 1896, the French Navy built a great base in Diégo-Suarez Bay, and equipped the port with an arsenal and a dry dock, the only ones in that part of the world. They served the commercial vessels of all flags disabled in those southern waters. In 1955, the port handled an annual traffic of about 100,000 tons.

Diégo-Suarez is the third commercial port of Madagascar, after Tamatave and Majunga. On the last day of 1958, there were 37,221 inhabitants in the city, of whom 33,060 were autochthonous, and 4,161 were described as "others"—meaning the French, the Créoles, the Indians, the Chinese; a few British subjects from the Seychelles, from Mauritius, and even from the U.K.; some Comorians, some Zanzibari, and a few Arabs from Yemen brought in to work the docks. Even so, the odd fact is that the port and the bay of Diégo-Suarez are of greater importance to the rest of the world than to Madagascar.

Up at the north end of the island, the bay and its town have little hinterland; a massif and a desert cut them from the rest of the island. It is a dry place; its Malagasy name, Antsirana, means "the City Lacking Water." In 1958, the French authorities hired a commercial well-digging company to drill through the underlying solid rock, but failed to strike a vein of water. An average of forty inches of rain falls annually on an average of eighty-two days in a hot and sticky climate that does not cool off at night. The French in residence prefer to live at 2,210 feet in altitude on the Amber Mountain in a suburban town of villas and gardens named Joffreville. The future French Marshal Joffre served as military commander there in 1897. From the Mountain of Amber he looked down on Diégo-Suarez Bay, shaped like a ragged four-leaf clover, its deep-blue waters studded with small islands among golden hills. The bay is as beautiful as its peers of Rio de Janeiro and San Francisco.

I have never heard a good word said for the port city. It is safe to say that Diégo, as the French familiarly call the town, is the worst place in Madagascar. And why limit it? It is one of the worst places in the world. The *Guide Bleu* describes it as "unfortunately, not yet a fine city," being treeless and shadeless, although built along the straight lines of modern town planning. True enough; but nothing else is straight in Diégo-Suarez. There is a special ugliness about it that seems to emanate from the local way of life. It is a dirty armpit of a town, inhabited, I am told, by the detribalized, demoralized, degenerate, undignified Malagasy, displaced from all over the great island; and by even worse French specimens. It was explained to me that cut-off Diégo, in the French times, had come to be a sort of public convenience for the civil service to which French soldiers, sailors, and functionaries were assigned, and to which the failures and remittance men and women drifted, when their professional ineptitudes and personal aptitudes for such things as wild sexuality had got out of hand. So, at a dead-end in Diégo, they had nothing to do but to let themselves go. *Se laisser aller;* it sounds tired, exhausted, on the skids and far down the slide, in French. Such is not the case for the French Navy, which, in the odd and impersonal way of the Services, assigns young French ensigns there for a tour of duty. Perhaps in their clean white uniforms, they escape the mess.

For mess it was in 1942. France was worn out; Vichy was trying to point with pride to "loyal" Madagascar. Great Britain and all the Allies needed the good news of victory—any victory. Those were black days in the war for the ultimate winners. So the invasion of Madagascar came about. There was nothing French in Diégo to threaten anyone, in those forgotten days; that is to say, except the magnificent harbor itself.

One look at the map makes clear that whoever holds the deep and sheltered bay at the northern tip of Madagascar threatens or potentially controls all the coast of East Africa from the Cape to the Horn, from Durban to Aden, and on into the Red Sea to Suez; into the Persian Gulf to Abadan; into the Arabian Sea to Bombay; across the Indian Ocean to Burma, Thailand, Indo-China, Indonesia; and to Australia, to New Zealand, into the Pacific. In our winter—their summer—of 1941–42, the Japanese had submarines in some or all of these waters. The Italians then controlled the Mediterranean Sea, *Mare Nostrum*. At that time, in the European theater, only the United Kingdom of Great Britain and Northern Ireland still held out, islands of an island country in northern seas.

On 18 June 1940, the French functionaries and colonials, or a majority of them, rejected General de Gaulle's call to the Free French, broadcast from London on the day after Marshal Pétain asked the Nazis for an armistice. Instead Madagascar chose to go along with Vichy. The Malagasy were not consulted. It was the decision of the bureaucrats in the Colonial Ministry, and the commanding officers of the defeated French forces of the earth, the sea, and the air. They made, of course, the wrong choice.

Why? How did it come about, this rejection of the future made far away and long ago? No hostile force put any pressure on Madagascar then; there was nothing like the coming ultimatum of the Japanese to order Indo-China to give in. The forgotten island was not involved in geopolitics like mandated Syria and Lebanon. To be sure, a day or two is a short while for a bureaucratic functionary to have to make up his mind; but it was long enough for the governor of the Chad to rally to General de Gaulle and take his central African territory with him. A day was enough for Félix Eboué, described in the latest edition of the *Petit Larousse* as an *"homme politique français de race noire,"* a black French man born in Martinique, the first to rally with his assigned colony to the Free French.

The Frenchmen in charge of Madagascar in June, 1940, arrived at their poor conclusions and made their bad decision to support a beaten government in Vichy not because they considered it their bounden duty as sworn-in functionaries (my-country-right-or-wrong principle), and not from any careful analysis of the state of war—although we tend to forget that reason alone was not enough, in 1940, to convince any man of the ultimate Allied victory. The British Isles held out, stood firm, and won. But as usual with those islanders, theirs was a triumph of character over the reasonable and the rational mind. Things looked good for Hitler that summer; the intellect alone could not alter the facts.

The French bureaucrats on Madagascar in 1940 did not want to lose their pensions. It was as simple as that. Most of them were senior in grade, getting along in years. Their personnel folders, and the money they paid into the retirement fund, were not with General Charles de Gaulle in London. They were in Paris, in occupied France; and Vichy had access to the documents.

Life is a tragic experience; and history may well be the opinions of historians; but both have their comic moments. This decision of the French functionaries governing Madagascar in the summer of 1940 seems to me to be one of the funny ones. Think of it—to save their pensions and their status in retirement (which, of course, they lost; for they later had to stand trial, and were sentenced to terms in prison or to periods of national indignity), this collection of civil servants and service officers chose defeat and dishonor as though they had no other way out.

As the whiting bites its tail, as the squirrel whirls its cage, the French bureaucrat turned himself into a *rond-de-cuir,* which is the outside Frenchman's derisive and descriptive phrase for an inside French functionary. A *rond-de-cuir* is a leather ring, a wreath-shaped cushion stuffed with feathers, cotton, wool, or straw, or rags, shaped like a doughnut; it has been supplanted of late by an air-inflated, exhausted breath-inflated rubber round, or by a foam rubber pad. The man who sat upon it to pass his life at his desk did so because it was popularly believed that in the course of his inactive action he had developed piles. Hemorrhoids, real or symbolic, appear to be an occupational disease of the bureaucrat. His work produces a fundamental *déformation professionnelle*—or did in the heyday of the French bureaucrat. In America, we get ulcers and have heart-attacks. The French *rond-de-cuir* cannot let go; bent over, or under, a lifetime of desk work, his involuntary muscular reactions atrophy; he cannot digest the mounting piles of paperwork; consciously and unconsciously, he blocks.

So the Colonial functionaries, those unhappy mediums of empire, tried to make Madagascar a preserve for their own vanishing kind— and they almost got away with it because those other mythical average men, the Frenchmen in the streets of Paris, have never shown the slightest interest in leaving them to live and work in such places as Diégo-Suarez. A motherland cannot create new life in a new land by parthenogenesis. It takes men who love a colony enough to live there and to die there—to invest themselves and their lives wholly in the land where they were not born. The majority of the French in Madagascar, and in the other colonies, would not give up France; thus they remained aliens in foreign climes, absorbed in making enough money as soon as possible—a reasonable sum, no more—in order to go back home. Thus they handed over the tedious business of government and of keeping the peace to the professionals—whom they then despised for doing the job delegated to them.

So a gulf formed between the French settlers and the French functionaries in such places as Madagascar. The settlers lived in a fantasy of France as it was at the moment of their departure, and as they hoped it would be when they returned to pick up where they had left off living there. The functionaries, barricaded behind their desks, tried to bring off a similar impossibility, which was to do nothing but their daily work. Each lived isolated in time and space from the island they happened to be living on.

So down there in Madagascar on 18 June 1940, the French bureaucrats, the French servicemen, and the French colonials, some of whom were "good" and some of whom were "bad"—as individual human beings—made their choice for whatever causes or reasons. Having done so, they tried to make do with it as best they could. They shared the forlorn hope that, as usual, Madagascar was so far away from the theaters of battle, and so little known to any man and any power, that whatever they did would pass unknown, be overlooked, be soon forgotten. They had the notion that they'd not be noticed down there. Out of the world's sight, out of the world's mind. They thought they'd get away with it, and ride out the war. And they might have, too, at that, if it had not been for a couple of things in that bleak early spring of 1942. First, they forgot about their great harbor of Diégo-Suarez; second, the Japanese seemed to be winning the naval battles in the East, and the Germans seemed to be winning the land battles in the West. The Allies longed for a victory, and looked around to find the place for one.

Perhaps, because in war anybody, including the members of the general staff, can find reason to believe even the most outrageous rumors; or because even the best secret intelligence is apt to be, is liable to be, incomplete or faulty; or simply because they needed an excuse to justify an invasion of the island, the British press in 1942 was allowed to print stories to the effect that Madagascar, already controlled by, was about to collaborate with, the Japanese. Indeed the conclusion might well have been logically arrived at from looking at the map and remembering specific dates.

On 7 December 1941, the Japanese Navy and Air Force had surprised the Americans in Pearl Harbor. On 10 December, off Malaya, the Japanese had used airplanes and torpedoes to sink the two greatest battleships afloat, *The Prince of Wales* and *The Repulse*—prides of the British Navy. On 11 December, the Japanese took Manila in the Philippines; on 23 December, they took Guam in the Marianas. On 2 January 1942, solitary Wake of the North Pacific fell. On 15 February, Singapore was overwhelmed. On 8 March, the Japanese took Rangoon. On 9 April, Bataan, and on 6 May, Corregidor surrendered. They took Indonesia in June.

So, to believe that the Japanese were in, or on the way to Madagascar was a logical if, in fact, a mistaken assumption. They had considered occupying this furthest western outpost of Polynesian, and thus Asian, culture. Madagascar should rightly have been incorporated in the Greater East Asia Co-Prosperity Sphere. Indeed, it is fascinating to speculate about what the Japanese might have done with their intense cultivation of the huge, empty island. But being realists, even if of a tormented and fantastic kind, the Japanese admirals and generals decided not to over-extend their forces. It is a long, long way from Tokyo, to Singapore, to Diégo-Suarez. In any case, as things looked to the most optimistic or pessimistic minds, soon the Western nations would collapse, and then Madagascar could easily be picked up, if need be, by the Japanese or the Germans.

In February, 1942, the Vichy French minister Benoist-Mechin made a speech saying that if it was, or if it became necessary, his government, the only legal government of France, would not hesitate to call upon Japan to defend Madagascar. Therefore, the British had good cause for their decision to get there first, in force, before the Japanese stepped up their infiltration.

74

Monsieur Armand Annet was the Vichy French governor of Madagascar; a senior career officer in the Colonial administration of the Ministry of the Colonies, at the time of the British invasion. Ten years later, in 1952, he published a book in which he took malicious delight in numbering the Japanese on the island in his time. There were two, an old maid and an old bachelor, she a servant, he a gardener, working for French families. But Annet says, the British, once they got ashore, persisted in seeing Japs everywhere. It is true that some of the highland Merina tribal people show evidences of Mongolian blood; they are yellow-skinned, with straight black hair and slanting eyes. And the people of mixed race are hard to identify. Annet says that one time a British task force arrested a Franco-Negro-Caribe Indian mulatto, a man born in the West Indies, a minor functionary in the government service, whom they took to be a Japanese. The colored man was furious; they had to let him go. As it went on, this small invasion proved to have more comic aspects than most battle actions. Perhaps in all, two hundred men lost their lives in it.

Two or three books have been written about it. K. C. Gandar Dower's *Into Madagascar* is a witty and a first-rate piece of writing. The small Penguin paperback, made of bad, war-rationed stock, is long out of print; it is hard to come by. I looked through the library catalogues in 1959 and 1960 to find more about the man, but had no luck until, in July of 1961 on the island of Samos in the office of the British consul, I came upon a pile of dog-eared back numbers of *The London Illustrated News;* in the issue of March 18, 1944, I found a printed photograph and a carefully worded note that he had been reported missing and was believed to have drowned in February, 1944. He was a Cambridge University graduate, a champion tennis player, good at billiards, and, in 1938, the amateur squash rackets champion of the United Kingdom. This book, written in 1942, and Rupert Croft-Cooke's *The Blood-Red Island*, of 1953, are the most entertaining and the best reporting. But Annet's *Aux Heures Troublées de l'Afrique Française, 1939–1943* is the most peculiar. It is a sort of apology for his life, published by a vanity press. After the war, the French tried him as a collaborator and sentenced him to national indignity, a bitter and a comic sort of penalty for a man who had tried, and tried hard, to find a formula by which to save face and to surrender his island with honor. From his book—dull stuff for the most part, except for the specialist—he emerges as an honest bureaucrat whose fault was his reliability. He clung to the channels he worked through. He carried out orders and did his best to execute the orders of the Vichy policy makers. Always he tried to ask the boss's advice, by cable, and then to abide by the decision. He was a good clerk when he might have been a minor hero. It seems unfair to have sentenced him to so mean a punishment as national dishonor when his fault was that he was born a follower and not a born leader. He was a functionary and a bureaucrat; the symbolism of power was to him power itself. He did not change his colors, but instead remained a neutral grey throughout.

The British tailors make and sell an all-weather, all-purpose man's garment; it is a tweed topcoat on one side, and a water-proofed poplin raincoat on the other. All government workers like Governor-General Armand Annet would do well to invest in one, for when is a turncoat not a turncoat? And how can a public man know when to come in out of the rain? The colors of this dual-purpose cloak are apt to be subdued, as for protective coloration, as well as against travel stains. It does good service in airplanes.

When I landed in Diégo-Suarez, I had been prepared for what I there dug up when the DC-3 of Air France had put down in Vohémar, the next stop before the end. It was a hot sunny day; the airfield is a grassy disaffected pasture, lacking runways, control tower, or one- or two-way radio communications, or much of anything. To let the pilot know the direction of the wind, a far-seeing Malagasy attendant fires a pile of damp hay or straw as soon as he spots the plane in the sky. A thick plume of smoke rises up and bends as the wind blows.

Along with the rest of the passengers in transit, I got out of the plane to stand in the shade of the wing while other passengers and cargo were loaded or unloaded. So, looking down into the long tough grass, I found a foot-long chameleon at my feet, and I encouraged it to climb the brown leather strap of my camera kitbag. Madagascar is incomparably rich in chameleons; two-thirds of all the known *Chamaeleontidae* live there, or about thirty-five species. One is two feet long. I cannot identify now the name of the fine reptile that climbed up my strap, gripping the edges with its Y-shaped claws. It was a small and gaudy dragon with independent eyes. So he looked two ways at once as he slowly came, hand over hand, straight up. He held his tail curled under in a neat spiral, and he tried psychological warfare. He was designed to amaze and bemuse, and he looked fierce as he launched his display. At first, having come out of the grass, he was green, intense, bright, sunlit green, with red-brown stripes. Then he puffed out his throat, as though swollen with rage, and put on a motley of blotches that turned sulphurous yellow as a ground for a long blue streak. I thought of dinosaurs; my hand wavered.

This high-strung, photosensitive, small lizard is a classic propagandist; he employs his own emotions as means of attack; he turns his own fright and fury into weapons to strike terror in the hearts of his beholders. Apparently his own colorful aggression is fueled by his own anxieties. As a last resort, he opened his jaws wide and stuck out his tongue. I was entranced, and he succeeded. I carried him carefully out of harm's way, to put him down again at liberty in the green grass of Vohémar. Chameleon in Greek means "dwarf lion," but his deliberate courage is giant size. I am six times as long as he, yet he set out to scale the vertical edge of what he took to be my ramparts. He did his best to scare me; I did my best to scare; so he controlled and directed me to do what he required me to do—for his own benefit, not mine. But mine was the pleasure. I did what I could do to save his life. This chameleon has nothing whatsoever to do with the British invasion of Madagascar, except to point out that his psywar effort succeeded with me because I was his willing target audience. The British tried a spot of propaganda to soften up Diégo-Suarez's resistance, but failed because the Vichy French were hostile. So the British left off dropping leaflets, and took to dropping bombs.

Back there in Vohémar, the passengers came out from under the plane's spreading wings, and got up into the over-hot cabin; we took off, cooled off, and soon came down upon the Diégo-Suarez airfield to taxi up in front of the monument to the British invasion of May 5, 1942—a rusty, half-unroofed steel hanger. It had not been repaired by February, 1958. The British and South Africans bombed it, strafed it, shot it up, and snowed it with propaganda leaflets before, during, and after the bright morning when their expeditionary forces came out of the Mozambique Channel and landed in the Baie des Courriers, west of Diégo.

That same day, the port fell to General Sir William Platt, of the

Army; Admiral J. F. Somerville, of the Navy; and Commander M. L. Taylor, of the Air Force. The French troops captured at Diégo were sent as prisoners of war to South Africa, where most of them joined the Free French forces; all the Senegalese soldiers did. General de Gaulle must have been pleased by this demonstration of the simple soldiers' loyalty, but he was most displeased with the British High Command, who had included him out of the invasion. Grandeur, remote magnificence, and glory are hard to work with; it may be that the British did not take Mongénéral into their plans for Madagascar because they remembered the bitterness of the Vichy and Free French clash in Syria and Lebanon of the summer of 1941, and the distressing failure of the Free French attempt to storm Dakar earlier on. Yet once they had captured Governor-General Annet, the British turned the island over to General Paul Legentilhomme of the Free French. And then the bureaucrats again had a choice to make. Some of the functionaries joined up with the Free French; and some, committed past all change to Vichy policies, preferred to become real enemies and prisoners of war. But the anonymous, durable, apolitical bulk of civil servants went on working, spreading bread and butter while the old government was carried past on its shutter. Come to think of it, the bread must have been pretty bad then, with not much wheat flour in the mixtures of maize flour, manioc flour, dry lima bean flour, and so on; and the butter practically non-existent. When I was there, most of that was imported from South Africa.

Thus the British and the Allies had their small victory; it can be called a tidy one, as victories go. But once in full possession of the bay and the port of Diégo-Suarez with the desert and the mountain hinterland, they found, possibly to their surprise, that they were stuck. The geography of the island imposed its own conditions upon the British demand for total surrender. But, as is their way, they chose to disregard the mountain, the desert, and the sea, and sent off a stiff request to Governor-General Armand Annet, in Tananarive, calling upon him to hand over himself, his staff, his office, his government, and his island. He took advantage of the delay imposed upon the invaders by the topography to send off what must have been frantic radiograms to his superiors in Vichy. Always he was an honest and hard-working civil servant; and while awaiting a reply, he temporized. Annet sent off representatives to parley with the British on the far side of the mountain—the massif of Tsaratanana, 9,524 feet high—and carefully instructed one emissary, the regular French Army officer who was selected because he had an English wife, to wear all the ribbons of his French and British decorations earned in the 1914–18 war. Annet objected less to the terms for absolute submission than to the wording of the document to be signed. English is apt to be bald in its phraseology at such times; all the Vichy French officials on Madagascar held out for was a little fancy language to obfuscate things, some gentle double-talk to hide behind, some qualifying clichés to save the surface and thus to save their face, and their touchy honor. Always they bore in mind the personnel action, the paper work, the notes that had to go into their dossiers back there in Vichy France. It wasn't much to ask for—a little gentling of the language to save their skins.

So the British had to mount a small but full-scale invasion of the entire island. They took the two main ports of Majunga and Tamatave, and on 23 September 1942 they reached Tananarive—doing the final ascent in the only incompletely sabotaged railroad. Meantime, Governor-General Annet and his staff had retreated down the highland road, heading south, to Antsirabé, to Fianarantsoa, to Ambavalao, and to Ihosy. This last small, dusty administrative center in the beginning of the dry lands is pronounced "Ee-oosh!" and that is what it must have seemed like to Annet, an unlikely cry of relief, a windy sigh such as a deflated balloon makes. On 5 November 1942, exactly six months to the day after the landing at Diégo-Suarez, the invasion came to an end with unconditional surrender. Then came the bitter phase of Armand Annet's degradation. He was shipped off a prisoner to South Africa, where he did his time, supported only by his conviction that he had behaved according to instructions as a proper functionary. In this he was deceived, for the fragmented French immediately following the victory shaved the heads and stripped the collaborating girls in the French countryside; tried and shot Pierre Laval (he was, indeed, a toadlike, evil man); and piled on Annet's head all the public indignities available. To be sure, they left him his life, and what is more (if I am not mistaken) later restored to him his pension. As time passed in the reasonable French manner, they also gave him back his freedom of speech and of the press. He wrote a book.

But at the time of the British invasion of Madagascar, except for the token resistance of a few heroic young men who died symbolic deaths for France in theory, the opposition to the British conquerors was reduced to felling the imported, hardy, ornamental eucalyptus trees growing along the highways in the French manner. Thus, the Vichy French defenders hoped to slow down the advance of the tanks, the armored cars, and the troop transports, and to give the artillery time to . . . to do what? Kill a few men? Gain time? Save face? Theirs was a lost cause. The British correspondents tried to make light of this lethal foolishness in their reports, but privately they were indignant. The British soldiers lost their tempers as they rarely do before the enemy —any enemy—in action. They felt the French in Madagascar to be contemptible.

The British planes, naval guns, and demolition squads did a thorough job on the arsenal, which went out of the war effort for the duration. However, with victory in Europe, the French had to get it back into operation as soon as possible, because the arsenal not only works for the French Navy, but also does the heavy repairs for the port machinery, the island's rolling stock and public works equipment, as well as to give service to all foreign and French commercial ships.

So in 1945 the authorities in Paris sent down to Diégo-Suarez a crew of skilled French laborers and specialists from the arsenal in Paris and the great French ports. This nucleus of men knew what they were doing; they hired local unskilled labor, and they got the Diégo arsenal back at work. These mechanics and technicians were members of the French labor union in the Confédération Générale des Travailleurs, the CGT, which was then thoroughly infiltrated and dominated by the hard-bitten Communists of the French Party. As usual, these Communists were very well organized; and they had their instructions. As they recruited and trained their Malagasy assistants for the arsenal, so they recruited new Communists for Madagascar, and set up cells, networks—the whole pattern of C.P. organization to bore from within.

Today, Madagascar harbors the only native, aggressive, systematic, and organized Communist Party in "Black Africa"—which is to say, with the usual disregard for fact, in Africa south of the Sahara and the Libyan Desert, and in Madagascar, the large, ancient, puzzling offshore island. The port, too, was a French gift from France to the emergent

people, part of the *Présence Française* and the *mission civilisatrice.*
"The white man is committing hara-kiri," said Mr. Blaze. And all the
"trouble" in Madagascar comes from Paris. Well, if Professor Jean-Paul
Sartre, the eminent Existentialist, allowed himself to be beguiled, how
could the nationalist and "anti-imperialistic" Malagasy patriots withstand the pitch?

Yet, as usual, nothing is simple. It is to be noted that, in 1945, the
French authorities in Paris sent down a similar nucleus of skilled
French Communist workers to Dakar, in Senegal, where the arsenal
had suffered similar damage. However, there the Party failed. The
African Negroes and Islamic Senegalese workmen, unlike the detribalized coastal Malagasy and the intellectuals of the Merina highlands,
as well as the Créoles of Madagascar and Réunion, did not take to
Communism as a way of life or as a weapon to use against the French
colonials and functionaries. Why? Why not?

I have a hunch that, with a few notable exceptions such as Paul
Robeson, the Negroes of Africa and America do not make good Communists, and vice versa. I guess that the explanation is to be found in
the existing Negro and Malagasy natures, in their different characters.
I know that I can be proved wrong, mistaken, and indefensible for
what I am about to say; and probably old-fashioned, reactionary, and
downright inaccurate. However, it seems to me that there are differences between the white man and the black man—and the Malagasy. Already I'm in difficulties over terms; but I find that I must use
the inaccurate and arbitrary "white" and "black" for what they're
worth. I think that these differences are more than skin deep. I have
been assured that such is not the case. And I agree that a white child
and a black child, born and brought up under laboratory conditions, all
other things being equal, would prove themselves to be as "identical" as
any two human beings ever can be. But in our imperfect state of evolution, there are inequalities separating the Negro from the other. These
are the acquired characteristics that, like family heirlooms, play so
large a part in shaping our inherited ways of life. Each man alive learns
to be what he is, or to become what he could be, while he is a defenseless human creature, a child.

I am not sure, but I think that, whatever his coloration, the man of
sensibility's and the intellectual's load in the United States right now

81

makes him . . . what? A man apart? It is not necessarily true that he be termed neurotic. Yet he is apt to be forced to withdraw, to live an internal life; to turn to the laboratory or the library, those twin ivory towers of our times, where he can escape to pressures to conform, and can find the freedom necessary to confront the unknown. Thus the mixed-up Negro, mixed in blood, mixed in social pattern, the black man who picks up the singer's or the intellectual's load, may be like his white opposite, atypical. Paul Robeson does not speak, in his tremendous dark voice, for the Negro race, no matter how hard he tries. He sings of Communism as he sings spirituals.

Even so, the character of the Negro, as he appears to be in Africa and in the U.S.A., is different from the character of the white man, as he seems to be today in Africa and in the United States. The difference is not that of a dark shadow cast behind the colonial whose day is done, nor by the attitudinizing "poor white trash"—whatever that means. The difference is a matter of character, which is to say, "The aggregate of qualities that distinguishes one person or thing from another . . . moral constitution. . . ." As things stand, the Negro has a nature of his own.

Here goes: Negroes as a rule are not intellectual, but are emotional. Many of them are artists—singers, dancers, actors, celebrants of mysteries. In Africa, most of them have a great gift for the plastic arts, and are marvelous sculptors, and in wood and ivory as well as in gold and bronze. They live in their emotions, in their sense perceptions, and respond to the pleasures and the pains thus offered. As yet they have not forced the knowledgeable mind to lead them along by the nose. They like to sing, to eat, to do what used to be called make merry. They are of good cheer, given less than half a chance. It is not just white teeth in a black face that makes the grin of a Negro a happy sight. He has a wholehearted delight in the moment. For the moment holds all the life that the Africans and many Americans can have. Negroes, then, are not, as a general rule, against the life of the body; they enjoy what happens to the flesh. So they take to horror and to violence, as in the Mau Mau rites. Whatever else the Negroes now are, they are not yet Anglo-Saxons, nor puritans, nor critical and analytical Frenchmen. Theirs is another sort of life, which, for whatever reasons or causes, is communal, collective, and external. But not Communist.

Perhaps the Renaissance has run its course; perhaps humanism has had its great days. The reason of the Age of Reason has lost its force. The Dark Ages put their faith in an omnipotent, omniscient, anthropomorphic God; the earth, where Jesus Christ was born, was, with heaven and hell, their boundary. We live in another age; time and space now are one. Even the sun has a limit of light-years yet to burn. The unknown has a life of its own again. Even so, most of us, being human beings, still live in the delusion that man is the center of the universe. We suffer from that old malady of "rational" thinking.

Karl Marx, the detribalized, exiled, intellectual German Jew, who seems to have been a loving husband and father and a happy family man, was seriously afflicted by the disease of thought; and his era was the time of rationalism. So Karl Marx's Communism, and his disciples', appeals in dialects as neat as early abstract paintings to the egotistical people who have pride in the mind, who believe themselves to be able to think straight and thus to control life through thought. And, to be sure, it appeals to the underdog who wants to be the top dog; to the men who like to handle power; to the bewildered who need reassurance; and to the lost who want to be led back into a firm social order. Communism's dead-end, idealism, argues for an achievable goal of man-made perfection, and the life eternal. And, as usual, the white man gave the black man these hard, smooth, and fixed old-fashioned theories to climb up on. But in Senegal and in the United States the Negroes have rejected Communism. Perhaps they do not feel at home in it. Is it too cold, too pure, too orderly for them? It is for me. It puts a cage around life.

The Malagasy are not Negroes; and although there is an unknown quantity of Negro blood in the coastal tribes, their culture was clearly Polynesian. Enough of them have accepted Communism to organize a powerful political force, and to control the province of Diégo-Suarez. What are the Malagasy like? To begin with names and numbers, the *Service de Statistique* lists the total *population autochtone* on 31 December 1956 as 4,842,010; one year later as 4,975,498; and on 31 December 1958 as 5,096,767. On that day, the separate tribes in alphabetical order numbered:

The Antaifasy, "the People of the Sands," who live at the southern end of the east coast, 28,453;

The Antaimoro, "the People of the Coast," who live in the region of Vohipeno and Manakara on the east coast, south of center, and who have some Arab blood and all but obliterated traces of Arab culture, 178,215;

The Antaisaka, short for Antaisakalava, which name means that they are an off-shoot of the once dominant Sakalava of the west coast; they now work readily for the colonists all over the island, although their land is on the east coast south of Farafangana, 302,354;

The Antakarana, "the People of the Rocks," who live at the northern tip of the island in the Diégo-Suarez country, a regressive mixture of Sakalava, Betsimisaraka, and Arab tribes numbering 35,556;

The Antambahoaka, "the Descendants of Rabevahoaka," the smallest of the tribes, who live near Mananjary south of center on the east coast, and who claim to be authentic descendants of the Arabs who settled there in the fourteenth century; they are not, however, Moslems, and they number 17,723;

The Antandröy, "the People of the Thorny Brambles," a dark-skinned, primitive, and attractive tribe who live in the arid south around Ambovombé, where the clawed acacia, the endemic euphorbias, and the long-thorned *Didiereaceae* grow, 277,144;

The Antanosy, "the People of the Island"—a small one in the Fanjahira River, in the southeast; these dark-skinned, flat-nosed, thick-lipped people were the ones who drove out the first French settlers of Fort Dauphin, in and after 1643. They number 148,132;

The Bara, whose name is a name with no certain meaning; nomads of the southern highlands around Ihosy and Betroka, they are the artists, the sculptors, the dancers, the cattle rustlers, and the athletes of the island, 215,026;

The Betsileo, "the Numberless Invincibles," a peaceful and hard-working peasant tribe of the central highlands around Fianarantsoa, they are dark-skinned Polynesians, wonderfully skillful at managing the water for their irrigated and terraced rice fields; third of the tribes, they number 637,661;

The Betsimisaraka, "the Many Inseparables," who live along the top half of the eastern shore, around Tamatave and Antalaha, who work the rich plantations, and who are in vanilla; the second of the tribes, they number 773,104;

The Bezanozano, whose name, "Many Small Braids," is descriptive of the way they wear, or wore, their hair, are Australo-Melanesians, thought to have arrived on Madagascar about 2000 B.C. They live in a pocket between the Betsimisaraka lowlands and the Merina highlands, and number 32,540;

The Mahafaly, a splendid primitive tribe of the desert southwest, around Ampanihy; they are dark-skinned, and their name means "Those Who Put Taboos on Things"—78,398;

The Makoa, also known as the Mosombiky, or "People of Mozambique," who live on the west coast opposite Africa, are the only truly African Negro tribal group of Madagascar; they are the descendants of imported slaves, 58,934;

The Merina, "the People of the Highlands Where the View Is Wide," the largest and most advanced of the islanders and the former rulers of Madagascar; their city is Tananarive. Malayo-Polynesians, they are divided into three main castes: the Andriana, or nobles; the Hova, or freemen; the Andevo, or slaves—of whom some were the Mainty, or "blacks." Some of the Hova are light-skinned with slanting eyes and straight or softly curling hair; the Merina are by far the most numerous of the Malagasy, making up a quarter of the total population, and numbering 1,248,531;

The Sakalava, "Dwellers in Long Valleys"; formerly the most powerful of the tribes, their lands used to include the western half of Madagascar; Majunga is their most important city. A tall tribe of dark brown people, they are on the decline because, it is said, they have chosen to reject modern ways—316,212;

The Sihanaka, "the People of the Swamps" around Lake Alaotra, the largest fresh water lake on the island, north of Tananarive, west of Tamatave, on the broad shelf between the highlands and the lowlands. Their swamps have been drained to make rich agricultural land; the Sihanaka number 107,133;

The Tanala, "the People of the Forests" which have been cut down to make coffee plantations on the slopes inland from Manakara on the east coast; they are still primitive people, and in the Rebellion of 1947 and its aftermath, many of them died of exposure, fright, and starvation; and they number 215,639;

The Tsimihety, "the People Who Do Not Cut Their Hair" (as a sign of mourning), in full expansion, energetic, and hard-working, they are brown of skin, but are thought to be in part descended from the eighteenth-century pirates of Libertalia on Diégo-Suarez Bay. Their territory lies in the center of the north; there are 363,897 Tsimihety, among whom President Philibert Tsiranana, of the Malagasy Republic, is number one.

These are the eighteen tribes of the Malagasy. However, there are three other listings among the autochthonous population; and these are the Saint-Mariens of the island of Sainte-Marie that lies off the east coast north of Tamatave; it is famous for its cloves and for its romantic history; and since 1754, when the Betsimisaraka Queen Beti, married to a legendary French corporal known as La Bigorne, gave her island to France, its very mixed inhabitants have been French citizens; there are 12,859 of them. A second listing is of 46,601 Comoriens—Islamic people of the Comoro Islands in the Mozambique Channel north of Madagascar, a French territory; they are of mixed Malagasy, African, and Arab descent, and most of them live in Majunga and in the towns along the west coast. Finally, the *Service de Statistique* lumps together the "Other Races," and I do not know who these people could be. In 1956 there were 6,418 of them; in 1957, 6,276; and on 31 December 1958, only 2,655. Perhaps they are orphans, by-blows not claimed by any parent tribe or group or race. Perhaps they are only statistical leftovers.

The Communist Party seems to me to be a cage. Most of us live in cages, anyhow—some of our own making, some of our own choice; some are made for us by our ancestors and handed down, some forced upon us by our ignorance, or feebleness, our human fix. Societies at their worst put us into cages; the least powerful are the obvious, material structures; the strongest cages are the unreasonable ones, the invisible conditions that are, perhaps, accumulations of past time and fixed space hidden away in the unconscious. These cages take shape as a pattern of life hardens. The cages then become a container of the old familiar ways. It seems to be a safe haven and a refuge. So all change is excluded from urn burial. Primitive tribal societies in mountains, and in jungles, and on islands are such as these. They serve until they crystallize; and then they shatter at a touch.

Periods of transition always bring along chaos, for the crowded mind and heart of man cannot make room for new ideas and emotions in a single generation. And even so, as like as not, the bewildered individual, thrust out of his cage, picks up the wrong or the mistaken notion of what freedom is, of what reality may be. It appears to be a trait of human nature to build up hatred for one's conquerors—and for one's teachers, good or bad teachers. We seem to retain only what we learn the hard way—through the emotions in a series of shocks that break open fissures in our armored personalities, through which new methods, new ideas, and new techniques seep in as opal and agate replace the perished wood in petrified forests. And, having lost the old serviceable, if inadequate, scale of values, we are apt to misapply the new and foreign standards handed out to us. I never can remember how tall I am in centimeters, nor how much I weigh in kilograms; and for all figuring, I have to go back to the names of the numbers in my native, mother tongue.

So the detribalized Malagasy (or some of them), dispossessed and broken loose from their ancestral ways and places, and able to absorb only a little learning at a time, at first looked to find, not freedom of choice towards self-determinism, but instead, a hard and fast organized society as much like the old tribal structure as could be. In the old days, each man and woman knew his and her place; they could start off from that fixed point to do what they had to do. Communism's tight cellular units fit the bill for them. In the highlands, the *évolués,* the French-educated Merina tribesmen and women who formerly had held the power, found another motive force. It was their resentment and hatred of the French, who conquered and humiliated them, and who, without being fully aware of what they were doing, set themselves up as being racially superior to the Merina and all the other Malagasy. It is no good to explain to the autochthonous population that the French are French wherever they are, and as such naïvely take for granted that they are superior to every other people, "race," or nation of all the colors and the creeds on earth. To them their innate superiority is Q.E.D.—one of the laws of nature. The fact that the Malagasy are black, brown, and tan, and that the French are white, has only accidentally lugged in the highly emotional corollary that the white Europeans are superior, now and forever, to the colored peoples of the world.

Communism, then, appeals to some of the educated—which means Europeanized—Merina as the answer to the problem of how to reestablish their own natural superiority, as well as a weapon to evict the French and the *Présence Française* from *their* island. All this is complicated by the political and emotional fact that the coastal tribes and the others of the highlands fear and suspect the worst of their former pre-French conquerors and rulers, the predominant Merina of Tananarive. And the Merina look down from their high place upon the lesser breeds. It is odd but understandable to see the spread of this supposedly intellectual, thoughtful, rational, and brainy system of political science and political economy, the Communist way of life, fueled by such violent, unreasonable, and blinding emotions.

In the decade before the Second World War, there was a sort of Communist Party of Madagascar active in the island among the Merina of the nineteenth-century monarchy. However, the French Party disowned it, claiming that the Malagasy Party members were not true Communists because they worked not so much in the interests of International—that is to say, U.S.S.R.—Communism as for local independence from the French. The Merina Communists were accused of using the Russian international apparatus in an attempt to reinstate themselves in the feudalism of the not so very ancient monarchy of the island kings and queens. Therefore, the French Colonial authorities had very little trouble with the first Malagasy C.P.; they suppressed it along with all other political activities, as well as the trade unions, at the outbreak of the war in 1939.

The present Party is a different matter. It is classic in organization; it is supplied with organized fronts, fellow-traveling groups, symbolic nationalistic political personalities, and active penetrations of the Malagasy unions, professional groups, government offices, and so on. Those imported French arsenal skilled laborers, many of whom had been tested in the Communist resistance groups, were hard-bitten, disciplined, tough, and experienced Communists. They brought with them all the decisions ready-made, and built a firm foundation for what they see as the eventual take-over of the island. The wonderful Bay of Diégo-Suarez is their first prize.

Having built the French Navy's arsenal into a Communist bastion, the French workmen were sent home. The Malagasy organization that they left in excellent working order is supplied, supported, encouraged, and directed not from Paris any more, but from Moscow and Peking. The couriers and visiting officials come into Madagascar, describing themselves as tourists, private businessmen, and members of government purchasing missions from the Iron Curtain satellite countries, or, indeed, from Belgium, Switzerland, Italy, France, China, or elsewhere. And, as usual, the French, who are good talkers and who like to talk, take pleasure in serving the Communist purpose by spreading the defeatist propaganda of the invincible C.P. against their own interests.

It is also in the pattern of the Communist Party's planned action to infiltrate the target country with a few schooled and controlled men and women to work under cover, to form the well known hard core, to act as fellow-travelers, or to serve in the support section of the Party's intelligence or political action enterprises—as cut-outs, as couriers, as fronts, as red-herrings, or as sleepers. Thus it is far too easy to believe that Mr. and Mme. Boniface, and Mr. and Mme. Guy, French business people of Tananarive, may be Communist plants, despite their obvious success in capitalistic enterprises. These two French couples, whose last names can also serve as first names, which trick is a familiar dodge in the compartmentation of any spy business, are known to have been involved when they were young in the Spanish Civil War on the other-than-Generalissimo Francisco Franco side. "Republicans" and "Loyalists," they may have been; "Reds" they ended up —and left France in 1938, after Munich, for the island of Réunion. There they sat out of the war—or rather, worked hard at their professions. Boniface was a building constructor, an engineer, a contractor. When nothing was to be imported from France, or from anywhere else, he kept busy on Réunion improvising patchwork repairs to keep the charming Louis XVI, Directoire and Empire houses from collapsing; they are pretty residences built in the heyday of the Colonial trade, single-story, neo-classic buildings decorated with pilastered façades, columned porches, arched porticos, balustraded flat roofs set about with urns and flame finials, painted in pale pastel colors, standing in shady ramshackle gardens full of romantically overgrown old roses, and shielded from the streets by fences of palings and posts hung about with swags and garlands; but they are tumbling down—for lack of slaves to keep them up in the destructive climate.

The Guys, who work as a team, are radio, phonograph, and electrical-equipment shopkeepers; and they kept themselves busy repairing and patching up the old sets that brought into the island the only news of the outside world to get in. They prospered; or at any rate, they apparently had a source of ready cash. For they began to collect Chinese carvings and porcelains, buying up the heirlooms of ivory, jade and rock crystal, and the vases, bowls, dishes, covered pots, and so on, of the Chin Dynasty potters. For the impoverished Réunionnais would sell these treasures to the newcomers, called in to repair radios and flat irons, or to fix the ceiling, as they would not suffer the humiliation of letting the local merchants pick them up. Indeed, perhaps all the gossip about their Communist affiliation may be a bunch of lies thought up in malice and envy, and spread against them by the decaying old families who had to sell their precious ornaments and status symbols of the great old Colonial days to the brash, tough, hard-bargaining, and hard-working newcomers, with money to spare.

In 1945, the Guys and the Bonifaces moved over to Madagascar and set themselves up in business in Tananarive; the Boniface son is a building contractor like his dead father, and the Guys opened a flourishing radio, phonograph and record, and small electrical appliance shop where they sell well known trademarked products from France, from the United States, from West Germany, of course from Holland, and lately from Japan. Recently they expanded into brand-new quarters on the ground floor of a new building on the main street of the middle city of Tananarive. The Guys are very much alive. They have two sons, the younger one studying painting in the Ecole des Beaux Arts, in Paris. His mother is proud, permissive, but distressed by his choice; he has won several prizes for his work, but as she says, looking around the impressive premises of the radio and phonograph shop in Madagascar, "*L'art, ce n'est pas une vie!*" One cannot live by art alone.

It is the classic, canny French bourgeois capitalistic parent's cry. At that, it might well be the complaint of a heroic Communist mother, for the art of the West, and in particular of the school of Paris—despite Picasso, the Spanish comrade—is classified as decadent stuff in Moscow, along with the frivolous *vie de Bohème*.

The married elder son is a trained radio engineer who works part time in the family shop, and part time for Radio-Tana where he services the state-owned equipment. He does his technical job well, for he went to New York in 1954 to take a proper degree from—I don't know, Cornell, Van Rensselaer, somewhere. The point is that to get his entry visa as a student in the United States, he had to swear to certain statements absolving him from connection with subversive actions, past or present affiliation with Communist or Fascist Parties, et cetera. He must have been about five years old at the end of the Spanish war; and so, even if his parents were then members of the Communist Party, perhaps he is guilty only of association with his mother and his father.

He is a well grown young Frenchman, wearing his tight Italian clothes as though he takes himself to be the very measure of the man around whom French republican individual freedom has been built. He makes it evident that he thinks well of himself, and that he is the center of his known world. In 1959, he had an adoring young wife (French) and a baby son. The young people live with the parent Guys above the shop.

Mme. Guy is a typically energetic French *femme magistrale* of a certain age—meaning 50-odd—competent, loud, knowing, hard-work-ing, and well dressed in all the accessories of feminine success. For instance, in 1959, the only noticeably red attribute about her was her luxuriant head of dyed hair; it was a brilliant scarlet; clearly it required constant up-keep. Nothing could have been more thoroughly artificial. It was a bouffant crowning glory of conspicuous consumption. It must have cost a lot in beauty care to maintain such a head of red hair. The touching thing is that her daughter-in-law, a pretty but an ordinary girl with only youth as her distinction, dyed her own medium brown hair to match her mother-in-law's splendid status symbol, just before the wedding, perhaps on the theory that two such reds make it right.

The elder Mme. Guy wears handsome jewelry, large local stones of deep golden-brown topaz quartz set in ample amounts of red gold. The colors go well with that flaming hair and tawny skin. Mme. Guy is not skinny. She is tall; she has wholehearted style. She goes on holi-days back to France as a good colonial should; and she combines business with pleasure as a buyer of new stock for the shop. Husband and wife rarely go together for the very good reason that somebody has to stay behind and tend to business. The husband seems to be a solid citizen, a quiet and, indeed, a less conspicuous person. Who knows whether they are through with Communism or not? All good Frenchmen are supposed to be radical when young, and conservative in middle age.

When, at the time of the 1959 Referendum to adopt the new constitution and the Community, Sekou Touré voted No, and took Guinea with him out of the French sphere of influence, Mme. Guy was outraged. She said that Sekou Touré had to be punished, to be made an example of, to be denied all French help of any kind. The rest of Africa and Madagascar had to be made to understand his crime. What ingratitude! What insolence! He would see just how much he had lost by rejecting the *Présence Française!*

Was all that more C.P. guile? Or was it only French Colonial hurt feelings and general fright? There is nothing like a successful business enterprise in the colonies to make a man or a woman into a reactionary. C.P. guile or French Colonial bile—who can tell the one from the other in effect? One of the nasty aspects of our times of fast transition is that the stain of past Communist affiliations won't rub off. Mme. Guy, like the Red Queen, has to run as fast as she can in order to stay in the same place as the life around her moves from left to right across the political scene. I, for one, hope that the only remaining red left on her mind is her flamboyant hair.

The acknowledged and recognized leader of the Communists, and the Communist Party, of Madagascar is a woman, Miss Gisèle Rabesahala, a member of the Hova caste of the Merina highland tribe, and thus a predominant Malayo-Polynesian stock. She has never married. Political action seems to be her one consuming passion. It is hard to find out much of anything else about her outside her public life or, rather, inside it. She protects herself; and like President de Gaulle, she knows that political authority must be coupled with a certain reserve, a remote and austere mystery, a conscious isolation in the center of turbulence. She keeps herself apart, and she is into everything—or as much of everything political in Madagascar as she can infiltrate.

Communism's subversive action has been likened to the spot of oil that spreads its colorful, or dirty, film over the water or along the warp and woof of interwoven fabrics. It is ironic once again to realize that this technique of the spreading spot of oil was first used in Mada-

gascar by the great French General Gallieni, the Pacificator, the organizer of the newly conquered island colony in 1896. He set up
oilspots of armed peace in the troubled wilderness to demonstrate the
meaning of French enlightenment along with the then most modern
techniques of agriculture, animal husbandry, trade and commerce,
sanitation and medical care, and civil law and order based on discipline, understanding, and self-control. Miss Rabesahala (her name
is pronounced "Rah-bay-sahl") does the same, but to the opposite
effect.

It is interesting to note that one of the proofs, or at any rate attributes, of Polynesian culture is the equality, if not the superiority,
of women in society. In Polynesia, matriarchy is usual, and property
and kinship go through the female line of descent. The last rulers of
the nineteenth-century kingdom of Madagascar were queens, three in
a row. Miss Rabesahala looks to be about forty, but she is probably
older. She lives in Tananarive, and she is highly *évoluée,* and thoroughly assimilated into International Communism. Educated in
France, she had traveled to Moscow, where it is said that Stalin himself received her. She has visited Prague; she has gone to Peiping as a
delegate of the Malagasy youth cultural and mutual assistance organization, called the Association Démocratique de la Jeunesse Malgache.

But how did she get that way? For she is a hater, an agitator, an
organizer, a concentrated, dedicated Communist. It is easy enough to
show up the faults and the failings of Colonialism, even of the French
variety—which is not primarily commercial, has never paid its way,
and was not determined by the economic necessities of capitalism as
described by Lenin. It is much too easy to say that Communism's appeal as a logical, rational, workable political system fills the power
vacuum left in the minds of a people freshly broken away from super-
stition, ignorance, and hard and fast tribal culture.

It has been suggested that Miss Rabesahala took to hatred of the
French as a result of some traumatic incident in her personal and
private life that may have caused her violently to reject France and
French ways, and, by extension, the so-called decadent Western world.
Orientals like to be on the winning side, as who does not? And part
of the myth of Communism is that its ultimate victory is inevitable.

Even so, the Party of Madagascar has never exceeded 650 members at most (or so I am reliably informed) out of a total population of some five million and more people, who enjoy the usual universal suffrage. There is not one known or suspected Communist in the government of the present Malagasy Republic. There are a few "Red" deputies elected from the Province of Diégo-Suarez to sit in the island's Parliament; but the minority has little real influence.

These so called, and perhaps actual, Communist deputies were elected by the C.P.-organized members of the labor unions.

Labor in Madagascar has always been against the government—whatever government is in power. That is to say, labor in the concept of labor as we know it has always been a problem. It is a foreign import, the idea of a man or a woman working not for himself, but for some superior who supervised, directed, and paid him wages; or enslaved him. In the very early days when the clan and the family unit prevailed not only as the basis, but also as the whole structure of society, the Malagasy had a secure life to lead. He knew what work he had to do at any given time; he depended upon nobody but himself; he knew who he was. He lived at peace—or as much as a man ever can live at peace inside his skin and his society. He worked for the food he needed. His wife wove the clothes for the family. He built his house; his wife tended it, and cooked the food. Each year, he worked no more than the equivalent of three months of forty-hour weeks.

Then the enormous island was large enough for everybody on it, with space to spare. How many inhabitants could there have been on Madagascar when the Arabs came in with the slave trade to put a price on a life of human labor? Perhaps half a million fewer. There is no way of knowing. Today there are 5,000,000 Malagasy people; in 1901 there were 2,299,000. Perhaps a century earlier, when the Merina began their conquest of the island, there were as many all told; but the constant wars of the nineteenth century killed off the young men and kept down the normal growth of population. It is said that in the thirty-three years of her violent and reactionary reign, Queen Ranavalona I, the Cruel, caused the deaths of 1,000,000 of her subjects and, of these, 100,000 were slaughtered in execution.

The Arab slavers did not introduce the idea or the practice of slavery to the Malagasy tribes. The captives of the constant inter-tribal wars were set to work as slaves of the winners. But the Arabs and the later European slavers established a trade and an economy based on slaves, and in effect set a price on human life and thus encouraged warfare. Tribal chiefs began to sell their own people as well as prisoners.

When the Portuguese discovered the island, they took slaves home with them. When the French came in the seventeenth century, they forced the Malagasy into slavery. It has been suggested that the Malagasy fear and hatred of the *vazaha,* the white men, comes from the brutal treatment they received at the hands of the Arab slavers, and the European sailors and settlers, when they first went out to welcome them as friends, and even as gods. The Merina conquerors had evolved a caste system in which neither the nobles nor the free men did any physical work at all; their whole way of life was based upon slavery and slaves—although in practice these laborers were not harshly treated, but were included in the family as perpetual inferiors who could almost never change their condition, but who could speak out and be listened to. The future Maréchal-de-France, Louis-Hubert Lyautey of Morocco, when he was a colonel learning his Colonial methods under Gallieni at the end of the nineteenth century in Madagascar, wrote that slave and slavery were not the words to describe the condition of the treatment of this working caste of Andevo and Mainty; yet they were not free men and women, and they did all the work.

King Radama I had encouraged the forming of guilds for the various craftsmen and artisans at the beginning of the Merina monarchy, when free men did skilled work. Later Ranavalona the Cruel destroyed any freedom within these guilds and lowered the condition and the status of labor by establishing the *corvée,* or a period of unpaid forced labor exacted from individual craftsmen or whole guilds. They were made to work for her, or for the Crown, for the duration of her pleasure—and if she was not satisfied with the results of the builders or the silversmiths, for instance, working in the palace, she had the men executed. Laborers came to live in fear and trembling; for from the queen they had no recourse.

When the French annexed the island in 1896, they abolished slavery, and found that by doing so they had abolished both workmen and work of all kinds, and had no means of raising taxes. They were forced to revive and adapt the old feudal system of the *corvée* by which each man from 16 to 60 was compelled to work fifty days a year for the government in lieu of taxes. Those Malagasy who had the money could pay an equivalent sum in direct taxation, or hire poorer men to replace them in the drafted labor force. The majority, however, spent their fifty days annually building roads or other public works; and they did not like it.

So Madagascar has always had a labor problem and a tax problem. Having no pool of workmen, there is a perpetual shortage of labor, whether skilled or unskilled, to work the privately owned plantations or in the very few small industries and factories, as well as in the offices and hotels, or as servants in the houses of the well-to-do, most of whom are foreigners. The colonists complain that the Malagasy are lazy, born lazy, bone lazy, and that they do not like to work. There is a certain amount of truth in the loud claim. Malaria is a debilitating disease; the Malagasy diet of rice and boiled green shoots, with only now and again a little fish or bit of meat, lacks protein. And the shores, the coastal plains, the arid south and west, and the lower highlands all lie well within the boundaries of Arnold Toynbee's pessimum climate, where the labor problem can be summed up as: Why work? It's too hot.

So their society, whose members worked only as need be to stay alive, was a happy one—superstitious, held down by taboos, suspicious, and fearful of strangers, to be sure, but only normally neurotic, with witch doctors, magic, sorcerers, and living ancestors to take care of these. There was, in the old days, always enough for everybody in the almost empty island; and, except in the highlands, there was no labor problem. The conquering Merina tribe of the nineteenth century changed all that; and the French brought in a trickle of the revolution of our times.

In the socialist days of Premier Léon Blum and the Front Populaire in France in 1936, organized and protective labor unions got started in Madagascar; they lasted but three years before the outbreak of World War II suppressed them along with their allied political action. During the war, Malagasy laborers were once again requisitioned, or drafted, or called up by the Colonial government. In the Vichy year of 1941 (according to a Communist "authority" named Pierre Boiteau in his book, *Madagascar, Contribution à l'Histoire de la Nation Malgache*) the Malagasy men were forced to donate, in all, 2,550,000 working days to the government—as porters, road builders, laborers in public works, and foot couriers replacing the broken down system of wheeled communications and carriers. This return to forced labor was justified as a replacement for the years of compulsory military service no longer required of the islanders of the French Empire. It was a logical, and even reasonable, solution to the problem of food production in Madagascar, cut off from the foreign imports for the duration. But the method revived unhappy and unfortunate memories. The Malagasy remembered another period of recent drafted labor.

From 1926 to 1936, the Colonial authorities made use of a *Service de la Main d'Oeuvre des Travaux d'Intérêt, Général,* or SMOTIG for short, a sort of civilian conservation corps but with a difference; it was an army of laborers recruited in the military fashion, trained in the use of pick, shovel, and so on, and sent where the government decided they were needed to do the work of building roads, railroads, harbor installations, and bridges, or as lumbermen to fell the forests, or to drain marshes or to control streams and rivers. On the surface of it, the SMOTIG was not a bad organization—except that the Malagasy had no choice in the matter of recruitment. However, corruption set in; powerful private interests put pressure to bear on the functionaries to divert contingents of this publicly equipped and maintained civilian labor "army" to work on the plantations and concessions of various individuals and of the great French Colonial companies; in other words, for private profit. What was good for the great landowners and the Marseillaise, the Lyonnaise, and the Société de l'Émyrne was good for Madagascar. But not necessarily for the Malagasy; and so SMOTIG was abolished. There is a long history of conflict between management and labor on the island; and the labor shortage continues. But the unions have come in to stay.

On my arrival in Diégo-Suarez in the late summer evening of 20 March 1958, I had taken a room at the Universal-Epochal Hotel in the center of town. The day was hot; the night was even hotter. It had been my intention to go to bed to try to sleep. But I could not. So, acting on the principle "if you can't beat 'em, join 'em," I had got up

again and gone down to the hotel's thronged corner bar; but, after a
moment of pandemonium, I fled out into the street to stand for a time
on the edge of a crowd of whatever sex and of all colors moving slowly
back and forth, up and down and around, going nowhere, but cluster-
ing under the powerful electric light of a single large bare bulb screwed
into a goose-neck fixed to the wall above the open door to the bar on
the corner. It was the only entrance to the Universal-Epochal Hotel.
The white light did not so much illuminate as blacken the surrounding
night; it was a heavy, a hot, and a wet night. A hundred or a thousand,
or—who knows?—a hundred thousand doomed moths and winged
bugs buzzed the light bulb; the biting and the stinging ones stayed in
the lower shadows, to suck a little blood, to feed on the juicy whores
and their sweaty clientele, parasites on the parasites in heat, or in love,
or in loneliness, or in boredom, or in need—anyhow, in the night.

For the corner of the streets of the symptomatic Universal-Epochal
Hotel was (when I was there) the meeting place, the market place,
the stock exchange for whores; it was the playing field, the drill field,
the proving ground, the *champ de mars* for all, or almost all, the
ambulatory ones, the street walkers; and inside the bar at tables by
the wide-open windows sat the sedentary bar girls of Diégo.

Here congregated the port's call girls—and all that a man need do
was call out in any tongue; or if mute, he could point to make his
choice, either inside at the bar, or outside under the naked bulb. They
sat or they strolled, chattering and giggling, their eyes always on the
ready, never alone, always in multiples, and never silent. Up and down
they went; Miss Marilyn Monroe cannot be held accountable for the
extravagances of her imitators. Perhaps they were trying to fan the
heavy night with their belling skirts, though come to think of it many
of them had on tight bottom-huggers. There should have been a breeze
around that corner; but there was none. Diégo is a disobliging sort of
port.

The pick-up in the bar blared out Elvis Presley's rock and roll at its
highest volume. A few sailors and nylon-shirted, blue-jeaned young
men danced, if it can be called dancing, in the little space left among
the girls on the sidewalk. The atmosphere was hearty, matter-of-fact,
and downright honest. I saw one young woman through the open
window sitting at a table in the bar—a vantage point that must have

been her place, her preserve, reserved for her. Black-brown of skin, tall, direct of speech and powerful of personality, she spoke correct French in a tough Parisian accent and announced to somebody out of my line of vision that she was a one-hundred-per-cent pure-blooded Sakalava; and she spoke with humorous pride. When she stood up, I saw that she wore a man's blue work-shirt, and a man's bluejeans; but she was not a man. She had a red bandana tied, workmanlike, around her head. She eyed the potential clients among the men. Each one of us she looked over with a professional dispassion to form a rapid estimate of his cash and equipment. Hers was a black but open market.

There was no modesty, no false allure in her attitude. So one professional soccer player sums up another. She no longer played the game for sport, she worked at it; but she enjoyed it still, and had an expert's pride in doing a good job; it was, after all, what she was paid for.

She left it to the other, smaller, girlish girls to make much more of being girls. Indeed, many of them were pretty, very clean, well fleshed, and toothsome, as attractive as a poultry yard in late spring to a hungry man—some were for roasting, some for frying, some for spitting, and some were for the stew pot to be fricasseed, or sautéed. They had their charms; in their pale and pretty off-the-shoulder summer dresses, of the colors of spring flowers, they were not bad-looking in their high-heeled strapless shoes that went click-click-click as they footed it. They brushed their hair in the "My Fair Lady" style. Hardly a single Malagasy, *métisse*, or Créole girl needs a permanent.

They represented, I should think, all the island ethnic groups adulterated and detribalized, but not assimilated. Along the sidewalk, in the street at the corner under the naked goose-necked light, among the crippled bugs and battered moths, in the hot and raucous black night, they idled, or they danced with their grinning clientele to the beat of the rhythm of the lo-fi. The Malagasy recognize no color bar; it is said that 8o per cent of the girls have the usual occupational diseases. Diégo is a nocturnal town despite the beauty of its bay. It is far off, exotic, sordid, and as dull as it can be. It is too bad.

For once a good man *almost* brought off a wonderful experiment beside this bay. Here in the late seventeenth century, he tried to cultivate a kind of *Candide* garden, which he named Libertalia; in it he planted the seeds of human freedom and good will toward all men alive. He was a pirate, a young man, a Frenchman of France's great days—the Grande Époque of the seventeenth century. No one knows his real name; he was a Provençal gentleman, well educated in the humanities, a literate man with an inquiring turn of mind, and full of extraordinary life and vitality. Misson is the name he is known by, a last name without a recorded first name; he is not well known. Yet he was a man much concerned with liberty, with individual freedom, with honor and responsibility, with order, and with human dignity. He had all the great French virtues, including the famous flexibility, courage, and witty ingenuity that operate in le Système D. He was a *débrouillard*. He took things as they came and made the best of them, and of himself. That is how he got to be a pirate.

Whatever else he was, Misson was a fundamental revolutionary. He began his career by trying to live according to the established laws and the social patterns laid down by tradition and put in force by older men than he. He joined the new French Navy when he was sixteen; that seems to us to be very young, but in fact he was older than the Service. Jean-Baptiste Colbert, Louis XIV's great minister of commerce, like Louis XIII's Cardinal Richelieu before him, a far-seeing statesman, knew that the only way to put his country's and his king's power and glory upon a solid, self-supporting basis was to encourage trade, to make the French people prosperous, and to bring in wealth. Therefore, he sent out explorers and colonists to India, to Africa, to North America, and even to Madagascar; and subsidized, in the king's name, a merchant fleet as well as a powerful royal navy to protect the trade and commerce on the high seas.

Misson, the educated young man of the French Renaissance in Colbert's brand new French Navy, made good fast; he was a junior officer before he came of age. Life in any navy is a firm dictatorship, based on the microcosmic symbol of the ship afloat on the wide seas. The ship's crew today is, more often than not, apt to be a contented unit launched upon the happy mystique of paternalism. But ship's discipline must be absolute. In the worst of the old days, the rule was often sadistic, mindless, brutal, and degrading. Misson learned all this at first hand; and, being a reader and a thinker, he had a standard of what a proper human government had been, and might once be again.

This young Frenchman, then, when he was barely twenty-one, appears to have made up his mind, and to have waited for his opportunity. For Misson was a thinking as well as a feeling revolutionary; he rebelled not just against what he knew to be bad, but he also worked toward the attainment of what he knew to be the good and proper man-made order. He knew that government imposed by one armed man upon the many under him ended in corruption and the capricious use of arbitrary power. Misson believed that true government is one which all men agree to rule themselves. Few historical figures have been so solitary, so right, and so practical. Yet he was born beforehand; he was ahead of his century by a full hundred years. Therefore, he indulged in no wild romantic outcry, but stayed alive and bided his moment; and he was patient. All this seems odd, for he was a Provençal, a man from the Midi of France, where young men are not known for their calm wisdom so much as for their tall stories, hot emotions, and quick tempers. Even so, Misson seems to have had his share of the famous Provençal charm. He could talk and charm the birds out of the trees—and did convince a priest to lay aside his cassock to join the active life.

It happened when Misson was a junior officer in the Sun King's frigate, *La Victoire*, on liberty ashore in Genoa. There he met up with an energetic young Italian priest, Caraccioli by name. They strolled through the town together, talking, gesturing with their arms outspread, and laughing. Misson persuaded Caraccioli to leave the confined but perhaps not then very religious life and join him in the uniform of the Royal French Navy for a life on the open sea. The two men remained good friends all their lives.

One day the time came for Misson to put his ideas into action, but at first it must have looked like a disaster. Off Martinique, Colbert's French outpost in the Caribbean Sea, where Misson's ship had gone to protect French merchantmen from the pirates of the Spanish Main, and from the English free-booters, *La Victoire* encountered an English man-of-war; for once again the French and the English were at war. It was a hard fight and it ended abruptly. The English raked the French decks with grapeshot. An accurate French shot reached the Englishman's powder magazine; the man-of-war blew up and sank. When Misson searched among the survivors and the dead to find his superiors, he found that of all the officers of *La Victoire,* he alone had escaped the English balls—he was the only one of them alive. The revolutionary Provençal, then in his early twenties, got to work; he did first things first—inspected the ship and saw that she was not seriously damaged, looked to the care of the wounded, gave the dead sea-burial, and cleaned the decks of blood, broken spars, and battle litter.

Then in the quiet among those green and mountainous islands rising out of the dark blue Caribbean Sea, he called the crew together and harangued the men; they must have been a tough, hard-bitten lot of seventeenth-century sailors. He outlined his plans, and asked the men to join him and Caraccioli, the earliest of his converts, not in a life of crime, but in a life of freedom. The means to this end was to be piracy. Misson apparently had no great trouble in convincing the men to help him steal the frigate *La Victoire* from the Navy of the greatest monarch then alive, to pull down the Bourbon ensign of gold fleur-de-lis upon a white background, and to haul up the Jolly Roger.

I wish I had been there to hear him; it would be interesting to know what the man said and to see what he looked like. The Provençals are dark, short, well made men and women, often with the straight and classic noses, fine eyes, and generous mouths of the ancient Mediterranean type; and the men are hairy. Both the men and the women are high spirited. Perhaps Misson was a born leader. Freedom, liberty, justice—all to be achieved by means of the dangerous and adventurous life of the pirate—it adds up to a heady subject; Misson seems to have done well by his passionate beliefs. Perhaps he had been wounded; perhaps he stood in bandages upon the bullet-scarred bridge of the bloodied ship, but talked straight to the men; his was a crew of old friends. Who has not wanted to be a pirate at some time in his life? And in those days, human freedom and individual liberty of choice were not ordinary birthrights. Only the wellborn, the rich, and the powerful ever reached them. Every man jack joined Misson voluntarily.

The next thing that he had to do was make good. He did. Misson was careful to make himself into a successful leader. He proved his ability as a pirate captain to his crew. They all made money.

So the converted frigate sailed the Spanish Main, and around the Cape of Good Hope to run up and down the searoads of the East Indiamen. They took prizes, which they sold, surely, under some workable merchantman cover in French, Dutch, and English ports; perhaps the middlemen were not finicky as to the provenience of the goods they bought and sold at a good profit. On the high seas, Misson and his crew, as buccaneers, got a fame for chivalrous magnanimity among the law-abiders. When they sailed in for the kill, he and his men made it a point to avoid bloodshed and to spare the lives of all but the foolhardy. Apparently they worked together as an efficient, well drilled team; every pirate knew exactly what he had to do, and did it rapidly. Misson and his engineers invented or improved the methods of grappling the one ship to the other, and of boarding and stripping the loaded merchantman of all easily negotiable valuables—gold, silver, ivory, precious stones, bolts of silks and satins, and the boxes and barrels of spice—they permitted the passengers and crew to go free in their undisabled ship. There was no rapine, no savagery, no walking of the plank, no kidnapping for ransom, no spite and no revenge upon society. If the ship had any slaves on board as cargo or as personal property, Misson made it a point to free them. (Later on he did his best to send them back where they had come from.) Then he got away, relying on his expert navigation and the speed of his rebuilt frigate to keep his cherished freedom of choice and liberty of action. Thus he became a sort of nautical Robin Hood, another outlaw in the right when the law was in the wrong hands. There was time and space enough in the forests and on the seas of those gone days for such gallant men to live out their short lives before the world's ideas caught up with them.

As he worked at his freebooting trade, he kept his eyes open for a likely base of operations, a place where he could put his ideas of social order into action, a safe haven where he could not be reached but would be within striking distance of the shipping lanes. The good pirate's first choice was Anjouan, the most lovely island of the coelacanths, the pearl of the Comoro Archipelago. He seems to have been well received, for there he married the sister of the Moslem queen, a pale-skinned, dark-eyed Arab lady, come originally from Muscat. He seems to have behaved with the expected and romantic Provençal chivalry, for he served and protected his sister-in-law by doing battle with her enemy, the Sultan of the neighboring island of Moheli. Misson won. Perhaps his war work was part of the marriage contract with the Anjouan royal family.

If so, it may be that he found the atmosphere of the absolute Arab rule constraining. He was a man much preoccupied with freedom, a liberal man, a revolutionary. It may be that this thoughtful adventurer in humanism did not like what he found at court; or perhaps the pirate had to get away from the intrigues of the reactionary, segregated, personal rule of petticoats. Islam was pretty well frozen tight in those days; the Koran left no room for growth. Or as a virile young man, perhaps Misson wanted to be the head of his own house.

So he left Anjouan behind him and sailed south, presumably with his princess-wife, although her fate is not recorded; he headed west into the empty Bay of Diégo-Suarez and landed on the deserted shore. How old was the man? Not yet thirty; his dates of birth and death are unknown, or unrecorded, but his life was spent in the last half of the seventeenth century. Misson must have put a lot of thought into working out his plan before he went ashore, for once on dry land he laid out a city and surrounded it with earthworks and palisades. He built his forts and residences of timber cut from the forests of the hills south of the bay. He named this capital of a new country Libertalia, and he called the inhabitants Liberi. He seems to have been an enthusiastic man with a fine sense of detail, as well as a sound organizer.

The Liberi of Libertalia, tough and seasoned sailors and pirates, were provided with a General Assembly in which they ruled themselves, although it is to be suspected that Misson's word carried more weight than the assembled voice of this early democratic experiment, and he drew the line between liberty and license. For instance, he "protected" the morals of his men and encouraged them to marry. They found wives from among the Malagasy girls, who seem to have been willing if, as things worked out, their tribal fathers and brothers were not. Furthermore, Misson did not permit his pirate crew to swear —neither to blaspheme nor to make use of obscenities. What's to be made from that? That he was a Christian and somewhat of a puritan? He was strong-minded.

To support his new state, Misson set the pirates to work. They planted gardens; they tended poultry; they kept herds of cattle. They must have had trouble finding a sure water supply. But at first it was a small community. What is the crew of a frigate? Thirty men? Fifty? To build up a population, Misson passed the word among the pirates of all seven seas, and sent out literature to advertise his Libertalia, and to invite all men of good will without distinction to join in the experiment as working citizens. In his recruitment, he once again showed the practical side of his political ability. He needed men. Therefore, he did not exclude, but was careful to include, all comers, and to offer them a new way of life. He had confidence in the human race, in himself, and in the validity of his experiment. He offered the dispossessed and the rejected a place to put down roots, and live. Did he believe that evil is but the absence of good, and that, given a chance, the good qualities inherent in all men will fill the void of evil? The fact is that newcomers liked the idea of Libertalia, and began to join in force. Perhaps Misson picked them up in *La Victoire* while he was out on raids to get the cash to finance his go at Utopia, and brought them back on his return to home. Perhaps a few complete pirate ships sailed into the Bay of Diégo-Suarez and dropped anchor.

In 1697, Captain William Kidd brought his leaking galley, *The Adventure*, into the harbor for repairs. Kidd, a Scottish New Yorker and a maligned man, was not a pirate but a privateer licensed by the British of London to prey on French merchantmen. The two countries were at war. But by 1897 peace had been declared, although no one knew so on Madagascar. When *The Adventure* proved to be unseaworthy, Captain Kidd scuttled it. Half his impressed crew of Cockneys chose to desert him and to join Misson's liberal experiment in Libertalia. So Kidd took over an Armenian ship sailing under French papers, perhaps in the Levantine trade, which he believed to be a legitimate enemy prize; with a skeleton crew, he sailed off in the *Quedagh Merchant* to be arrested for piracy. His noble backers abandoned him; he was unjustly tried. He was hanged in London.

One of the important new members among the Liberi was Tom Tew, an American pirate from one of the British colonies along the Atlantic coast. He, too, essentially was a social man and an idealist. Libertalia casts an odd light on piracy and pirates, who seem not always to have been swashbucklers or men of uncontrollably criminal natures. Perhaps they soon realized that piracy is an indefensible way of life; to be sure, it has no future. Enough of them jumped at the chance to settle down in what might well be a last colony of Athens drawn up in imitation of the classic city state where humanism and democracy began. Tom Tew, the American buccaneer, soon took his place alongside Misson, the gentleman from Provence, and Caraccioli, the once Italian priest; they made a sort of triumvirate to govern the Liberi. For a time, the Greek revival prospered.

Who knows what Madagascar might have been had Libertalia survived and spread the Liberi ideal south along the shores and into the highlands of the great island? It did not; perhaps for the same causes and reasons that the French civilizing mission more recently has not. Apparently neither Misson nor the later arrivals could work out a sound and viable economy to support their experiments. Perhaps evolution refuses to be nudged along, but must move slowly, in fits and starts, according to its own calendar. The Greeks might have seen in Misson a doomed man, challenging the gods. The irony is that he was brought down not by a thunderbolt, nor by any French or British or Spanish punitory fleet, but by the Noble Malagasy Savage, whose daughters had married the crewmen.

One day when Tom and Misson, with the greater part of the able-bodied men, were out of the bay on a pirate enterprise to fill the Libertalia treasury, the Antakarana, the men of the rocks, came down out of the forests of the Mountain of Amber, and, perhaps to recover some dark Helen, swarmed over the palisades, massacred the Liberi, and razed the well ordered town. Then, taking the widows and their children with them, they returned to their wilderness of rocks and trees, and to their own native ways. I hope that President Philibert Tsiranana, of the Tsimihety tribe, and of the Malagasy Republic, is descended from one of these Liberi children who escaped death. Misson's experiment was too good to have been totally erased.

When Misson, Tom Tew, and the pirate crew sailed back, laden down with booty, into the beautiful and peaceful bay, no voice called out to welcome them home; the Anjouan princess was dead; Caraccioli was dead; the town was burnt; the gardens had dried up; there was nothing there. So he went back on board the old *Victory* and sailed away. Misson, *La Victoire,* and the men vanished. It is thought that the bottom of the ship was torn out on a coral reef in the Mozambique Channel, driven by a storm and helpless in the treacherous currents separating his island from Africa. Tom Tew, who seems to have kept the command of his own ship, was captured in the Red Sea, and hanged.

On the morning of 21 March 1958, a Thursday, I woke up in my dim bedroom of the Universal-Epochal Hotel at 5:30. I was wet. It was my own sweat. The dismal mosquito net smelled of stale human bodies. The iron bed was big enough for two—for three. Its elegant blue linen sheets had soaked up the trickles that ran down my sides. I got up and walked barefoot across the sticky red tile floor, and found a single, large, blond cockroach in possession of the wash basin. My towel, not big enough for modesty in size, had fermented in the night. The single tap ran brown water at body heat. The water closet, housed in a dark room of the dimensions of a dug grave, did not perform its function; and there were other guests in the hotel besides me.

I went back to my room past the open doors of naked sleepers, packed my bag, and headed for the staircase of this dormitory annex in the back of the building containing the public rooms. I stepped across two full-grown, panting boxer dogs, and went down. As I turned the newel post, I got momentarily caught and thoroughly scratched by one of the untrained tentacles of a giant "crown of thorns" plant (*Euphorbia milli,* endemic to Madagascar, but now found all over Christendom), growing, and growing exceedingly well, in a box on top of the post. I crossed the animated courtyard peopled by grinning Malagasy men in shorts, cackling poultry of many mixed breeds, and several snarling cats; and an iron wire clothesline, fortunately slack, caught me across the Adam's apple. I backed away, ducked, and went into the kitchen full of flies flying in lazy circles.

In the dining room I found a ten-year-old fat Créole boy, surely somebody's son, who eyed me with a knowing speculative look, as though he had last viewed me through a keyhole. In the center of the hotel desk stood a vase holding a single branch of immaculate, untouched, white-petalled camelias blossoming among fresh, clean, dark green, glossy leaves. Behind sat the patron of the place, a flacid Créole wearing khaki shorts, buttoned up, as his tan shirt was not. Runnels of early-morning sweat ran down his sallow thorax. Even his eyes seemed to be diluted. I asked him to send me breakfast, and then crossed the slippery floor of the unswept corner bar, and sat down outdoors at a rusting iron table on the sidewalk.

In the level morning sunlight, I watched the various Malagasy employees of the town's shops and offices, and the arsenal, walking down the street to work. The Indian merchants began to unlock and roll up the corrugated iron shutters of their open-fronted shops, and to set out their wares for the day's bargaining. Diégo is a depressing place. The bookshops do a thriving trade in horror comics, printed on cheap stock, written in simple French, and illustrated in crude colors.

On the walls of the buildings is pasted up the word for Diégo. They are advertising posters, small ones, lettered in bright and terrible neon colors, reiterating the trade name of a bottled soft French drink. It is another offering of the *Présence Française;* it attempts to discourage the young from drinking even watered wine or harder alcohols. In shocking pinks, violent magentas, acid greens, sulphurous yellows, and lipstick reds, the letters spell out "PSCHITT. . . ." That's the portmanteau word for Diégo-Suarez.

The Pleasures of Discovery

Once again up in the air of Madagascar on the way to Nosy-Bé, flying through the sunlight of the first day of the Austral autumn, I looked down upon the great blue Bay of Diégo-Suarez, shaped like a crumpled four-leaf clover but unlucky to the French, I reflected that, had an English or a Scottish pirate founded a colony on those brilliant golden shores, he would not have called it Libertalia; but he would have made a go of it.

The British pirate colonist might have named his town New London, or New York, or Nova Scotia; or, if he had a sense of humor, New Caledonia—for, after all, his was to be a thieves' market town. Whatever name he gave it, he would have carefully come to terms with the tribal chieftans, first keeping them at bay with beads, calico, brummagem, and rum. In the end, he would have annihilated or annulled them, either by hunting them down and killing them off, or by rounding them up in reservations and subjecting them to games—cricket! Eventually, because what was good for his business was good for the colony, from his cantonment outside the native quarter, he soon would have organized the blacks and been knighted. Thus a hit-or-miss sociopolitical *modus vivendi* would have worked itself out, with law and order enforced in a reluctant mutual admiration and respect, and with some sort of working justice for all.

Soon the many sterling virtues of the British character would have come muddling through; filtering down from the top, human decency would have spread out to cover the whole of the island, by then colored pink in Victoria's realm. When the costs of Pax Britannica reached the point of diminishing returns, and the tide of empire began to ebb, the independent Dominion of Madagascar would have opted to remain in the Commonwealth, with visits from the queen. Then, after the Second World War, the Independent Malagasy Republic would have entered the United Nations with a strong voice in Afro-Asian affairs. There is no way to understand the British; in them, character emerges triumphant over reason. Thus the British Isles survive against all thinkable odds. Evolution must have invested heavily in the Angles, the Saxons, the Celts, the Jutes, the Picts, the Normans, the English, the Scots, the Welsh—and, anyhow, in some of the Irish.

As the British have made a mystique of muddling through, so the French have made an emotion of logic. A heady and a brilliant race, the French are addicted to thought. They are passionately fond of analysis and synthesis. *Ecstasiés devant* the Goddess of Reason, whom they adore and venerate, they nowadays seemingly rarely put her attributes to use in the practical purposes of self-government. So they work out admirable plans for action—clear, logical, balanced, and reasonable, *French* down to the smallest detail. There is never a loose end left untied. In the outline of their Colonial, or French Union, or Community policies, as in the five Republics' constitutions, everything is fixed; all the parts fit together in a masterly design, admirable in itself—and unworkable. The completed plan of action completely cuts out the action it plans.

With enlightenment for dynamism, the moving idea of the nineteenth-century French Empire—the Civilizing Mission—was both grand and glorious. But in the implementation, it did not work. Colonial policy fixed itself for all time in a static pattern applied to nature. The orderly, logical organization, thought out and imposed by Paris, proved to be inflexible. With no room left for growth according to its own nature in root or in branch, the grafted colony did not flower with a life of its own in its foreign climate. The bureaucrats of Paris spun their filaments in their corridors, as spiders spin their webs in trees, and caught the soaring mission of French enlightenment, and sucked it dry.

Even so, illogically, unreasonably, France gave her dark people the best that lay within her gift; and that was liberty, of which freedom of choice, for good or for ill, is the cornerstone. Therefore, as in France, when methods and traditions hardened to become bad habits barring the way, revolution (again as in France) cut the key to the locked door. When Europe exploded in 1939, Asia, Africa, and Madagascar took fire; they burned with a light of their own.

In theory, nothing much is fundamentally wrong with the *mission civilisatrice;* for the offer of Western culture, on the whole still the best in the world, is valid. In action, the fault lay in a curious withholding, not of French culture, but of the French themselves. In France, the French kept France apart from the sum of the parts of the empire. When General de Gaulle, recognizing the fault, devised the Fourth Republic's French Union and the Fifth's Community, he tried to impose France as the first among equals on the Colonial peoples—and on the French themselves. It was too late. The idea of equality, along with that of liberty, had already taken hold; but not fraternity. The French can call no other man brother.

They had gone out to the colonies as soldiers, as adventurers, as teachers, as exiles, as remittance men. They had gone out as hard workers, laborers. Some, indeed, went out as saints, and some as lovers. These last were the ones most bitterly hurt by . . . by history, which they took to be defeat and rejection.

The fact was that any French Colonial, or Overseas, or Community policy drawn up upon the theory of the civilizing mission had to be as fixed in pattern as is a solar system in the universe, with France as the sun around which the planets and the satellites revolved in immutable order. The sun, however, has always set on every empire. It may be that history, like the heart, has its own reasons.

So I reflected as I looked from the airplane down upon a wasteland of barren hills and valleys made beautiful in an arid way by patterns of erosion like cockscomb flowers, or, indeed, like slices of a human brain excised for study. Then the source of a stream came into sight, a cultivated watershed of curving terraces following the lie of the land. Rice is the Malagasy staple, as wheaten bread is the French staff of life. Rice grows in a shimmering pattern of wet emerald green paddy fields man-made in the dry red earth.

Further along, the streams trickling in the small valleys joined to make a slow river of thick red water wide enough for islands. The islands took the shape of Brancusi's bird in flight. Perhaps sculptors are right, and painters and musicians are right. The eye should see forms and colors in their own relationships of mass and space; the ear should listen to the sound of music. The human mind should not try to put what the eye sees and the ear hears into words. History is history, complete in itself. French is a lapidary language, most moving when carved into monuments.

NOSY-BÉ

Nosy-Bé is a South Sea Island small enough to fit into the imagination. Of volcanic origin, it is rich and green with a name pronounced Nossy-Bay, meaning "Great Island." Its wooded peak. Kokobe, rises 1,075 feet above a blue and coraline bay off the northwest shore of Madagascar, eight miles away. Its fertile soil and its climate are excellent for spices. The French got Nosy-Bé before its bigger neighbor. In 1840, the Merina armies came down from Tananarive and drove the heiress of the Sakalava, once the dominant Malagasy tribe, from her territories on the great red island, and reduced her to one small green island domain. Tsiomeko was her name; she was young, and she was black and comely. She was safe on Nosy-Bé if not secure, because the Merina in their highlands had forgotten how to manage their ancestral outrigger canoes. They built fortresses along the coast and began to consolidate their gains.

In her plight, Queen Tsiomeko first appealed for help to the Sultan of Zanzibar, the Sakalava's old ally in the slave trade. He sent along a ship of his fleet; but after a year or two, he withdrew it, along with his protection, from Nosy-Bé waters. He was a merchant prince, and he saw which way the wind was blowing—down from the highlands and out to sea.

In 1817, the British on Mauritius had convinced the enlightened

King Radama I, of the Merina, to put a stop to the slave trade of Madagascar, and had agreed to pay the king "the Equivalent," an annual sum—a thousand dollars in gold, another in silver, stated amounts of gunpowder, flints, and muskets, four hundred surplus British army uniforms, and a full-dress array for Radama—to replace the lost revenues in slaves. Later on, the British made similar arrangements with the Sultan of Zanzibar—and took in exchange his African mainland possessions of Kenya, Uganda, and, still later, Tanganyika, although they left him his islands of cloves.

Queen Tsiomeko, thus abandoned on Nosy-Bé, threw herself upon the mercy, and, it is said, into the arms of a chance-come captain of the French Marines, whose ship, the *Colibri*, had put in to explore these waters. The captain proved to be a cautious fellow; he promised to speak to his superior officer, the governor of the island of Réunion—once again called Bourbon under Louis-Philippe. The governor's name was Admiral de Hell; when he listened to the story told him by Tsiomeko's lover, the captain of the Marines, what did he say? Hell, yes? So the pretty island fell like a ripe plum into French hands.

A century or so ago, tropical sugar and spice islands made money, and a Colonial economy aroused no moral indignation. Perhaps, indeed, Admiral de Hell decided—as a Marxist might interpret his action—to take over Nosy-Bé and Tsiomeko's reduced Sakalava tribal people as a sort of preserve, a stud, a well stocked reservation to insure a steady supply of field hands for the French planters of Réunion-Bourbon. With the British of Pax Britannica patrolling the sea roads, slaves were hard to come by. The Sakalava are tall and muscular. The dark-brown bucks and wenches made prime slaves to work the sugar cane. But perhaps, on the other hand, the French took Tsiomeko under their protection because, in those delightful days of yore, love conquered all, and along with love went a certain responsibility.

In any case, Admiral de Hell had a precedent for the take-over of Nosy-Bé. A hundred years earlier a similar chance, and a greater love, had brought to France another Malagasy spice-island, Sainte-Marie of the cloves, whose inhabitants have been citizens of France since 1750.

Jean-Onésime Fillet was this lover's name. He ended as a king, but he began life as a Gascon, and later was made corporal in the private army of the French East India Company. Sent out to fight the other mercenaries, those of the British East India Company, near Madras, in a clash between those two privately owned commercial companies then building the French and the British eighteenth-century Colonial empires, the corporal was both shot and sabered. He must have been a robust and a fortunate young man, for he survived the field of battle to be invalided back to the French East India Company's base on Bourbon-Réunion. There he made a quick recovery. His fellow soldiers in the barracks, perhaps in deference and in admiration of his natural qualities, gave the Gascon ironman a descriptive nickname—"La Bigorne." A *bigorne* is a French meridional anvil with a horn.

One day, or perhaps it was by night, La Bigorne's commanding officer came home unexpectedly in the classic manner and found the young corporal in bed with his lady-wife. La Bigorne leapt from the bed in the alcove, ran through the high rooms of the colonial house, climbed the wall of the shady garden, and, with or without the active or the tacit help of his cuckolded officer, the lady-wife, and his delighted barracks mates, stole a small boat, and with two runaway slave men, he set out for Madagascar—some 375 nautical miles across the Indian Ocean. The currents and the prevailing winds carried him along. On the fifth day, waterless under the hot sun, close to death, he sighted a land bird, and then, to the west, a palm-fringed island beach.

Through the rippling waters reflecting the blazing sunset skies came swimming out to save his life a handful of smiling, glistening, brown-skinned girls. One of them was named Bety; she was the princess and the heiress of the island. She cherished him. La Bigorne married her. He made an ideal husband and an enlightened consort. He built roads, brought in clove and coffee trees, built trading posts, established local industries, and dispensed justice in the shade "Underneath the Fatatra Tree"—which is the meaning of the name of the island capital. Queen Bety ceded Sainte-Marie to the French on 30 July 1750. A Frenchman in disgrace, in exile, in love—even if he be the king of an exotic island realm—is forever a man of France.

On that other island, Nosy-Bé, two centuries later, I walked along a shady road through a diminished stand of hardwood trees, giants of the original rain forest, tamed and overcivilized, their trunks at the base set about with peppercorn vines. *Piper nigrum* has a strong habit of growth. The thick-leaved vines swarm up the tree trunks for ten or a dozen feet to make, in effect, a dense green flounce, a sort of petti-coat or pantalette ruffle for the noble and high-branching trees. Thus the pepper grove may suffer a poodle-dog indignity, a humiliation of nature; but it makes a very funny sight to see.

Black pepper comes from the dried berries, called peppercorns; they grow in clusters, first green and then red; white pepper comes from the husks. In the Renaissance and in the Age of Reason, pepper was worth its weight in gold. In the nineteenth century, it was the best of the tropical cash crops. In 1950, a kilogram sold for 980 francs CFA; but by 1958 the price had fallen to 340 francs CFA—less than a dollar a pound. A very good harvest for a planter of Nosy-Bé amounts to forty tons.

From the circus of the peppercorn grove, I went out into the sun-light of the sugar-cane fields—flourishing, free of slave labor, but no longer economical. The intricacies of sugar are too much for me, but just before independence for Madagascar and Nosy-Bé, the French government in Paris underwrote the Colonial crop—and thus bought sugar at a price higher than that of the arranged, or rigged, world market. By then, the former empire, the present French Union, had be-come one of those famous French luxuries, an *article de Paris*.

At the end of the lane beyond the thick cane fields, I came upon the most beautiful beach that I have ever seen, or that I expect to see—crescent-shaped, clean, its pale sand as fine and as soft as silk slipping through the fingers. Coconut palms grew—as surely they still grow—just above the reach of high water. I think that coconut trees are the best of palms. They are not stiff, but instead they curve and bend as they grow, it may be, like thinking reeds. Even so, they hold up their heads. The sun shining straight down on them casts shadows like splashes of ink on the white sand. The wind blows through the fronds. It *is* a dry sound in a wet world; but the wind is a gentle, warm wind. It ruffles, but does not break, the surface of the mild water; the water is as green and as blue as jewels and enamels.

Among the splashes of shadow across the smooth sand, in and out of the sunlight, walked a couple—a French man and a French woman—clearly in love; their own shadows moved about their feet. The smaller belonged to the girl—to the young woman, I mean to say. She was perhaps twenty-five years old, an adult, as feminine as only French women, being mindful, know how to be. She had long hair, dark and thick; and she had braided it. She wore a pretty bathing suit of lovely colors; it suited her; the colors were not primary. I found her beautiful to look at. From time to time she turned her head to look up into the man's face. They were smiling; they were in love, and it was knowledgeable.

He was older by ten years or so, a total Frenchman, going as nearly naked as he might go, covered but not concealed by an adequate black fact. What is it all about, this French acceptance of the human condition, of the self? Of the flexible skin, the perishable flesh, the bone structure and the nerves and the muscles of the given members, topped by a head containing a brain, all for use, all inhabited and infused with intangibles—the spirit, the soul, the character and immortality: a life on earth. I am told that both monkey and man, shot by bow and arrow, transfixed, take the shaft in the hands.

I passed them on the beach, I walked my way to come upon a group of slim young French mothers and their very French children digging in the sand for clams—the smallest clams that I have ever seen, miniatures. It took, I'd say, a hundred or so to fill up one of the bright-painted toy buckets, imported from France. The *Présence Française* here had on flowered bikinis. One of them told me that the clams made an excellent soup.

At the blue water's transparent edge, hermit crabs scuttled away from my feet in their borrowed shells as I walked to the end of the beach; for the beach did not dwindle, it came to an end in a thirty-foot cliff rising up like a rough wall. Thick-leaved ficus trees had dug in on top to send down their strangling roots to search out fissures in the volcanic rock. Their heavy level branches like awnings cast a shade illuminated by reflections from the rippling bay. In the pockets of the porous cliff a hanging garden of begonias grew, a blossoming of pink flower sprays among green winged leaves.

I turned my back and walked along the curve of sand, burning hot underfoot at midday. So I took to the water, dived and swam about, came out, and stood in the sun for a bit to look out to sea. I saw a neat limpit of a green island, far off, all by itself with but a single house upon it—designed by a Frenchman but thatched with banana leaves and walled by woven palm-fronds. It stood back of the cleared fields among great-leaved trees, some wild, some cultivated.

There there lived a Frenchman, a white man civilized in France, with his *ramatoa*—his Malagasy woman, his wife, neither *évoluée* nor *assimilée;* they lived in chosen isolation. Yet it was my good luck to meet the *ramatoa* on one of her rare departures from their island, a small and self-contained, a private place, where they could grow almost all the necessities of their way of life. She had come over in a dugout canoe to Nosy-Bé to barter for such things as salt, medical supplies, cloth—whatever she and her husband could not find at hand or produce on their island, not large enough nor so placed as to be strategic. She had brought with her an offering to sell for cash.

Although I had been told the story and therefore looked at her curiously, this Malagasy woman, handsome in her late twenties or early thirties (which is to say mature, already well along in life) did not seem remarkable to me. She was brown-skinned; she had parted her tribal hair in squares and tucked each tuft in a coil to make (in effect) a squad of soft snail-shells upon her well shaped head. She wore a washed and faded pink cotton dress, and she carried a basket, undoubtedly of her own expert making. Out of it she unpacked a pair of pottery birds, fat guinea fowl, recognizable at once but simplified, sun-baked of hand-shaped red clay, then blackened with graphite rubbed on, each indented spot of the plumage whitened with chalk.

I picked one up and saw that the black and white came off on my fingers. They were wonderful birds. I laughed out loud, and the *ramatoa* smiled in pleasure. She evidently knew all about guinea fowl, very silly birds but good to eat when young. She must have trapped and cooked and eaten a great many.

Guinea fowl flock wild in Madagascar. To catch them alive, the Malagasy find a flat rock in the bush, and, out of wet clay, they shape a ring to form a feed pan on it; this the sun bakes hard and dry. In this circle, the hunter scatters a handful of grain; then he retires, out of sight.

The silly guinea fowl come up to investigate the snare. They find the corn. In their immoderate greed and haste, they peck away so hard and fast at the grain on the stone feed pan that, gobbling, with their own bills so close to their minute brains, they knock themselves out. Then the Malagasy hunter comes up, picks up the idiotic birds, and goes home laughing to a feast. I bought the pottery pair and I have them still—chipped a bit, to be sure, for the sun-baked clay is friable.

The Great Red Island

I forget how much I paid the *ramatoa* for them. I do not know what she bought with her earnings.

Her French husband, as a very young man in 1938, had set out upon what promised to be a brilliant career in the Colonial service when he had gone down, with his French bride, to work in Madagascar. Munich came and went. The war broke out. This thoughtful, reasonable, well educated, disciplined young man then opted for Vichy after the Fall of France in June of 1940. With him, so I was told, the deciding factor had been not a matter of the pension but of the principle —my country right or wrong. After 1942, he had made matters worse for himself by refusing to give in—neither to the British invaders, nor to the Free French liberators. So, back in Paris after 1945, he was tried, found guilty, sentenced to national indignity, and to prison, stripped of his rights as a French citizen—for a time—and disgraced for as long as a memory serves. His wife left him with their two sons— and she was described to me as "*une vraie* pin-up," red-headed, green-eyed, white-skinned—for she had backed a winner, not a loser, when their families had arranged the match. She had the money; he had had the distinction and the name.

So, released from prison, cleared but in bad odor, he had gone back to Madagascar to buy himself an island and to find himself a faithful *ramatoa*. Together they had cleared enough of their small island to build terraces and to plant rice, maize, manioc, and some quick- as well as slow-growing fruit trees—bananas, papayas, mangoes, and, as far as possible from the sea, oranges and lemons; pineapples, too. He almost never leaves the island. I do not know whether or not he and the *ramatoa* have children; if so, they will be Malagasy and free, not French, not freighted with two thousand years of culture. I wonder, though, if—like Paul Gauguin on another island—when he looks at his pink beaches and Polynesian girls as beautiful as fruit and flowers, he sees France?

Back on my crescent beach, I picked up my schnorkel; I put the flippers on my feet; I swam out to some likely rocks, and I looked down. What is the use of waterproof watches? There is no time under the sea. Undersea time came to an end long ago. Prehistory (a word of poverty) has no meaning underwater. Space there is liquid; so is light; man and time there are displaced. For long ago evolution gaffed him, or so the scientists now say; there is nothing to be done about the sea. In it, man is alien. "The French have no business in Madagascar," I said aloud, but to myself, submerged.

Down there among the corals I was all eyes; there being no sharks nearby, I did not qualify as food; displaced, I had no weight to speak of. Desperate, I brought thought to bear, and fancifully said to myself that, soon after Adam left with Eve, a corner of Eden slid into the sea, a far corner—not where the orchards grew. I looked down to give common name to the bright coral—fan coral, brain coral, stag antlered and branching coral, coral in reefs, coral alone, alive, alive O! growing in all the coral colors, red and black and lilac and drab. Coral's an animal, a polyp in motion, a flower of flesh, a sensitive predator. It traps and absorbs microscopic sea food.

Down on the rippled sand-floor, trepangs crawled slowly about. The pale kind of this turd-like vermiform holotherian is as nasty to step on as is used chewing gum. At low tide, the Sakalava tribesmen harvest the sea cucumber, the blackish *bêche-de-mer,* dip it in boiling water, dry it out, and export it to China along with sharks' fins for soup— two minor articles of commerce in the *Présence Chinoise.*

So are the seashells. The pink, pointed, spiraling, turban-like troches and the great ocean pearl-oysters are made into buttons. But most of the shells have no use, except to collectors and to the mollusks them- selves—the limpets, the augers, the harps, the conches, the murices, the clams, the scallops, and the coweries. All sorts of all shapes of shell, with the life intact inside, lived down there, as did gardens and whole forests of seaweed—but *weed* is a landlubber's word. In and out of the fluent groves, red, brown, and chlorophyll, swam the fish— the big and the little fish, red, gold, silver, blue, black, striped, streaked, spotted, blotched, mottled—the slow, stately swimmers, the darts that flashed by, the fat ones, the thin ones, the flat ones, the pencil-like, and the chunky ones, all full of life that is not my life, compact, hydrodynamic, finned and scaled, swimming solo or in schools, almost free of choice. I am informed that fish are a noisy lot, but I looked on in silence. Crabs there were, crayfish, and shrimp—some have their eyes on stalks; some do not. Some are fanged; some secrete poison; some are electric. So much for the sea.

Majunga

MAJUNGA is the oldest of the Malagasy harbors. Lying on the northwest shore at the mouth of the Bombetoka Bay at the end of the Betsiboka River, it has been a trading port since long before Madagascar was discovered and named Madagascar. Whatever navigators came down from India, from Persia, from Phoenicia, from Egypt, from Pelasgian Greece, from the Byzantine Empire, from Arabia, and, before the rounding of the Cape of Good Hope, from Medieval Europe, sailed into land at Majunga to do business. Today, although ocean-going vessels must still lie off its silting, shifting waterfront to load and unload in lighters, Majunga is the second port of Madagascar, handling 200,000 tons of merchandise in a good year (to Tamatave's 300,000 tons).

Majunga is a pretty place; its name, from the Arabic, means "City of Flowers." The French enjoy living there; it has the pleasant atmosphere of an old established colony. It is a sunny town of regular streets and squares planted with thick shade trees and named after Richelieu, Colbert, France, Liberty, the Republic, Gallieni, Jules Ferry, the Church, the Liberation, General de Gaulle—and even after George V, Nicholas II, and the Slaughter-house. The pretty villas are built against the heat—Majunga is the hottest place in Madagascar, varying from 58° to 90° Fahrenheit in the shade. The shade is thick in their flowering gardens, and the houses are painted in the pale colors of ice cream and water ice. I learned to go out early in the morning or in the cool of the evening, either on foot or riding in a rickshaw pulled by a fellow man. He did not mind—although at first I did—because he makes a living. He has been organized and so he earns as much as an internal combustion taxi-driver. He wears a wide-brimmed characteristic straw hat, and he clangs a bell against a shaft of his livelihood to catch the eye of a potential customer, or to clear the way. He is a big black man as a rule, running barefoot in shorts and shirts.

In 1952, there were 42,000 people living in Majunga, of whom 17,000 were Sakalava. The land of this once dominant Malagasy tribe, "the People of the Long Valleys," runs down the west coast opposite Africa across the Mozambique Channel, and goes inland through the flat and rolling bush to the highland foothills. Thus it lies under the wind and gets little rain; it is a wilderness and a wasteland of dry plains and thick, low forest growths, almost empty save for the long, fertile river valleys, now being brought into scientific cultivation. The deep alluvial soil, cleared and irrigated, is planted to government-sponsored but privately owned commercial crops, such as a kind of cotton brought in from California to produce the highest yield of excellent fiber in the world. Along the Mangoky and the Tsiribihina (the "Man-gook" and "Cheery-bean") Rivers, Maryland tobacco grows in French *regie* monopoly.

So the Sakalava hinterland is being surveyed, mapped, and counted. The average population of the entire island in 1958 amounted to but 22 inhabitants per square mile. However, the Malagasy are now in the act of "demographic explosion," with an annual birth rate of 2.5 per cent. Forty per cent of the islanders today are under fifteen years of age—because the French health authorities have put down malaria, wiped out smallpox, almost eliminated leprosy and the bubonic plague; and they have got tuberculosis and the respiratory diseases under control, and also the venereal or social diseases. A short time back, it was said, 80 per cent of the wild tribal people carried congenital syphilis, left behind by the seventeenth-century pirates of the Spanish Main. The next campaign—in 1959—was to have been an all-out attack on the virulent liver fluke, the snail-borne trematodes of bilharziasis (a disease oddly associated in my mind with William S. Hart of the early wild Westerns). So the French were midwives to the Malagasy population boom.

The Sakalava for the most part are still pastoral, although the Vezo clan are fishermen. They are tall, very dark-skinned, muscular, with African hair and Polynesian and Arabic features—left behind by the slavers from Muscat and Oman, and later Zanzibar. Supplied with muskets, powder, shot, and steel knife-blades, the Sakalava—those who were not sold for export—became paramount among the eighteen tribes. They dominated the island in the seventeenth and eighteenth centuries, but they made no attempt to organize their conquests into a political entity, as the Merina of the highlands did.

The end of the Sakalava domination came in 1840—when Queen Tsiomeko fled Majunga for Nosy-Bé. Foreign anthropologists now say that the Sakalava are today in rapid regression—which is to say, they are committing tribal suicide. Apparently, they refuse to . . . what is the word? To adjust. They have opted for death, and not for a watered-down life. In their refusal, which is reaction and rejection, a truly deadend and die-hard conservatism, there is something admirable, something noble, something dignified and even aristocratic. The Sakalava are a tribe of heroes—in the ancient Greek sense of that difficult word.

To be sure, it is old-fashioned nonsense to elect to cease. Even so, I found it encouraging to come upon a tribe of men and women who will not change their ways; they are convinced that their way of life suits them, as is. I wonder if all free choice boils down to "No!" Maybe, so it may be, in personal freedom. On the last day of December, 1959, there were in all 316,091 Sakalava men, women, and children, who found it better to be dead-black than, say, red, white, and blue. But on the other hand, the 1950 census counted them as 275,000. So perhaps the Sakalava have changed their minds; or, more likely, they are wild and independent human beings who refuse to stand up to be counted—or rather, to lie down and let the statistical cybernetic machine roll over them.

When I was in Majunga, the French added up to 2,500 individuals. On Sunday evenings, it was the wont of the young and younger (meaning older) members, and the *évolués* and *assimilés,* and the by-blows, to gather at the Greek-owned Grand Hotel on the waterfront, to dance. The girls and the young women, dressed to kill, drifted in in small coveys, or in pairs, or alone; the young men, likewise in sexual segregation, came in bands, or in flights, and now and again in prides and parades, and they wore sport clothes, or, indeed, bluejeans and T-shirts—working dress.

Once on the wide verandah or in the enormous room, the sexes sat apart, the girls in the light near the dance floor, the men on the periphery in the dark. Even the drinks were masculine or feminine— hard likker or beer for the men, orangeade, pop, or syrops for the girls. The young men laughed and bantered noisily in their corners; the girls smiled, spoke quietly, or sat, saying nothing except with their smiling lips and glancing eyes; they were as decorous as flowers in a summer garden. The young men scraped their chairs on the wide floor-boards, stretched, scratched, and generally made it clear that each one was carefree, fancy free, and meant to stay that way. To be sure, they were no freer than humming birds are free of long-throated crimson flowers.

The music played. All conversation ceased. The dance began. Each young man made a bee line to his chosen partner, and, without a word spoken, he claimed her as though he knew what he was doing. Despite the empty Mozambique breeze, the night was hot, as was the Caribbean music played by five Martiniquese. So was at least one of the girls, a coffee-and-cream beauty, who had touchingly, although mistakenly, obeyed an impulse to dip her wooly head into a dye pot. It had come out flame red; and in effect, it was as troubling as a conflagration in which a house burns down. She sweated at the airpits of her very tight bodice, above a swirl of petticoated short skirts. To be sure, I was sitting still and sweating, too; but with a difference.

To me, and to the young Frenchmen, the most attractive—she was the most popular—of the girls was a tall, slim Sakalava, dark of skin and elegant in a very pretty dress of flowered silk. She had long hands and wonderfully long legs, and she had presence. She looked at eye level straight into her partner's eyes, and she smiled and talked as she danced; she danced beautifully. She was a joy to see.

In the dance, each knew exactly what to do at all times, as in true ritual. The pattern took the form of an oval garland inside the rectangular space, woven and formal; indeed, ceremonial. There is nothing left primitive about the French, I thought, my toes jumping inside my shoes; even their blood is Gallicized as it filters through the brain on its way back and forth from the heart. I shifted in my seat, wondering at what point in history the French rejected the undisciplined unknown. And once again the irony of their civilizing mission struck me. This Negro music, come into Majunga from Spain, Africa, Arabia, and the East by way of the hot Americas, beats in the forests of the night, and not in the forest of Fontainebleau. There are differences indeed among the trees, I say, despite the eminent French parthenogenesist Jean Rostand's proof to the contrary. Who wants us all to be alike, bred in a laboratory, born by a bottle?

Overcome by loneliness, I got up and walked away from the dance. Through the thick and moonlit night, I followed the corniche to the Crocodile Point, a high cape where the town planners had built a French *terre-plein*—a level space enclosed by balustrades set about with sweet-smelling shrubs and vines. There at this vantage point I took my stand, to look down at the harbor. Below me to the right I made out what seemed to me to be an admirable construction, a long, straight jetty thrusting into the thick currents of the Bombetoka Bay. But no ships lay tied up at this dock in what seemed to me to be a sheltered and an admirably secure port. The harbor was empty in the still and moonlit night. I took my mind away from the dance, and realized that I was looking down at the notorious, the infamous Schneider jetty, to build which, in 1939, the equivalent of more than a million dollars had been wasted—or as wasted as money, once spent, or stolen, or given in bribes, or lost, ever is wasted. Part of the plan to modernize the harbor installations, this jetty had been badly placed across the currents. Thus it attracted to itself all the silt of the slow river; it lay buried in mud. The jetty was a total loss—except, possibly, as a monument to mankind's imperfection, to the human capacity for error, or to someone's corruptibility. The jetty failed to control the river currents or to balk the tides.

There being, thus, no comfort in the sight, I turned and headed back the way I'd come along. And I stopped to look up at the ancient baobab tree growing (in our time, but not when it was planted) in a traffic island in the center of Poincaré Square at the end of the Avenue de France, on the waterfront. In 1959, when I visited Majunga for a second time after the successful Referendum that kept Madagascar voluntarily within General de Gaulle's Community, I saw that the enormous, huge, thick-branching tree carried a neat white OUI lettered on the scarred bark of the tremendous trunk.

By then I had learned that a French authority on such a matter as the trees of Madagascar, H. Perrier de la Bathie by name, had estimated that this particular baobab was at least ten centuries old, and that it served as a kind of trademark. A thousand years ago, Arab slavers had planted this imported African tree—*Andansonia digitata,* and not the local baobab variety, *A. madagascariensis,* which has a different habit of growth. It was their sign, and perhaps it served as a landmark to let newcomers to the port, in their generations, know that others before them had prepared the ground and worked out mutually satisfactory commercial treaties with the local tribal chief. The Arabs bartered, in exchange for Sakalava slaves—a merchandise that they carefully handed and well—their own brand of civilization. Islam was then past the peak of its achievement and expansion; it was hardening for the long decline.

The earliest Arab navigators from the north must have sailed into Majunga in the reign of the Caliph Harun al-Rashid, the greatest of the Abbasids of Bagdad. And, it is supposed, Scheherazade, wife of the Sultan of India, had heard of the island; for in her *Arabian Nights Entertainment,* she told of Sinbad the Sailor and the fabulous Roc. That giant bird of the book, able to seize a full-grown elephant in its talons and fly off, was thought to have nested on Madagascar, although ornithologists now say not. Zoologists likewise discount the elephant native to the island. Madagascar always has been a legendary place.

In the tenth century before Christ, David and Solomon knew vaguely of the island; as did, later, Martin of Tyre, Aristotle, Pliny the Elder, and Ptolemy; all the great Arab navigators and geographers knew that a big island lay in the hot seas off the east coast of Ophir. They gave it various names: Phebol, Cernea, Menuthias, Medruthis, Sherbezat, Camaracada, and the Island of the Moon.

Before they were discovered, the Malagasy had no name for their own island, which was everything to them, home and fatherland, continent and earth, universe—and even heaven, too, for the Malagasy soul had no better place to go for the life after death, no ethereal unknown perfection elsewhere. Madagascar was everything to them;

and it was satisfactory, it was all they knew. Today, for outer space, they have had to take in French words for place names like Asia, Australia, Africa, Europe, and the Americas.

Indeed, when they speak of their island, Madagascar, and of themselves, the Malagasy make use of foreign nouns; they were named by mistake. In error, Marco Polo in his Pisan prison dictating his book of reminiscences of a long adventurous life apparently confused the island with the mainland port and hinterland below the hook of Africa—a city now called Mogadishu in a country now called Somalia. He spoke of "Madeigascar" and he gave the place untold wealth—in gold, in ivory, in tortoise shell, in jewels, in elephants, camels, and giraffes. Marco Polo has proved to be notably accurate about the roads he travelled and the lands he saw for himself; but he never knew at first hand Africa, and never saw the island he named. Of these places, he recounted hearsay got in Xanadu in the time of Kublai Khan from Arab merchant-navigators. What language did they have in common, the Venetian traveller and the Oriental storytellers?

Later, Italian cartographers of the Renaissance changed the spelling and put Madagascar on the map. The mineral deposits there have proved to be disappointing; there is a bit of almost all the ores, and many of the lesser stones, but almost none in quantity and quality profitable in large-scale exploitation. The animals of Madagascar are rare and fascinating, but only to the specialist, not to the white hunter on safari.

However, and although Marco Polo got it wrong, there were commercial possibilities in the island; the Arabs made a good thing out of Malagasy men and women, boys and girls, in the export-import trade. They sailed down in the monsoons of the Boreal winter, laden with hardware for exchange; they sailed home again to market in the trade winds of the Austral winter, carrying prime slaves.

By chance, in side-effect, they introduced along with firearms their lunar calendar and the names for the days of the week and the months of the year. Before them, the Malagasy had no use for time, as such. And the slavers left behind them other forms of slavery: the use of paper for the written word; the human and the divine words of the Koran; powerful magic, both black and white; and the patriarchal system of family and clan rule in a man's world. However, neither

Islam, nor purdah, nor the word took hold, although the earliest known island records are books of magic written by Antaimoro sorcerers in their Polynesian Malagasy language making use of an adapted Arabic script of the sixteenth century. The Arabs, then, did not stay. They came to do business; they left a little of their blood behind; they went with the winds.

Nor did the Arabs introduce the practice of slavery to Madagascar —a solution to the labor problem that seems to be at least as old as time. The Sakalava chieftains, long before the Arabs came, waged wars to capture and enslave prisoners; and in tribal justice they condemned their own law-breaking, and thus criminal, fellow men and women to slavery for life. The Arabs, working in harmony with the chiefs and the kings, merely introduced and organized the export trade. They made first-quality goods, these tall and muscular, often magnificent Sakalava men and women, thought to be a mixture of melanic Polynesians and African Negroes.

Perhaps because there was no onus attached then to slavery— although, to be sure, no man or woman chose to be a slave—the extended slave trade did not in itself corrupt the tribal society of Madagascar. The French Revolutionary ideas of personal liberty, individual human dignity, and the rights of man made slavery indefensible; and the machines of the industrial revolution made it uneconomical. There are several dates to put to its end: the British freed their slaves in 1838; the French of the Second Republic in 1848 gave French slaves French citizenship; Abraham Lincoln's Emancipation Proclamation of 22 September 1862 was ratified in December, 1865. Domestic slavery went on in Madagascar until the French annexed the island in 1896.

Throughout the eighteenth and the nineteenth centuries, the reserve of slaves in Madagascar was to the Malagasy currency as the gold in Fort Knox is to the American dollar. Then gold was valueless, for all the gold (not much) of Madagascar belonged to the Vazimba, those mysterious, black, pygmy earliest inhabitants. Gold was taboo. The metal was untouchably reserved for the adornment of the Merina kings and queens, who wore it as an emblem of their inherited divine right to rule worked with red coral (likewise taboo) in heavy crown jewels (on display in the Museum-Palace); and likewise as proof of their descent from the deified Vazimba. The Malagasy were, and most of them still are, ancestor worshippers. To be sure, in their Christian decadence, the last of the Merina rulers gave gold-mining concessions to the French—who went broke, perhaps in divine punishment. In 1958, Madagascar produced a total of 24.8 kilograms of gold, or about 656 Troy ounces.

When imported silver coins began to circulate in Madagascar in the eighteenth century, everything about them was foreign—the metal (which does not exist in the Malagasy state of nature), the obverse and the reverse of the coin, the concept of coinage as currency in trade, as a gauge of wealth, as a basis for the economy, and as personal adornment. Thus there were no taboos attached to the minted dollars —Spanish, or Mexican, or Yankee—nor to the French five franc piece that was officially established in 1855 as the unit of currency for Queen Ranavalona the Cruel's realm.

In 1817, when what a slave fetched in the market for export set the price of things, the unit in the bartering was a keg of gunpowder, a small keg, weighing forty pounds. Retailed by the Arabs, the keg sold for 240 dollars. The silver dollar in Madagascar then was worth a French five franc piece; and that was worth four English shillings, or one American silver dollar. A prime buck or wench for export, f.o.b. Majunga, was worth fifteen silver dollars, seventy-five francs, or two and a half pounds of gunpowder. It is always interesting to know the price of anything at all times, but it is almost impossible to establish a really equivalent value of one slave in the currencies of, say, 1960. There is no use in trying to figure things out in the price of bread, for the Malagasy eat no bread. However, in the uncertain slave market of 1850, eight or ten turkeys, or a score or a couple of dozen fowl in the poultry yard, cost one contemporary American dollar. A zebu steer on the hoof cost five dollars. An ordinary run of the Malagasy slave cost fifteen dollars. Today at inflated prices in Malagasy paper money, the same quality beef steer costs the equivalent of twenty dollars on the hoof.

I do not know what a fatted animal for export was worth a century ago, but in 1850 a prime slave cost from $30 to $40 in Majunga; the same slave, once exported to Réunion to work in the sugar cane plantations, retailed from $200 to $240, and that amounts to a 500 per cent mark-up, a practice that incidentally agrees with the local cost-times-five formula now used to arrive at a retail price for any goods or product of Madagascar offered for sale in New York.

If the War Between the States had gone the other way (I figure, but I cannot guarantee my figuring), a slave offered on the auction block for sale today in the Port of New York would fetch from $300 for a small boy to $2,000 for an adult. The actual price would depend on the male Malagasy slave's age, his physique, his condition, his health, his proved potency, his docility, his character, and his skill. These figures agree with the outrageous prices, as I remember hearing my Southern ancestors speak sorrowfully of being forced to pay for new blood just before what my New England ancestors, having won the final battle, called the Civil War.

The most expensive slave I found listed in the books written by nineteenth-century missionaries and world travellers about Madagascar was a highly skilled woman, apparently middle-aged, especially talented in the weaving of fine silk cloth, *lambas* and *lambamenas*—shawls, scarfs, and shrouds. She fetched a price equivalent to that of a good used Cadillac, although perhaps not an El Dorado convertible. Nowhere in any of my reading and research did I find the slightest hint that virgin boys and girls were sold to specialists in sex. I think there may have been no demand for such a slave to supply. And, indeed, all the experts agree that the life of a slave in Madagascar was not so bad; on the contrary, it was very good, as slavery went and goes.

But of course, the institution is destructive; it destroys both ways. In Madagascar under the Merina monarchs, all manual labor as well as all the wars of conquest were carried out, won or lost, by slaves of the Andevo and Mainty castes in the rigid tribal order. The nobles of the Andriana and the free men and women of the Hova castes were removed from reality; they were prevented by the system from lifting a finger to help themselves; thus, helplessly they were made dependent upon possessed inferiors. Thus the symbiosis of the owner and the owned destroyed progress, made freedom meaningless, and eliminated liberty. In their filanzana, chaired on the shoulders of slaves, the once dynamic Merina were carried to the edge of the abyss; there they stood. The French came along, in 1895, and gave them a nudge; the whole social order crumbled. Freemen and enslaved men, all fell over the cliff into chaos.

By then the Merina tribe had fixed itself in an elaborate structure. On top stood the royal house of kings and queens; next came their distant cousins; then came the nobles—all members of the Andriana— the lords. They were exempt, they lived above the law of the ordinary courts, and they had the power of life and death over the lesser peoples. In the early days, the lords had worked for a living as governors and generals, examples, keepers of the peace; but in the end, like their counterparts in that other court of Versailles, the noble Andriana had great privilege but little real power.

The Hova caste of Free People made up the majority of the Merina. They were lighter in skin color than the royalties—whose darkness came from their divinity—they had, or so they claimed, married into, and thus absorbed, the ancient Vazimba, the original ancestors; and certainly they had exchanged dynastic brides, before the absolute Merina dominance, with the royal families of the lesser, darker coastal tribes. The Hova of the Merina showed their predominant Malayo-Polynesian blood lines; the tribe came from Sumatra and Java and from the Malay Peninsula where for a century or so before they left, their ancestors had lived under Hindu influence. Today the Hova, short and graceful people, have straight or curling hair, almond eyes, and almost Mongol-Chinese "yellow" coloring. Yet, oddly, unlike the other Polynesians—say, the Tahitians and the Samoans—among outsiders, the beauties of the Malagasy appeal chiefly to the dispassionate ethnological eye. As a rule, the Hova are unremarkable, except for the quick intelligence that informs their faces. This majority caste was subdivided into the Hova, those born free; the Hovavao, who were wholly emancipated slaves; and the Zaza-Hova, once free, but reduced and sold into slavery for debt, or as a punishment for political —later religious—offense.

The caste of slaves had an élite—the Tsiavondahy, those owned by royalty. The majority of the Andevo—"the Lost"—may once have been free men and women, but who in time had lost whatever semblance of freedom serfs, caste of workers tied to the land, may have had; they were people born to work; but even so, they were considered members of the Merina tribe. Below the Andevo came the Mainty—

"the Blacks"—who, if their name was descriptive, presumably were not Merina much reduced, but were men and women of the other, darker, melanic tribes captured in war, or purchased, or even imported from Africa. They were accumulations incorporated into the tribal caste system, and even recognized as members of the individual slave-owning families. I find no record of rebellions or of slave uprisings.

The other tribes of Madagascar were less elaborately caste-ridden. Apparently the Merina stratified themselves as they left their nomadic ways and settled down in the highlands to live fixed lives in walled villages surrounded by irrigated rice fields and burnt pastures. In the late eighteenth century when the king of a dominant clan conquered first his Merina cousins, and later the Betsileo, the Betsimisaraka, and the Sakalava, he overextended the family unit. Thus sophistication set in, and perhaps decadence. Even so, the Merina monarchy had a century of a certain primitive glory. Madagascar gave it space enough—empty, timeless space. The Malagasy then, like the lemurs, had no natural enemies (except one another). Thus in their way of life, they lived as in a *vase-clos*, as under a bell jar. Natural history struck a balance, almost motionless in equilibrium (until the foreigners came in).

But it was not quite a static society; there was a certain freedom of choice, with consequences. Members of the different castes could intermarry. The children of such mixed but recognized unions automatically were born into the lower caste of the lesser parent. A slave, if his owner gave him both permission and help, could earn and save enough money to purchase himself as well as the freedom of his family down through the generations. At the very top of the heap, the intermarrying, inbreeding royalities stagnated in the blood; the men, at least, lost their force. Thus a family of the Hova caste of freemen, Andafy-Avaratra by name, assumed and held the real power as hereditary prime ministers. The last of these, Rainilaiarivony, chose and elevated to the throne three of the Merina queens in succession (the last of their line). Thus he proved not so much that love will find a way, as that there was a certain flexibility in the hierarchy, although, indeed, he stretched things to the very limit by marrying them, one after the other of the royal ladies in turn. The marriages were, to be sure, morganatic and, at least to him, convenient. According to the caste system, which he was bound to respect and maintain as the framework of the state and the skeleton of his personal power, he would have undermined the establishment had he sat down upon the throne, by day. So he ruled by specialized immobility.

Following their conquest of 1895, the French decreed the end of slavery at the bottom, and the abolition of the monarchy at the top. So fell the caste system. The royalties went into exile, but the bewildered men and women newly freed had no place to go in liberty; they had no capital to invest in freedom of choice, and nowhere to house self-determinism. They were, in fact, at liberty, lost outside of the familiar enclosure where they had felt physically, spiritually, and psychologically at home.

On the other hand, the former free men and women and children —the Hova—lacking slaves, literally could not get out of bed, comb their hair, or put on their clothes. They could not wash themselves. They did not know how to draw water from the wells and public fountains, nor how to light a fire to boil the kettle or the pot. They could not cook, let alone find food and eat it. They were abject, and many of them would have died if some of the old slaves had not preferred to return to live the only life that they knew. Independence, perhaps at best an illusory thing, was impossible to imagine. Worst of all, high and low and in between, the Malagasy found themselves to be detribalized by foreign intervention; so they never forgave the French for their enforced, unwanted gift of liberty. Freedom, it appears, can neither be given nor imposed; nor can it be withheld. It must be taken. The French once knew this fact.

In the light of the Lenten moon in Majunga in 1959, I walked away from the Arab slave-traders' planted African digitate baobab trademark tree, and from the white OUI calling upon the enfranchised Malagasy to support Charles de Gaulle in the Referendum for the Fifth French Republic, which has proved to be not quite a democracy. In Madagascar, Lent comes at the end of the hot and humid summer. Easter is a moveable autumnal feast. It coincides with the annual outbreak of a localized disease, endemic, epidemic, and known as *"la majunguite."* Then Majunga enjoys ill health, and is bedridden. Majunguicitis is a fever in the blood, a seasonal disorder, and it is catching; but unlike nymphomania or satyriasis, it does not persist. It comes on at Carnival, and dies down as the cool weather sets in, and it is followed by an eruption of scandal and a rash of divorce. None is immune; although the very young and the very old, perhaps because of their antibodies, usually escape the contagion, all human flesh is susceptible. The early symptoms are idleness, boredom, and restlessness. But once the incubation period is over, the afflicted feel wonderfully well; the hair takes on a luster, the eyes light up, the lips perpetually smile, the skin glows with a lovely bloom; all the muscles move in tonic flexibility.

As I walked back from the baobab, I caught a glimpse of two young people held in the grip of the malady; that is to say, they seemed to me to be in love. The girl was beautiful; she was radiant. She stood poised on a doorstep under an arch cut in a high white wall, a garden behind her. She shone in gentle illumination—but she could have withstood the lighting of an operating theater. She was young, she had the perfection of a hybrid flower, she was breathtaking. Her hand on the latch of the open door, she had turned to look back and down at the young white Frenchman, who stood, transfixed, key in hand, caught by her beauty as he tried to lock the door of his small white Dauphine. He gave up and abandoned his cast shell.

I wonder if, in empire, the segregation and the separation of the races is essential?—white and black, superior and inferior, leader and led. In a civilizing mission, the European colonists leave their Fatherland, the power, to go out to the colonies to offer the natives a Motherland (France, for instance), from whom all blessings flow. Fatherland, Motherland—the image of Colonial empire is certainly confusing to all concerned in spreading the seed of enlightenment.

Father, mother, lover and beloved—is sex necessary in a Colonial set-up? The whole affair appears to go against nature (as they say); and yet *"Vive la difference!"* is the French battle cry in the war between the sexes where, as elsewhere, all is fair.

So "Fair play!" is the British cry in their form of sport. Instead of intimate games, the British empire-builders introduced empirical cricket—and as a basis of human encounter, they made it work. They had learned how do to so on the playing fields of Eton and on the battlefields of Waterloo.

The French never did see their empire as a ball park. Thus when the British captured Diégo-Suarez in 1942, they were disgusted to find no playing field, no pitches, no courts, no greens, no links, no pools—no facilities for games, none at all. They shook their heads and scornfully dismissed the French as colonizers, colonists, character and empire-builders. Without teams, how could the French expect teamwork in the mutual enterprise of empire?

After the war, when the French turned Madagascar over to the Malagasy Republic in 1959, they had built 42 stadiums; 146 football fields and two more for Rugby; 68 basketball courts, some of which were covered with a roof; 78 volleyball courts; 21 swimming pools; 10 yacht clubs, on the sea as well as inland on lakes; 12 judo and fencing clubs; and 78 tennis courts. To play on all of these, they had organized 152 football teams, 28 Rugby clubs, 38 basketball associations, and so on, down to 10 teams for ping-pong, 9 bowling clubs, and a single group of fencers. And in both world wars, as well as in the lesser wars inside the Colonial empire, the French took Malagasy conscripts into their army as soldiers in Colonial regiments that proved in action to be distinguished for exceptional courage against the common enemy.

In Majunga, in the morning, I came upon a soldiers' monument standing in an out-of-the-way knoll in a small and shady square, near the cemetery. Erected in honor of the young men who died in glory, it is a discreet war memorial, a modest obelisk of stone on which stands a wingèd victory cast in metal—iron, probably. For recently it had been given a coat of aluminum paint; therefore, it glittered, as though brand-new. Angel and obelisk stand on a truncated pyramid of three steps of stone, supplied with three sets of dates. The first, and, I judge, the only numerals the monument builders had in mind at the time, are 1894–1895. They are cut into the middle step. Later another hand carved in 1914–1918 on the bottom step, but they are chiseled in the same eternal style. Thus there was no room for 1939–1945 on the pedestal; these numerals are cut into a separate slab, a small rectangular makeshift, leaning on a slant against the little pyramid. Anyone could pick it up and carry it away.

In the French conquest of Madagascar there were no Malagasy troopers in the detachment of Marines sent ashore on 12 December 1894; nor in the bigger expeditionary forces that arrived in Majunga

on 15 February 1895 in the hot summertime of heavy rains, to fight
their way 375 miles by road to Tananarive. The only thing was that
there was no road in those days; so the French engineers set out to
build one; it proved to be a mortal enterprise and it took six months.

As usual with all outbreaks of war, nothing makes good sense in
retrospect. The history of it is that throughout the nineteenth century,
the British and the French had been jockeying for power and place
in Madagascar. Therefore, the Merina kings, queens, and hereditary
prime ministers, all of whom thought that the island belonged to them,
had learned to keep their independence by playing off the one foreign
power against the other.

The Malagasy downfall was precipitated from Europe, where, in the
Franco-Prussian War of 1870–71, Napoleon the Less lost out, and
Bismarck won. The Iron Chancellor of the German Empire pulled
great weight and disturbed the balance of power on the continent.
By so doing, Bismarck not only humiliated the defeated French, but
also excluded them from their old cultural emprise in the vanished
little courts of Germany, in Italy, in Austria—and diminished them in
Russia. By containing France in Europe as inside a wall, Bismarck, by
chance, sent the ambitious young Army and Navy officers forth to
conquer Africa, Asia, and Madagascar, there to regild the tarnished
grandeur and glory of the Motherland on Colonial fields of battle.

These French officers proved to be so successful in the land-grab
that Bismarck, who had no interest in acquiring colonies, was forced
in 1884 to pick up the Cameroons, Togo, a piece of West Africa, and
Tanganyika as well as Ruanda-Urundi—as makeweights in the balancing of power at the conference table. Thus this imperial German statesman turned out to be the father of both the German and the French
Colonial empires of the nineteenth century. Victoria was not much
amused.

For Bismarck thus disturbed the British, who found it prudent to
settle their small, outstanding Colonial differences with the French.
They took over Zanzibar and the Sultan's hinterland—Kenya and
Uganda. The French got Madagascar, more or less—as a kind of protectorate. Then Bismarck called the Conference of Berlin in 1884–1885
to answer the African Question, and in particular to settle the problem
of the ownership of the Belgian Congo. The arrangements made by

the European Colonial powers lasted for a generation—until the Treaty of Versailles.

The first Franco-Hova war began in May of 1883 when the French Navy, operating from bases in Réunion, in La Bigorne's Sainte-Marie-de-Madagascar, and in Admiral de Hell's Nosy-Bé, took Majunga. France decided to claim the Sakalava port and tribal hinterland as part of the territory ceded by Queen Tsiomeko on Nosy-Bé in 1840. The French forces occupied the Merina royal capital of Tananarive in June of 1883. Back in Paris, the French Chamber of Deputies, confronted by a *fait accompli*, decided on 27 March 1884 that France had the right to "protect" the whole island of Madagascar. By the treaty signed with Malagasy prime minister and queen on 17 December 1885, France took outright possession of the Bay of Diégo-Suarez and its shores; and in return agreed to protect the Merina kingdom from all (other) outside and foreign enemies. Other clauses had to do with overseeing the keeping of the internal peace, and to establishing trade and commerce with exclusive French monopolies. There was some truth in the French claim that by so doing, they improved the living conditions of the lesser tribes of Madagascar, then subject to the whims of the highland Merina's absolute and irresponsible power.

The first French resident in Tananarive was a career officer in the French Colonial service named Charles-Marie Le Myre de Vilers. He arrived at his new post on 14 March 1886. Although many streets and schools in Madagascar bore his complicated family name in 1960, things did not go well with him in his own times. His trouble came from the wily prime minister, the queen's consort, Rainilaiarivony, who refused to listen to (French) reason unless it was backed up by the active presence of the French Marines. Incident followed insulting incident; in January, 1894, the Chamber of Deputies in Paris voted to use force if necessary to uphold the terms of the protectorate. Rainilaiarivony decided to test Le Myre de Vilers' strength; his name means "the Father of the One Who Holds the Flower"; he wanted to see which man held the power. Le Myre de Vilers decided on a strategic retreat; and, aged sixty-one, he took up the French flag and, on 27 October 1894, walked out of Tananarive at the head of the entire French Community, to take the trail for Majunga.

The exodus comprised 100 French civilians, 146 French soldiers, and 31 native porters—277 men in all. Perhaps the women and the children had been sent home earlier on. But they took 53 animals with them, most of them cattle on the hoof to be eaten along the way. The men were civil servants, businessmen, explorers, scientists, teachers, missionaries, and possibly a tourist or two, as well as the officers and the men of the Marines, and the Malagasy whom they owned or hired or could persuade to go along to help out, and as guides. The footpaths led through wild, rough, almost empty, highly accidented country; the party reached Majunga in 26 days, on 21 November 1894, reduced by 52 men, who did not fall by the wayside but instead dropped out on their own. Of the 225 who went the whole way, some went home, some crossed to Nosy-Bé, or further, to Réunion; and some waited to join up with the coming French expeditionary forces on 15 February 1895.

According to the official French communiqués, the conquest of Madagascar was thrust upon the French, whose government, patient and reasonable over a period of ten years, had no choice but to take disciplinary action. However, to the French electorate, the punitive expedition did not make sense; the invasion of Madagascar was unpopular from the start. The French people, who, it might be assumed, were represented in the Third Republic's Chamber of Deputies, the Senate, and the Cabinet, rejected the invasion and the conquest with considerable violence. They had no need for, and wanted no part of, Madagascar. Thus the military had to fight a sort or rear-guard action against hostile public opinion in France the while they fought against the Malagasy, the climate of Madagascar—and the famous Generals Hazo and Tazo ("Forest" and "Fever"), who led the defense in depth. The invasion, then, represented not the will of the French people, but the will of the French military caste backed up by a few ambitious statesmen-politicians.

For, by the end of the century, that curious anomaly of the French form of democracy had established itself: in the Republic, the elected deputies no longer represented their constituents as such, but instead spoke either for the powerful special interests in their electoral districts, or for their political parties—or for themselves, alone. As things worked out, the unheeded voice of public opinion was right. Madagascar has never been of real value to more than a fractional minority of the French; and French glory and grandeur never flamed brightly there. Thus the conquest of the island illustrates once again the peculiar fact that the French Colonial empire belonged to the Army, to the Navy, and to the permanent bureaucracy of France, and their dependents (including the *colons* and the colonists), but not to the French people, who paid the price.

Most of the French voters did not even know where Madagascar was, and they did not care—until their husbands, their sons, their lovers and cousins and brothers and young friends died there. The newspapers of France knew; and except for the pro-government papers, the journalists and publishers of France attacked the invaders and the invasion. To be sure, few editors based their protests upon principles or scruples. The French press cannot be called disinterested (what newspapers or news magazines can?); most of the newspapers of those days were bought and paid for to serve special interests of their own—such as, in one or two instances, foreign powers.

Therefore, Madagascar soon became known in headlines as the Red Cemetery—"red" from the color of the lateritic soil, the silted Betsiboka and Bombatoka water, and, inaccurately, for the spilled French blood. But, in truth, 9,337 plus 14 French conscripts, professional soldiers, North African riflemen, and Foreign Legionnaires, most of them young, were buried along the road of invasion. In the six months that it went on its slow way, the expeditionary force as a whole lost 46 per cent of its effectives, and the engineering corps, given the hardest work to do—building the road, building the bridges —lost 64 per cent of its men. So the emotional and eye-catching headlines were, in effect, right to miscall the island the Red Cemetery; and the muddy river and bay that pour their blood-red waters past Majunga to stain the blue salt-seas took on the symbolism of pathetic fallacy.

Into these thick red waters were poured 14,773 troops, of whom 11,000 were Europeans, most of them young Frenchmen, brought down from the twenty-six-year-old Suez Canal, into the gut-shaped, hot Red Sea, and around the Horn of Africa, steaming into the tropics, across the Equator, and into summertime. They all wore government-issue woolen uniforms and stout leather boots. Some of these men were doing their stint of military service—they were, then, from eighteen to twenty-one years old, being hardened to defend their native land. Troops were not pampered then with suntans and ice cream.

Of these, in the almost exactly six-month period of the campaign—from 15 February to 21 August—9,337 (5,787 white Europeans and 3,550 Algerians) died of tropical diseases such as malaria, dysentery, and heat exhaustion; 97 were wounded, and 14 killed outright in active warfare. There is no record of the number of Malagasy casualties. All this took place about sixty-five years ago, only three years before the Spanish-American War, only nineteen years before the First World War, only forty-four years before the Second World War. It was a luxury, indeed.

The French invasion of Madagascar began exactly thirty years, a full generation, after the American Civil War had ended. Military strategists now all agree that whatever else, and whoever else, died between Harper's Ferry in 1859 and Appomattox in 1865, modern warfare was born on the intervening battlefields. Yet the French invasion of 1895 turned out to be an old-fashioned sort of war despite the French High Command's conviction that they had with them the very latest piece of modern war matériel—the wonderful Lefebvre wagon. Putting all their eggs in that one basket, they hoped to make of it a kind of blitzkrieg. It was to have been a fast action, a short and mobile war. At the time, from Paris, and in a different sort of way, the Lefebvre wagon looked to be as foolproof and as functional as the Maginot Line; but it proved in action to be as dangerous and as destructive to the French.

The *wagon Lefebvre* (and who Lefebvre was, I do not know; both the man and the wagon have vanished) was a ready-made, prefabricated, two-wheeled iron cart, standardized in all its parts, and demountable for easy shipment from France, and for rapid assembly in the field. Once set up, it was designed to be powered by an ox, a horse, a mule, or, in case of necessity, any number of men. There were no oxen trained to the yoke in Madagascar, although there were some 8,000,000 head of zebu cattle running almost wild—something like three to each man, woman, and child on the island. There may have been as many as a hundred horses—introduced as mounts to carry the missionaries on their rounds; but horses do not thrive in

Madagascar; the climate and the ticks kill them off. In 1958, there were 2,049 of them, luxury animals, bred and trained to the saddle and the sport of kings. All the mules had to be imported from Missouri by way of Marseilles and Majunga; I have no figures on the casualties in mules. When men started pulling the Lefebvre wagon, it behaved like the Juggernaut chariot.

Once in motion, the Lefebvre wagon was prepared to transport everything a solider or an army needed in active combat (in Europe) or behind the lines: ammo, weapons—both small arms, rifles, and mountain guns—all other equipment and supplies—food, wine, water, road-building picks and shovels, spare uniforms, blankets, tent canvas, and its own spare parts. It could do service as an ambulance or a rolling dispensary; it could be used for troop transport; it carried a portable altar on Sundays and Saints' days; it saw service as a hearse. Thus it was accepted as an indispensible and an efficient war machine; and the invading generals were delighted with it. It proved to be a lethal weapon, too; but not to the Malagasy.

To get the Lefebvre wagon rolling out of Majunga, it was necessary first to find a road. There were no roads in Madagascar in 1895—not one, none. In all the 226,600 (approx.) square miles of highlands and lowlands, not one of the 999 miles from north to south, not one of the 350 miles (at the widest) from east to west, was paved; there was no dirt road, no wagon trail, no wood road, not even a pair of wheel ruts, for there were no carts. The Malagasy had not invented the wheel, not even as a toy; and it was royal policy not to make use of the vehicles that had been given them; it was strictly forbidden to keep up the few highways that, earlier on, had been laid out.

Seventy-five or eighty years earlier, Radama I, the last strong and liberal king of the Imerina, had brought in wheeled transports for which he built a system of highland roads around his capital; and in the early days of his widow and successor, Queen Ranavalona I, more were put through. But according to the ubiquitous British missionary, the Reverend Mr. Ellis, all these had fallen into impassable disrepair. In Tananarive on its hill, washouts and gullies six feet deep and more ran up and down and zigzag across the steep, unpaved city streets. The queen and the prime minister fostered the neglect. At night it was too dangerous to walk out because these chasms had begun to undermine the retaining walls of the terraces and houses. Frau Ida Pfeiffer, the intrepid Austrian world traveler, reported that these were the worst roads she had ever come upon; she said that the Malagasy of a century ago had less of "the comforts of life" than all but the American Indians of the Oregon Territory—and she had been everywhere.

The Malagasy did not mind; they had footpaths. They like to walk about. But it was a matter of royal policy in the latter half of the nineteenth century not to build roads and not to keep up the few in and around the highland towns. The reactionary, isolated queens and their prime ministers reasoned that they, themselves, had nowhere to go, except on an occasional royal progress. Then they and their court of nobles and well-to-do Hova were carried in chairs on the shoulders of slave porters, and accompanied by more slaves and retainers, sometimes to the number of ten or even thirty thousand—of whom from two to ten thousand were counted upon to die on the way. It had always been so.

So the Lefebvre wagon went on crushing soldiers for 147 miles from Majunga to Superbieville, a town now called Maevatanana, "the Fine Village," but then named after the Frenchman who worked his gold concession of 3,600,000 acres, more or less, from 1885 until 1895; and then on further to Andriba, "Where There Is a Wall," 231 miles from Majunga. Here the French generals came to the conclusion that they were on the wrong track. It had taken them six months—187 days in all—and 9,337 lives to convince them that the Lefebvre wagon was not much good in Madagascar. The average Frenchman and Algerian is not tall—perhaps five feet six inches. Thus the wagon road killed them off at a rate of 23¾ men per mile, a high rate of speed for those days.

On the 21st of August, the generals changed their tactics and formed a flying column of 4,500 men, whose motto was *"Marche ou crève!"*—Tananarive or bust. They left the end of the road on September 14th; they got to their destination on September 29th. It took them fifteen days to cover the remaining 102⅓ miles of roadless wastelands, and to cross the cultivated fields and burnt pastures of the highlands in the cool and pleasant weather of early spring. The flying column hauled along a couple of cannon; with these they took the island. On the last day of September, 1895, at 3:30 in the afternoon, the last Merina queen of Madagascar, Ranavalona III—born in 1861; crowned on 22 November 1883, her twenty-second birthday; dethroned on 27 December 1896; and exiled to Algiers, Algeria, where she died in 1917, aged 56, and was buried; dug up and transported, in November 1938, to be ceremoniously returned to her native land for reburial in the royal Merina tomb of the Rova in Tananarive—gathered her court around her and took her stand on all that was left her of her domain, the hilltop crowned by the royal citadel.

There she stood in the pretty gardens of the Blue Forest, provided with fountains and flower borders, among a scattering of palace pavilions, one of which, a gingerbread Victorian cottage named Manampisoa, "Beauty's Increment," is as charming as a toy; and the biggest of which, Manjakamiadana, "Where It Is Meet to Reign," is now a museum of dead royalty and natural history; and another of which took fire and flamed up to convince her—to surrender herself, her people, and her island of Madagascar to the French.

From her high place, she looked out onto a wide view of the shallow green valley ringed by purple hills. The gardens are protected by stone balustrades edging the declivity. The queen, a slim young woman, little, with a charming brown face, wore, it may have been, a trim-waisted, tight-bodiced, royal red velvet gown, full-skirted, gold-embroidered, cut to give the queen both height and presence, and sweeping the ground as she walked along the paths in the elegant and end-of-century French fashion (one such, made by Worth of Paris and practically as good as new, is on display, filled out by a headless form, in a glass showcase in the Throne Room of the museum); and perhaps she had on her few diamonds (a necklace had been presented to her by the French government) as well as her royal orders—but perhaps not the Grand' Croix of the Légion d'Honneur hung around her neck by Le Myre de Vilers in the name of the Third Republic (now vulgarly called "the Slut") on 20 November 1888—when she struck her red ensign and hoisted the white flag.

She did so after three French melinite shells from the mountain guns had burst among the fretwork palaces and pretty gardens; and a fourth, an anti-personnel shell, had showered shrapnel on a sunken courtyard to kill her own Life Guards, tall black men magnificent in uniform, before her eyes. That shell accounted for thirty-five Malagasy casualities; the other three killed eighteen. The island colony was formally annexed by the Chamber of Deputies of the Palais Bourbon on 6 August 1896.

Madagascar is bigger than France, Belgium, and the Netherlands combined; but few in France rejoiced in the victorious conquest. In the *caf'conc'* of Montmartre in those great days of the Belle Époque of Toulouse-Lautrec and of Yvette Guilbert, they sang sad little songs, *complaintes*, like the one Edith Piaf used to sing to mourn her lost legionnaire. Gallieni had counted on the young women of France, the fiancées and the wives of the survivors among the French Colonial troops, to go out to join their men and to settle down on acreage allotted them for the homesteading. That was the way the Roman had settled and civilized Gaul, although those earlier legionnaires had married native women. But the young women of France rejected the chance to demonstrate the virtues of French culture and of French civilization to the Malagasy; and few of the Frenchmen on the island made permanent attachments in Madagascar.

Tananarive

A CHILD can take in the sunny landscape of the Malagasy highlands at a glance, and happily start to play with all the other children— fragments of the demographic explosion, dark-skinned, light-skinned, black and brown and white and golden, from Africa, from Asia, from the Mediterranean and further north, and from the South Sea Islands (unless, to be sure, his parents forbid him to do so). The Imerina ("Ee-mairn") around Tananarive, where the Merina children live with their unprejudiced mothers and fathers, is as pretty as a picture book. On the ride into town, the vistas open up, page after page of luminous scenes, clean but not tidy, full of incident. The golden sun shines down from a heavenly blue sky as the sun should shine down on childhood to illuminate a lovely, rolling, cultivated landscape, sparkling with water, set about with steepled towns on gentle hills, all painted in clear colors—sky blue, earth red, the emerald green of growing rice or the pale straw yellow of the harvest, leaf-green, brick-rose, tile-brown, the soft grey of weathered wood, and the flower hues, shaded and shadowed as the white clouds, flat on the bottom, fluffy on top, sail peacefully through the clean, clear, high atmosphere. And the air is kind to the skin, soft enough to put a bloom of peaches, plums, grapes, and blueberries on the distances.

It is a fresh and pleasant land, almost, but not quite, familar, agreeably unreal, wholly delightful, restful, kind to the eyes. The good French road winds like a black and satiny ribbon up and down and around, festooned with French telephone and electric-light wires fixed to French porcelain insulators on the arms of the grey-painted, French-erected, metal posts. The road leads through plantings of mimosa-acacia-wattle trees, golden and silvery, feathery and fragrant in May and June; and through shaggy, plumy groves of taller eucalyptus trees, smelling of childhood remedies. It goes up and over arched bridges spanning straight canals bordered with rows of trembling poplar trees connecting the still waters of shallow ponds in pastures where herds of cattle graze. Why does a zebu have a hump? To store up a reserve of fat in the good season.

All the towns are charming. The houses facing upon the road are family houses, prim Victorian brick cottages, two stories high, adorned with wooden verandahs like aprons, trimmed along the eaves and the gables with edgings of wooden fretwork like tatting, topped with ripply roofs of pantiles. It is a landscape as proper as a well-brought-up young lady's watercolor sketch.

In window boxes, in pots on the steps, in the dooryards blossom together all the summer annuals and the flowering plants of all the hemispheres, north, south, east, west, in a fine confusion of the seasons: morning glories, trumpet vines, geraniums, begonias, marigolds, carnations, cosmos, zinnias, lilies, asters, daisies, nasturtiums, chrysanthemums, strawflowers, crimson cockscombs; dahlias of all the shapes, the sizes, and the shadings; roses—trees, bushes, climbers, and ramblers; nice little fruit trees—peaches and plums in November and December (cherries refuse to grow in Madagascar); grapes in January; apples later on in March, April, and May; and pears (all the fruits are small); and the exotics—jasmine, diurnal hibiscus, crass bougainvillaea, great bushes of crimson velvety poinsettias, orchids in the shade; mangoes, papayas, bananas—oranges, lemons, lichees, and pineapples grow further down the slopes of the escarpment; and in the dry places, comical prickly-pear cacti and armored clumps of century plants, some in bloom.

The tooting, honking, shrieking cars and trucks are all recognizably French, as is the driving: beetling quatre-chevaux, elegant Dauphines, bucketing deux-chevaux, shark-like I.D.s and D.S.s and the others. Dogs bark and run away; energetic chickens flap their wings and scatter. But nothing in the impatient traffic alarms the men and women walking along the highway into town, and walking very well. There is nothing about the people to frighten a child—not even one already prejudiced in parentage. Few in the highlanders are tall, few are ugly, few are beautiful, and none is fat. The young men wear whole light-weight suits; the young and the old women wear cotton or silk dresses, sometimes flowery, sometimes dark, but most in pale and pretty tints. A very few of the old men still wear striped pajama suits, trousers and long tunic tops. The young women and the old women, and the old men, wrap shawl-like or scarf-like *lambas* around their shoulders; the old men wear straw hats; the women walk in the bright shade of pretty silk parasols, the loveliest of which are red.

The prettiest girl of all the girls, perhaps eighteen or twenty years old, her lustrous, curling, dark hair braided in two thick loops pinned up in back, carried such a parasol; and in the crook of her arm she held a bunch of nodding pink and white cosmos, long-stemmed, lacy-green-leafed. In the other hand she carried her elegant, high-heeled French shoes. Barefoot, light-brown-skinned, in a pale and pretty dress, she walked in her moving spot of rosy shade, smiling, French rouge on her generous lips, a glint of golden dentistry in her white and even teeth; her almond eyes smiled in her small face, too. Where could she be going? Who could she be?

No, there is nothing to distress a child along this road, neither in the picture-book land, nor in the reality. Not even the once ominous great bulwarks—the massive, sloping, twelve-foot-high ramparts of smooth, hard, red adobe surrounding what used to be cattle pens and remote farmhouses—for they are crumbling, riven by neglect, eroded by the rains, no longer functional. The French stamped peace upon the face of this high land. Before they came in the last days of the Merina monarchy, bandits, outlaws, dangerous gangs of desperate men attacked the outlying properties and villages of the feudal Hova and Andriana. But that is as it should be in a children's storybook.

The road went up and over a gentle rise, and it came down in the wide, round, fertile Betsimitatra plain, emerald green with rice fields, glinting in the sun, ringed by purple hills. And there I saw Tananarive, a city on a knoll, centered upon this shallow earthen bowl, a piling-up of houses and shady gardens like an offering of harvest fruit and flowers. There is no human habitation in the world more agreeable to come upon.

146

Tananarive is an unexpected place, a delightful end to a long journey, a pleasure to discover. It is like nowhere else I know. Its name means "the City of a Thousand"—although no one is certain whether the thousand is the number of the lesser Merina towns of the highlands, or the thousand palace guards surrounding the first of the conquering Merina kings. The old spelling is Antananarivo—*An* means "the," and the final *o*, as with almost all terminal vowels in Malagasy names put into an adapted and phonetic Anglo-Franco alphabet, is mute. The shortened name is pronounced "Tahn-ahn-ah-reev" with a rising French inflexion. In 1959, the people who lived there numbered 206,324, more than three quarters of them Merina tribal people, all of them now free men and women, most of them descendants of the caste of Hova ("Ooov"). A very few of the Andriana royalties and nobles now remain; and no slaves, none at all.

The Merina, "the People of the Land of Wide Prospects," or, to give them their other name, the Ambaniandro ("Ahm-bahn-ee-ahndr"), "the People Who Live Under the Sun," are highlanders, and thus not wild jungle men. In every way they hold themselves to be superior to the lesser and the lower tribes of the island. Indeed, they have proved themselves to be the most energetic, the quickest to appreciate the French gifts, thus to educate themselves; and they are the hardest-working to change their ways—the most successfully assimilated into French culture. Thus perhaps it is natural for them to be the most fervent nationalists. The Merina make up a quarter of the total island population—there were about a million and a quarter of them at the time of independence. Perhaps because their highlands are healthy, they are the most prolific of the tribes.

Nobody knows exactly when these latecomers from Sumatra and Malaya came some three thousand miles across the Indian Ocean, bringing with them their almond eyes, light skin, and lustrous hair; perhaps it was as little as five centuries ago. The legend is that, because of their late arrival, they found no free land along the coast; thus they were forced to make their way up into the almost empty highlands where the soil is thin and the living is not easy. Hard work turned the Merina into thoughtful people, who planned their way of life according to the seasons of rice culture in a cool climate.

Now almost treeless, once, perhaps, the highlands were forested; a few mossy stands of primeval trees still grow—severely protected by the French Forests and Waterways—in the folds and dells of the highest mountain slopes, put aside as national parks. Either the lightning of thunderstorms or the early hand of man set fire to these forests long ago, if, indeed, they grew. Today fifteen hundred kinds of tree grow on the island, covering but 10 per cent of the enormous surfaces. The denuded land is classed as *savoka* ("sha-vook"), which names a sort of brush-grown steppe—invaded by bamboo and various others of the grass family, tough pasturage seasonally fired to make way for new and tender shoots for the herds to graze upon. Thus the nomadic herdsmen destroy seedlings and saplings, and burn the organic topsoil. Experts—foreigners—in the field of conservation say that to control erosion and to restore the Malagasy land in such climates and conditions, at least 30 per cent of the surface must be given over to stands of trees and forests. Madagascar lies 12° below the Equator; the Tropic of Capricorn crosses the south.

And yet only 3 per cent of the island is cultivated; thus 87 per cent varies from burnt pasture, to steppe, to wasteland, to desert, and to bare rock. Four million of the Malagasy grow the crops and herd cattle along ancestral lines; and in their cult of ancestor worship, these inadequate and even destructive ways are fixed almost untouchably in the grip of divine approval. There is almost no topsoil left except in valleys along the eastern escarpment. To hold what remains of the highland loam, the French passed severe laws against fire; and they introduced the thick-barked eucalyptus and the tenacious wattles from Australia. But they were weed trees, and although they survive, the desert spreads.

Another spreading desert long ago sent the Polynesians, Melanesians, and Malayans from their other islands across the Indian Ocean onto the Malagasy shores, and up into the highlands. As the Gobi formed and spread to dry up the grazing lands of what is now Mongolia, the desert sent out wave after wave of mass migrations, moving west, south and east. One such wave piled up at the base of the Himalayas, new mountains—formed, it may be, when Gondwana broke up and the ocean troughs sank to corresponding depths. This Mongol people found a pass and poured through the mountain barrier down into what is now India and Burma.

Running ahead of them—for the invaders were, to be sure, enemies, unknown—the earlier inhabitants fled south through Malaya into Insulasia. There on the islands a growing demographic pressure turned "Those of the Many Islands" and "Those of the Black Islands" into seafaring people. So Polynesians and Melanesians crossed the South Pacific to the Hawaiian Islands, to Easter Island, and indeed to Mexico and down to Chile and Peru; and others crossed to Madagascar and the shores of Africa. The ocean currents and the prevailing winds carried them along.

Proof of these pelagic migrations lies in the language and in certain identifiable artifacts—for example, the two valved bellows used in forging iron that is known to be an invention of the Malayan Peninsula, and which turns up in these islands, and in East Africa. The other major proof lies in the basket- and mat-weaving culture of the islands, and in the fact that the Malagasy dressed themselves in tapa and in cloth woven of vegetable fibers or raffia or fine split reeds, but not in the skins of animals or wool, as in Africa and Europe.

Proof of the possibility of such a voyage—how long did it take? what did the people eat? how did they carry or collect fresh water?—came in 1883; when Krakatoa, a small volcanic island between Java and Sumatra, blew up, after "several months" some of its pumice stone floated onto the shores of Madagascar. A century earlier, when Captain James Cook encountered the Polynesians, they came to get him in war canoes holding two hundred men. Even though they were in the decadence of their achievement, they were still powerful enough, in the Sandwich Islands, to take him and ritually to ingest him, thus to absorb his magical and powerful white flesh.

In Madagascar at about the same time, an adventurous European named Nicolas Mayeur climbed the forests of the eastern escarpment to discover Tananarive. There he was the first white foreigner to be presented at the court of the Blue Forest—on 15 September 1777—to Andrianamboatsimarofy, the predecessor of King Andrianampoini-merina, the Conqueror. And that can serve as the date when history came into Madagascar; Mayeur found "in the center of the island, thirty leagues from the sea . . . a country, until then unknown, surrounded as it was by wild and savage tribes . . . with . . . lights . . . commerce, and an . . . active political organization and administration. . . ."

The enlightened line of highland kings began with Andrianjaka in 1610. He was followed in 1630 or so by his son, Andriantsitakatrandriana, who was followed in 1650 by his son Andriantsimitoviaminandriandehibe, et cetera, father to son, for six more enormous names, down to Nicolas Mayeur's host, who ruled from 1774 to 1794. He of Analamanga, "the Blue Forest," then was conquered by his distant cousin from nearby Ambohimanga, "the Blue Hill," a mystic town, the source of the Merina strength. So Andrianampoinimerina ("Ahn-dreen-nam-pou-ee-nee-mairn"), described as "a savage of genius," took over and united the Merina highland tribe, and began the conquest of the whole island.

His name means something like "the Lord in the Heart of the Highlands," or "the Prince Worthy of His People and His Country," and it is his official title for life after death. He chose it himself. At birth he was not given a name, but instead was called something or other— perhaps Filth, perhaps No-account—to cheat the evil spirits of the surrounding air. Later, having survived, in childhood he may have been called by a descriptive name. I knew a small boy called Difficult —and so he was. Still later, after adolescence, he chose a name for himself; I do not know what it was, but it probably was just a man's name like Alexander (which means "Defender of Men") or Arthur ("Admirable, Marvelous").

The French called him Nampouine; and he was forty-nine when his victorious army defeated an enemy of 20,000 men, to unify the Merina tribe. From all accounts, he was a capable leader. He disciplined his men; he gave them confidence in themselves—and in him. He held the tribe's attention. He seems to have been an imaginative, unhampered man, able to make use of the habits and the customs of the Merina in order to bring them along behind him in his expansion of the tribal structure to take in all of the enormous island. At least once, perhaps because, as with all born leaders, he knew he had the Lord on his side, he took great liberties with what sociologists call the ethos of this tribe in order to put new heart into his highlanders.

The conqueror had decided to invade Majunga, there on the battlefield to challenge the supremacy of the Sakalava. It is true that the big black warriors of the then dominant tribe were in their decline; nevertheless, they were still formidably armed with Arab muskets from the slave trade. And although their aim may have been inaccurate, their black gunpowder flashed and banged, and their lead bullets killed an enemy far beyond the reach of spears.

Perhaps the Lord in the Heart of the Highlands smiled as he worked out his plan to put an armor on his men against a panic fear. To do so, he made use of his royal ancestors and his inherited divinity as well as his divine right, and he got away with it. The king made himself demonstrably immune to death by musket ball.

First he called his royal sorcerers together and gave them his instructions. Next he selected a straight-shooting—and straight-faced —Merina rifleman, and told the crack shot what to do. Then King Andrianampoinimerina assembled his army on the parade ground and told the men that with the help of the Fragrant Lord and the divine ancestors, the sorcerers were going to make him and all the other soldiers of the tribe invulnerable to Sakalava bullets, and thus invincible in battle. He then distributed prepared amulets—hollowed-out crocodile teeth filled with nameless substances ground to a paste.

While the royal sorcerers cast their spells of strong magic before the soldiers' eyes, the king turned his back and popped a bullet in his mouth. He then turned to stand in all his majesty as a test for the potent magic and a target for the sharpshooter. The astonished army in terrible silence heard the musket shot ring out, and saw their king spit from his smiling mouth the bullet into his cupped hand. He held the bullet for all the men to see; they saw that it had not harmed their leader and their king. The army began to cheer in bursts of shouting laughter. The Sakalava lost the battle; it is not recorded what the divine ancestors said of this legerdemain to their impious but victorious son and heir.

Fighting then in Madagascar was not regimented warfare. Two howling, shouting hordes of naked enemies mixed together and killed one another with spears or any other weapon they could use; but they had to be worked up in a battle frenzy. Mayeur describes one of Nampouine's failures before Tananarive; the assault was disrupted by a plague of locusts—a greater enemy than either of the opponents. Thick enough to cloud the sky and hide the sun, the airborne army came in for a landing.

A human armistice was at once declared. Each man and all the officers threw down their arms; all the women of the towns and farms ran out to join them. They beat their drums, they beat on pots and pans, they waved their shields and *lambas,* they lighted fires of damp brush, and they shouted to keep the swarming grasshoppers from lighting on the tender blades of rice growing in the irrigated fields and terraces and from laying waste the crops. The Malagasy have never been single-minded, bellicose warriors. Like other mild and gentle people, they can go berserk, as they did in the Rebellion of 1947. But rarely can they sustain a cold-blooded, disciplined attack in the art and the science of war.

In the palace museum in Tananarive, there hangs a damaged life-size, full-length portrait in oils, said to be a likeness of the Conqueror, but if so it was painted from memory after he died. It shows a slight figure of a primitive man, pale-skinned and lightly muscled, wearing a *salaka*—loin-cloth—and a red-bordered, white *lamba.* He stands against the sky in what the painter took to be a properly warlike attitude. The hand of his bare throwing arm holds a *sagai*—spear—in hurling position, the other arm outstretched in balance. There is no enemy to be seen, but, brows knit, the king looks steadfastly off on a tangent to the left, beyond the frame. He has just come from the hands of his hairdresser, who, having greased his dark hair with zebu suet, has arranged a fringe on his forehead of ten or so flat, spiral curls; two or three corkscrew ringlets hang free in back of his head. He wears a close-clipped, Hollywood star's moustache and a tuft of beard on his lower lip. A disc of mother-of-pearl on his brow shows that he is a warrior. But clearly the stand-in model had got tired of the pose.

However, Andrianampoinimerina was a mighty man; he had an end in view, which was to push the frontiers of his united kingdom down to the island shores. "The sea must be the limit of my domain," he said. So, once more he tried to take Tananarive; again he failed. After the shouting and the howling had died down, Mayeur saw the families of the defeated dead men come out onto the field of battle to bargain with the victors for the bodies of their fallen fathers, husbands, and sons, so to give them proper burial in the family tombs, the "cold houses" usually strongly built of stone, well roofed over. The houses of the living were much flimsier—even the palace of the king in the painting was built of wood and thatch. One stays in one's tomb longer than one lives in one's house; and the living must ensure the repose of the ancestral souls.

Mayeur reported that the widows and fathers paid as much as 20 *piastres* (or silver dollars) for the most distinguished of the fallen warriors. But because the Merina have always had a sound business sense, the victors often dismembered the bodies of the men they killed to offer them piecemeal to the survivors. It was a seller's market.

Yet Nampouine was not a monster. He triumphed over his cousin-chieftains only to bring order to the island. Once victorious, he set out to establish peace and prosperity. He encouraged the intensive cultivation of the newly conquered territories. Once he said, "We are identical, Rice and I. I tell you that Rice is the ally in whom I trust, because, if I have formed and organized you Merina as befits a great people, it is he, Rice, who feeds you, and, consequently, who gives you life." He was addressing a *fokon'olona*—a sort of tribal or town meeting called to discuss current events and to decide the issues; or perhaps he was haranguing a *kabary*—an extraordinary rally called for a special purpose. At another such occasion, the king said, "I have made Rice my best friend, because it is on him that I count to make you people live. You are my kingdom." Then he made his remark about the sea being the only natural borders of his rice fields—which was his term for his island kingdom. The king literally owned all the land, the rice fields, the pastures, the woodlands, which he gave in trust to his subjects to work for their lifetime, but not to own or to inherit. Rice is the word for food in the Malagasy language; and rice field was the term of motherland or fatherland. There was then no concept of a nation or a country, one among many. Madagascar was to the Malagasy the whole world, and their universe—until the foreigners began to trickle in.

Andrianampoinimerina was a wise man of his time and place. To work his increased rice fields, he took up the concept of forced labor, and used the system of the *corvée* in lieu of taxes; it was a kind of feudal obligation in which each male citizen had to donate a month or more of work each year to plant, cultivate, and harvest the rice fields that belonged to the state—that is to say, to the king. He even set up a kind of competition in which he set one community against another to see which of their various incorporated sub-tribes could produce the best quality and highest quantity of rice; the winner was rewarded with appropriate honors and privileges. In return, he organized and guaranteed a steady supply of water in an improved system of irrigation. He himself worked with the engineers to build dikes, levees, canals, dams, drainage ditches, and reservoirs. He established a special corps of guardsmen to patrol the water works. Four hundred men each year were excused from military service to maintain and police the irrigation system in the rice fields surrounding the capital. In 1810, the city had a population of about 15,000.

These guardians of the rice fields had the right to call up the farmers to make emergency repairs in time of storm or other disaster. They had to contend with the rats and the fresh-water crabs and shellfish that undermined the embankments. If one of the Four Hundred failed in his duty, and was found guilty, he had his skull split open. The king even regulated the methods of growing rice. In those days, the Malagasy had not invented the plough. Instead, to turn the earth, they herded cattle into the flooded rice field, and drove them round and round. The king forbade this practice; I do not know why. He distributed a narrow-bladed iron spade, more like a spear than a shovel or a fork, and recommended that his subjects wear out the new iron *angadi* in short order.

All that has survived about him reveals him as a good king, not a revolutionary but an organizer, a conservative man, able to develop the old, traditional ideas, and to extend the existing tribal institutions and practices to accommodate change. He codified the laws—which still serve the Malagasy Republic (enlarged and modified by the Code Napoléon). He was enlightened, but he was wise enough not to force his people beyond their abilities to absorb new ways. So he made his people happy and yet brought his country to the new frontier of modern times.

He was the image of a highland king. Therefore, the Merina had faith in him. They followed him. His innovations worked out well. This Malagasy conqueror, a contemporary of the great Napoleon, was born at the right time in the right place. An administrator and an executive, he stretched the tribal patterns, but he was careful not to break their barriers. Thus, as a leader, he conducted the energies that had built up among the prolific highlanders, whose minds had begun to work, out of the past and into the future. He captured the popular imagination, he fired his subjects, he motivated them, he gave them work to do; he gave them direction and he released their powers. The Prince Worthy of the Highlands satisfied the Merina. It is understandable that he came to think of himself as infallible and omniscient.

He gave the people what they wanted in a king—he had the essential quality: he was *masiaka*. This Malagasy regal epithet translates as hard, stern, ill-natured, threatening, absolute—but just, and right.

The Merina people in their tribal society knew at all times exactly what was expected of them; thus they felt at ease and (to use that damned word) secure. When times began to change around them, they were lucky in the man they found to lead them. They thrust power and glory upon him; he shouldered the load. It is, then, understandable that he began to believe himself to be incapable of fault—he *knew* what was best for his people, and for their next leader and king, his son and heir. As a father, he was terrible and mighty; thus he proved himself to be a human being—he destroyed his son.

The future King Radama I was the child of his father's prime, of his greatest and most energetic years. Andrianampoinimerina was forty-seven when his heir was born in 1792, two years before the successful taking of Tananarive. Thus the boy grew up at the time when the king could do no wrong, in the crescent period of his father's hardening self-confidence. He saw that the boy was handsome, physically fit, intelligent, and able—already, at fifteen, a gifted general on the field of battle. In all ways he was a fitting prince, save in the essential: Radama lacked the *masiaka* quality.

He was reasonable, he was thoughtful, he was sensitive, he was gentle, he was considerate, he was good. So the father set out to savage this overcivilized boy, who had to be made *masiaka* for the good of his country, and his people. The fatal lag between the private thought and the public act had to be knocked out of him; it was tragic flaw. The father set about remaking the son in his own image.

Radama I came to the throne in 1810 when he was eighteen; he ruled for eighteen more years, half his lifetime; he died when he was thirty-six—killed by his father's dead hand. When Radama I ascended, he had to contend with more than the rice fields of Madagascar; he had to work with history, then firmly in the grip of the British. Napoléon had won his battles, and had lost his empire. He left France confined within reduced borders. The British, that Nation of Shopkeepers, backed by the victorious fleet, then began to develop the industrial revolution, the Middle Classes, social reforms, the parliamentary system of self-government, and European capitalism—and to spread them throughout the world of Pax Britannica. The British Navy had taken the Mascarenes from the French in 1810; and although, in 1815, they returned the island of Réunion, they kept Mauritius, and made of it a base for the expanding British Empire.

Robert Townsend Farquhar, a canny Scot (later to be knighted), was appointed to govern the new crown colony in 1810; he regarded the French as his opponents, if not his enemies and his rivals, in those waters. As an active British Empire builder, he set out at once to win over Radama, whom he addressed as the king of Madagascar; thus the British recognized the Merina monarchy. Sir Robert did so not because he believed that Radama was indeed the king of the entire island with all the tribes, but to establish the fact that Madagascar did *not* belong to France, as the French claimed. For if Madagascar was established as an independent native realm, it became at once a fair prize for any European Colonial power able to take it and to hold it. After the Congress of Vienna, the French had brushed off their very dusty, half-forgotten claim to the Great Island—"Oriental France"—so named by Louis XIV and Colbert when they called it the brightest jewel in the Sun King's crown, and abandoned it, in 1686.

In August, 1816, Sir Robert sent his first official mission to Tananarive—which city the British still persist in calling Antananarivo—to sign a commercial treaty with Radama. All went well. In December, "Sir Farquhar," as the French persist in miscalling the British knight, sent a mission of thirty soldiers commanded by a Captain Lesage, with whom Radama went through the most sacred Malagasy ritual of *fatidra*, or blood brotherhood. The rite of "the Bleeding Incision" ties two men together in bonds stronger than the family ties of birth.

Fatidra requires seven symbolic ingredients, appropriate actions, and the services of a sorcerer. The two men, blood-brothers-to-be, gripped the handle of a *sagai* spear and held it over a rice basket containing seven dry grass plants, roots and blades, to represent the seven deaths to visit the man who betrays his blood brother; a grasshopper with its head wrung over its back to show that the faithless one would never more be able to see ahead of him; a dry cow flop from a mother-

156

less calf to show that the perjurer would be reduced to ordure; some water from a failing spring to indicate that the oath-breaker's life and wealth would dry up; a rifle ball to kill the violator; an old bone to show that such a man could never expect proper burial in his family tomb; four pinches of earth taken from the cardinal points to show that the mother of us all would refuse her products to the betrayer, and that wherever he turned he would find damnation. The spear they jointly held made clear that their brotherhood was a matter of life and death. Having sworn to maintain good faith, the two men drank the mingled drops of their blood that fell into a porcelain bowl from the incisions made in their epiglottises; after which they feasted, and presumably went their way linked together more or less like Tom Sawyer and Huckleberry Finn along the banks of the Mississippi.

However, it was Sir Robert's third envoy who came to share the life of the king as his constant military adviser. Sergeant James Hastie, an Irishman of the garrison of Mauritius, arrived in Tananarive on 16 August 1817. It was a stroke of genius on the part of Sir Robert to name Hastie as his political agent—today he would be called an ambassador—to Radama's court, the Rova of Tananarive. The Irish sergeant proved to have real ability as well as a talent for friendship; he comes off the printed page of history as an attractive man of good will. He drilled the Merina soldiers and accompanied the king on the expedition of 1819 against the western Sakalava clans, and in 1820 he led a disciplined army of 14,000 troops once again against the Sakalava. In 1824, he went with Radama to take Majunga in a successful action to break the losing tribe's resistance.

When Hastie first arrived, in 1817, he brought along a number of gifts fit for a Merina tribal king—some blooded English horses, perhaps the first to be introduced to Madagascar; a compass; a handsome chiming clock; a splendid dress uniform of soft green leather boots, tight blue trousers, a frogged red jacket, and a black cocked hat with a great white plume, along with all the gilt trappings, in which the king stood for his life-sized portrait.

But these were toys; Radama outgrew them. As a ruler, he continued his father's work of conquest; but he soon learned that, once he had brought all the island's tribes together, he would have to find a suitable government and administration for his new land.

If his father, the conqueror, was a "savage of genius," his son,

157

Radama I, was the first modern man of Madagascar. The one knew what he was doing; the other knew what he had to do. The father unified the Merina tribe and pushed his rice fields to their natural boundaries—the seas surrounding his united island. In so doing, he brought the tribal system to its culmination; he stretched this small, familiar way of life to its own natural limits, which were also limitations. He then tried to fix his achievement for all future time. Radama, the son, saw that he had to introduce another and a foreign way of life —the modern times and techniques of Europe. To do so, he was compelled to destroy much of his father's ancestral structure in order to build a foundation for the new political order. As an enlightened ruler, he was forced to be revolutionary; as a leader of his tribe, he was called upon to fill the image of a classic *masiaka* king of the Merina. The effort killed him.

Even so, in the eighteen years of his reign, half his lifetime, the king introduced the outside world to Madagascar, and thus gave his island its then dangerous, but now forgotten, place on the map of the geopolitical world. He drew the attention of the European powers onto his kingdom, and thus entangled himself and his rice fields in the struggle between a France in containment and a Great Britain in dominance.

These famous treaties between Sir Robert Farquhar and King Radama I—between Great Britain and the Merina monarchy—that did away with the slave trade for a while, the first signed in 1817, the second ratified in 1820, had less to do with the rights of individual man and inherent human freedom than with London's plans to demonstrate to the world the British liberal humanitarianism behind its course of empire, and even more to do with Sir Robert's scheme to destroy the old-fashioned plantation economy of French Réunion that was based on a steady supply of slaves. Pax Britannica was then in its early days; the excuse to police the seas in order to stop the slave trade, and at times to interfere in the disorderly internal affairs of little nations lying along the route to India, served as a reason why Britannia had to rule the waves and, if need be, to keep the oceans' peace by force of naval might.

The French reacted to this encroachment on what they held to be their sphere of influence. In 1817, Sir Robert had sent Sergeant Hastie into Madagascar to take his place at the king's side; two years later, the French governor of Bourbon-Réunion sent in the French Sergeant Robin to be the king's private secretary. He seems to have been a good man too; the year of his arrival, he opened the first school in Tananarive and gave classes in reading, writing, and the French language. The Sergeant Robin brought off a real triumph; he taught Radama I, aged twenty-seven, how to read and write—and think—in French, and thus gained the first victory in that small cold war's battle for the king's mind.

Sergeant Hastie, the king's military adviser, recognized this coup brought off by his rival, and wrote off to Sir Robert on Mauritius, who in turn appealed for aid to the London Missionary Society—and got quick action. On 4 October 1820, King Radama gave audience to the Reverend Mr. David Jones, the first of the combined British political agents and men of God—the Protestant kind—to establish himself in Madagascar. A second young Welshman, the Reverend Mr. David Griffiths, followed Jones, and brought out both men's wives and growing families of small children; one of the wives and several of the infants died of "fevers" in the next few years. But the Welshmen indeed did good works.

The missionaries joined forces with Sergeant Robin, perhaps at the king's suggestion to settle a dispute, and altogether they adapted a Roman alphabet of twenty-one letters to the Merina dialect of the Polynesian language spoken by all the eighteen Malagasy tribes. Their language, by the way, despite its many words of Bantu or Arab derivation, and despite the many, strongly marked differences and usages among the tribes, is the single strongest proof that the Malagasy originally immigrated to Madagascar from Polynesia. The alphabet still serves; and it has established the Merina highland speech as the official spoken and written language, along with French, in the Malagasy Republic. French perforce is the language of international relations, commerce, and higher education.

The spelling is phonetic, but it takes getting used to, what with the mute terminal vowels and the swallowed syllables. It has been said that Radama, to settle one dispute between Welsh Jones and Griffiths on the one hand, and French Sergeant Robin on the other, allotted the consonants to the English language, and the vowels to French pronunciation: A B C D E F G (hard) H (mute but aspirated) I J K L M N O (*oo* or *ou*) P R S (both *s* and *sh*) T V Y (for the pleasure of the eye as a final letter, for it is pronounced *ee* as in I) and Z. The French pronunciation, to be sure, now dominates both consonants and vowels; but the Welshmen get the credit for the hard spade work. They devised a grammar, and compiled a Malagasy-English dictionary, and saw them through the printing presses. And the Franco-English, or Anglo-French, battle for the schooling of the young Malagasy ideas stepped up its pace. They taught by precept and example; and both French and British missionaries and political agents doubled in brass as reporters, botanists, explorers, architects, engineers, doctors, farmers, and representative European human beings.

But to the young king goes the credit for bringing literacy, education and the written words of history, along with all the benefits and drawbacks, to his people. Meantime, both Paris and London backed up their local representatives by sending a series of what seem to me to be extremely puzzling gifts to King Radama I. In 1820 came an oil portrait of King Louis XVIII, and a series of engravings of scenes from French military life. And from King George IV came a gold cup, two ceremonial gold lances, and a pair of duelling pistols. In 1821, fifty young Merina men were sent to learn navigation in the British warships of the Indian Ocean, although Madagascar never has had a fleet. Others went to London to learn how to play martial music.

The British seemed to have drawn ahead. In 1822, Radama sent off an ambassador to the Court of St. James's, and that same year proclaimed that henceforth there would be no more territorial concessions to any foreigner without the express authorization of himself, the king. In 1825, he decreed that both the British Navy and merchantmen could make use of the ports of Madagascar, and any British citizen who chose to do so might reside in the island. That same year, he set up a royal customs service; and perhaps to keep the British on their toes, Radama then named Robin, the seconded sergeant of the French Army, to be Grand Marshal of the Palace, as well as Commander in Chief of the East Coast.

Meantime, the Merina wars of conquest, in which the seconded sergeant of the British Army, James Hastie, served as military adviser to the king, were going very well. On 14 November 1824, Radama proclaimed, "Today, the whole island is mine! Madagascar has but one master." The facts were not quite so, for the southern peoples never were brought under effective Merina discipline—when attacked, they vanished into their thorny euphorbia forests and spiny opuntia cactus thickets. Yet Radama was in effect the king, and most certainly the all-powerful paramount chieftain of the eighteen Malagasy tribes. Therefore, the 14th of November, 1824, was a great day, a moment of triumph for Radama, an enlightened king, and for James Hastie, a brilliantly successful ambassador. Both men died soon after, in Tananarive; Hastie on 8 October, 1826, and Radama two years later, on Sunday, 27 July 1828, aged 36. He was the first of the Merina kings and queens to be buried in the new royal tombs inside the Rova of the Blue Forest, the hilltop of Tananarive.

All his wives were beautiful, or so James Hastie had said in praise of the man whom he liked and respected; and among the dozen wives there was a conquered Sakalava princess. But Radama had no sons or daughters to succeed him. Radama was a conqueror. He was a drunkard.

Andrianampoinimerina, the Prince Worthy of the Highland People Under the Sun, made his son into an alcoholic, and, in effect, cut the young man's throat. Cause and effect as the basis of reasoning have never fully been understood in Madagascar (and elsewhere) and are not yet part of Malagasy thought processes. The father had in mind only the son's good, which was the country's and the people's good, when he set out to alter and correct the boy's good nature. The old man wanted to toughen up the young one, to prepare him for his future, to provide him with a princely education, to fit him for his destiny as king, to carry on the good work of unifying Madagascar. He did his best to destroy the weaknesses he saw in the future ruler's character, to excise the reasonable and thoughtful nature, to erase the too sensitive imagination, and to instill the missing essential requisite. Radama I had to be made to carry on as a mighty king. The boy had to be made to measure up to his divine ancestors. The father tried to remake the son in his own image, to lick him into shape as a harsh, cold, stern, cruel, terrible and mighty man. For Radama lacked these indispensable royal qualities; Radama was not born *masiaka*.

Therefore, the father set out to inculcate the stern and terrible *masiaka* traits while the boy was still malleable in adolescence, and, when he was fifteen or sixteen, the king, then aged sixty-one or sixty-two, turned his heir over to a group of hard characters for schooling. They were young aristocrats and minor royalties—a hard lot of libertines, dissolute, tough and self-indulgent, with a taste for sexual violence; and they liked rum. They were privileged; the king protected them. Whatever this gang of young lords did, they did for the king's pleasure. The king gave them instructions to debauch the crown prince —for his own *masiaka* good. It says a great deal for Radama's innate good sense and strength of character that, although, it may be, he was made sterile, and turned away from his dozen wives, and certainly left with a craving for alcohol, he made an excellent king. He managed to survive the effects of his savage and *masiaka* father's tutoring to rule for the good of his country. And had he survived to live as long as his father had—another thirty years—he might have brought Madagascar through its transition out of the primitive Polynesian and Arab tribal pattern, to lead the Malagasy into a way of life of their own. Radama might have brought his rice fields into a modern political, social, and economic whole by combining the Asian, African, and European traditions, and allowing them to grow. But he died young; he did not have the chance.

The old, absolute, infallible Andrianampoinimerina put an end to that. He, the living ancestor, the *masiaka* king, tried to go on ruling, dried up and mummified, wrapped in his red silk *lambamena,* from inside his cold house tomb. On his death bed in April, 1810, just before he "turned his back" the conqueror called his successor, the eighteen-year-old Prince Radama, along with the boy's number-one wife, Ramavo, his cousin and his senior by two years—the future Queen Ranavalona I, the Terrible, a truly *masiaka* ruler—and the dying king gave his instructions that tied up the inheritance. He said of his niece, "If she is not greedy to eat the zebu hump, the kingdom will belong to her after you. These are my wishes. You will not forget them."

Before his time came to die, Radama I, the reigning king, tried wisely to go against his father's wishes; he named a well-trained young prince of the royal house as his successor. But his wife Ramavo had not forgotten; and although she proved indeed greedy to eat the zebu hump

—the choice meat of royal power—she feasted quietly and carefully. She ate in secret with a patient hunger; and to her meals she brought men whom she could trust, the reactionaries, the conservatives who did not like the foreigners whom Radama had brought in, and whose power grew as the king listened to their counsel. The future Queen Ranavalona I gathered together her own court of malcontents, and she waited for her time to come to strike.

She spent hours, days and nights, and long months alone in her cabin palace inside the Rova while her husband was off living the solider's life in his wars of conquest. She could neither read nor write, so she passed the time by thinking about things. She looked about her, and she began to talk; so she worked out her intrigues. She was getting on for forty, a dangerous age, it is said, in idle women. Ramavo was the king's cousin and wife, and next in line; and she was childless. By setting her aside, the king, her husband and her cousin, helped her on her old-fashioned way. He had named as his heir to the throne his nephew, the son of his oldest sister, a boy whom he had had educated in the English mission school, and who already showed signs of an open, able mind, thinking along the liberal and progressive lines in politics. His choice alarmed the devout old men, his dead father's companions in arms, who remembered the conqueror's doubts about his son, the thoughtful Radama. They joined the growing circle around the reactionary *masiaka* Ramavo, the replaced next in line. When her time came, she was ready.

In November, 1827, Radama I, at the head of his victorious troops, climbed the cliff to his highland capital from the port of Tamatave, where he had led an expeditionary force to put down a Betsimisaraka uprising. It was hot down there in late spring; the anopheles mosquitoes were thick in the rain forests. They bred in the still waters of the lagoons now being joined to make the inland waterway of the Pangalanes Canal. Perhaps the king brought back in his veins the protozoans of malignant malaria; or perhaps the disease in his blood turned into black water fever. Once inside the Rova of the Blue Forest, he threw off his gaudy uniform, and lay down on his bed. Throughout the summer, all through the fall, and into winter, he got worse. He could no longer stand up on his feet to preside at court, he could not sit erect on the throne to conduct the affairs of state. His hands shook.

On 27 July 1828, a Sunday, in his bedroom, well supplied with rum, clouded by the black depression brought on by his disease, and cast down by his success as a ruler, tired of the demands of his own intolerable enlightenment—in his lucid moments, he must have heard through the blood beating in his ears the slanders spreading from his neglected, scheming cousin-wife—he reached out of bed, perhaps to grasp the rum bottle; but in his fit of *delirium tremens,* he touched instead a handy knife. His fingers closed around the smooth haft. Perhaps its old familiar balance felt good and comfortable to him. He took it up and cut his throat. He died almost at once.

As queen, Ranavalona I, the widow Ramavo sat down hard on the throne. Six days later, while her dead husband's body lay drying out in state, she put to death his closest relatives—his designated heir, his other nephews, his half-brothers, his cousins, and even his mother, the queen mother, the widow of Andrianampoinimerina. Her name was Rambolamasoandro; the others were called Rakotobe, Ratefy, Ratefinanahary, Ratafika, Ramananolona, and Rafaralahy. "Ra" is an honorific prefix meaning "sir" or "lady"—monsieur, madame, or mademoiselle. They were all strangled with silken cords, or shut up in prison and left to starve, for royal blood must not be shed.

Ramavo means "Miss Yellow." Perhaps she was fair in coloring. Ranavalona ("Rah-nah-vah-loon") means "the Lady Who Has Been Folded"—like a precious silken *lamba,* put away in a safe place to be brought out and worn only on great occasions. The queen chose as her name for eternity Rabodonandrianampoinimerina, but she is known to history as Ranavalona the Cruel. I do not know exactly what the ceremonial title means, something like "the Lady Queen Worthy of the Highlands." Clearly, her intention in selecting it was to hark back to the good old days of her father-in-law, whose great name she incorporated in her own. Thus she at once declared her policy of state, and reinforced her legitimate right to the throne she had preëmpted.

On August 13, eighteen days after Radama had cut his own throat, in great ceremony, Queen Ranavalona I had her husband's corpse put in the royal tomb at nightfall. She buried him in a coin silver coffin, made by melting down Spanish *piastres,* French five franc pieces, and Mexican dollars. In his tomb—built by a Frenchman, Louis Gros, and

164

made of dressed stone—the widow-queen surrounded him with all his worldly possessions—one hundred and fifty-five uniforms, all their ceremonial swords and regalia, the pistols, the muskets, the bandoliers, the powder horns, the gorgets; and on the walls she hung a portrait gallery of his peers; Frederick the Great, of Prussia; Napoléon the Great, of France; and George IV, of the United Kingdom.

Having satisfied the traditions and conventions, Ranavalona I set to work. It became evident at once that she had already made up her mind on several policies of state. Before the funeral, she published a code of forty-eight laws based upon the ancient and conservative Merina customs. She then set out to prove that she was *masiaka*.

On November 28, 1828, she refused to recognize or even to receive the new British political agent-ambassador, Mr. Robert Lyall; and she declared that she was in no way called upon to uphold the terms of any of the Anglo-Malagasy treaties signed by Radama I. In August, 1829, having got word that the French were sending from Réunion a military expedition to insist upon their "rights" to representation in Tananarive, the queen raised an army of 14,000 conscripts and sent them off pell-mell down the escarpment, to stop the invasion at Tamatave. The expedition failed; the French succeeded in their Show of Force, and thus they taught the new queen that she had to put up with foreign powers. . . . She learned that she could not yet turn off the outside world. She found that she had a great deal to do before she could reign, rule, command, and be obeyed as she intended.

The fact that she was a woman, and thus a queen, ruling over men presented no great problem. The ancient Polynesian tribal system was matriarchal—women in the South Sea Islands have always been free and equal to any man. However, since the Arabs from the seventh to the fifteenth centuries had introduced their concept of male dominance as tribal chieftains to the coastal peoples, Ranavalona had to make sure of the legitimacy of her position. Thus she had herself declared to be a member of the male sex, and a king. She had herself crowned Ranavalona *Manjaka* (the word means king *or* queen), by the Grace of the Fragrant Lord, Ruler of Madagascar, and Defender of the Customs of Her Ancestors.

To such a new state there were drawbacks. For instance, it became unthinkable that she should remarry. However, it was decided that she might take whatever lovers she saw fit; and any child she might in consequence bear would be declared the son or the daughter of Radama I, in his tomb, it to be announced to the island people that the living spirit of the dead king, still intent in watching over the welfare of his rice fields, had left his cold house to return by night to the queen's palace chamber, there to beget his heir. Such things were thought perfectly possible in the fetish and ancestor worship then in its elaborated and sophisticated decline. Neither Andrianampoinimerina nor Radama had let religion get in their way, although both made use of sorcery, witchcraft, and the public credence to influence their soldiers and subjects, and so to rule effectively. Ranavalona, who announced firmly for the religion of her ancestors, seems to have been able to manipulate her devotions according to the way her faith furthered or obstructed the ends she had in view—her royal pleasure.

She was pleased to be a king in abstract and concrete authority to rule; she was pleased to be a queen in the flesh. On Wednesday, an auspicious day, 23 September 1829, she bore her dead husband a son and heir—her only child, born to her late in life, nearly fifteen months posthumously. She called the child Rakoto, "Sir Boy." And everyone agreed that it was good and natural. In those days in Madagascar, very little was known for sure about the unobserved internal anatomical details of procreation; the Malagasy have a flexible sense of time, and they accept magic and the supernatural. They are said to recognize and to respond to an imperious sexual need; and they like children— both as children and as the future caretakers of the ancestral remains. In any case, who was there to ask leading questions of the queen?

In fact, the boy's father was one of the lady's lesser lovers, a general named Andemiatza, who was assassinated by his successor in the first year of his royal son's life. The expediter was another military man, General Rainiharo, of the powerful Andafy-Avaratra family, freemen, not nobles, who ruled Madagascar through, by means of, and in the names of the queens whom they selected, elevated, lovered, or married morganatically for the next sixty-six years.

When the Queen Ranavalona I promoted Rainiharo, it may well have been that she exercised a personal choice; but this action of her private life had public consequences. Rainiharo belonged to the middle class of the Merina tribe, to the majority—he was an Hova, and not an Andriana, and he was a reactionary. So long as he held the power, he resisted change, tried to block social evolution, and did his best to maintain the static tribal system. In the highest peaks of the highland in the coldest nights of August in midwinter, a skin of ice forms, once every few years, on the surface of the still and quiet pools. So the queen and Rainiharo tried to freeze themselves in place on top. In the fixed order of the caste system, he never could become king; he dared not break through the rigid and stratified order. He was a commoner. Yet when he ascended to take the real power of the monarchy, he brought it down out of the hands of the Andriana; and thus the caste of royalties and nobles began to wither; the force went out of them and they were left with the empty privilege of their high birth. They became ceremonial figures. However, Queen Ranavalona I, who ruled for thirty-three years, was a powerful and *masiaka* woman, able to keep her men and ministers in their subordinate positions, and to do as she pleased.

Or almost as she pleased; for chance played its part in the destiny of the queen, and in the history of her island, as chance does. The single most important event of her reign was an act of God, or of circumstances; or at any rate, of the weather. She had no hand in bringing it about.

One stormy late spring day in November, 1831, a shipwrecked Frenchman, aged twenty-five, was cast up naked on her coasts. When he got to his feet, he stood up, a staunch and life-sized *mésure de l'homme*—in the true proportions of French civilization. He served throughout his life as the standard and the criterion of nineteenth-century French culture in Madagascar. He lived thenceforth until he died in, on, and for the island; and he died rich, aged seventy-six. From the day of his arrival until seven years after his burial, in December, 1878, the history of Madagascar and his own personal, private, and public history were inextricably entangled. And as such things go down there, from 12° south of the Equator on beyond Capricorn, he got to Madagascar by mistake. His name was Jean Laborde.

Not a freak, not a reformer, not a compulsive, not an explorer, not a land-grabber, he was a most attractive sort of universal man of his moment. He was a Gascon, like La Bigorne, and like him a resilient man, venturesome. Born in Auch, down near the Pyrenees, the county seat of the department of Gers, he has had a street named after him, the rue Jean-Laborde. It is not an important thoroughfare; it is not an important town despite the fine cathedral with carved Gothic wooden stalls. His father was a cartwright and a wheelwright. The son learned the family trade and taught himself how to manage tools, to deal with iron and wood, and to do the precision work of an artisan and craftsman. He made wagons, carts, coaches, carriages, and the rest of the wheeled vehicles of his day. He learned to put his hand to making almost anything, and to see the work through from beginning to end.

But life did not seem large enough for him in Auch—the conservative, iron-bound, solid-oak closed circle of the life of a good provincial citizen in a reputable craft and trade. That part of Gascony is not a rich country; it is only now being brought into good production by the large-scale modern methods of agriculture introduced by the French farmers who have returned from Morocco and Tunisia. They buy up the fragmented fields and cut down the hedgerows, and find fertilizers and crops to suit the chemistry of the soil and the climate.

So in 1827, when he was twenty-two years old, Jean Laborde left home; he went to India where France still retained a half-dozen trading posts left over from Colbert's commercial empire, the factories and enclaves of Surat, Mahé, Karikal, Pondichery, Yanaon, and Chandernagar on the Arabian Sea, the Coromandel coast, and the Bay of Bengal. In three years, Jean Laborde made enough money to buy and outfit a ship, and to set out on a hunt for the treasure of a sunken vessel lying on a reef in the treacherous Mozambique Channel where it had foundered on the way home from India to France with a load of gold, diamonds from Golconda, emeralds from Jaipur, sapphires from Kashmir and Ceylon, rubies from Burma, and Oriental pearls, jades, and porcelains from China and Japan. But it had run into a storm, holed its hull on a coral reef, and gone down in the shallow water of a lagoon. So far as it is known, neither Jean Laborde nor anybody else has found the treasure; but who knows?

Laborde's ship, in which he had invested all his earnings and savings, likewise ran into heavy weather in those uncharted southern waters—that Jean Parmentier, another French sailor, in 1529 called *"la Mer Sans Raison,"* "the Unreasonable Sea," "the Senseless Sea," of inexplicable, unthinkable winds and currents. Laborde and his crew had to run for shelter off the southeast coast of Madagascar, where they met a cyclone, and were wrecked north of Fort Dauphin—the site of the disastrous first attempt of the French to colonize the great island in 1643. The east coast is a notoriously inhospitable shore; the escarpment plunges abruptly into the Indian Ocean depths where the great sharks swim. I do not know who else made it, but Jean Laborde reached the narrow beach alive, and was promptly taken captive by the dark-skinned, wild, and naked Antanosy tribesmen. But he was not killed; the Antanosy acknowledged the Merina rule.

By Ranavalona's royal decree, all shipwrecked castaways of whatever provenance automatically became royal slaves as soon as they touched dry land, and they belonged to the monarch; Laborde entered Madagascar as the queen's personal and private property. The purpose of this law was to discourage further European exploration of the coastal waters, and to prevent any sort of unauthorized landings, forced or voluntary. The effect was to save the lives of the unlucky mariners; it was to the best interest of the Malagasy tribesmen to take good care of the queen's property, and to speed him on his way to Tananarive. Anyhow, Jean Laborde, a young man, a Gascon, and an adventurer, was bound to swim through those dangerous waters and to land on his feet. Somehow, he found his way north along the east coast to the Frenchman Napoléon de Lastelle's plantation and sugar cane fields, south of Tamatave.

When Jean Laborde got to Napoléon de Lastelle's plantation, the rum distiller first obtained the freedom of her white slave from the queen, and then he sent the young man up to Tananarive, where Ranavalona I received him at court, and where he made history. Late in November, 1831, on the recommendation of de Lastelle, and in the presence of the great dignitaries of the kingdom, Jean Laborde signed a contract with the government to manufacture rifles and cannon for the Malagasy Army. To do so, Laborde had to start from the ground, from the subsoil, and build up; he had to get the ores, build a blast furnace, collect the fuel (he used charcoal), design the molds, and so on. He set to work. Thus, on de Lastelle's rum distilleries and on Laborde's iron foundry and guns was the industrial revolution brought into Madagascar; those were the instruments of change. From that moment on, until she banished Laborde and all the foreigners from the kingdom twenty-six years later, the queen showed a strong preference for the Gascon's company. Soon the English and the Welsh of the London Missionary became jealous of his influence over the queen.

And to be sure, the legend is, and the French story goes, that he became her lover. What were they like then, this young but experienced and knowledgeable Frenchman, this artisan and adventurer, this good man of his epoch who came to be known in Madagascar as *"le grand français?"* And the illiterate *masiaka* queen? I have seen no portrait of him in his youth. There is a photograph of him in his old age, from which a bronze bust has been made to serve as his official memorial. It is set up on a marble base in the small hillside park, named for him, in front of his former town house in Tananarive's high town below the queen's palace and the Rova. All three—monument, park, and house—are modest in their ways. The square is now dominated by a huge contemporary school building in the fenestrated slab style, the Lycée Gallieni, where all students of all nations and races who fulfill the stiff requirements are admitted for French instruction, as in France. A plaster copy of the bust stands on a pedestal in the hallway of the Institut de Réchèrche Scientifique, a building in the botanical garden by the Tananarive zoo.

In his old age Jean Laborde was photographed wearing the elaborate, tight, stiffly gold embroidered French diplomat's dress uniform, for he had been named Consul de France in Madagascar in April, 1862, under the Second Empire. The Third Republic treated him shabbily, retiring and replacing him without warning on 7 November 1877, one year and fifty days before he died of dysentery and a disease of the bladder; and then, once dead and buried, using his last will and testament as a cause to wage the first Franco-Hova War of 1885. The stiff photograph and the three-dimensional portrait bust show a bemedaled and bestarred, round-headed man, snub-nosed and stocky, once muscular, but a far from heroic French figure of a man. He wore an "imperial" moustache and goatee, grey and white; he had got very thin on top. He seems never to have been a handsome man. Nothing about the photograph or the bronze suggests a dashing, light-hearted, brilliant hero, a great lover with an organizing mind. On this small evidence, it is hard to imagine Jean Laborde as a romantic figure.

But perhaps when he was young he was a *beau garçon,* having that quality of smiling energy, of self-confident vitality—that compact, concentrated, and spring-like force of personality that makes a man attractive and, it may be, brings luck his way. He was full of life, tough as leather, durable, and flexible. And to be sure, when he was twenty-six, he lacked the accumulations and the accretions, the scars of failure that slow a man down. The photograph is an official portrait, anyhow. Young, he had gusto, totality, and endless enterprise, and that quality now specified as libido. He liked to live; his energies flowed out of him. He was *débrouillard,* but steadfast. Jean Laborde was a good man. He had a happy influence over the young prince, the queen's multiple-fathered son, who called him his spiritual father. Laborde stood up as a sponsor for the boy at the ceremonial circumcision in the winter of 1835. This solemn male rite, probably an adaption of the Islamic religious practice, takes place among the Merina in the cold season (to help the wound to heal) when the boy is from six months to a year old. In other tribes, there is a mass ceremony once every seven years.

The queen was in her forty-third year in 1831, overflowing with the energies that come to a woman of her age; and she had had to be careful when her neglectful husband was alive.

Whatever it was that went on between them, Laborde and the queen established an enduring relationship. The effect of their personal polarity cannot be called either good or evil; it was, it now is, historical. French influence predominated; the British lost ground.

They lost out not because none of the men, being missionaries, good fathers and husbands, and early Victorian puritans, saw fit to make a burnt offering of his body upon the altar of his country and his God, but because the London Missionary Society was giving hope and direction, education and Christian salvation, to the Andevo serfs and slaves, and to the most thoughtful of the free men and women of the Hova caste. The British missionaries were informing and illuminating the ignorant Malagasy mind and soul. The queen was shrewd, although illiterate. She saw that these foreigners were educating her people—teaching them to read, to write, and what was worse, to think, and to protest.

Then in the seventh year of her reign, in the summer of 1834–35, Ranavalona, aged forty-nine, was stricken with a frightening illness. She thought that she might die. Her first action, when she felt well enough to leave her sickbed, was to go in solemn homage to thank the presiding and protecting geniuses of the Merina royal family, the twelve fetishes, or *sampy*, for her recovery. Ranavalona was devout as neither of the kings had been. Radama I, who tolerated all forms of religious belief, and had introduced Christianity along with education to the island, was a skeptic. He had neglected the family idols; he paid little attention to the witch-doctors and the sorcerers, or, apparently, to the missionaries' God. He had broken with the ancestors in order to open up a future for his people, and to introduce progress—or, at any rate, history—to Madagascar.

His widow tried to put a stop to all that he had begun. As she grew older, she increased in fervor; she worshiped her own divine ancestors. She had no need to think about her faith, nor to examine the nature of her nebulous, Sweet-Smelling Lord, Andriamanitra, nor that of Zanahary, "the Creator." Ranavalona was content to leave the unknown. She followed her emotions, and she believed that she was wise. Therefore, in her climacteric, she went to enlist the help of the twelve royal *sampy*.

These neglected fetishes were enshrined in a traditional, steep-roofed cabin-palace, doubly holy because Andrianampoinimerina had built it as his own residence. Thus his divine soul returned to it as needs be to aid the queen. Neither men on horseback, nor hogs, nor Europeans could enter the sacred hut.

The most important of the *sampy* was named Kelimalaza, "He Who Is Small but Most Famous"—nicknamed the Sampy Maditra—"the Stubborn Fetish." He was made of three pieces of wood wrapped in white silk and kept in a wooden box wrapped in red silk banded with blue cloth. His guardian sorcerers claimed that when he was angry, he allowed none of them to lift the lid of his coffer. Having thus given the sign of his displeasure, the Stubborn Fetish demanded appeasement—a ceremonial soothing of his ruffled feelings, brought on by some careless action or other, it does not matter what. So the sorcerers asked his pardon in a sort of blanket request for absolution of the unknown sin. Then the fetish was graciously pleased to unlatch his lid, and to allow the reverent hands to lift him from his box to perform his special magic.

Another fetish was named Rakelimalaza; he held a bird in peculiar horror—the Vorondolo, "the Bird of Death," a kind of owl (*Tyto alba*). But the fetish whom the queen went to thank for her recovery was Manjakatsiroa, "the Peerless Sovereign." He took the form of a little sack, a sachet, a small bag of sand brought by a famous sorcerer from Matitanana, a most holy place. He was the talisman carried by a reigning king into battle.

Ill in bed and alone, Ranavalona must have given way to black and terrifying thoughts. Refreshed by her visit to the *sampy,* she embarked on a series of reforms. First she turned her attention to righting the wrongs brought in and spread by the missionaries, to whom she addressed a message on February 26, 1835. She enjoined them to respect the customs of her country. She told them that they were free to follow their own religion, but that henceforth they were to abstain from baptizing any of her subjects. On 1 March, a royal edict prohibited the practice of Christianity in the land. On June 18, she expelled all the British missionaries from Madagascar; and she shut down their schools. She prohibited education.

Then the queen turned violent. The next year she began to persecute the Malagasy Christian converts who would not adjure their new faith. On 14 August 1836, she ordered the public execution of the first of the Malagasy Christian martyrs, a woman of thirty-seven named Rasalama, who spent the last night of her life on earth in church, praying. Next morning, she walked to the place of execution on the edge of a high cliff, singing hymns. Then she knelt and began to pray; she was speared to death before she got to the Amen. The executioner's *sagai* was named Tsitialainga, "Which Liketh Not Lies." Rasalama's body was hurled down onto the rocks below, where dogs and carrion birds ate her flesh, and her bones bleached. Other martyrs were enslaved; others burnt at the stake. At the place of execution there now stands an English Protestant Memorial Church, built between 1863 and 1868.

Next, Ranavalona, who knew now that she could rely only upon herself and her divine ancestors, revoked her dead husband and dead father-in-law's innovations in the administration of justice by impartial court of law. She brought back the old, the tried, the true system of trial by ordeal to determine the innocence or the guilt of her subjects suspected, or accused, of guilt.

To judge by the numbers of men and women whom she had put to the test, she had a low opinion of the human race. It has been estimated (by the French) that a tenth of the population, then numbering between one and two million Malagasy, were forced each year in one or another of the ordeals, to prove their innocence. And of these the chances were that at least half did not succeed, but instead died. Thus one out of five of the total population was proved to be criminal. In the highlands, no less than fifteen thousand people and perhaps as many as twenty thousand so were killed in one generation. Between 1823 and 1844, in the period of Christian martyrdom, at least 150,000 men and women suffered death in ordeal; and of those who were found innocent, many lived enfeebled lives as a result of the poison used to judge them; and of these, many were doomed after death, for they were sterilized, made impotent—prevented by *tanghena* from begetting and conceiving children to attend their souls.

The poison of suspicion spread. If the queen, or a noble, or a member of the court or of the government felt indisposed after a meal or suffered from indigestion, all the household slaves were put through ordeal to prove that they had not put a specific poison in the food. And to be sure, all members of the palace guard were tested periodically for reasons of security. Ranavalona had begun to see personal as well as public enemies lurking in all corners of her green rice fields, behind every blade of grass in her highland pastures, and in the rooms and corridors of the royal citadel.

The converted Malagasy Christians were her special enemies. She put them to the test in wholesale trial by ordeal. These men and women were made to testify against themselves, to prove their innocence, or to confess—and thus be executed. The queen believed that Christianity and education were her mortal enemies; and she was right; but her concomitant belief that human beings take to corruption as naturally as the sparks fly upward can be questioned. It is true that the Christian missionaries and school teachers had made great headway in converting the low and lesser middle castes. But neither the queen nor the ministers brought themselves to examine the faults in their government and the Malagasy society, thus to correct them and allow for growth; instead Ranavalona took to reaction, and ruled by force of terror.

There were several forms of trial by ordeal. The most innocuous and perhaps the most interesting was based on the power of auto-suggestion and in effects on the involuntary muscular action of the accused—the power of the unconscious mind over matter. The defendant, already in a state of terror as he confronts his accusers, his judges, himself, the unknown, and their (or his own) ancestors, gods, or God, was forced to drink a bowl of water in which an idol had been dipped, or a piece of gold, the taboo metal, untouchably reserved as the exclusive possession of the queen and of her mysterious ancestors, the Vazimba. In this ordeal, known as *rano volamena*—"gold water"— the man was shut up for twenty-four hours to fast alone in the house of trial—time enough to cultivate the fungus growth of anxiety. He knew, and all the judges, the sorcerers, the witch-doctors, and the queen knew, that if he was innocent, no harm would come to him from drinking the strong medicine. But if he was guilty—in his own eyes of anything at all—he would not be able to contain the holy potion, or would vomit it up, or would pass it; or it would turn his bowels to water. Thus his belly was made to testify against his tongue.

In another form of ordeal, usually reserved for men accused of stealing cattle—those quasi-sacred, certainly valuable units of wealth, prestige, and status—the man accused had to touch his tongue seven times to a red-hot iron spearhead. If he did not burn, he was proved innocent, and suffered no further harm. Women were not allowed to witness this ordeal. The judge-executioner sat on a stone stained with the blood of a sacrificed red cock; and, of course, it was he who fired the iron spearhead to the degree of heat he chose.

In still another ordeal, that of man-eating beasts, the man on trial was made to swim across a river of crocodiles. If he got to the further bank, he had to plunge in and swim back. The innocent, protected by the gods or the ancestral spirits—some of whom liked to return to crawl the earth and swim its rivers inside the armored reptilian's hide —emerged unharmed and whole. The guilty vanished out of sight beneath the thick red river waters.

But the most elaborate, most certain, and most frequently used of the ordeals was trial by *tanghena*, or *tanguin*, in which the accused was made to swallow the poison of the fruit of the *Cerbera venenifera,*

175

an apocynaceous shrub of the dogbane family, resembling its more beautiful cousin, the pink, rose, or white single- or double-blossoming oleander—likewise a poisonous plant. The *tanghena* ordeal was most satisfactory because no man or woman went through it unscathed. Even those who demonstrated their innocence, and who did not die at once, suffered for the rest of their natural lives. They learned that right and wrong, innocence or guilt, are arbitrary in their special meanings; they learned that black is white if black, who has the power, says so. They learned that the man with the strongest stomach is the right man for the right time.

The ordeal was a tremendous spectacle conducted by specialists, themselves above and beyond their own law, high court functionaries who were men apart, sorcerers, magicians. And it may well have been that, despite the trickery—at least one act of dishonesty was essential to the performance of their task—these executioners, called *ampitanghena*, were not in themselves bad men (although the surviving witch-doctors today are notably greedy men), but only products of their own profession, itself founded upon the shaky basis of an act of faith, a belief in the absolute righteousness of their calling. Who is not capable of self-delusion? They sought out enemies of the state, heretics, bad or weak men and women, public enemies of the existing order. When Andrianampoinimerina died, all the Merina tribe was made to swallow the *tanghena* to prove that no man killed the king. There is no known antidote for the poison, twenty or thirty grains of which prove fatal. That is a great amount of poison to make a man swallow down; and it allowed the executioner to kill or save foe or friend.

The trial began with a prologue in which the officials made a show of testing the impartial and lethal strength of the *tanghena*. The officiating judge picked up the chosen nut and, by means of a small, ceremonial, ebony-handled, sharp *sagai* spear, scraped the dry fruit so that the gratings fell onto a square piece cut from the shell-like bark of a banana plant. Then, having invoked the presiding spirit of the ordeal by poison, whose name was Manamango, he asked the aid of the gods to guarantee that the test be successful. Next, he took up one of the two live fowls lying ready at hand, ligated for the purpose, and forced the grated poison down the throat of the bird. He then did not wait for the *tanghena* to take effect, but, making sure to prove his point, which was that the poison itself was not the instrument of justice, he made use of a magician's sleight of hand to strangle the struggling cock. Thus he proved that the innocence or the guilt of the accused man or woman, aided and brought forth by means of the ritual poisoning, was the determining factor in death or survival. A rooster or a hen knows neither right nor wrong; but human beings do know, and must be held accountable. To make his point perfectly clear, the judge then picked up the second bird, again invoked the spirit of impartial justice, and made a show of forcing more of the grated poisonous nut down its gullet—the while he did no such thing. For this hen had to survive, or otherwise the ordeal had no virtue in it.

So a man's life, his innocence, and his eternity were weighed against his death, his guilt, and his damnation on a fixed scale of grated poison rigged by two fowls and the executing sorcerer's magic thumb. Such values pleased the queen, who meant to rule in security.

The purpose of the fraud was to crush all hope out of the man on trial—to bewilder the mind, to excite the glands, to speed the beating heart, to wind the nerves, to squeeze the lungs, to snarl the guts—and to float up out of the brain's dark crevices those submerged faults and guilts, the sins of omission and commission that every human being brings to life as he walks his way along the edge of the cliff. He thus was made to be his own judge and his own jury. Who among us knows himself to be wholly innocent, who is without fault? And what man can live according to his own ideals? So a desperate man was made ready to disgorge a judgment upon himself.

Next came the action. The accused, who had been made to fast for twenty-four hours, was isolated in a cabin empty of furniture, an enclosed place. The sorcerer then went into him accompanied by his aides, who carried the machinery of justice—the venomous nut, a spoon made of bark, the ebony-handled spear, and three bits of chicken skin, each about half an inch long, cut from the back of a fat hen. The women of the accused man's family took up their assigned places to surround the cabin; and, kneeling, they began to chant over and over a formula, a prayer: "If in reality he has committed the crime, let him die. If he be innocent, let him live!"

Inside the hut, the man was stripped of his clothing, and, naked, made to sit upon the earthen floor, facing east. The standing *ampitanghena* then carefully explained the nature of the oncoming ordeal. Then the man was given to drink down a bowlful of thick and white ricewater to act as "a bed to receive the poison." The sorcerer directed him to sprinkle several drops of it on his hand, on his chest, and on his feet. Next, calling for his instruments, the *ampitanghena* grated the poison, determined the amount he needed, spread it on the fat side of the three bits of chicken skin, rolled them into a ball, and handed that to the man to swallow.

Once he got it down, the sorcerer took up the familiar prayer by which he passed the buck to the gods. He proclaimed that henceforth the outcome of the ordeal was a matter of divine wrath or mercy; he was but the frail human instrument made use of by omniscient forces above and beyond his control. So he invoked the divine wisdom of impartial justice, and called upon Manamango to take upon himself the responsibility of the ordeal. But his final act before he relinquished full control was to hand the man one more full bowl of thick rice water— the mystique of rice, the staff of life, was also made to serve. The man accused had to drink it down in order to enable him to throw up the evidence and the proof of his innocence or his guilt—those three bits of poisoned fat hen-skin.

But in the lapse of time filled in by the incantation, be it a long prayer or a short one, between the swallowing of the *tanghena* ball and the offing of the emetic, lay the moment of truth. Thus, as he covered himself with divine protection, the *ampitanghena* in fact killed or cured the tested man—condemned him or allowed him to demonstrate his innocence. The while he prayerfully denied it, the judge held firmly onto the outcome of the trial by ordeal. He manipulated justice under cover of the hokey-pokey. If the abracadabra was drawn out long, the man died; if it was cut short, he had an even chance to live.

For after the accused had swallowed the emetic rice water—and to be sure, although the system and the sorcerer deny it, a man forced to undergo any ordeal is implicitly accused of sin or crime—he had to retch and vomit in a prescribed style into a shallow basin handed him for the purpose. Outside the cabin, the surrounding women stepped up the rhythm and the volume of their chant to help the man to heave. The judge-diviner then bent over the bowl of spew to find, or not to find, all three bits of the fat hen's poisoned skin. If all indeed had come up in requisite order, then the ordeal was over and the man was proved innocent. If one or two or all had not come up, the man was doomed; he was forthwith transfixed by spears.

But, as usual in any ordeal, although innocence in action must be arbitrary and abrupt, guilt has many facets to catch the light. There is but one way to be good! But there are many ways to be found evil. If before the man gaped and retched, the fingers of his hands curled inward, it was a fatal sign; and if the man did not vomit by the rules, and shoved aside the ritual basin when it was offered him, he was likewise executed on the spot. Such things happened often enough to be recognized and given proper names: the first was *mamoly landy;* the second, *manosi dovia.*

Likewise if, although his belly contracted, he did not regurgitate all three bits of skin, no matter how many buckets of rice water he got down, and no matter how often he vomited forth; and if, finally in complete exhaustion, he could no longer swallow any more emetic, he was then put to death. Again, if having successfully delivered up the three skins at the first vomiting, he could not stop, but gagged again and again to go on incontinently retching and spewing—perhaps in disgust, perhaps in involuntary criticism, certainly in disrespect of the gods, the sorcerer, and the trial by ordeal, perhaps in shock— the disgruntled lie-detector declared that the man, who had proved himself by bringing forth the three skins of his innocence, had come through the ordeal aided by the puissant black magic of his personal talisman, or because he had the good luck to lack any sort of moral sense. Such a man revealed himself to be a hardened criminal—a hidden malefactor, and evildoer, a transgressor, a man better off dead— and he was speared upon the spot.

Even the "innocents" who came through the ordeal in the correct response suffered. Some walked out free to die of the aftereffects of the poison they had swallowed and absorbed before they vomited up the skins. It was a painful and a prolonged death of intolerable agony that came in spasms of recurrent pain. All were damaged, some were paralyzed, some were sterilized, all were diminished, and most remained suspect; for some of the mud stuck. And the scars hardened; it was an ordeal by trauma, as well as by *tanghena.*

Those found guilty and then executed, once dead, could not escape.

Their dishonored bodies were dragged through the streets so to be made to serve as terrible examples. The dead body was then to be not excused; it could not be buried in the ancestral tomb, for the spirit had to be eternally damned. The corpse was put, head turned towards the south, in a shallow grave covered with an inch or two of dirt soon to be scratched away by the wild dogs, the rats, and the carrion crows, and fed upon—perhaps made to serve, being poisoned flesh, as an exterminator. Thus his ghost was condemned to roam forever; it was denied peace. And his survivors, his family, guilty by association, were made suspect; they were ostracized.

So the queen, in her endeavor to fix her way of life forever, in effect destroyed it with suspicion; she blighted its natural growth. By means of the *tanghena,* the queen poisoned herself, her country, and her people. In her world, a good man had to have a strong stomach to survive. He had to learn how to vomit forth at will. Above all, he had to get in mind by heart the point beyond which he could not bring himself to step and know himself to be a man alive. Many may well have said "Better Red than dead." But some did not, even when death came in ordeal, filthily.

And so the queen failed. Most notably, Christianity, reinforced as is its way by martyrdom, did not perish. Nor did education. Meantime, the queen refused to learn to read or write, and with the help of her divine ancestors, the dozen fetishes, and her gods—along with the power of her official lover, the gigolo prime minister—she made herself increasingly *masiaka* (but not just).

In this chosen guise, she stood (she did not sit) for a royal portrait painter. She put on her new crown, a massive affair with a lining of red velvet, adorned in front with a fantaisie of seven gold spear-points fanning out above her brow; and it was topped by a golden bird, its wings outspread—a falcon, the royal Malagasy emblem, "the Bird of Strength," *voromahery,* a bird of prey, *Falco peregrinus.* And she had it on straight, like an ill-advised hat, a clumsy adaptation of a foreign high style. It sat on her head; but, like the ladies say, it did nothing *for* her—to soften the marks of time's passage across that once-lovely face. However, in the cut and the line of her clothing, she was not looking for elegance and chic. The crown served her purpose, which was not to turn herself into a Byzantine icon like the Empress

Theodora, nor into a mother-image of steady value and all human worth, like magnificent Queen Mary. Ranavalona the Cruel, in her copied royal trappings, looked like what she sought to be—a Malagasy matriarchal *masiaka* fetish; and she struck terror. Yet it turns out to be of an oddly modern kind, for she is as alarming as an overdressed ogress—an angry Mom on the warpath in a towering rage. Under all those yardgoods, she wore the pants in her tribal family.

There is no doubt that she liked power. She brooked no denial of her will. Ranavalona was cruel when disobeyed. She ordered one young man and wife to adjure their new faith and to return to the ancestral ways of fetish worship. But the converted Hova "freeman" and free woman refused to deny Christ; thus they defied the queen. In so doing, they cast doubt upon her ancestral and divine right to rule absolutely, as she saw fit, over the bodies, the minds, the souls, and the eternity of all her subjects. She ordered the pair to be burnt alive in public, not at the stake, but bound and thrown onto a pyre of wood. The young woman was in her ninth month of pregnancy. She gave birth in the flames. The executioner picked up the child, held it, thought a moment, and then tossed it back into the fire.

Against all this unfathomable horror, Jean Laborde worked patiently and tactfully. He did not waste his time to protest; nor, before this brown Mrs. Behemoth did he give way to wroth or malice. Perhaps he knew that a man can do no more than be himself as best he can. So he set out to demonstrate the virtues of his own world by working hard to bring in all he could of Western culture, French civilization, and the industrial revolution. He was a reasonable man. He worked constantly and well. He made progress.

In November, 1831, he signed a contract to make rifles for the royal army. Early in 1835, he was put in charge of the logistics of an army that the queen sent to conquer the southern tribes. For the first time in Malagasy history, Laborde used ships to transport food and matériel, the munitions that he had made himself, and the reserve troops, from Tamatave by sea to Fort Dauphin on the southeast coast. When he got there, he found the Merina army in great confusion. Therefore, he took charge, assumed the command, and led the expeditionary force to victory. He did not work with serried ranks of disciplined men in red coats, in horizon blue, in field grey, or in khaki. He had to bring order to a horde of miscellaneous dark-brown men from sixteen to sixty, conscripts, slaves, or mercenaries, next to naked, armed with spears—or with his own rifles. They had been ordered into battle from Tananarive, and told where to go; but they had to get there on their own, living off the country, and supplied with neither rations nor transport—nor protection. If ten thousand set out, and if two thousand arrived at the theater of war five hundred miles to the south that was well and good. The rest had disappeared on route—died of disease or malnutrition, been picked off one by one in the forests or on the savannahs, or had deserted. So many had so little stomach for warfare that, in 1821, Radama I had found it necessary to pass a law condemning any soldier caught withdrawing, retreating, or fleeing the field of battle to be burnt alive. Jean Laborde proved equal to the task of winning the queen's wars.

On 24 May 1835, as commanding general, he led his troops in an attack against the southern Sakalava and their allies in the Bay of St. Augustine, below Tuléar on the southwest shore.

Two years later, on March 28, 1837, he began his great work by signing a treaty with the Merina government—one man and one country as partners—to create an entire city and what is now called a complex—the manufacturing town of Mantasoa ("Mahnta-shoo"), twenty-five miles today by excellent road from Tananarive towards the east. Laborde's city no longer exists, but another town of the same name does, built up around the dam and reservoir constructed by latter-day French engineers to supply the capital with running water. The forest-planted borders of the lake, the wooded slopes of the watershed, and the town provide the well-to-do with a weekend resort where they repose in charming modern houses, swim, water ski, sail from the yacht club, or fish for black bass.

In 1938, the Geographic Service of French Madagascar resurveyed Laborde's manufacturing city of factories, blast furnaces and kilns, foundries, warehouses, streets, residences, farms, gardens, reservoirs, canals, shops, and all the other needs and necessities for the industries and the workers that he organized; and the modern engineers found it all good. Laborde's contract of 101 years earlier called upon him to create a cannon foundry, a sugar refinery, an indigo dye works, a soap works, and a silk industry from the cocoon to the woven fabric. "I also engaged," he wrote later on, remembering the past, "to produce several acids, alum, sulfate of iron, Prussian blue, et cetera. Ten days after the contract was signed, the queen sent me 20,000 men [forced laborers] . . . whom I put to work at once building roads, jetties, canals, a great reservoir, leveling a site for a factory, and doing all the necessary groundwork for a large establishment."

So Jean Laborde built a city of 10,000 permanent workers, who were not consulted, and who did not like the life. But they worked. On 29 June 1843, Laborde fired the blast furnace. On 12 July 1844, he saw the first of his cannon leave the arsenal. Before long, the new strain of silkworms that he had introduced were spinning sufficient filament to weave into three hundred pounds of cloth a year. Soon his heavy industry began to turn out hydraulic engines for the queen's rice fields, as well as pumps and conduits to bring a steady supply of pure water to Tananarive.

There seemed to have been nothing this Gascon from France could not put his hand to. He introduced meteorology and the lightning rod to Madagascar, an island of violent thunderstorms and cyclones. And, although it is recorded that an American named William Marks introduced the first glass window-panes to the country, in 1874, thirty years later, where the then queen, Ranavalona II, had them set in the windows of a now-vanished pavilion, Kelisoa, a "small treasure," in the Rova (and that's all I know about William Marks), Jean Laborde baked bricks and tiles, and thus revolutionized the domestic architecture of the highlands. He changed the way of life inside the houses by setting up a glass factory and a pottery where he trained his forced workers to blow bottles and cut tumblers, and to produce a glazed earthenware—his decorated dishes and plates resemble the charming eighteenth-century wares of Rouen and Strasbourg; but only one or two examples—a covered soup-tureen, a serving dish—have survived.

He built a paper mill, a tannery, woodworking shops and a furniture factory, and a cement works. And he erected all these shops and factories in their proper places according to an orderly, rectangular master plan; for Laborde laid out his city of Mantasoa in a rational, reasonable, and logical French design.

Nearby, to the west in a hill with a view, he planned a residential garden city, and built it not within a square but in the arcs of a circle; it centered upon a country residence for the queen set down on the high point. To the north where he had space and the land was good, he built himself a house and an experimental model farm, which he stocked with imported prize cattle from the established breeds of milch and beef cows and bulls of Bordeaux, of Gascony, the Garonne, Brittany, and Normandy. These he crossbred with specimens selected from the local zebu (*Bos indicus*) stock. Thus, between 1840 and 1860, Laborde produced the *rana* strain, now breeding true. There are today some thirty to forty thousand head of cattle in Madagascar, descendants of Laborde's experimental animal that he created to combine the qualities of the beef and milch cows and steers from France with the stamina and the ability to resist the parasites, the diseases, and the climate of the long-naturalized hump-backed Malagasy cattle. So he brought in the scientific methods of animal husbandry and agronomy. He bred horses too.

He set out and supervised the care of orchards of European fruit trees—apples, peaches, pears, plums, for instance, all adapted themselves and survived. He brought in the various berries, garden vegetables, and flowers, originally from Europe, America, and Asia, but now cultivated wherever they will take root all over the world. On his farm, he raised swine; he smoked and salted hams; he made all sorts of cheese; he set out vineyards, and made wine; he distilled brandy and rum; he brewed a sweet, thick, and—I should think—nasty syrup from the fruit of the tamarind tree—named *Tamarindus indica,* but most probably native to Madagascar.

And into the ornamental waters, the ponds and the canals, which he designed for the queen's and his own country houses, he introduced (in 1861) the goldfish of Europe and of China, the *Carassius auratus,* so thinking to amuse the queen. He brought in seven of them, and at first kept them in a fish bowl in her palace on the hill of Tananarive. But she grew bored with them and told him to take them away. So he carried them down to the little lake of Anosy, then on the outskirts of the low town, where, on the little island that gives the lake its name, there then stood a royal summerhouse. It has been supplanted by the towering stone and bronze Monument aux Morts, without which no French city is complete—a war memorial, and a most effective one, erected to recall the French and the Malagasy of the island who died in the 1914–1918 World War; and by extension and addition, those of the Second World War. The charming lake is surrounded with a line of jacaranda trees from tropical America, their showy clusters of blue-lilac flowers reflecting in the quiet waters in the spring. The goldfish there grew large and escaped into the irrigation canals that supplied the near rice fields; they lost their bright color and reverted to ancestral shape. They are now carp, which the Chinese once fed, it is said, on dry blood and so produced the red-gold and fantastic pop-eyed and fantailed little monsters, none of which amused Ranavalona the Cruel. Carp have become food-fish today in Madagascar.

Jean Laborde was a good businessman, too; he bought and sold all sorts of commercial products. He became a banker—and lent money to his royal godson, the increasingly irresponsible crown prince. He taught the boys of the royal caste how to ride the horses he gave them. He instructed the barbers by showing them how to cut hair and trim moustaches and beards in the current French style—and haircuts are still unmistakably French in Madagascar. There seems to have been nothing this man could not do.

Laborde introduced the use of cut and dressed stonemasonry as well as brick and mortar. He served by appointment as architect to the queen. In 1839, Ranavalona the Terrible, the Cruel, commissioned him to build her the "Queen's Palace" that still dominates Tananarive, although Laborde's construction is no longer visible. At the command of Queen Ranavalona II, this wooden palace was encased in stone. James Cameron, a Scottish missionary, architect, soap-maker, and handy man, did the job—although Jean Laborde was still alive, and had ten more years to go. But he was out of favor; and on 2 October 1862, he had been named French consul in Madagascar. In any case the British influence in the Merina monarchy had become dominant once again; and the second Ranavalona, along with her prime minister-consort, had themselves baptized into the Anglican Protestant Episcopal Church on 21 February 1869.

The palace as it stands today is a very silly structure, having a tremendous, high-pitched tile roof set with dormers in vertical rows, and trimmed along the edges with a stone balustrade. Each of the four corners is supplied with a square tower, of which each outer surface has been provided, in descending order, with one bilobate Byzantine window, one bull's-eye (that of the left-hand front tower having been filled in with a clock face), and two mid-nineteenth-century-Greco-Roman-Renaissance pedimented and pilastered windows, one triangular, one arched; and the sides between the towers of the rectangular, two-story, masonry revetment were then provided with two built-in arcades, one above the other, of Roman arches held up by square pillars adorned with engaged columns, of which the capitals are most eclectic. Yet, inside this hard shell, Jean Laborde's original wooden palace-sized hut still stands preserved as it was built to order for the terrible, reactionary Ranavalona the Cruel.

His was a bad but significant structure. He had to build a palace fit for his special queen; so he designed a monument to her and to her reign. It was enormously over-extended, but it was a traditional Malagasy native wood and thatch cabin on the grand scale. Thus he preserved the quasi-sacred plan of the single-roomed ancestral residence, in which everything had its fixed and meaningful place; but at the same time, he enlarged its dimensions as the conquering Merina kings and queen had enlarged their dominion over the other tribes to take in the whole island. The palace was, then, a reactionary structure, a place in which the queen hoped to hold sway over time and space. She named it Manjakamiadana—"Where It Is Comfortable to Reign."

As is the function of architecture, the palace suited the Queen's name and nature down to the ground; it reflects its moment in Malagasy sociology and history. Ranavalona the Cruel made terrible demands upon her people; the construction of her monstrous cabin-palace made cruel demands upon the laborers whom she condemned to build it. She put her Official Lover, the prime minister and general of the armies, in charge of assembling the lumber. In such a traditional structure, the essential element is a master post to hold up the rooftree, and to support the weight of the heavy thatch. The curtain walls of wood are hung on a framework held up by a grove of lesser tree trunks. To find this key timber and the other logs, the prime minister had to send an army of workmen down into the Betsileo tribal lands of the eastern escarpment, where the few remaining virgin stands of jungle hardwoods grew. The men in this *corvée* were neither paid nor provided with food or shelter. Authorities differ as to the number of men employed to find the trees, fell them, trim and dress the lumber, and transport it through the trackless rain forests, up the cliff onto the highlands, and across torrential streams, ravines, hills and valleys, and rocks and erosions, some three hundred or more miles, and one or two thousand feet in altitude to Tananarive; and there to set them up in place on top of the Rova hill. One "eyewitness" records 10,000 laborers, and says that it took them nineteen days—and that 2,000 workmen were either killed outright, or died of exhaustion. Another lists 5,000 men, who did the work in twelve days, and 1,000 died. The first "authority" was a British missionary named Radlay; the other is the French Communist and former Colonial functionary, Pierre Boiteau. Neither writer can be called disinterested.

Yet the fact is that the monodendritic central column, which still supports the anachronistic rooftree of the palace, is made of ebony—a wood too dense to float, and too hard for termites or decay to bring down—and was cut from a single tree of the *Diospyros* genus. The timber measures 39 meters, or 128.7 feet in length; the tree from which it was cut must indeed have been gigantic. To this day, the master pillar remains a notorious piece of wood; it has been personified— "Vola Mihitsy" is its name. "It Is Worth Its Weight in Gold," we would say in English, although the metal of the Malagasy name is silver. It cost one or two thousand human lives. Such was the queen's pleasure.

Even so, Jean Laborde worked within the given framework of his time and place for the good of Madagascar. History used him. He was European civilization personified in his prime; and he enjoyed special favor.

In 1845, he and de Lastelle were among the very few Europeans in Madagascar—to be sure, there were then probably not more than a hundred or so on the entire island—to be exempted from the royal decree that made all other foreign nationals liable to the laws of the land, including the *corvée* and trial by the ordeal of *tanghena.* In the next few years, Laborde followed the queen at court and on her royal processions. On one of her pleasure trips, she was accompanied by an escort of 10,000 soldiers; and on another, she, all her court, and a similar army, paid Laborde a visit at his industrial city of Mantasoa.

He seems to have been on good terms with the family of the Official

Lovers, for when Rainiharo, the first of the hereditary prime ministers died on 10 February 1852, Laborde was commissioned to build the family mausoleum, still one of the monuments of Tananarive. To judge from the similar architectural style, at about this time he built his own tomb at Mantasoa—one of the few things, along with the blast furnace, to have survived to this day. Neither his nor the prime minister's tomb can be called handsome, being somewhat Hindu-Mogul-East Indian, and certainly exotic in effect. Each is climaxed by a single pillar curiously topped by a blunt cone finial—unmistakably phallic to the cluttered Freudian eye, but puzzling. For it is not clear whether this memorial assertion of the masculinity of the dead and gone men who were the queen's Lovers was a conscious and witty comment on the queen's tyranny, or an unconscious protest against the matriarchal rule.

If Jean Laborde built the tomb of the prime ministers to insure his place at court, he most certainly did so because the queen asked him to. No man—and no woman, for that matter—dared gainsay her request. Laborde had committed himself to the life of Madagascar; it was *his* life. Yet, a white European foreigner, a displaced Frenchman (but not an expatriate), he had constantly to prove his good faith and his good will; he stood on slippery ground. Intrigue seeped like spilled blood from under the closed doors of the cabins of the royal Rova. Life in the queen's entourage had come to be a perpetual ordeal. Jean Laborde saw to it that he survived.

However, at about this time in the middle of the century, the Grand Frenchman's life in Madagascar reached its climax. Then things for him began to go bad—perhaps because he put his hand to shaping history instead of to forging such things as lightning rods. History has to be let alone to run to earth along its own lines.

Jean Laborde's godson, "Mr. Boy," the queen's one and only son, the crown prince, was then twenty-five years old, adored, overprotected, heavily insulated from real power—yet able to get away with almost anything because in the eyes of his all-powerful mother, he could do no wrong. He was, in fact, a frivolous and a trivial young man, although his heart was in the right place; he was a Mamma's Boy, tied to her apron strings, protected behind her full skirts. From his place, he set out to bring about what was to have been a revolution from on high; but he did not understand what he was doing. So he began to pull wires that came loose in his hands, wrapped themselves around his throat, and strangled him.

The princeling was understandably impatient to take over the rule of his much mismanaged state, and to recover the royal powers from the prime ministers, those Official Lovers, who had usurped them. He knew that under his mother, the affairs of state and those of the royal household had merged. The queen, then aged sixty-six, could see no difference between her personal whims and the monarch's obligations. She was no longer interested in the exercise of power as the dynamics inherent in the principles, the theories, and the abstract ideas of rule. She believed her rice fields to be but the source of revenue to support her queenly way of life. She had no understanding of the political economy of her realm, although she kept a firm grasp on the purse strings. She tried to manage her island like an inexhaustible private feudal estate.

Although self-indulgent and weak, Rakoto was—or so it has come down to us—an educated, enlightened, intelligent, and generous young man, motivated by all the best of what he had learned from Jean Laborde and Napoléon de Lastelle. In effect, what he had learned amounted to pure treason.

On 14 January 1854, the crown prince wrote a letter to Napoléon III, the emperor of the French, to ask him to send aid and assistance from France to Madagascar to put an end to the barbarous conduct of the queen's ministers and advisers. In other words, the heir to the Merina throne considered his mother, the queen, Ranavalona the Cruel, to be a captive on her throne. Thus, he invited the ambitious lesser Bonaparte to send an expeditionary force to invade the island, and thus to free it from the existing state of savagery to which it had been reduced by a petticoat rule. The prince's act can be seen as a most enlightened call for help; but nevertheless, it was an act of treason.

The prince trapped himself in treachery by trying to make practical application of that Jesuitical notion having to do with the end justifying the means. In June 1855, Jean Laborde brought into Tananarive secretly, and against the law, a French Jesuit priest, who lived in plain clothes in Laborde's townhouse, where, on 8 July 1855, the Prince Rakoto went to take part in the first Roman Catholic Mass celebrated —in secret, illegally—inside Madagascar since the expulsion of the missionaries and the royal edict prohibiting the exercise of the Christian religion almost exactly twenty years earlier.

Whatever the dominant motivation that moved him to attempt revolt against his mother, the queen, Rakoto had reason to be alarmed by the current state of Malagasy affairs. In the twenty-seventh year of her terrible thirty-three-year reign, Ranavalona the Cruel had come to suspect everyone near her of evil intent toward her—except her treasonable son and her old friend Jean Laborde. She no longer had any illusions on the subject of her Official Lovers' love for her. Two years before, the old one had died. She had buried him with all due pomp and ceremony, but she had not been given free choice in the elevation of the new one, the old man's son. Raharo, known officially as Rainivoninahitriniony, had assumed the family power behind the throne; as Premier and Commander-in-Chief, he could afford to let the function of the Official Lover fall into desuetude.

But the queen had learned the bitter side of absolute power and arbitrary privilege. She had put her faith forever in her son and heir, but she could no longer bring herself to trust any other man or woman of her palace, her court, her bodyguard, her government, or her people. She stood alone, and sometimes she dared not eat for fear of poison in the food. In her suspicion, from time to time, she killed a cook. Always she was vigilant.

Even so, the crown prince found a way to send his letter off to France, thus inviting Napoléon III to invade his mother's realm. Nothing immediate resulted from Rakoto's enlightened act of treachery. Napoléon III had made commitments in the Crimea, in Mexico, and elsewhere; therefore, he was unable to accept the crown prince's invitation to invasion. However, the proper authorities in the French bureaucracy filed Mr. Boy's letter in the pigeonhole marked *"Pending"*; and their successors took it out for action later on when, after 1870, the French Army wanted to refurbish France's tarnished *gloire* by adding Madagascar to the new Colonial empire.

If European and personal history caused the emperor to lay the matter aside, current events brought another Frenchman to be the Man of Destiny, the French instrument in the hands of the flighty prince. This was Joseph-François Lambert. He was a live wire. In June, 1855, the ambitious young businessman, then aged thirty-one, accompanied by the disguised Jesuit priest, arrived to install himself in the confidence of the heir apparent. Lambert came prepared with letters of introduction to Jean Laborde; he had seen to it that everything had been properly laid on for his takeover. He was a go-getter. He was a bad man, although to do him justice perhaps he did not know it. However, he knew what he wanted; he wanted success. He came to be the prince's evil genius.

On 19 June, a week or two after his arrival in Tananarive, the queen received him and that other disguised subversive element, Father Finaz, the Jesuit, who went under the name of Mr. Hervier; and a week later gave a great banquet in honor of the two newcomers and her old friend Jean Laborde—not in the Rova, but in the house of the prime minister. Lambert had already made contact with the prince, who gave him his friendship and royal favor. In the middle of a three-day bullfight staged by his mother, the prince on 28 June 1855 signed the Lambert Charter; it proved to be his own death warrant. Lambert then was an active thirty-one; Laborde was fifty; Father Finaz was eternal; Ranavalona the Terrible was sixty-seven; Rakoto was twenty-six. It was a century and more ago. The bullfight took place in a courtyard of the citadel. A matched pair of lyre-horned, hump-backed male animals gored one another to death.

Lambert was the right man in the right place; he sold himself to the prince. He struck while the iron was hot. So Lambert came to embody all good foreign things to the spoiled son of a domineering mother, a credulous and trusting young man with no authority to do what he did and no idea of what he was getting into. But soon the gossips began to whisper words that got around, were heard, were noted, and were remembered. During his short reign as King Radama II, and on the occasion of his death, the whispered rumors came to the ears of the wordly British missionary, the Reverend Mr. Ellis, who gives us to understand in his book, *Madagascar Revisited, describing the events of a new reign and the revolution which followed,* that a highly personal contact connected the flighty and frustrated princeling with the energetic and unscrupulous French businessman. But, according to the French, the Reverend Mr. Ellis was a British secret political agent; and perhaps it is all defamation of character. The reactionary prime minister, who got rid of the prince when he was king, and who

191

tried to abolish the Lambert Charter, was inimical to the parties of the first and of the second part, whatever their private relationship.

I do not know what the two protagonists—the agonist and the antagonist—in this tragedy looked like at the inception. Time has put masks before their faces. That is as it should be; for these two men of the nineteenth century, the one a "black" South Sea Island Afro-Asian, the other a "white" French European, have come to represent more than themselves in history. And, no doubt about it, the action between the two involved dirty work. The notorious Lambert Charter gives evidence in itself of that. When he signed it, the crown prince was the heir to the throne, no more than that. He had no official position otherwise, and no voice in the government. His role in the grim fairy tale Merina monarchy ruled by an ogress-queen was that of a minor. Until his mother died and he succeeded, he lived below the age of consent. He had no legal right to give himself and the raw materials—the mineral wealth, the forests, the great plains—of his mother's kingdom to the upstart from abroad. But hard sell or soft sell, the prince bought what Lambert had to offer; both men signed the charter. Their business began.

In truth, the Lambert Charter was a standard business contract of its time. Today we have learned, we have learned the hard way, that it was a bad business. For, to carry out its already obsolete terms, the French government and army made use of it (along with Jean Laborde's contested will) to justify the first Franco-Hova War of 1883–1885 and the subsequent unworkable French protectorate; and the second Franco-Hova War—the invasion and conquest of 1895, and the annexation of Madagascar as a French colony in 1896. In brief, the Lambert Charter gave the young Frenchman a personal and private monopoly to exploit all the minerals, all the forests, and all the unoccupied lands of the enormous and almost untouched island of some 228,600 square miles. For this exclusive right, Joseph-François Lambert engaged to pay the crown of the royal Merina government one tenth—that is to say, 10 per cent—of his private company's profits. It was to be capitalized and managed in France. There was nothing stipulated about international or governmental inspection of the books.

It is true that Madagascar's subsoil has proved to be surprisingly barren, its forests far from rich, and most of its topsoil unfertile. But to this day, the island has not been efficiently prospected. There are few investors, few producers, and fewer consumers of the island's few ores and crystals. There have always been almost intolerable management and labor problems; the costs of shipping are high. Madagascar is a faraway place. Lambert knew nothing of any of this when he drew up and signed his classically evil contract, and sold it and himself, as representative products of European culture, to the prince.

Two days after the secret signing, on July the first, 1855, the queen, wishing to demonstrate the civilization and the culture of her country, and the magnificence of her court, gave a state ball. The path up the hill to the palace citadel was lined by the queen's bodyguards, standing at attention; they were tall, dark-skinned young men dressed in white loincloths, and armed with bayoneted muskets. In the courtyard, under a spreading scarlet silk umbrella with a gold knob on top of it— the emblem of her royalty, held up by a tall slave—the queen stood to receive her distinguished foreign guests, Jean Laborde, Lambert, and "Mr. Hervier," the Jesuit priest. She never set foot to the ground outside the Rova, but was carried, always sheltered by the red umbrella, in a portable gilt throne.

At one such occasion, Ranavalona the Terrible wore a purple and green plaid silk crinoline, much flounced; and over it, as a sort of regal cloak, she had put on a dressing gown of green velvet lined with crimson satin. Her head, her ears, her throat, her breast, her stomach, her wrists, and her fingers were adorned with gold and red coral. She liked her guests to dress up, too. At one reception, the Grand Frenchman and his métis son Clément, recently returned to Tananarive from his education in France—the father was fifty, the son twenty-two, in 1855—were dressed in Arab costume. They wore robes of scarlet and orange silk, with immense turbans to match upon their heads, and on their feet bright slippers with turned up, pointed toes. The Reverend Mr. Ellis (the reporter) preferred to maintain his British missionary dignity in a black frock coat, striped trousers, black boots, and a stovepipe hat. One time Laborde entertained the company by sending up fire-burning, smoke-and-hot-air-filled, brightly colored paper balloons. He made looking glasses, and flashed the sun's rays across the valleys. Mr. Ellis had a camera, and he took likenesses; he cured the fever with doses of quinine.

At these royal banquets, the guests ate from porcelain plates, and used proper silver knives, forks, and spoons. The tables were spread with lace-encrusted linen napery and adorned with artificial flowers (not for lack of the natural kinds, but to show imported elegance) in rooms hung with foreign mirrors in gilt frames, and furnished with Louis-Philippe and Victorian chairs. The liveried servants walked silently because they were barefoot. To make the silverware, Malagasy silversmiths, trained by Jean Laborde, melted down Mexican dollars, Spanish *piastres*, and French five franc pieces supplied from the national treasury; and if their work displeased her, the queen had the silversmiths speared to death. She did not pay them.

A menu for a state banquet has survived. The queen gave her guests roast beef, roast veal, steaks, cutlets, chops, *carbonades*, meatballs, stews, and other stuffed and sauced and sautéed viands; roast chickens, turkeys, geese, wild duck, guinea fowl, pigeons; and all sorts of fish; with "made dishes" in great variety, vegetables, pastries, well cooked rice, well baked bread, and fresh or cooked fruit. Very little wine was offered, but tea in quantity. All was set forth and consumed with the utmost propriety and elegance of deportment—although the ladies, afterwards, withdrew to chew snuff and spit tobacco juice into porcelain basins and silver spitoons, conveniently placed to the purpose beside the chairs and side tables.

The day after the secret Mass celebrated in Jean Laborde's townhouse on 8 July 1855, Lambert, the signed charter concealed upon his person, left Tananarive for France, to be the secret intermediary between the Heir Apparent of Madagascar and Napoléon III, and to offer the emperor of the French, in Mr. Boy's name, the protectorate of the island—bigger than France and Belgium and Holland combined. When Lambert got to Paris, a month or six weeks later on, he went at once to the Tuileries and gave the emperor the prince's message. Soon the agents of the British Foreign Office sent in their detailed reports. From London, dispatches and instructions went out around the Cape to Mauritius and from there to the Reverend Mr. William Ellis, in Tananarive. He went and told the queen, Ranavalona the Terrible, all about how Jean Laborde, Father Finaz, and Joseph-François Lambert had seduced Her Majesty's son and heir. The British missionary and the ruler talked together on the verandah of the "Silver

194

Palace," another two-story wooden cabin of great size; it must have taken place shortly before the Reverend left, on September 26, for home. He took back to England with him an orchid plant, *Angroecum superbum*, one of the 685 species that grow in Madagascar. It has a large white bloom, one of the first of which to open in England formed the center of the princess royal's bridal bouquet at her marriage to the crown prince of Prussia.

Meantime, in Paris, Lambert had begun his conversations with French businessmen and bankers to implement the Lambert Charter. However, when he was informed that the Foreign Office in London had got wind of his schemes, and had sent instructions to their agent in Tananarive, Lambert broke off his negotiations, and took ship for Madagascar. He arrived in the capital on 30 May 1857. Three days later, the queen gave him audience; he offered Ranavalona the Terrible rich gifts from Napoléon the Little—an elaborate music box made by Husso-Buthod and Thibonville, of 254 rue St.-Martin, in Paris; it played several selections, including a song of farewell. And he bought a chiming clock, some silverware, some Sèvres porcelain, and so on. The queen accepted them; she knew what she was going to do; she had made up her mind; she was biding her time.

Ranavalona I and her prime minister, Raharo, had known about the Lambert conspiracies for nine long months, during which time she had done a good deal of emotional reflecting about Lambert, Ellis, the rest of the French and the British, and Jean Laborde above all— Jean Laborde, for so many years her favorite, a man she thought she could trust, almost one of them, a Madécasse if not a Malagasy, with a métis son twenty-three years old, only three and a half years younger than the prince, his father's godson with whom he had grown up. The queen had made exception after exception in favor of Laborde— who, to be sure, had been useful, and who had worked to enrich the island and the monarchy. He had been a friend—until Lambert arrived along with the secret Jesuit. Now Laborde had joined the enemy, he had gone too far; she had had enough of him.

On July 7, 1857, five days after she had given Lambert audience, the queen decreed exile from Madagascar for all Europeans; and she confiscated their possessions.

What took place in those five days between the queen and her prime minister and the three Frenchmen, Laborde, Lambert, and Father Finaz? We know that she blamed the foreigners for what the prince and Lambert had conspired to do. They had tried to destroy her! She could not bring herself to believe that she and her fierce and arbitrary rule were mistaken—that she, herself, the *masiaka* queen, who had been crowned as a king, and who loved her son, had caused the prince's reaction to her own reactionary acts. She knew what was best for Madagascar, and she knew what was best for her boy. She could not bring herself to blame herself—it was not her fault, as queen and as a mother, that her son had been a foolish boy. He did not have her long experience with foreigners and their evil, subtle, and perfidious ways—she knew them. So, throughout those five days, and for the remaining four years of her life and her reign, she proved herself to be an adoring and a forgiving mother, fierce as a tigress to protect her cub, her kitten, her boy. She refused to listen to anything said against her son and heir. It was *not* his fault. And so she banished the secondary cause of discord—the corrupt foreigners with all their wiley talk of progress and enlightenment.

As soon as she expelled Jean Laborde (he and Lambert went to Réunion), the Malagasy laborers at Mantasoa—Laborde's industrial complex, his manufacturing town—rose up from their forced labor in the machine shops, the iron foundry, the various factories and kilns and furnaces, and all ten thousand of them, condemned to slave away in modern industry for life, took the place apart. They wrecked the machines, they razed the buildings, they ruined everything, they laid waste the town. The queen's prime minister, the Commander-in-Chief of the armies, the Official Lover, sent his son in charge of a detachment of troops to demolish whatever remained standing among the ruins, so to obliterate Jean Laborde's memory, and to wipe out his influence from the face of Madagascar.

Only a single animal from his private zoo escaped Laborde's disgrace. He had brought in from Africa apes and monkeys, gazelles and antelopes, birds of all sorts, a camel from Egypt, and one hippopotamus from some highland lake or river. The workers took up spears and killed them all in their cages—except the thick-skinned hippo; male or female, it escaped through a broken barrier, and took to the papyrus thickets growing in the shallows of Laborde's lake-reservoir.

There the solitary animal lived on for years; it turned into a fabulous beast, and is said still to be alive, browsing in the night. Earlier in that year, on 27 February 1857, Napoléon III had recognized Jean Laborde's service in promoting the Christian Roman Catholic religion and French civilization in Madagascar by creating him a chevalier of the French Legion of Honor.

Four years later, Queen Ranavalona I died in Tananarive on August 18; some say she was eighty-one years old, but probably she was about seventy-three. She had reigned for thirty-three years; her son, proclaimed King Radama II, was certainly thirty-two years old on his next birthday, September 23.

He strangled no other contender to the throne, although he did exile Prince Ramboasolama, his mother's nephew and adopted son, his cousin and foster-brother. On 1 September 1861, the new king passed a series of new laws to suppress the Ordeal by *tanghena,* and to permit his people the freedom of worship. He showed the court that he intended to be a liberal ruler. On 12 October Radama II welcomed Laborde and Lambert, accompanied by two Roman Catholic priests in their right robes and proper names (Fathers Jouen and Weber; I do not know what happened to "Mr. Hervier"—Father Finaz); they entered Tananarive with much honor and a ceremonial escort. The king and Lambert, then aged thirty-seven, resumed their old relationship as though nothing had happened in the past five years. This time, the renewed Lambert Charter, properly signed and sealed, was a legal document; it was dated 3 November 1861, and it called for the establishment of La Compagnie de Madagascar. Its terms were the same— 10 per cent royalties to the king.

For himself, Lambert received, besides the monopoly to exploit the realm, immense concessions of land grants; exemption from export and import duties and taxation on whatever the company sent out of, or brought into, Madagascar; and the right to mint and issue money. In brief, he took over the resources, the economy, the finances, and the treasury of his friend's kingdom; and he was ennobled and entitled Duc d'Émyrne—Duke of Imerina, Duke of the Highlands of the Far Horizons and the Long View. There seem to have been no clauses in fine print in this handwritten document; but the king should have read the handwriting on the wall.

Queen Victoria, Emperor Napoléon III, and Pope Pius IX sent proper representatives all bearing gifts to the coronation, held on 23 September 1862; for the new king had reestablished foreign relations and had invited the missionaries to return. An English bishop, a British general, the Reverend Mr. Ellis and seven members of the London Missionary Society; a French baron, an imperial minister plenipotentiary, and several Army and Navy officers, and the Pope's priests, all gathered in Tananarive. They brought among many splendid European gifts, including a handsome Bible, a large silver vase, and a solid gold beer service—a pitcher and I do not know how many steins. And they sat down after the private Roman Catholic religious ceremony, followed by the solemn public enthronement, to a splendid banquet of a hundred coverts. The next month, Napoléon III named Jean Laborde the consul and agent of France in Tananarive, and gave him a salary of 30,000 gold francs, plus another 30,000 for expenses; 30,000 gold francs was then roughly the equivalent of 6,000 gold dollars, U.S.A.—a handsome salary in 1862, in Madagascar. On 22 November, Radama II named Clément Laborde his minister of foreign affairs.

But the Andafy-Avaratra family of the hereditary prime ministers liked none of this; they began to group the forces of reaction around them. Many of the Andriana nobles and the Hova freemen disapproved of the young king's headlong rush to change the way things had been for thirty-three years; they stood to lose their power, their feudal wealth, their tribal way of life, and their ancestral gods and fetishes. They disapproved in particular of the king's favorite, Joseph-François Lambert, Duc d'Émyrne. On 7 April 1862, back in France, Radama II's roving personal ambassador Lambert ceded his monopoly, for a good price, to a French Société Anonyme, a privately owned, limited stock company, a commercial—not a cultural or government-sponsored—enterprise, the Compagnie de Madagascar, *foncière, industrielle et commerciale,* capitalized at 50,000,000 gold French francs, with headquarters in Paris. It was already at that time an old-fashioned thing to do, an archaic exercise of capitalism. Yet Lambert sold the kingdom of Madagascar to French private interests to exploit for their own personal profit.

The British had by then found that their East India Company

(which though a private enterprise was controlled by the British
government, which owned the largest block of shares) had run its
course. The Sepoy Rebellion of 1857 proved, among other things, that
private citizens and businessmen of one country no longer could run
"native" realms, no matter how uncivilized or corrupt, for profit; thus
Victoria became Empress of India in 1877. But in France in 1863, no
one apparently found Lambert's sale of Madagascar to be questionable.
After all, in 1859, another group of private citizens had organized the
Suez Canal company, which survived almost its full contract of ninety-
nine years as a highly profitable "living fossil" (see the coelacanth);
and, in its death throes, provoked an obsolete, and doomed, punitive
invasion. So Lambert killed his friend the king.

Back in Tananarive, the Prime Minister Rainivoninahitriniony, early
in March, prepared a revolution, which broke out on 8 May 1863. The
dead queen's old lover struck at the king indirectly; he attacked the
"menamaso"—the group of young men close to Radama II, his
favorites. For he had surrounded himself with mignons as had another domineering mother and queen mother's son, Catherine de
Médicis' boy, Henri III, likewise assassinated. The king of Madagascar's favorites were, it is said, handsome and enlightened young
men, properly casted companions to the thirty-four-year-old king. His
mother had married him to a second cousin, Rabodo, some fifteen
years older than he; both had the same maternal grandmother. When
he was young, he had married, somehow or other, a slave girl, Mary,
who, to judge from her name, must have been a Christian. Thus, in
full Oedipal rebellion, Mr. Boy had broken still another taboo.

The description of the short-lived king that has come to be accepted as historic fact is that of a sentimental, weak, emotional, easily
influenced, impulsive, vacillating, self-indulgent man, a suspect, an un-
Malagasy ruler. That description cannot be called dispassionate, for
it is recorded by his victorious enemies, the king-killers; and by the
visiting British missionary and political agent, the Reverend Mr. Ellis,
a proper Victorian, upper-middle-class gentleman. To be sure, Radama
II chose his friends badly—but that act of faith is always a matter of
good or bad luck, if character is destiny. And whatever else Joseph-
François Lambert was he seems to have been a charmer; undoubtedly
he gave the prince, and then the king, the business economically,

culturally, financially, and politically; and in enlightenment, the Frenchman knew what he was doing, as the other man did not. Yet Radama II's laws and decrees give evidence that he was a good king for the two years in which he was permitted to rule. Perhaps his motivation was an unconscious reaction and revolt, as with children in the onslaught of adolescence, against his terrible mother and her arbitrary ways. It may be that the power of his office, had he lived, might have totally corrupted him. A ruler has to have the respect, the confidence, the admiration, the love, or the fear of his subjects. None of this was the case with Radama II.

There is no direct evidence of public opinion rising against him, but his death was heralded by an odd phenomenon—a sort of mass hysteria arose. It took the form of an epidemic like St. Vitus dance, a collective dance of death known as *ramanenjana*. This mysterious choreomania broke out near Ambondrombé, a mountain in the highlands where the shades of the Malagasy dead used to go to live their afterlife. From afar, the chance voyager, if he is a true believer, can see their houses and shining palaces on the mountain slopes; and sometimes he can see groups of eternally young women dancing—he can hear the music. At times of discord, he can hear the rumbling of guns. But if he runs to get closer to the vision of delight, it vanishes, and he finds himself in a forest among rocks like ruins.

The dance of 1863 began when Queen Ranavalona I's still vigorous ghost, displeased to see her son rushing headlong into reforms betraying her established traditions, decided to return to the land of the living so to put order in the house her son had inherited from her. As she went toward the gate opening out of the mountain fields, she encountered the spirit of her dead husband, Radama I; he took up a stance to bar her path. For he, unlike the Terrible, the Cruel woman between them, approved the work of his posthumous son, begotten upon her by his spirit, but not by his flesh. The father and the son were in agreement as to the reforms essential to Malagasy progress. Ranavalona proved to be more than a match for her dead husband and her living son. She did not stop, she walked through her husband's older and less substantial shade; and, on a summer night in February, 1863, her powerful spirit left the mountain in a burst of music; and accompanied by an escort of the reactionary dead in torchlight procession, she took the road for Tananarive. Thus the faithful among the living heard her approach, and all began to dance.

At the first human village under the mountain, the ghostly porters handed over the queen's *filanzana* to be shouldered by the living; hallucinated runners went ahead from village to village carrying the phantom baggage and announcing the passage of the queen's displeased ghost. So the dancing spread up and down the land. On March 26, she made her entrance into the capital. The dancing men and women looked up, wide-eyed, to see her in the steep streets. They were then struck dumb; they stood still, paralyzed, it may well be with fear—and so the dancers got their name of *ramanenjana,* "the rigid."

The queen's shade took her rightful place upon the sacred coronation stone of Mahamasina in the center of the level meeting place under the palace-citadel, the Rova of the Blue Forest. Dancing, her loyal subjects came to honor her, and to bring offerings of sugar cane and bunches of bananas. The plain filled with the possessed, who plucked their round and hollow stringed-instruments and sang while they danced until they dropped haggard, hollow-eyed, and absent. Others danced along the ridgepoles of the steep, thatched roofs, as sure-footed as somnambulists; others clave to a single spot and writhed. Some walked barefoot upon the thorny cactus plants and felt no pain. The most devoted men and women danced at night among the tombs —and saw the spirits of the recognizable dead applaud them. So she doomed her son; he joined her in death in the night of 11 May 1863. I do not know whether they went back together to the mysterious mountain of Ambondrombé.

But it is known that near the Silver Palace in the Rova, the king was set upon by Rainivoninahitriniony's, and by his brother Rainilaiarivony's, men, and strangled with the silken cord. Most of his favorites were later hunted down and transfixed by spears. After his death, his elevated widow-cousin, the new queen, ordered any dancer of the *ramanenjana* to be constrained in irons. The choreomania abruptly ceased, as though by magic.

For the energetic and victorious Andafy-Avaratra brothers of the long and honorific names declared, in the daylight of May 12, that Radama II had committed suicide when he heard of the rounding up of his *menamaso* mignons; and the brothers announced the elevation of Queen Rasoherina. Her chosen name means "the Chrysalis" and probably it makes symbolic reference to her belief that the human body is but the sheath of the immortal soul, and the pupa but the momentary and motionless stage ended when death releases the imago.

Rasoherina emerged as a queen skilled in the surface play of diplomacy; she established cordial international relations with France and Great Britain. But two weeks after her coronation of 15 September 1863, the Malagasy government formally refused to recognize Radama II's and Lambert's and, by extension, Madagascar's and France's commercial and cultural treaty of 1862. She rejected the Lambert Charter and its subsequent monopolistic French Colonial company. Joseph-François Lambert, Duc d'Émyrne, drops out of the picture at this point. Laborde stayed on as French consul and political agent. Rasoherina signed a treaty of "Peace, Friendship, and Commerce" with the representatives of the United Kingdom in 1865; and a commercial treaty with the United States in 1867. The French government, through Jean Laborde, the consul, protested the abrogation of the nefarious Lambert's charter and subsequent arrangements with the dead king, and proceeded in a high and mighty manner; a Great Power then brought its full military, naval, and diplomatic pressure to bear on the small powers in its way; it was the thing to do; it was the only thing the natives understood. France demanded an indemnity for breach of contract to be paid by the Malagasy Merina monarchy to the French private citizens, the businessmen, bankers, and investors who had bought up Lambert's monopoly and made of it the anonymous and private Compagnie de Madagascar.

On 31 August 1865, the year the American Civil War ended, Rasoherina and the Andafy-Avaratra brothers paid up. If I ever knew how much cash changed hands, I've forgot. In the statistical light of today's national debts, loans, gifts, conscience money, blackmail, and grants in aid, the sum paid out was at once much too much, and derisory. Queen Rasoherina contributed half the amount from her private fortune—a fact that informs us that Queen Ranavalona the Terrible, however disastrous she may have been as a ruler, was astute enough to enrich herself and her family throughout the years of her long reign.

In December, 1865, the original Lambert Charter was taken from the Merina state archives and burned in the presence of the government officials and the court dignitaries; and the British came back to the fore as the dominant foreigners in Madagascar. Two missionary-architects, James Cameron and William Poole, were asked to build the queen a new residence in the Rova; they began work on 25 April 1865. *Manimpisoa*—"a Blossoming of Beauty," or "Beauty's Increment," as the palace was named—still exists; it is a charming Victorian cottage two stories high, made of wood, its gables and verandah porches trimmed with gingerbread fretwork like crochet lace. Architecturally indefensible—a confusion of fluted wooden pilasters, Ionic and Corinthian capitals, a steep Malagasy pitched roof, and marvelously inlaid parquet floors of ebony, rosewood, pallisander, and some sort of hard and yellow wood—it is a thoroughly delightful, a very badly planned house. A pavilion of the museum now, it is jam-packed with trivial bits and pieces—glass as well as real semi-precious jewelry, nicknacks, worn ceremonial finery, swords and spears, a crown or two, bric-a-brac, mementoes, leftovers, portraits, souvenirs, curios, and those puzzling objets d'art and de virtu given by distant European sovereigns at state occasions. It all makes a charming display.

Rasoherina reveals herself as a pleasant woman. For example, she insisted that no lock be fixed to any door of her palace. She was superstitious in a nice way; and, wanting to live happily among friends, she made her British Christian missionary architects avoid all dimensions containing either of the numbers six or eight, because the word for six—*enina*—is rooted in the verb *manenina,* which means "to be sorry," or "to repent"; and the word for eight—*valo*—rhymes with *fahvalo,* which means "enemy." As she built her palace in the Rova, Queen Rasoherina consulted her mother before she made any decision; the royal women went together to select the lumber and the planks for the framework and the inlaid floors. Together they consulted the sorcerers to choose the lucky day favorable to begin any new piece of work. Rasoherina, then, was as mother-ridden as her dead husband had been, but less disastrously. How old was she? Fifteen years senior to Radama II, she was forty-nine when crowned, and fifty-four or -five when she died.

The great event of her five-year reign was the accession to total power of Rainilaiarivony, the last of the prime ministers, the brother of the one before, with whom he clashed, and whom he overthrew; and the son of the founder of the Andafy-Avaratra dynasty. Rainilaiarivony—"the Father of the One Who Has the Flower"—was, indeed, a queen-maker; he selected, elevated, and married the last three, beginning with Rasoherina, whom he married in open secret. To do so, he divorced his Hova wife, the mother of his sixteen children—the first son among them, I suppose, being the one who had the flower. I do not know what sort. None of the queens bore him a child. There is no evidence that the prime minister-consort, of the Hova caste, and thus not eligible for crowning, was a husband in more than name only. But he was after real power, and so, who knows?

Otherwise, not much notable took place in Rasoherina's short reign, except that she made a royal progress from Tananarive to Andevoranto, down on the eastern shore. She left on 20 June 1867 in the cool season, and took along an escort of 12,000 men as bodyguards, as well as a mobile court of at least 60,000 ladies and gentlemen in waiting, friends, relatives, attendants, servants, suppliers, camp followers, and hangers on. Jean Laborde went, too. The queen returned to Tananarive on 6 October; more than 10,000 men died as a direct result of the excursion, but an enthusiastic crowd of highlanders gathered to welcome her home.

The queen began to fail in health two months later in December; on 24 January 1868, she was "mysteriously" transported from Tananarive to the holy royal town of Ambohimanga, and then to the prime minister's country residence at Amboditsiry; there would be nothing remarkable about any of this moving about—after all, they were husband and wife—if a plot had not been brewing since June to unseat the queen and get rid of the prime minister. The coup d'état failed on 27 March 1868; the conspirators had wanted to break the prime minister's power, and to elevate a royal Merina man to be a proper king of Madagascar.

On the first of April, Rasoherina died; on the second of April, Rainilaiarivony elevated her cousin to the throne as Ranavalona II; and he married her. Rasoherina had been baptized into the Roman Catholic faith on her deadbed, on April Fool's Day. Jean Laborde sponsored her; he was her godfather.

On 28 January 1869, the prime minister and his second queen were baptized by a Malagasy, Pastor Andriambelo, into the Anglican Protestant Episcopal religion—and thus the prime minister set the pattern for his future foreign policy. He played no favorites; instead, he set the French against the British, and thus tried to balance the two encroaching powers. At the end of July, the queen laid the cornerstone of the royal chapel in the Rova; on 3 September, the Protestant Episcopal Church of England was made the official state religion of the brand-new Christian country.

It is not known what Ranavalona II thought about all this. As the Princess Ramona, she had been a minor royalty all her life—the second cousin of Rasoherina, the granddaughter of Ranavalona I's mother, and thus a first cousin once removed of the terrible queen, third cousin twice removed of Radama I, second cousin of Radama II—all on the distaff side. When unexpectedly raised to the throne, she was a portly valetudinarian aged thirty, apt to give no trouble to anyone if allowed to enjoy ill-health in peace.

So then the queen and her premier brought out the royal family's fetishes and burned them in an educational display to show the Malagasy people that the old time religion had had its day. From then on, there was a time of ecclesiastical construction. Today perhaps one-third of the Malagasy people are, at least nominally, Christians; and of this approximate 1,666,667 men and women, about half are Roman Catholics, and the other half Protestants—Lutherans, Methodists, Episcopalians, French Calvinists, and a few Quakers and Seventh Day Adventists; and possibly a few Jehovah's Witnesses and Latter Day Saints.

The various missionaries got together and made peace by dividing up the island into spheres of influence, the Protestant overlay superimposed upon the Catholic, or vice versa. Thus the various Catholic orders—the Jesuits, the White Fathers, the Marists, the Lazarists, the Dominicans, the Franciscans, the Fathers of Our Lady de la Salette, and the various nuns, have their separate geographical allotments; so do the aforementioned Protestant sects. It is not known how deep these variations of Christianity have penetrated into the Malagasy tribal unconscious—or, indeed, the conscious intellect. However, the Protestants all sing the good old hymns, in translations, but not very often in harmony, and the Catholics cross themselves and genuflect. Sorcerers and witch doctors, however, still do a thriving business.

Yet progress indeed was on its way in. On 2 October 1874, Ranavalona II freed all the Negro slaves imported from Mozambique since 1865, in which year, by means of the treaty with England, her predecessor had once again stopped the exportation of Malagasy slaves. In consequence of their various treaties with Radama I, when the slave trade was first outlawed, the British had paid the king an annual "equivalent" in money and gifts to replace his lost revenue from the sale of human merchandise; this time no new "equivalent" seemed necessary. To be sure, neither the queen, a member of the royal clan of the noble caste, nor the prime minister, a member of the free caste of Hova, then went ahead to free the Andevo caste of serfs, nor the Mainty slaves. These bondsmen had to wait until 1896, the year of the French conquest and annexation.

To stave off just such an invasion, already in view in 1876, the prime minister brought in British and French military advisers and instructors to try to inculcate proper European discipline in the wild and naked conscripts of the Malagasy standing army. Two years later, he established a sort of militia to police the towns and to keep the peace in the provinces harassed by cattle rustlers and other thieves. To this day among the Bara tribe, the young men must "prove" and demonstrate their virility by stealing at least one head of cattle before the girls will agree to marriage.

But the most notable event of the reign of this hypochondriac, dipsomaniac queen was the death, in 1878, two days after Christmas, of Jean Laborde. He died in his Tananarive townhouse of dysentery and a disease of the bladder, in his seventy-fourth year. In that last year of his life, the French bureaucracy in Paris had treated him shabbily. He had been scrapped as French consul, perhaps not out of personal spite with malicious intent, but as a result of his being associated with the Second Empire and with Napoléon III's pretentious failures.

The chief reason for Laborde's replacement, however, must have been the obvious fact that he was a friend of Madagascar and of the Malagasy; and, having lived constantly on the island (save for the four years of enforced exile on Réunion nearby) for forty-seven years, he no longer represented France and the French way of life. He had loved Madagascar and—it may be, when he was young—the fearful first queen. He had married a Malagasy *métisse* (it is true, he had divorced her); he had begotten and raised his son to be a Malagasy—even though the boy was predominantly French by reason of blood. Thus Jean Laborde no longer could be said to have the best interests of France, and of the new French Third Republican government, uppermost in mind and heart. He was suspect; he was found guilty of and by his long associations.

The French army and the French politicians of Paris had begun to make plans inimical to the Merina dynasty, to Malagasy independence, and to the old-fashioned, out-of-date Frenchmen, those who believed in the ideas and the ideals of the French Revolution of 1789, and the French First Republic. So, without warning, Jean Laborde, on the morning of 7 November 1877, had opened a dispatch and had read that he was herewith summarily retired as the consul and agent of France in the kingdom of Madagascar. The Grand Frenchman had been dismissed as of no further use to his native land.

Then Laborde died. Once dead, he was—or rather, his material possessions were—found to be of the greatest possible value to the Colonial and military functions of French politics. When he died, Laborde was found to have been a rich man, richer than any other Frenchman of Madagascar has ever been. It is impossible to estimate his wealth in the equivalent values of, say, 1960. But in 1878, he left 1,138,600 gold French francs in cash on deposit in Madagascar. Laborde owned several houses and estates all of which were equipped with fine nineteenth-century furnishings (the Louis-Philippe armchairs and settees of the townhouse salon now serve the presbytery of the Roman Catholic cathedral in Tananarive); he had quantities of solid silver knives, forks, spoons, and services, porcelains, crystal, napery, carpets, chandeliers, mirrors, ornaments, draperies, chairs, tables, beds, chests-of-drawers and wardrobes full of a great many full-dress uniforms. His experimental farms were stocked with prize French stock as well, cross-bred, and zebu cattle. He owned orchards in full production, as well as sugar plantations, distilleries, workshops, factories, and slaves. He held great land concessions, he owned whole jungles of rare hardwood, and square miles of mineral deposits with their working mines. There is no way to arrive at a statement of his wealth.

Rainilaiarivony and Queen Ranavalona II promptly confiscated the Laborde fortune—the cash, the personal possessions, and the real estate. The Merina government denied the validity and the legality of the testament. The prime minister based his action on the traditional Malagasy law that the entire island of Madagascar belonged to the queen, who could assign territory as concessions to individual Malagasy or foreigners for use during the lifetime of the tenants; but not even the queen could give these holdings to her subjects or to any outlander to own outright. Thus each man and woman in Madagascar had but a life interest in the land. Heirs did not exist; they had no rights. The French, to whom possessions are almost sacred, were outraged.

The prime minister was a wily man. Swollen with his own brand of small-minded acumen, he miscalculated both his own strength and the French weakness. He might have got away with his claim to the Laborde mineral concessions, plantations, and other real estate; but neither the queen nor the government had any right to the money and the personal possessions; indeed, a strong case could have been made for Laborde's right to own, and thus to leave to his heirs, the houses built upon the land he had been granted, and that undoubtedly he had improved.

In any case, the French government, still rankled by abrogation of the Lambert Charter, took up the cause of Jean Laborde's will. The Army and the Navy sent a show of force, which, by 1883, turned into the first Franco-Hova war and, in 1885, the French Protectorate (although it was never called such) of Madagascar. Jean Laborde, once dead, served as a reason to resurrect the French claim to "Oriental France."

The alcoholic Queen Ranavalona II died on 13 July 1883, aged only about forty-five. In her official portrait, she looks like a stout party, exceedingly overdressed in robes of state far too heavy for the island's mild highland climate. Pale of skin, she had lovely, fine-fingered, small and delicate hands, with which, apparently, she had lifted up far too many brimming cups. Of what? Rum, most likely—but perhaps of cognac and Scotch whiskey, too, imported in trade agreements with the two contending powers. France and Great Britain at that time were rapidly coming to terms on the convulsive land grasp of unclaimed Africa.

1. ABOVE: King Radama I, the good king with the tragic flaw.

2. ABOVE: Rainiarilarivony, powerful prime minister for three queens.

3. BELOW: Queen Rasoherina, who would have no locks on the palace doors.

4. BELOW: Queen Ranavalona III who died in exile.

5. ABOVE: Fort Dauphin: beyond the radioactive sands and the shark-infested sea lies the south pole.

6. BELOW: The French call this granite rock "La Brioche," as in "Let them eat cake."

7. ABOVE: In the southern highlands, on a summer day in January.

8. BELOW: Diégo-Suarez, a red port on a blue bay.

11. Nosy-Bé: Peppercorns in cluster.

9. Antalaha: Green beans on the vanilla orchid vine.

10. Antalaha: First quality vanilla beans, cured, bundled, ready for sale.

12. Mole 4, Tamatave, the chief port.

13. Planting rice in the highland valley of Betafo, in January.

14. A Sakalava singer, Belo-sur-Tsiribihina.

15. A Betsileo rice farmer, near Fianarantsoa.

16. A Vezo fisherman, off Morondava.

17. A Betsimisaraka in vanilla, in Antalaha.

18. A Sakalava matron, of Nosy-Bé.

19. Mahafaly housewives in American housedresses, fetching water from a spring on the flamingoed beach of the Bay of St. Augustine.

20. TOP RIGHT: Majunga—the old streets give way to the town planners.

21. MIDDLE RIGHT: Ranohira—high noon in the Horombé.

22. BOTTOM RIGHT: Ambalavao—"Newtown," built of early 19th century red bricks.

23. BELOW: Tananarive, February flowers in the Zoma.

24. Tananarive: The Queen's Palace, where once a blue forest grew.

25. BELOW LEFT: Ilafy: a wooden pleasure house for Radama II.

26. BELOW, RIGHT: The Highlands: a one-family house designed by Jean Laborde.

27. BELOW: Fianarantsoa: bucranes of wrought iron and gilt on the doors of the Palais de Justice.

28. RIGHT: A Betsileo cenotaph, monoliths and zebu horns.

Tananarive, town house, *c.* 1900.

30. Ampanihy, country house, *c.* 1960.

31. ABOVE: Near Morondava, on a sand dune, the tombs of the Vezo kings.

32. BELOW LEFT: At Ankirondro on the Tsiribiniha, the portrait of a Sakalava queen standing on her grave.

33. BELOW RIGHT: Inland from Fort Dauphin, a boatload of Antanosy on an anecdotal, biographical tomb post.

34. ABOVE: In the Taboo Forest of the tombs of the Mahafaly kings and queens, *Aloalo*—tomb posts, soul perches.

35. BELOW: Ambatolamphy—a Merina "cold house," the long-term residence of mummified ancestors.

36. ABOVE: Didiera trees in a forest of euphorbias.

38. BELOW: A baobab, the big-bellied mother of the forest.

37. BELOW: A tamarind in Belo-sur-Tsiribiniha.

39. ABOVE: Ampanihy—a kid in the cattle
    market, one Easter.

40. LEFT: A *Lemur catta* in the zoo
    of Tsimbazaza.

41. BELOW: A chameleon on a fence
    in Majunga.

42. LEFT: Colbert, Louis XIV's great minister of commerce.

43. RIGHT: Gallieni, the greatest of all the men of Madagascar.

44. LEFT: Jean Laborde, the universal man.

45. ABOVE: One of the martyrs, Dr. Raseta, on the left, arrested in France.

46. Mr. Philibert Tsiranana, first President of the Malagasy Republic.

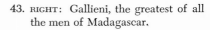

When his second queen died, Rainilaiarivony had already made his choice. For his third and last queen, he chose his dead wife's great-niece, the Princess Razafindrahety, who was also her fourth cousin, once removed. In succession, the princess's mother was next in line; but the prime minister liked young women. So Ranavalona III, who had to marry the man who elevated her to the throne, and who was younger than all but the youngest of his sixteen children, was crowned on her twenty-second birthday, the 22nd of November, 1883. The prime minister was fifty-nine.

The new queen was a fragile little thing, not more than five feet tall, and, from her royal portrait, not a happy bride. At her coronation, she wore a magnificent royal garnet red velvet mantle, lined with ermine and charged with heavy gold embroidery in designs of crowns and ears of rice ripe for the harvest. It was a French creation from the Maison de Haute Couture, Lemoine, in the Boulevard de Capucines, Paris, France; it was made to order and sent by the future President of France and his wife, M. and Mme. Sadi Carnot (he was assassinated by an anarchist in 1894). Ranavalona III was frightened of her much-married old husband; and on the whole, she was much relieved when, a dozen years later, the French invaders deposed him and sent him into exile in Algiers. She hoped she did not have to marry his complaisant replacement, the new Prime Minister Rainitsimbazafy, an even older old man. The French, victorious, did not insist upon it.

From the start, things went bad in Ranavalona III's reign. Her husband thought he could keep up his successful double-dealing, but he could not. He lost the first Franco-Hova war in 1885; and his wife was forced to cede Diégo-Suarez and the northern coast to France. To be sure, the newly established French bank in Madagascar, the Comptoir National d'Escompts de Paris, immediately lent the Merina monarchy 15,000,000 francs to pay off the debt. The rest went to settle most of the other costs of war. The prime minister was made to pay 560,000 gold francs to Jean Laborde's two nephews, a settlement that in itself admitted the royal contention that the dead and gone Grand Frenchman had had no right to will the Malagasy land that he had worked for his lifetime to any heir.

Even so, Rainilaiarivony, like the Restoration Bourbons, had forgotten nothing and had learned nothing from the experience. In his blind and idiotic refusal to face facts, he brought on the 1895 invasion and conquest. After thirty-one years in power, the old man's government fell on 15 October 1895. He died on 17 July 1896, aged seventy-two, in Algiers, where he had lived briefly in princely exile in the Villa des Roses, in the Mustapha Supérieur quarter, attended by his grandson Ratelifera. On 4 October 1900, his remains were brought to Tananarive and ceremoniously deposited in the monumental family tomb under its curiously phallic pillar. The then Governor-General Gallieni made the funeral oration.

Gallieni, another truly great Frenchman of the nineteenth century, took the occasion to make French propaganda of the dead old man's entombment. In his speech, he tried to show the Malagasy how much better off they were living as they then did in a colony of the democratic French empire. He began by quoting a Malagasy proverb: *"Tsy mety miady amam-paty,"* which translates "Don't argue with a dead man," or perhaps "Don't whip a dead horse." The Merina monarchy survived the death in exile of the Father of the One Who Has the Flower, in the Villa des Roses, by less than seven months.

To judge by the prime minister's ceremonial court-dress, and by the wardrobe of embroidered uniforms that have survived him, Rainilaiarivony ("Ray-nee-lay-ar-ee-voon" no accent) was a dapper little, self-important man, as preposterous as any man in history anywhere, at any time. Small and small-minded, he moved in a fantasy of total power; and he lost his grip on reality in the delusion that he was the one and only right man at the right time in the right place: on high. So he had, perforce, to surround himself with a buffering of yes-men who, in their natural function, concealed the corruption, the wet rot, the dry rot, and the fertile, secret growths that go on in the thin shadow of an aged dictator, who holds ceremoniously still.

The old man had but one political maneuver in his diplomatic relations, both defensive and offensive, with the encroaching Colonial powers; it worked for a while, and then it ceased to work. It was a policy of brinkmanship. He lived in a perpetual crisis of threatening European invasion; and so he played one power off against the other. First he gave a bit to the British; then he yielded a fraction to the French; always he had no intention to fulfill the agreements or the terms of the treaties enforced upon him. He played his weakness into a semblance of strength that, even in those days before radio, wireless telegraphy, and the international telephone (he had allowed one wire to be strung between Tananarive and Tamatave, but it was at best an uncertain means of Morse-code communications) fooled nobody but himself. Yet he got away with it at first; then, having no way to imagine what the great outside world was like, soon he found himself caught in his own trap. There was no way out except into the clouds of delusion. So, high in place on top of the hill in the Blue Forest, he denied the existence of the devil, and closed his eyes to the deep blue sea lying below his closed horizons.

To the French resident and to the British envoys, he went on saying "It may be," and "Perhaps." He never said "No!" He would never say "Yes." It was always, "I shall think about it, or "We shall see." Or "I shall consult Her Majesty the Queen, and let you know her decision tomorrow," and tomorrow. Then he went off to look into the mirror, perhaps because such a glass reflects the man against his past, and therefore makes an excellent screen against the future. In a mirror a man is able to delude himself for all time—if such is what he is looking for.

To do him justice, the prime minister must have been a handsome young man. From his portraits, it becomes clear that he was especially proud of his thick, gently curling, dark and lustrous head of hair, cut, trimmed, brushed and combed to perfection. He had wide-open, almond-shaped eyes, a straight nose, and a thick moustache. He had an oval face and a slim, trim body. Like all dictators and like the most successful leaders, he had a strong sense of the dramatic and the symbolic act, and he was vain. When he was displeased, he made a show of it. He did his paper work—heard or read reports—in a small office of Rasoherina's playhouse palace, in the mornings; then he emerged to give his orders to his "government" officials. When he decided the time was ripe for an angry scene, he used to put on a bright red dressing-gown; it came to be the symbol of his personal, initimate, and absolute rule; it was an appropriate uniform for the queen's Official Lover and morganatic husband. According to the label on the glass case in the museum of the Queen's Palace, where this red robe is on display. when he came out of his office in his special dressing-gown it was a sign that "Rainilaiarivony was going to shout and storm about."

This man was born on a Thursday in 1824; and had things gone on then as they traditionally should have, as soon as he was born the infant boy would have been exposed—put down in the hoof-marked dirt in front of the gate to the cattle corral, so that when the zebu herd was released through the high red adobe walls to get pasture, their cloven hoofs would have decided his fate. For he was born on a *fady*, a taboo day. A Thursday child is unlucky; he brings disaster to his family and his people if he is allowed to live on un-exposed to the decision of the cattle hoofs. Most such babies were crushed to death; the few over and around whom the bulls, the cows, and the calves stepped were purified of malevolence—marked out as worthy of the ancestral gods. The future prime minister escaped this test because when he was born, in the enlightened reign of Radama I, the practice had fallen momentarily into abeyance. So, according to his own reactionary and traditional thinking and believing, the baby, father to the man, survived against the rules—to live to destroy the Merina monarch and Malagasy independence. Radama I, then, by forbidding the *fady* ritual of infanticide four years before this little man was born, proved (it may be) that enlightenment is wrong, and that the dark forces of the unknown are right.

So the 103 years of the rule of the Merina dynasty of kings and queens ended at one o'clock, at thirteen hours, on 28 February 1897 (it was a leap year), when Governor-General Joseph-Simon Gallieni, the Pacificator, more famous for his taxis of the Marne, sent Rana-valona III into exile in Algiers, Algeria, with a suite of royal relatives, where she is still remembered as a charming and popular little person. She loved the scent of white heliotrope, and was particular about her style of dress—French high style, fashions from Worth, of Paris.

Her predecessor and great-aunt, Ranavalona II, the Valetudinarian, the Sot, found herself the easiest way to enjoy royal ill-health. *Her* predecessor and distant cousin, Rasoherina, "the Chrysalis," the widow of a strangled Mamma's Boy fifteen years her junior, the first queen-wife of the hithertofore hereditary Lover *en Titre*, the queen-maker Rainilaiarivony, had died mysteriously as a coup d'état broke out and failed. Radama II, the good androgene, had been seduced by his admiration of things French in the person of Joseph-François Lambert, an adventurer and businessman—and the king died violently as an extended result. His mother, from whose place among her sheltering petticoats he had revolted, Ranavalona I, the Terrible, the Cruel, had killed or caused the deaths of—it is said—roughly a million of her subjects, half the island's guessed-at population, in her thirty-three-year reign of terror. But she had, it may be, loved, and certainly sponsored Jean Laborde, the Grand Frenchman, a good man, a castaway. Radama I the Great died young by his own hand—he slit his throat in *delirium tremens*, because he was not, by nature, the *masiaka* king his father had tried to make him by teaching him bad habits. The first of them, the father of his country, the Seignior Worthy of the Highlands of the Wide Horizons. Andrianampoinimerina, the Conqueror, was all that—terrible, awe-inspiring, just, powerful, and mighty —and more, he was a wise Merina tribal chieftain.

The images, attributes, and old clothes of all these royal men and women are now on suitable display in the rooms of the palaces of the Rova on top of Tananarive. In the basement, under the throne room of the Palace of the Queen-Museum, *Manjakamiadana* by name, "Where It Is Easy to Reign," are displayed the rearticulated, mounted, sub-fossil bones of that native, endemic, and unique Malagasy struthious bird, the flightless aepyornis, the biggest bird on earth, that, in recent times, until the swamps dried up, or until the earliest arrivals on Madagascar, a once desert island, hunted it down to eat its gigantic drumsticks, bigger than an average modern man, used to lay eggs that still are to be found—a specimen is in the Field Museum in Chicago. They held as much meat as a two-gallon demijohn, or *dame jeanne*, or Lady Jane, holds any sort of liquid. The ratite Malagasy bird is now extinct, but noteworthy, as are the little, light-brown royalties, burnt up in the bright, hot, gem-like flame of nineteenth-century French glory.

Gallieni; The Queen's Bath; Bastille Day

In the Merina highlands, there were a thousand towns grouped around Analamanga, "the Blue Forest" on top of the hill, now the High Town of Tananarive. In the woods orchids clung to the bark of the trees, and great spiders sat in their webs spun among the branches, where some birds sang, and some birds worked. In the spring of the year, red "cardinals," small weaver-birds, flew busily about in their best-dressed plumage. They still do. Once mated, the males change to a neat suit of serviceable grey, and they get down to work to weave their well constructed nests. The *Foudia madagascariensis* of the *Ploceus* family like town life.

There are three hundred kinds of birds in Madagascar grouped in fifty-nine families: pigeons and doves, hawks and falcons, many sorts of duck, guinea fowl, quail, partridge, cocks-of-the-forest, parakeets, flamingoes, cuckoos, king-fishers, crested hoopoes, swallows, black-birds, larks, and the various herons, some blue, some white, some brown. Most of the birds have left the Blue Forest and the nearer towns under the hill as the spreading city has absorbed the villages although their names remain as quarters and districts of the capital.

One such is Ambohimitsimbina, which means "Be Careful Here." Once it was a last stop, and often a place of respite and release, for prisoners coming from torture and going toward death. What is to be made of the chosen means of execution in those tribal days? The condemned Malagasy was thrown from a high place, over the cliff,

214

down onto the jagged rocks below. "Be Careful Here"—await in dignity for death, or for reprieve, or for pardon—is now a charming residential quarter, tree-shaded and flowery; it affords a great, wide view of fertile rice fields in a green plain ringed by purple mountains; but the pretty villas stand on the same edge of the cliff.

Further along is Ambohipotsy, "the White Quarter," named for the bleached bones of those who did not escape the spears of the executioners, nor the rocks below; carrion crows ate their flesh. The place has been cleaned up; from on high, there is a fine view of Anosy, "the Island Lake," with the 1914–1918 Franco-Malagasy war memorial standing on the island among bougainvillaea vines and jacaranda trees. Beyond, in abandoned rice patches being filled with red earth, the new buildings for parliament and the government of the Malagasy Republic are to arise. At the bottom of the cliff, already a race track and a football stadium have been built. On the other slope there is a steep step-street called Tsiofakantitra, which means "the Old Can't Make It." And above the little lake there is a very good address called Isorakaka—"Out of Breath."

Many other quarters take their names from rocks: Ambatonakanga, "Guinea-fowl Rock"; Ambatomena, "Red Rock"; Ambatovinaky, "Cleft Rock"; Ambatomitsangana, "Standing Rock"—a kind of menhir. The temporary quarters of the Houses of Parliament, in buildings left over from a fair, stand beside the botanical gardens and the zoo. The small, deep lake in the middle of the hilly park is called Tsimbazaza, "Not For Children."

Antaninandro means "Out in the Full Sunlight." Anakely means "In the Grove" and it lies at the bottom of a narrow valley; it is the central marketplace to which a pair of opposite step streets descend, or ascend; one is named for Lambert, the other for de Lastelle. The days of the Malagasy week, named from the Arabic (and beginning with Sunday) are *Alahady, Alatsinainy, Atalata, Alarobia, Alakamisy, Zoma* and *Asabotsy;* and Friday has always been Tananarive's market day, although the Zoma operates every day today.

The Zoma is the prettiest sight of the city. From above in the shady park of the Place Colbert, it is a pleasure to look down at the triangular market with the red-brown, high-peaked tile roofs of the permanent stalls—for dairy products, meats, fish, poultry, drygoods, and handicrafts—surrounded by rows of white octagonal parasols, as big as tents, shading the displays of bright vegetables, fruits and flowers. The French health authorities saw to it that the Zoma was kept clean; nobody was allowed to sleep there or to spit there; all of it was hosed down and scrubbed at night.

On Fridays, the Zoma overflows its triangle to run down both sides of the wide Avenue de la Liberation; there, under the arcades and out on the parks, cheerful Malagasy women offer their embroidered and lace-encrusted napery and bed linen—delightful nineteenth-century needlework taught them by the British and the French missionary ladies and nuns. Others make displays of woven stuffs—baskets, boxes, hats, bags, mats—of many intricate designs in straw, raffia, reeds, split palm-fronds, some colored, some left plain. In the bargaining, the matrons and the matriarchs sing a three-note negative; but they smile as they come to terms. An important tablecloth with a dozen napkins of Belgian, Irish, or French linen and much fine lace costs $100 and more.

I was on my way to "the Blue Hill," Ambohimanga, the birthplace of the Merina kings and queens, a royal country town; it was a clear, cool autumn day. The road took me through flooded fields, sheets of water carpeted with water hyacinths, most beautiful with round green leaves and upright spikes of misty lilac bloom, all gently rippling and sparkling with a life of their own. It is a noxious life and an indomitable weed. *Eichhornia crassipes*, native to northern South America, here escaped from ornamental garden ponds to invade the warm waters of the world. The pretty aquatic plant chokes the rivers and the ponds, kills the fish, breeds insects, and destroys the rice.

But in Madagascar, some good has come of the invasion and takeover. The humped cattle have learned amphibious ways; they wade out, belly deep, and deeper, halfway under, they browse on the floating green salad. The zebu have ticks. The submerged ticks crawl up above the water line. White herons, *Bulbulcus ibis*, fly out and come down to perch on the brown cows' ridged backs. They pick off and eat up the ticks, and that is why they are called *pique-boeufs*, or tick-birds.

I left the rippling pasture sparkling in the sun and drove into dry highland scenery to stop and park outside the stone walls surrounding

Ambohimanga, a royal village set upon a moated hill. The portal is framed by crudely rectified monoliths, one stone to either side with another for a lintel, as simple as pi—or, rather, two pis—set in the thickness of the ramparts, back to back. Between them is a grooved space for the gate itself, which does not slide but rolls to close the way. For the door is another monolith, a thick disc like a rough millstone standing on edge—a rolling stone that has gathered if not moss, then grey and orange lichens, since Governor-General Gallieni abolished the monarchy and exiled the last queen on February 28, 1897.

The unimproved royal road spirals through the pretty country village to come to a dead-end on top of the flattened hill before the gate on the massive stone walls of the Rova. Inside the royal enclosure, the neglected summer cottages of the queens still perch on the solid mansonry of terraces, sunken gardens, and pit-like courtyards, some bridged, some planted with arched allées of giant ficus trees of a sort reserved to cast thick shade on kings and queens. The neglected flowerbeds are now overgrown with tremendous poinsettias, crimson and velvety in May and June. The *Euphorbia* (Poinsettia) *pulcherrima* was introduced so many years ago from its native Mexico that the Malagasy, mistakingly taking it to be indigenous, call it *Euphorbia madagascariensis*, and have made it the national flower.

On the ramparts and retaining walls, the flimsy pavilions, giving way to rot, were built to the queen's taste, which was late Victorian. Her chamber is furnished with a matching bedroom set of carved black walnut, like great-grandmother's bridal suite, bow-legged tables, marbled-topped, and all. The figured wallpaper has come loose from the damp wall; the looped and fringed silken draperies hang in shreds. But from the many-paned high windows, her view is still wide and free over highland hills and dales, with Tananarive in the distance, fifteen miles away. She had no proper bathroom, to be sure.

But all the Merina kings and queens took an annual ceremonial bath in a corner of the throne room. There in the presence of the court and the tribe, the living monarch was washed in holy water as in a communion, perhaps to establish the body of the king or the queen as the spiritual abode of all the divine ancestors, and thus worthy of the fealty of the tribe.

The Great Red Island

General Governor-General Joseph-Simon Gallieni suppressed this national and mystical rite on 5 March 1897, five days after he had sent the last queen into exile. He then imposed upon the conquered and annexed Malagasy people, to serve in its place, the French National Festival of the 14th of July, in commemoration of the taking of the Bastille in 1789, and the end of despotism. In doing so, Gallieni acted like a tyrant as absolute as any Bourbon; but his benevolent purpose was to bring peace and order to the new colony.

Gallieni was the greatest of all the men of Madagascar, and the most inaccessible. He did more for France and for the Malagasy than any other of the island rulers. I find it almost impossible to understand the man. He and his life are crystal clear; yet like a crystal dropped into pure water, he vanishes inside his work. There is no way to separate him from his achievement. He was a professional soldier; he used his uniform to its purpose—as a covering to obliterate the private personality; as work clothing identifying the wearer with the work. He was as anonymous as he could be among a race of individuals. Khaki is the color of dirt; in India it means dust and dusty. Horizon blue absorbs a man in a perspective. Even military full-dress, which can be gaudy, is designed to fit the man to an idea and an ideal, such as glory and grandeur, and not primarily to enhance the private person of the wearer.

The French love glory; the French prize grandeur. As a nation, they adore logic as they venerate reason. French culture is man-sized, as French civilization releases the whole man's virtues. The French are proud of their soldiers; they honor their heroes; they respect individual human beings. But how the French hate and suspect the pure, the austere, the incorruptible, the puritan, the man who, in self-control and in self-discipline, lives his life wholly according to his own chosen values and standards—the man whose self-imposed conditions do not include self-indulgence in the various human faults and failings.

Gallieni was such a man. He knew what power was, and he used it impeccably—as a tool to secure Madagascar, a colony achieved after 254 years of fitful, petty effort. Having pacified and organized the island, for France, he relinquished power and he went away, free of it. The French found his integrity abnormal. Five years dead and buried, belatedly he was elevated to the august company of the French marshals. In 1960, for reasons not made public, his completed statue was not placed in a niche in the row of other great French soldiers in the Napoleonic façade of the Louvre along the rue de Rivoli.

Yet Gallieni was a great Frenchman and a great French general in the great French tradition. A nineteenth-century rationalist who lived according to the dictates of his mind, he ruled himself; and the French did not take to him. Unlike his disciple, Marshal Louis-Hubert Lyautey of Morocco, who learned his trade in Madagascar, Gallieni refused to make use of public relations to fire the popular imagination. His remote and chill integrity bored them. Some of the French—the venal politicians and businessmen—hated him, and knifed him in the back, because he was inviolable. He put up with them; it was part of his job. But he did not give in.

The *grandes dames,* the elegant hostesses of Paris (whom, it is true, he scorned when they set out to lionize him at the dinner table) despised him—for these ladies love to think that momentous affairs of state arrange themselves around their boards or in their beds. Others, the bureaucrats, destroyed his work, when, in their daily paperwork, they lost sight of his goals.

The year after the conquest, Gallieni had to be called in to save the chaotic situation in Madagascar. He did so; he brought imaginative common sense to bear; and with the help of a handful of young French officers, whom he had formed, and with six hundred professionals of his "beloved" Foreign Legion, he saved the island for the French empire, if not for the French people.

What was he like? It is hard to say. In studio portraits, buttoned and hooked and belted in a tight uniform, he appears to have been a thin, flat-bellied and flat-backed man, with a force of will more robust than this physique. He was not handsome. He had plenty of chin. His mouth was half-obscured by a thick moustache, by no means chic. His nose was longer than need be—even to support the ridiculous pince-nez that may have clarified his vision, but certainly hid his eyes; his ears were large; his forehead high and clear. Surely he wore steel-rimmed spectacles hooked in place in the field. A second lieutenant in the Franco-Prussian War of 1870–1871; a first lieutenant on the island of Réunion in 1874; a captain and a major in Senegal and the French

Sudan in 1876 and 1883, and in Martinique where he was commanding officer; a lieutenant-colonel in French West Africa in 1886; a full colonel in the mountains of Tonkin in 1892; a general in 1896 and the first governor-general of Madagascar from 1897 until 1905; Gallieni was a Marine.

Not a headquarters man, he was a field officer, not a conniver; and yet he got his promotions regularly, according to the slow advancements of those days. His men found him to be good company in the mess. In him, they knew they had an officer they could trust. He assigned each of his subordinates a job of work to do; and then Gallieni left them free to do as they thought best—and he backed them up. He asked of his men only the best that they could do. Of himself, he asked perfection. Lyautey described him as a masterly leader, a large-minded, understanding man, both intelligent and forceful. "He never for a moment loses sight of the over-all idea; life takes on a joyful meaning in this man's company." Gallieni once remarked, "*Moi,* I do not believe in great men." He did not consider himself to be essential. And from his residence in Tananarive, on 6 February 1889, he wrote, "No man is indispensible"—although in that same letter he asked for dedicated and gifted men to be sent out to Madagascar as colonists.

An intellectual man of action, this vegetarian Marine, who drank water, once remarked that in his life, "*Je n'ai jamais été ému.*" He had a wife, a daughter, and a son; he knew great moments in the history of France. What could he have been talking about? He said, in translation, "I have never been moved by the emotions." He read John Stuart Mill, Charles Darwin, and Herbert Spencer; with them, he was a nineteenth-century Rationalist. Perhaps he meant that he had never felt emotion in a crisis; or perhaps that he had never been swayed by an emotion in the making of a decision.

According to those theories, he made mistakes—or so we now believe. He thought that the black and the other "colored" "races" were, in their nature—it being no fault of their own choice, but instead a scientific fact—inferior to the "white" man, less intelligent, more emotional. Thus, according to those "laws of nature," Gallieni thought that the Negroes and the Malagasy had been left behind in and by evolution—never to catch up with the favored "white" sports and mutations of the human race. He likewise accepted as viable as well as inevitable that dubious Spencerian phrase, "the survival of the fittest." The fittest to survive were French.

Thus he believed that a colony of colored people in their own natural habitat should be administered for the good of the French. To be sure, it was the obligation of the innate, white, superior beings to manage the lesser, darker men and women for their own good. Thus, willy-nilly, in a way like God, Gallieni saw his duty as a supreme power to protect the Malagasy from their baser natures—as well as from the rapacious, ill-advised members of his own white race. He was never arbitrary in his stay in Madagascar; only the French Jesuits, the English merchants, and the Merina nationalists had reason to complain of prejudicial treatment. He was never doctrinaire. His worst fault was that he set impossibly high standards for those, in the system, who came after him. He was a perfect patriot; France was to him the best of all possible countries in the as yet imperfect world.

Remote and self-contained by nature and by choice, Gallieni kept an intimate journal in three foreign languages; and he gave it, oddly enough, a name: *"Erinnerungen* of my life *di ragazzo."* It has never been published, except in quoted fragments, such as this item in curiously chi-chi English jotted down when he was twenty-seven in Senegal, just launched upon his Colonial career: "Negroes sweet, life charming." Soon he wrote, *"La bonté ne vaut rien pour personne; elle est trop souvent prise pour la faiblesse."* Work at it as I may, the statement comes across into (my) English as "Kindness" or "Goodness"—or perhaps "Kindheartedness" or "Benignity"—"is worth nothing to anyone; it is too often taken for weakness." And that sounds like a classic statement of French cynicism. Did something happen in the jungles to make this young man lay aside the chancy emotions and put his life into his mind? For all his perfect love for France, Gallieni was a realist. His love for France was alarmingly abstract.

The French, who did not take to him, may have found something excessive and alien in his Gallitude. He was too coldly logical, too purely reasonable, unnaturally unemotional; he was the specimen of all French national virtues, in French uniform. But the fact is that Gallieni was not French, except the hard way—by conscious choice. Born in 1849 at Saint-Béat down in the Pyrenees near the Spanish border, his mother was a Catalan, and his father Italian. This man, Gaetan Gallieni, revered Napoléon Bonaparte; in 1805, when he was born, the future Emperor was the President of the Republic of the Milanais; thus from his birth, he was republican. Later, when called up to serve the Hapsburgs in the Austro-Hungarian Army, Gaetan Gallieni got away—he crossed the Alps to join the French Army, in which he became an officer and a French citizen. He married, retired from the Army, cultivated his vineyards, and was elected mayor of Saint-Béat. When he was forty-four, his son was born.

At the age of eleven—two young to have exercised free choice—Joseph Gallieni entered La Flèche, a celebrated military school. At nineteen, he went on to Saint-Cyr, the French military academy. Two years later, as a second lieutenant of the French Marines, he was honorably wounded and captured at Bazeilles, in the French defeat of 1870. So destiny—shaped by the Prussian Iron Chancellor, Prince Otto von Bismarck—sent him out to conquer and to administer the African, the Asian, and the Malagasy colonies for France. In Madagascar he was called the Pacificator. He spread peace all over the face of the troubled land by means of Oil Spots—the *Taches d'Huile* —which is what he called his system.

When he arrived in Tananarive, in his forty-seventh year, he had spent most of his life in French outposts of empire; as a result of tropical diseases and hard work in bad climates, his health was precarious; but he was at the peak of his powers. He knew what he had to do to put down the revolts fostered by intriguing Merina royalties, and to break the gangs of patriotic bandits, the Eights. Indeed, he had to finish the conquest of the island; the Merina had never brought the wild tribes of the south under effective control. He sprinkled his spots of oil; it is the nature of a spot of oil to spread.

A *tache d'huile* was a fortified strong point, sometimes a real garrison, but often an outpost staffed by a sergeant or a corporal and two or three soldiers; the men were left to their own devices and their own resources; but their task was to spread enlightenment along the line of peace. A typical oil spot took the form of a self-sufficient model farming community—a farmhouse with appropriate outbuildings and workshops. The peasants among the soldiers cultivated a kitchen garden and planted an experimental nursery to see what European and Asiatic or African plants, trees, cereals, berries, vines, fruits, vegetables, and flowers would grow in the highland climate. The stock breeders set to work to build a cow byre, a sheep fold, a pig sty, a rabbit hutch, and a poultry yard (the rabbits, by the way, did not thrive, and still do not, in Madagascar). The purpose was to supply the outpost, and to show the local people how things were done in France, and how to make use of each animal's produce.

Next came the workshops—carpentry, cabinet making; a forge and smithy to work iron and other metals; a brick and tile kiln; a room of spinning wheels and looms; and any other shop in which the men of the garrison could practice their own trades and skills, and show the Malagasy how to do the work. A dispensary was admirable, but a school was essential; for the native peoples had to be taught the French language. In fact, the construction of the schoolhouse took priority after the building of the farm itself.

Such was an oil spot; from it spread the arts and sciences of peace, and consequent law, order, and prosperity. Each blockhouse became an outpost of French civilization, a lighted window in a dark night. Like a drop of oil spilled upon a woven fabric, this enlightenment then spread along the warp and the woof throughout the length and the breadth of the land.

The French and the Foreign Legion soldiers were given scope to use their own abilities and native good judgment; Gallieni knew how to delegate authority, and how to communicate his own enthusiasm for the task in hand. Some of the officers and men found themselves dispensing justice, trying Malagasy brought before them and accused of civil disobedience, thievery, and even murder; there was no other authority, and no one else, to listen, to weigh the evidence, and to make judgment.

Some of the troops, to be sure, did their military duty and fought the *Favahalo* bandit insurgents. But Gallieni instructed his men to shoot to kill only when necessary to maintain the peace and the power of France. Captured rebels were not—if possible—to be executed; those resistants who honorably surrendered were set free to live in voluntary —or enforced—cooperation. There was to be absolutely no burning of towns, no reprisal, no punitive displays of French might, and no act of vindictive cruelty. The pacification of Madagascar was to be peaceful.

It must indeed have been a joy to work with this imaginative general, who encouraged his men to put to use that most famous French national quality of improvisation, of looking about, picking up what lay at hand, and making do to accomplish the mission. In New England, something similar was called Yankee ingenuity. In French, it is the *Système D—D* for *débrouillement,* or for *démerdement*—by means of which a gifted, lively man untangles the snarled-up situation, breaks through the red tape, short-cuts the military channels, gets the work done—pulls out a plum or two for himself, and gets away with it. There must have been a great snafu in stocking these oil spots; supplies from France most certainly did not arrive in good condition on time in Tamatave. The journey up the roadless escarpment must have been hard on the new men and the imported stock. So the soldier-teacher-farmer-worker-spreader of French civilization had also to live off the land and keep himself alive in good working condition. He was a pioneer. He knew what he was doing—and so did his commanding officer, General Gallieni.

The objectives in sight were three: one, to make use of the professional aptitudes and the good will of the French soldiers; two, to instruct the Malagasy in modern methods of agriculture and stock-breeding—to teach them how to work regularly and systemically, so that they could go out and put more of the uncultivated land into production, thus to populate the almost empty island, and thus to enlarge the oil spot; and three, to prepare the way for what Gallieni hoped would be a wave of select French colonists, for whom he hoped to build up a pool of labor to work their land grants and concessions. In this, he failed. As General Governor-General he had to go back to the Merina kings' and queens' hated system of *corvée,* by which all men from sixteen to sixty were forced to give fifty workdays of labor each year to the government, to build roads, or to be indentured to private plantation owners. It was a form of feudal taxation, lifted for life if the man contracted to work for a year or more in a private enterprise. Each male Malagasy between these working ages (if any government authority could catch him) was given a pass-book in which a record of his labors was inscribed. It served as a kind of identification paper.

So, with the pacification of the island complete, the oil spots, having spread, should have joined to cover the surface of Madagascar; and thus all the natives and the natural wealth would then be ready and waiting for the expected intensive French exploitation—which did not follow through. Incidentally, the autochthonous peoples would have been shown how to lead orderly, productive lives at peace; and, through participation, to prepare themselves eventually, but not just then, to take over the problems and the responsibilities of self-government.

It was a good system; but it did not work as expected—although, in the long run, it has proved itself. With all the obvious and avoidable failures of the French Colonial empire, it is notable today that some, if not all, of the new and independent African and Malagasy "republics" do have a few, a handful, of native-born, French-educated leaders willing to cooperate among themselves and with their former motherland to keep the peace in their period of transition. The great quality of Gallieni's oil spots was the inherent dynamism of the system; he left room for growth. It is true, he did not foresee the nature of that development—away from, and not towards, France. Yet he was a reasonable man, an evolutionist; and he could be, were he alive, content with the work he started, he and a tested nucleus of his Foreign Legionnaires.

This odd fact I cannot get over: that the colony was put in order by professional soldiers and foreign mercenaries, often outrageously tattooed. The men were reliable, expert, disciplined—and dedicated not to France, nor to the French, nor to the civilizing mission. Their loyalty was limited to the Foreign Legion, and, it may be, to an officer like Gallieni. They did the work the French refused to do—for example, they carried out Gallieni's order to suppress the Malagasy National Festival of the Queen's Bath, and in its place to impose Bastille Day, along with fireworks and dancing in the streets.

In the reign of Queen Ranavalona III, she bathed on November 22—her birthday and her coronation anniversary—although originally the bath seems to have been a New Year's festival. In the days of Radama I, the monarch shrieked when the holy water touched his naked body. He shouted, "Let me be sanctified!" Again he screeched as his attendants dried the royal flesh, and he cried out, "Bless me, O my Lord and my Creator! Thanks be unto You!" Each time, the courtiers and the tribe echoed the king—or, at the end of the Merina monarchy, the queen.

Then, gowned in rustling red silk—by Doucet or Lemoine—and

jewelled in full regalia, the queen emerged from the curtained corner of the throne room. In her hands she carried the hollowed white horn of a zebu bull, filled with holy water from her bath. With this water, she aspersed her people. So she shared her sacrament.

The queen then took her place on the throne to receive homage and fealty, and to preside at a ritual feast of *jaka mialin-taona*—dried beef that has "slept for a year."

As Roman candles and rockets on the 4th of July now replace the original bombs bursting in air, so this jerked beef of the ceremonial banquet had come to replace the flesh of the body of the dead king. The Vazimba, whom the Merina absorbed in their progress to the highlands, practiced the manducation of their dead. Thus they preserved the precious virtues of the father of the king; the son and heirs ate up the dead parent's flesh. So they took his divine and immortal soul into their living bodies, to gain strength, and to protect their inheritance, thus not to let the body and the soul, which were then one and indivisible, be wasted in the earth or in the air, in fire or in water. Thus death was a renewal, not an end, to life, in perpetuity.

The Queen's Bath, then, in the beginning was the laving of the body of the dead king before its assumption by the living ruler and the tribe. It had come to be a Eucharist, a partaking of the body and the soul of the living and divine ancestors, linked to the person of the living queen for eternal life on earth. It was a ceremony celebrating the continuity of life, in the succeeding generations, an identification of the present with the past.

Gallieni broke that human chain. He exiled the queen and he put France, the motherland, in her place, with himself, the *masiaka* representative of her power, in position to rule, with a promise of liberty, equality, and fraternity to come. There is no question of the value of the gift; France at that time, at the peak of French achievements in Humanism, stood at the high point of French modern history. The Malagasy tribal system had gone as far as it could go, feeding on the past, partaking of the dried flesh of its ancestors. It had come to a dead-end. So Gallieni went back to the source of French enlightenment, and brought the revolutionary French discoveries of the rights of man into the island along with the National Festival commemorating the end of despotic power and the fall of the Bastille.

The French of France refused to honor his gift to the Malagasy in

Madagascar. In 1900 Madagascar was an underdeveloped island with few easily accessible natural riches to export to France; and consequently the island had no immediately available source of internal revenue. Therefore, to finance the pacification and the organization of this new and enormous French colony, General Governor-General Gallieni asked Paris for funds. He wrote that the "economic advancement of a country is the only justification for colonization," and that the native people had to be brought into Colonial development so to be encouraged in commercial, social, and political progress. The funds he requested were denied him.

In 1900, the French Chamber of Deputies passed a French law prohibiting the government of France and the French empire from spending the French public revenues, obtained from taxes levied upon and paid by the French electorate for the purpose of paying the cost of French government, outside France to develop the colonies of the French empire. The penny-pinching thinking behind the law was to put the burden of paying the cost of empire upon the conquered Colonial peoples themselves—thus each colony was to be made to pay for the French *mission civilisatrice* imposed upon its people. The Colonial peoples had to pay their own way; the colonies had to be made self-supporting. France then was gorged with gold; the French were the bankers of the world. To this day Madagascar has no heavy industry, and very little light.

Thus cut off, Gallieni put his Foreign Legion to work building roads, and schools, and hospitals; with his Legionnaires he policed the island and he went on spreading his oil spots—the French way of life. Of his two enemies, the Andriana and the Hova of the Merina were less dangerous than the politicians back of him in France. Even so, Gallieni did his work like a man who straightens out a snake, and then goes ahead on the assumption that if a snake sees reason, and if a serpent chooses to, it will go straight ahead. Snakes, politicians, and evolution do not get along that way. He knew so; but according to the nature of his task, he set about building the highways between two points, along which French thought, French civilization, French order, and French culture were, indeed, to come into the island. There are no venomous serpents down in Madagascar. Gallieni left Tananarive to go home to France in 1905.

In 1911, he was offered the supreme command of the French armies.

227

However, acting in character after thought, he declined the honor and the culmination of a soldier's life.

He argued that he was too old and in too poor health to take on such responsibilities; he proposed another man to be the French generalissimo—Joseph Joffre, then a general, later a Maréchal-de-France, who had served under him in Madagascar as commander of the Diégo-Suarez military district. On 24 April 1914, Gallieni reached the age limit, his sixty-fifth birthday. He retired to the house he had built for the purpose in St.-Raphael, a quiet town on the Côte d'Azur. His wife died suddenly on 27 July 1914. On the first of August, he was recalled to headquarters in Paris. War broke out. On 26 August, Gallieni was named military governor of Paris. On the night of the 2nd and the 3rd of September, the French government left for Bordeaux. Joffre had withdrawn to the east of the capital; the city lay unprotected from the German advance, unprotected except by Gallieni, who said, "I have been given the mandate to defend Paris against the invader. This mandate I shall carry out until the end."

As a soldier, he knew that Paris had been sacrificed to tactics and to strategy. From headquarters, he watched the conduct of the battle. At about midday, he saw his chance, and in a stroke of *débrouillard* genius, he mobilized the taxis of Paris—the taxis of the Marne, as odd a fleet of vehicles as ever carried reserve troops to a surprise flank attack —and to victory in the night of the 3rd to the 4th of September, 1914. The irony here is that, although Gallieni is best remembered for these taxis of the Marne, no one knows for sure whether he or some other flexibly quick-thinking improviser hit upon the notion of calling in the tough old French taxi drivers and their moving cabs (one of which is now a museum piece on display among the ancient artillery, the tattered banners, the war trophies, and a few specimen crippled veterans in Les Invalides) to save Paris, and perhaps the war. But it is known that when Hitler's *Blitzkrieg* took Paris in that implacably beautiful June of 1940, and France fell, one of the first acts of the Occupation was to throw down and break up the monument to Joseph-Simon Gallieni, *Maréchal-de-France*.

More Pleasures of Discovery

ON my second visit to Madagascar one February, I hired a Simca Ariane and went for a highland drive. I drove south, thinking about Gallieni and about personal integrity, honor, glory, grandeur—words and meanings, it may be, that are no longer functional today. They were to Gallieni. It struck me that his individual incorruptibility worked against him, and against Madagascar. His personal and private—and public—virtue showed up the venality of the expedient French politicians of the Third Republic. Thus he threatened them; if he was right, they had to be wrong. Yet not all of the opponents to Colonial expansion, and thus to Gallieni, were bad men. Georges Clemenceau, "the Tiger on the Left," pursued his own visions of French glory and French grandeur.

Be that as it may, one peculiar fact about the French Colonial empire of the nineteenth century emerges clear from Gallieni's life— the dynamics of its course. Whenever France was defeated, as at Waterloo, and later, in the Franco-Prussian War, the humiliated French Army officers went out and collected a colony—beginning with Algiers in 1830—to lay at the feet of . . . of France. But *which* France? The face of the Army's France seems hard to identify. In less than a century, the Army served France in three republics, a Restoration of two Bourbon brothers, a variant monarchy with a bourgeois king, and two Napoleonic empires, the great and the less, as well as in something called a *Directoire*. In all this domestic confusion, it is understandable that the French people looked with suspicion at the Army's piling up of Colonial gifts at what they took to be their own feet. They tried in the July Revolution of 1830 to reject Algiers; and sixty-five years later, they wanted nothing to do with Madagascar when that colony was brought to them.

I drove along through the cool and luminous highlands, thinking that whatever else the island is, it is a collector's item. It is a beautiful place; and on my highland drive I found two perfectly beautiful exotics, one fish, one flesh. Both imported by the French, neither willing nor able to naturalize themselves, each came originally from the Americas. The first were the rainbow trout flashing in the primeval forest streams running swift and clear and cold down the slopes of the massif of Ankaratra (8,725 feet in altitude).

Introduced in 1926, the *Salmo gairdnerii* of the far west were, in 1958, hatched lovingly in rectified, spring-fed ponds where ferns and mosses grew under the podocarps and pines. Both fish and forest used to be vigorously protected by the French foresters of the Colonial Eaux et Forêts. Therefore, in the eyes of the extremists among the Malagasy nationalists, most of them young highlanders, these pampered trees and rainbow trout took on the hostile aspects of . . . oh, of that other Poisson, la Pompadour—extravagantly protected luxuries. Therefore, in the turbulent days of agitation, Yes or No for General de Gaulle's Referendum, some few of the most violently anti-French nationalists set fire to the forest reservations. The pools and streams among the flaming trees boiled up and cooked the rainbow trout—indeed, *au bleu*, but not to eat.

I drove on; and further south, in Fianarantsoa, the highland capital of the Betsileo tribal country, I went, one evening, into a flatiron of a building where, in a bookshop, I bought, in fact, a book. I cannot recall the title or the author, but I remember clearly the young woman who sold it to me. At first she sat behind her desk; then she stood up and walked towards me.

She was tall, five feet eight or nine; she carried herself well, and she had presence. Her dignity and her composure made it clear that, notwithstanding her great beauty, she was a thoughtful, capable businesswoman of thirty, with a mind to put to work, and no nonsense: a *femme-de-tête*, it may be, but what a beautiful woman! Everything about her was harmonious, from her fashionably controlled dark-brown hair to her long, high-arched feet in very high-heeled red shoes. She wore a red dress that fitted her and suited her. She was altogether memorable, with long-fingered, narrow hands. Her clear brown skin was the color of the end of a splendid summer on the beach. She asked me, efficiently, if she could be of service. I remarked that I was looking for something to read—a truth—but then (I wonder why?) I added a fact—that I was American.

"So am I American," she said, speaking educated, cultivated French; and, having surprised me, coolly added, "Central American, from Martinique."

"Have you ever been to New York?" I asked. It was something to say.

"No," she answered drily. "You have odd notions on the subject of colored people—" (She held out her left hand, waist-high, palm-down; the oval nails were painted red; and with the index finger of her right hand, she touched the smooth brown skin) "—like me." And having pointed out her reasoning, she glanced up to look at me, and to smile.

In Washington, the State Department interviewers used to ask aspiring American diplomats how they would handle similar, but hypothetical ensuing silences; one such man, having replied that he would tell the regional truth, abruptly ceased to aspire to the diplomacy. On the spot, I said that indeed Madagascar appeared to be free of such odd notions (and I repeated her own phrase, *"drôle d'idées"*).

"Indeed, you are mistaken," she corrected me, and in the French of the Comédie-Française explained that a pale-skinned highland Merina of good family will not marry a man or a woman of the darker tribes. As for herself, she disliked equally strongly the very white and the very black. The blue-veined Nordic and the blue-gummed Negro were equally distasteful to her. She liked a bronzed skin.

But even so, she added, thoughtfully, it is not a question merely of color, for she did not much enjoy the company of the Malagasy, few of whom as yet were really civilized (she used that word, *évolué*). To be sure, in time—but neither tomorrow nor the day after—the Malagasy would learn how to think and to lead cultivated lives like other people. Already those in the civil service often were most distinguished men. She regretted that such could not be said for most of the women, who were, as yet, ill at ease in European company. They had uncertain manners, and no conversation—none.

It having become apparent that this extraordinary, beautiful young

231

woman was conversant with the world, and that she had manner, we talked. I learned that she was a French citizen; that she was the daughter of a judge; that she had divorced her French husband from the Midi— her marriage had not turned out to be a match; and that she lived with her two small daughters in the largest house (which she hoped to sell) in the town, where, things being slow, and nobody having much business of his own to mind, everybody minded everyone else's—or everybody's else.

"In these uncertain times," I asked, "who will buy your house?" and asked if she intended to stay on in Madagascar after Independence.

"I wonder?" she replied; and answered, "I think not."

ANTSIRABÉ

ANOTHER French provincial city of the displaced nineteenth century is Antsirabé, a spa of radioactive mineral springs, both hot and cold, and bubbling and still. It lies in the center of the highlands in the middle of green fields and rolling pastures, with pine woods covering the round hills. Even the sky is a mild French sky, full of soft white and grey clouds bringing the blue down closer to mankind. Its waters are as good as any of the cures of France.

"The Vichy of the Indian Ocean" has a thermal establishment; a gently steaming, open-air swimming pool; a nine-hole golf course; a hospital for the hydrotherapy of poliomyelitics; and an old-fashioned hotel of great, high rooms and wide verandahs—all meshed in flowerbeds and easy walks laid out for the delectation of the celebrants of the water cult. But the mystique failed at the Antsirabé source, perhaps because the Malagasy rarely suffer the patriotic French complaint, liver trouble. Only the thoroughly assimilated among them drink the wines and eat the sauced cuisine of the true initiates—and they make the pilgrimage to France to take the waters. The national

Malagasy dish is boiled rice and boiled *brèdes*—the tender shoots of various bitter green-leafed vegetables—with now and again an egg, a bit of fish, or a little meat. None of this is conductive to the mineral-spring mysteries.

If, indeed, architecture is a branch of pastry cookery, the Malagasy climate has apparently encouraged neither the arts founded upon the nature of stone or clay or bronze, nor those founded upon the native belly. I strolled along the shady streets of familiar name—Voltaire, Lafayette, Danton, Gallieni—all set about with pretty French villas in their gardens, and I found myself walking along the rue Benyowski. Who was he?

Graf Moritz August von Benyowski was a king of con men in the Age of Reason, a wild promoter, a Hungarian count in the suite of Stanislas Poniatowski, the last king before the total partition of Poland. Catherine the Great exiled the Magyar to Siberia when she took the Pole to bed. Benyowski kept on going east, and found a ship to escape from Kamchatka to Madagascar. He landed in the Bay of Antongil in 1772, and he sent a letter to the king of France. Louis XV wrote back to name Benyowski commander of the Island of Madagascar—still claimed as Oriental France, and called the brightest jewel in the French crown.

The Hungarian's first official act was to lay out a capital named Louisburg, and a port, Choiseul. His extravagance aroused the jealousy and the suspicion of the neighboring Mascarenes, whose French governor sent back derogatory information in unfavorable reports from Mauritius to Versailles. At once, Benyowski sailed for France. There in a stormy audience with the king he did not deign to defend himself—instead he attacked his petty critics, and demanded to be named king of Madagascar. That was in 1775. Benyowski was expelled.

He then went to Vienna to offer *his* island to the Holy Roman emperor; but Joseph II, brother of Marie Antoinette, declined the gift. Benyowski went to London, to see George III, who, being himself subject to insanity, might well have listened; the British, busy with the American Revolution, refused Madagascar. Benyowski took ship for the brand new United States, where, radiating confidence in those exhilarating days, he sold himself; he found backing, formed a company, sold his stock, bought a ship, raised a crew—and sailed out of

Baltimore, not as count, not as king, but as emperor of Madagascar, to land again in the Bay of Antongil. Although he liked the Malagasy and they loved him, he had a short, disputed reign.

The tottering Ancien Régime of France could not brook the defiance of so outrageous an upstart. Louis XVI, who had seven years ahead of him before the guillotine, ordered out the French Navy and the Marines. They shot and killed Benyowski, the emperor of Elsewhere, in a battle on 27 May 1786. Nobody knows where he was buried; his towns vanished. But the shareholders in his enterprise got their money back, with profits, from the sale of his best-selling, posthumous *Memoirs*, of 1790. Somewhere in Madagascar a mountain is named after him.

I walked along Benyowski Street in Antsirabé and stopped to look at a nice little house, its neat little door flanked by a pair of begonias —I cannot name the variety, but I have seen similar plants, potted and flourishing on farmhouse window-sills in the state of Maine, the kind with wing-shaped, spotted leaves and clusters of waxy, crimson blooms. In Benyowski's street, the winged begonias shot up higher than the doorstep, higher than the door, higher than the upstairs windows, higher than the eaves and the rooftree. They were gigantic begonias; yet the French woman who peeked out from behind her starched white window curtains to find out what I saw to make me stand and laugh out loud was not a dwarf. Madagascar is an enormous island.

FIANARANTSOA

BEFORE Hitler thought up the Final Solution of the gas chamber, in 1940, the Nazis played with the humanitarian idea of cleaning out the European Jews by transporting them to Madagascar, there to live a tribal life of their own. The notion proved to be impractical from the standpoint of logistics. The French, who, in defeat, still owned the almost empty island, would not have concurred had they been consulted. Nor, to be sure, would have the Jews. In 1917, Chaim Weismann had rejected the highlands of neighboring Kenya as a National Home. Yet, had other things been equal, the Jews, as in Israel, might have worked wonders developing Madagascar. Indeed, had the Japanese got there . . . but they did not.

Madagascar's great luxury is space, luminous, beautiful emptiness, mile after mile of grassland, brush, and woodland, broken by craggy mountains. Inside the encircling horizons, pillars of smoke arise by day, and burning bushes flame up by night, fired by the nomad herdsmen.

In the Betsileo tribal land, the almost empty, black, and well constructed highway is strung with small and pleasant human habitations, all pretty much alike. One sticks in my mind for its brass band, glittering and golden in the sunlight. I stepped on the brakes to find myself surrounded by dark-brown instrumentalists in immaculate white uniforms, all buttoned up. The young were solid; the old were slight. Their coiling, writhing horns hurt the eye; their blaring music hurt the ears; but they were fine and dandy—black and white and brassy, full of life. They marched north; I drove south.

The Betsileo, third in number of the tribes, are described as the peasants of Madagascar; dark of skin and muscular, they are peaceful and hard-working, famous as hydraulic engineers in the construction and management of their terraced rice fields, but bad as soldiers. Thus they did not resist the conquering Merina, their northern neighbors. I came to a red-brick town on a ridge named Ambositra ("Ahmboostr"), set about with flowers, famous for handicrafts. The pretty place has an ugly origin. Its name means "the Place of Many Eunuchs." When Prince Radama won a battle there, a century and a half ago, he killed the old men, castrated the young, and herded the women and children into slavery.

On I drove, into pine forests, down steep slopes, up again into the wind where the rain falls, to come to the Betsileo capital Fianarantsoa, pronounced "Fee-anna-rant-soo," called Fianar for short, and meaning "Where a Man Learns Virtue" (more or less). One afternoon I left the hotel and, seeing a hill, set out to climb it on foot. A steep and winding narrow road took me between rows of neat brick houses into a small marketplace where Malagasy women—the middle-aged and the old—sat about in the sunshine and gossiped, the while they kept a weather eye out to see what was going on. I found that *I* was going on. They stopped talking to observe me. Younger women, shaplier in more recent European dress, put aside their household chores to look at me through open doors and windows. Old men, well wrapped up, studied me from their sheltered corners out of the wind. Young men, neatly dressed in trousers and sweaters, hanging around and talking, some leaning their backs against sunny walls, some sitting at tables under trees playing a checkerboard game, looked over, looked up, and looked away. A great many small, delicate, wide-eyed brown children wearing skimpy European clothes were playing in the square. As I came along, they grew wary, stopped their games, stood still, and eyed me. Some gave way to fright and ran. One ten-year-old, a girl with two long braids and a baby brother or sister riding in a sling made from her *lamba* on her back, got up from where she sat, turned, glanced over her shoulder at me—the spread-eagled baby did so, too—burst into giggles, shouted with laughter, took to her heels, and ran around a corner.

Out of a house came one small boy of six or seven, his left arm in a heavy plaster cast slung in a triangle round his neck; confronting me, he froze. Standing on the stone stoop of his red-brick house, he looked up at me in round-eyed consternation, lost his equilibrium, and tumbled over. He fell flat on his belly on the cobbles of the street. Slowly he began to make a gentle moan, but he did nothing about getting himself back onto his feet.

Without thinking, I took the stride or two to him, and, while making soothing sounds (in French), I bent down, picked him up, and stood him upright—all of a piece, rigid with terror. Then a young adult Malagasy, neat in a European suit, a felt hat on his head, came up and, hand in hand, took the boy away, without a word spoken or a backward glance.

Wondering if I had broken some taboo, I stood still and I took stock of myself. Was it my relatively enormous height that dismayed them? I looked myself over—proper shoes, black slacks, black sweater, right mind, and not, I think, an outlandish physiognomy. I gave up, turned, and walked the uphill road to come to the top; there I found

a *château d'eau*—a covered masonry water tower and pumping station
—built into what had been the royal citadel, the Rova, and manned by
a well dressed, white-collar Malagasy of my age. I was very pleased,
indeed, when he greeted me with courtesy (in French), and we began
to talk.

He asked me if I liked the view as much as he did—and I did. It
was a green and spacious view in the cool of the evening, of forested
mountains and cultivated valleys, with a glint of water in the plain
under the dome of the sky, and with the town spread out below us.
Not even Tananarive has a better view, said he, and added that he was
an Hova from Tananarive, a member of the civil service. He wondered
if I were, perhaps, a functionary, too, it might be, from Paris.

I learned my French in Paris, but it is not that good. "I am American," I said, "from the United States, born in Massachusetts."

Silhouetted against the highland sky, he turned his back to the view
to face me; he tilted back his head; he looked at me. Clearly he was
absorbed in what he saw, and he saw me. As though to himself, he
said, *"C'est comme ça."* Then in sober surprise he commented, *"Voilà
la tête d'un Américain."*

"Yes," I said, "this is what one American looks like."

He went on examining me, not in the least discourteously—a specimen American, the first he'd seen face to face. I saw that something
puzzled him. He asked me, "How does it happen that you are white?"

In truth, I am not very, although I am a paleface of English,
Scottish, French, and Dutch descent, and not a redskin. Before I
could find the answer, he asked me another question: "Where are
your feathers?" In disappointed tones, he asked me, *"Où sont vos
plumes?"*

Where are they? In 1950, among the one hundred and fifty million
Americans of all the states, 343,410 were Amerinds of all the extant
tribes, two-tenths of 1 per cent. In Madagascar, the proportion is
roughly 100 to 1—five million Malagasy of the tribes to fifty thousand
French and Créoles. To my friend, an Hova of the Merina, an *évolué*,
a (then) French government employee at the waterworks of
Fianarantsoa, I was not a real American. I was, instead, a full-blooded
European, not a brave, not a native, not indigenous, not autochthonous,
without a single feather in my cap.

237

I thought it best to change the subject. So I asked him why I—for all they knew, a Frenchman—had frightened the children on my way up the hill; and then I told him about the boy with the broken arm.

He reluctantly explained. First, it was the matter of my size and height; but that was secondary. It seems that had I been an Indian chief, bare-chested in war paint, an eagle feather bonnet on my head, and whooping, I could not have terrified the child more than I did when, dressed in white shirt, black sweater, and black trousers, and murmuring in French, I bent down to pick him up. Then I was to him a nightmare image encountered in broad daylight, the terrible archetype of arbitrary, incomprehensible, destructive power—the white man, an ogre. Once the European had been as Prospero, with magic in his presence. But since the Rebellion of 1947, in the collective unconscious of the Malagasy, he had turned himself into cruelty incarnate. The child with the broken arm imagined that I had come to pick him up, carry him off, and . . . what in hell do ogres do to children? I forget, if, indeed, I ever knew.

The Rebellion of 1947

AT 12:30 the next day, Palm Sunday, I sat down in my reserved rattan armchair up front in the self-propelled, Diesel-powered Micheline on my way from Fianarantsoa to Manakara on the coast. In comfort I looked through plateglass windows at the jungle scenery of the escarpment—steep rain forests on ridges, in ravines, on shelves, with torrents and waterfalls, and now and again a cultivated patch. In four hours, the narrow-gauge, zigzag descent of 102 miles crosses a display of bridges in great variety and length, and goes through 49 tunnels—the longest (3,531 feet) almost as long as the cliff is high (3,700 feet). It is a specimen of imaginative French railroad engineering, put through unimaginably difficult terrain, and it took from 1926 to 1936 to complete. The Malagasy laborers had to be conscripted—diverted from military service. The railroad serves the coffee region.

Coffee beans grow on pruned evergreen-shrubs set out in orderly rows in terraced plantations; the soil is rich and well drained; the rainfall is plentiful. Like tea, coffee was introduced to Europe in the seventeeth century, perhaps from the Sublime Porte to the Sun King's court. Towards the end of the eighteenth century, the coffee houses of London, and the cafés of Paris had created a demand that spread the commerce and the cultivation of the bean to all the hot and hilly regions of the known world. Then the delicate variety that produces a brew of the finest flavor, *Coffea arabica,* native to Ethiopia and Arabia Felix, was introduced to Madagascar from Mauritius and Réunion. In

239

the nineteenth century, Merina landowners worked big plantations by means of slave labor, and they made money.

In 1878 a fungoid disease, *Hemileia vastatrix,* came into Madagascar from Ceylon. The blight attacks the evergreen leaves and kills the susceptible *Coffea arabica* variety. By 1901, Madagascar's coffee exports fell to 117 kilograms of beans; and by 1904, to six kilos—13¼ pounds. Meanwhile, the planters of the eastern escarpment, where the heavy rains favored the spreading fungus, rooted up the delicate and dying Arabica plants, to plant the Kouilou and Robusta kinds, tougher trees, resistant to the blight although their beans produce a harsher, bitterer coffee. And thus Madagascar lost out to drier, higher tropical regions, as in Brazil, which country in 1949 produced two-thirds of the world crop, or 1,068,283 tons of coffee beans.

Then came the Second World War; and after the war came the widespread popularity of Nescafé and all the other instant coffee powders. It was discovered that the strong Robusta and Kouilou flavors survived the processing—and were much improved. Therefore, in 1958, Madagascar exported 47,800 tons of coffee beans worth $32,324,000; and coffee once again became the greatest source of foreign revenue.

There would have been by then many more tons of beans to export had the Rebellion of 1947 not destroyed so many of the plantations, and frightened so many of the planters from their cleared lands inside the jungles of the Tanala tribe, wild men. Therefore, instead of increasing (although in fact coffee is overproduced everywhere), the Malagasy crop declined; and it still declines now that the Rebellion of 1947 has belatedly achieved its ends. Business in the independent Malagasy Republic is slow.

The rebellion took everyone by surprise in 1947. Not even the rebels, let alone the great majority of the peaceful Malagasy, knew what to make of it. Nobody was prepared, although the handful of conspirators had made careful plans. Their aim was to clear the French from Madagascar, and to recover the island for the Malagasy.

The troubles began at midnight between the 29th and the 30th of March, from Saturday night to Sunday morning, at Moromanga, 74½ miles from Tananarive, a railroad junction on the Tamatave line, from which a branch takes off to serve the rich agricultural region of Lake Alaotra. There is an important military installation at Moromanga. The authorities, mistakenly, thought at first that it was all just another brawl between the resentful Malagasy men and the French Colonial soldiers out on pass and in pursuit of girls.

It was not so; it was part of a large plan. Similar surprise attacks had been timed to explode simultaneously in Tananarive, in Tamatave, in Diégo-Suarez, and in the important towns of the central highlands and east-coast lowlands. In Moromanga the Malagasy rebels—nobody knows how many there were, one hundred, several hundred—most of them stripped down for action to loin cloths or shorts, and armed with some rifles, a few machine-guns, and not many revolvers, but with many *sagai* spears and *"coupe-coupe"* machetes, stormed the barracks, storerooms, arms and munitions dumps, and headquarters of the French Colonial Army. Their leaders were a few professional Malagasy soldiers, noncommissioned officers for the most part, trained in the 1939–1945 war in France and seasoned in the night fighting of the maquis and the resistance against the occupying Germans and Italians between the Fall and the Liberation. Behind them were all the resentful and enraged witch-doctors and sorcerers of Madagascar, out to get back their waning magic hold; still further back were a handful of professional agitprop Communists; and to the rear were all the Malagasy of all the tribes who had ever been injured, hurt, scorned, or diminished by the French or the Créoles, as well as the envious, the dissatisfied, and the bewildered. Among them on all fronts were the thieves, and those who like a fight. Together at Moromanga they killed twenty-three soldiers including nine French officers and non-coms, eleven Senegalese, and three Syrians; the rebels were repulsed. How many of them were killed in the action, I cannot say; in the countryside that night and in the next few days of confusion, forty-nine civilians were massacred, most of them peaceful, pro-French Malagasy men and women.

At the time of the rebellion, the Liberation of Madagascar and the break-up of the French Colonial empire was, indeed, being planned; but it was envisaged for the far-distant future. No exact date, such as the year 1960, had been set. Therefore, the rebellion had to fail. In fact, it failed because the rebels failed to take Tananarive—as, indeed, other rebel groups failed to capture the port of Tamatave or an arms-depot in Diégo-Suarez. The island did not rise up; the wild and primitive tribes of the arid south did not take fire; the various Sakalava of the west remained calm; the Betsileo of the southern highlands, and the

Tsimihety of the north, did not all join in. Apparently, the organizers mistimed the uprising; they had ambitions way beyond their potentials to achieve. Nobody can say with certainty, because no master plan, no table of organization, no charts, no battle order, and no communiqués have ever been discovered.

It is known, however, that the capital of Madagascar and the center of the French Colonial government was saved by chance; by pure chance the steep streets of the delightful city of Tananarive of (in 1959) 200,000 inhabitants, one-tenth of whom are Europeans— French, Créoles, Greeks, British, Norwegians, Americans, and one or two from most of the other "white" countries—did not run red in the night from the 29th to the 30th of March, 1947. The city lay asleep at midnight; there is little to do at night in the town. The functionaries and servicemen, family men as a rule, have always kept themselves to themselves—they stay apart and save money to spend in retirement back home in France. The government people had a great load of work to do in organizing the new French Union of General de Gaulle's Fourth Republic. Perhaps their paperwork had caused them to lose touch with the islanders whom they governed.

The newcomers from Paris had not yet become used to the island conditions; and the old hands were tired, waiting to be replaced, ready to go home. They were sound asleep. Perhaps a few bachelors prowled; but by midnight they had either made their connections, or given up and turned in.

To be sure, earlier in the year various well known Malagasy national-ists had been, as usual, writing articles and making speeches denouncing the French, demanding immediate freedom, and generally inciting the Malagasy people to take violent action against foreign oppression. This all was old stuff; there was nothing new in it; most of it was discounted as the usual and familiar propaganda and political fireworks brought on by the elections of 1946. The French did not take these open attacks upon themselves seriously; they were used to the same sort of thing back home—a part of the French passion for free speech, and a proof of the success of the *mission civilisatrice*. They all knew that the Malagasy were not yet ready for the responsibilities of self-government in total freedom.

It is a matter of record that the Governor-General's office had received reports that a group of rebels had scheduled a revolt against the

Europeans to take place in the night of 29 March. The proper department had disseminated the information to the various provincial governors according to the correct procedure. But the Intelligence people had dismissed the report as one more unlikely rumor having no real basis in fact—to be noted for what it was worth.

The leader of the uprising in Tananarive was a Malagasy lieutenant of the regular French Colonial forces. His name was Randriamanana; that is almost all that I know about him; from his choice of action at the moment of crisis, he seems to have been a prudent, an imaginative, and a cautious man—not a hothead, and not a vainglorious leader; and not lucky. I do not know his age; I know nothing of his war experience; I cannot say what happened to him—whether he was killed, or captured, or executed, or whether he lived to fight another day. He may still be alive, but I doubt it.

My guess is that he was not an Hova nor an upper- or lower-caste member of the Merina highlanders. I think he belonged to one of the coastal peoples. It may be that he was chosen to lead the revolt in the capital for that reason.

It is notable that the Merina people—the intellectuals and the politicians, of all the tribes the most civilized in the French manner, and thus the most eloquently nationalistic and the most vocally anti-French—did not, on the whole, take active part in the actual fighting. The rest of the Malagasy tribes distrust their former conquerors and rulers; and for this reason, the Merina-Hova may well have been left out of the secrets of the rebel high command.

Lieutenant Randriamanana—whoever he was, and for whatever causes and reasons—was chosen to lead the attack on the key city of Tananarive. He was given full authority and full responsibility. He brought in his men, all volunteers, all fully motivated, the élite of the rebels—and thus the experienced and the disciplined men, trained in underground commando action—into Tananarive, and he disposed them in secret in all the strategic places. To succeed, the rebels had to take all the centers of communication—the central office of the Postal Telephone and Telegraph service, Radio-Tananarive, military headquarters, the residence of the Governor-General, and all the main government buildings as well as the railroad station and the intersections of the main highways.

Having made his plans, Randriamanana went in to take up his observation post in Tananarive to watch the life of the city throughout the day. I wonder where he hid out. In what room in what building? It must have been high up on one of the hills. I think he must have been able to watch the traffic on the road south—the road, then hard-surfaced, that I later took down into the southern highlands. Or perhaps the lieutenant chose a secure and unremarkable house where he could receive couriers bringing in reports from other observation posts, and from which he could go unobtrusively to see for himself any unusual action on the part of the enemy. All that afternoon and on into evening, one such unforeseen movement of French forces took place under Randriamanana's eyes. He watched as the afternoon went by, and he grew increasingly thoughtful.

It looked very much like a concentration of reserve troops called up and brought into the capital to defend the French Colonial government of Madagascar against just such a surprise attack as he was waiting to lead. It seemed to him that he had been betrayed.

Not so. It happened that on 29 March 1947, "several elements"—perhaps two or three hundred French and French Colonial soldiers of the regular Army—had finished their ten-day or two-week period of rest and recreation at Antsirabé, the town of thermal springs in the mild, green landscape south of Tananarive. They had been assigned duty in the garrison of the capital, and had left Antsirabé in the morning packed into all the available trucks and troop transports that could still roll after eight and ten years of hard service on the rough and neglected roads of Madagascar. Throughout the war, the Occupation, and the Liberation, the vehicles had been made to serve without replacements or spare parts brought down from France. They rattled and banged; their tires were thin, their inner tubes patched and repatched. The Army mechanics had had to make use of the famous Système D to hold them together and to keep them on the road.

So the convoy of average and over-loaded troop transports set out from Antsirabé to cover the 106¼ rough miles to Tananarive. One after another of the trucks broke down. The soldiers got out and sat on the grass and waited while the mechanics tinkered with the engines and tried to make running repairs, cannibalizing one wreck to get the best of the lot on its way. Meantime, the others went on ahead with orders to unload their troops and to turn around and drive back to pick up the stranded men under the shade of the tree—or from the café-bar of the nearest village. It must have been an enjoyable outing for the rested men; no one was in a great hurry. But to the tense and nervous observer, Lieutenant Randriamanana, able to interpret military actions, the unexpected and irregular traffic of troop transports coming and going along the highway to Antsirabé throughout the long sunny afternoon seemed to be not the result of the mechanical failure of worn-out Citroëns and Renaults. He logically and reasonably recognized it as a shuttle service bringing up reinforcements to protect the city from his own surprise attack. He concluded that all his plans were known to the French authorities. He was, in fact, mistaken. Yet at eight o'clock in the evening, 240 minutes before the midnight H-hour, the rebellious lieutenant called off his action in the rebellion; he thus doomed the Malagasy revolt—the first of the French Colonial uprisings after the Second World War—to failure. In 1947, the French had something like 6,500 regular Colonial troops in Madagascar; 4,000 of them were either professional Malagasy soldiers of island conscripts in their term of military service. Another 1,000 were Senegalese, regular soldiers. The remaining 1,500 were French officers and non-coms of the cadre.

The rebellion failed at 8:00 P.M. on Saturday, the 29th of March, 1947; it went on failing for another three years. The reactionary and fanatic sorcerers and witch-doctors took over when the soldiers and the intellectuals gave up; they had everything to gain, and nothing to lose. They wanted to get back their frightening hold of total power upon the ignorant and wild tribes, such as the backward jungle people through whose lands I traveled in the Fianarantsoa–East Coast railroad train. The Tanala ("Ta-nal"), "the People of the Forests," numbered 200,535 in the census of 1959. They, and the other primitives, went into battle crying "*Rano! Rano!*" which is to say, "Water! Water!" but not because they were thirsting. It was a magic formula given them by their witch-doctors and sorcerers instead of steel armor plate. "*Rano! Rano!*" was supposed to change the bullets of the French rifles, automatics, and machine-guns magically into drops of water. The water of Madagascar is soft water; there are almost no calcareous rocks under the lateritic soil that stains the rivers red.

The Tanala and the other tribal warriors wore amulets likewise guaranteed to bring them victory alive. One such was a crocodile tooth hollowed out and filled with dust and powders, bits of hair, nail pairings, spit, and excrement powerfully spoken to, and bound together with wild-nut oil and melted zebu suet. Another was the tip of a bull's horn decorated with woven patterns of colored glass beads, and stuffed with ugly and filthy substances. By such magic talismans, the dispossessed witch-doctors and sorcerers thought to pit their black magic against the French enlightenment, and to retribalize the Malagasy. They wanted nothing of independence, or free choice, or self-determinism. They wanted the old familiar security of taboos and totems, and the fetishes of their ancestors. So they directed their bitterest attacks against the *évolués* and the *assimilés*—the Malagasy who had taken up with the Christian foreigners. Of the 8,500 big and little private plantations destroyed in the Rebellion, only 1,500 belonged to the French and Créole settlers. The rest were the enterprises of the educated Malagasy who had turned their backs on their own tribal past; such men and women and their children were slaughtered as apostates.

By May, 1948, Paris had sent down an additional 11,500 reliable officers and soldiers to raise the army of occupation to an effective of 18,000 men. In all the three years of the sporadic rebellion, the French lost a total of thirty settlers, most of whom were Créoles, some of whom were brutalized, all of whom were murdered; and 1,000 soldiers, not all of whom were Frenchmen from France. Nobody knows how many Malagasy died or were somehow killed. It has proved to be impossible to collect any sort of accurate statistics, but a conservative educated guess puts the casualties at 80,000—seventy-seven and one-half dead Malagasy to each French death. Of that great number, not many died quickly or violently. Two or three thousand only, maybe five, were shot, bludgeoned, cut up with knives, speared through, or cruelly tortured; and only a very few were executed.

The rest—and it may be as many as 120,000, or as few as 50,000—died of exposure, starvation, fright, and that strange and primitive form of suicide, the failure of the will to live, the choice to die, the refusal to survive. Whole villages and clans, entire regions, abandoned their flimsy huts and settlements; they ran from their rice fields, their manioc patches, and their bits of garden; they left behind their stores and granaries, their hens, their wells and springs. In panic they ran off into the forest and out onto the dry *savoka*. There are no gazelles in Madagascar, no greater or lesser antelopes, no zebras—there is no game; there are no laughing hyenas to eat the carrion. Perhaps a few families of lemurs—gentle nocturnal spirits in the trees, they have the liveliest of curiosity—may have watched the helpless, lost, demoralized, and desperate people die. Long ago in their tribal order they had relinquished their abiilty to adapt themselves to changing conditions. Over them flew rose-pink, sapphire-blue, and bottle-green dragonflies in the sunlight; and at night, the silent and wide-winged moths. The Malagasy call them *lolo*—"lool."

One of them, *Acherontia*, the Sphinx moth, is marked on the thorax with a death's head; such a *lolo* is the unhappy, wandering soul of a Malagasy deprived of rightful burial in his ancestral tomb. There are 800 known varieties of butterflies and moths in Madagascar. From the eighty thousand dead there arose a plague of ghosts to haunt the French.

In the last Sunday and Monday of March, and on into April and May—into winter—after the French awoke to find their island in rebellion, they came through their bewildered disbelief, and, being frightened, being shocked, they reacted in outraged fury—now and again with ferocity. There are a great too many stories about one cellar torture-chamber in Fianarantsoa, used to extract confessions.

General Pierre Garbay, a professional French soldier, a graduate of Saint-Cyr, who had rallied to General de Gaulle in June, 1940, from his command in Central Africa, and who in 1958 and 1959 served as military governor of Paris, led the expeditionary force sent in from France to put down the Malagasy Rebellion of 1947. In Paris he came to be called "the Butcher of Madagascar."

It is, I think, a misnomer, indirectly the result of the known and remembered German occupation—the betrayals, the denunciations of the collaborators and the Resistance; and of the work of the Gestapo and the Vichy militia; and of the scramble for place and power in those first chaotic years after the war. Those were the great days of the Existentialists of St.-Germain-des-Prés. Their bleak philosophy, itself an intellectual response to the long humiliations of defeat, then set the style of French thought. Existentialism went along with Communism in the state of mind of Jean-Paul Sartre, who tried his best to make sense of man alive on earth. Indeed, so did General Garbay, a man of military discipline in another state of mind. Each knew the other's ideas of order to be inimical. I do not know what names, if any, the general called the philosopher.

The direct cause of General Garbay's being termed a butcher was the unfortunate attempt of the Colonial authorities in Madagascar and in Paris to suppress the facts and to keep reports of the Malagasy Rebellion out of the newspapers of France, and of the world. A misapplied censorship angered all the journalists, silenced the free press, and gave the French Communist newspapers the chance to make a good thing of the tormented and slaughtered Malagasy patriots. *L'Humanité*, the Party organ, played it up, and gave it to be understood that those numberless, defenseless, faceless tribes of gentle and blameless people—driven to rebellion by Colonial, imperialistic oppression, and led by enlightened men of good will (what would a Communist do to a witch-doctor?)—were being bombed and strafed out of their own forests, driven like a battue of game into their own wide and open pasture-lands where tanks and ranks of men armed with machine-guns waited to mow them down—men, women, and children—in fusilades, in hecatombs. After Mussolini, Hitler, and Stalin, it is easy to believe anything, and very hard not to.

With the Fall of France in Europe in June of 1940, the Frenchman in Madagascar—the *vazaha*, the "Look-at-That!" the white and godlike man from across the sea—toppled from his high place and turned into a suffering, bewildered, and inadequate human being like the rest of us. In the crisis only General Charles de Gaulle maintained his *masiaka* grandeur and glory—and he came to propose freedom for the Malagasy (in central Africa his carved image is worshipped as a fetish).

The shock of disillusionment—or awakening—had its greatest effect among the young Malagasy men of the classes of 1938, 1939, and 1940 called up in Madagascar for military service in France as soldiers and laborers in the French Army; they took part in defeat and spent the war years in France and Germany. Some 8,000 Malagasy soldiers and 7,000 workers lived to be repatriated in August and October of 1946. These young men were eighteen, nineteen, and twenty when they left their tribal lands; they were the strongest and the most intelligent Malagasy of their generation.

Down south, I later got to know one of these much experienced men, the Reverend Mr. Jean-Albert Mahatoto ("Mah-toot"), a sober patriot, a serious, hard-working, middle-aged man of forty-two when I met him at Easter of 1958. He is the pastor of the Norwegian-American-Malagasy Lutheran church in Ampanihy ("Am-pan-ee"), a small administrative town of the arid province of Tuléar. There he took care of the spiritual, and the political, needs of some five hundred parishioners, although not that many came to listen to him on Sundays. The wooden pews were very hard to sit upon. The tall, narrow, somewhat Gothic church has a high stone steeple topped by battlements. Church and steeple tower above the well grown tamarind trees in the church yard and over the surrounding native huts, shops, administrative buildings, residences, and the rival Roman Catholic church.

It is cool inside the thick walls of stone and mortar where Pastor Mahatoto used to get himself, his parishioners, the American missionaries, and the Lutheran Protestants in periodic hot water with the jealous petty authorities, the Malagasy in the government bureaucracy, by preaching fiery political sermons until they put the law on him. They may have been rival Christians, educated anti-clericals—"freethinkers" in the French tradition—or old-fashioned ancestor-worshipping pagans; those were the days of French dominance under the French Union. Perhaps the small functionaries were afraid of losing their well paid jobs when total independence came—for such was the subject of the Reverend Mahatoto's sermons. The Malagasy in the civil service were paid on the same scale as the French; such a man could earn as much as $280 (in CFA francs) a month; the pastor was paid 5,000 French-African Colonial francs a month, or about $23.00; the money came from America. In 1958 there were in Madagascar 201,531 "adherents" to the Norwegian Lutheran sect out of a total of 923,959 Protestants; the Roman Catholics numbered 1,026,770. The rest of the Malagasy—3,049,271—were pagan.

Before I met Pastor Mahatoto and the Norwegian-American Lutheran missionaries, I had heard about them in the hotel bar in Manakara at the end of the train ride down the eastern escarpment. There I had a beer and talked with a prematurely bald French police commissioner, who had worked in France throughout the 1940–1945 war and German occupation. By day he had collaborated with the

Gestapo on the surface; by night with the French underground Resistance. He had learned to trust no man. In Madagascar he saw enemies and spies in what seemed to me to be unlikely places; he informed me that the Norwegian-American Lutheran missionaries, half from Norway, half from Minnesota, were sent out by a great international Protestant cartel with money to burn to convert and subvert the Malagasy. He said they consciously undermined the tribesmen's respect and admiration for the French, and had actively encouraged them during the Rebellion of 1947; the missionaries were not friends of France. And anyway, he knew for a fact that they had got their Protestant parishioners among the miners to steal samples of the radioactive thorianite and monazite ores to send off to— The police commissioner did not tell me where; he remembered in time that he was talking and drinking with an American and probably a Protestant and possibly with a spy. He was a plump and friendly man.

Protestants protest, among other things, the infallibility of godlike authority on earth. Pastor Mahatoto did so, conscientiously. When I met him, I saw a dark brown man, short and muscular, his thick white hair clipped close to his round head. He spoke excellent French and wore western clothes—a white cotton shirt and dark cotton trousers, fresh in the morning, rumpled at night—the work clothes of an active man. He told me with dignity and pride that he is a pure-blooded Antandröy, a tribesman of "the People of the Thorny Land," who are wild, primitive, and most attractive.

Forty-two years earlier, when he was born, his father wore a loin cloth and his mother a greater length and width of cotton. Although most of the Antandröy still go nearly naked, the pastor's wife wears a proper summer dress, as do two of their small, fat and healthy children; the two-year-old plays naked and chocolate brown near his mother as she stands to pound the husks from the rice in a classic wooden mortar and pestle. Her kitchen is all outdoors—an iron kettle hung over a fire of sticks. Their house of two rooms and a porch is stone-built, iron-roofed. The pastor puts on steel-rimmed spectacles to study at night in the light of a hurricane lantern. The rush-bottom chairs and deal-table were handmade of local wood.

Born in 1916, schooled by the American Lutheran mission, in 1938 he graduated from the École Pastorale, the Protestant theological school for Malagasy pastors in Fianarantsoa. At twenty-two, he felt himself to be no longer young. His brothers and cousins were already husbands and fathers, primitive and helpless pastoral tribesmen living in the thorny, desert land. He meant to go to live among them, to do the job for which he had prepared himself. But, having been deferred to complete his education, he was called up for military service; before the three-year period was over, the war had broken out in Europe. The French Army does not exempt priests, pastors, and monks, but assigns them to the medical corps as orderlies, stretcher bearers, ambulance drivers, and nurses; or of course as chaplains and grave diggers; or to some other non-combatant work—in the offices or canteens. Pastor Mahatoto went off to France; in the spring of 1940, he was assigned as a male nurse to a military hospital in Liège. One clear spring day in May, in the *Blitzkrieg,* he was taken prisoner along with the several thousand other French Colonial troops at Charleroi in the Ardennes. The long, forced march southeast to Luxembourg was for him no great physical hardship; the Antandröy are famous walkers. But to be packed into cattle cars too tight to lie down, and to be transported the long way by rail to a concentration camp in East Prussia, was bad.

Despite their confidence, the German victors had not counted on taking so many and so varied a collection of prisoners all together; they had not prepared themselves to handle the wide range of assorted French Colonial troopers, although they planned to keep them separate from the French for purpose of future use in propaganda. Besides the Malagasy, the haul included North African Arabs from Morocco, Algeria, and Tunisia; African Negroes from Senegal, Ubangi-Shari, Guinea, the Ivory Coast, the Cameroons (formerly a German colony), and the Congo; from Indo-China, Tonkinese, Annamites, Cochin-Chinese, Laotians, and Cambodians; and perhaps some South Sea Islanders as well. There were among them a group of "Republican" or "Loyalist" or "Red" refugees, Spanish war veterans who had crossed the Pyrenees in 1938, and who were taken on as laborers in 1939 by the French Army.

All these men of all races and political colorations were put together in what had been a prison camp, intended only for anti-Nazi civilian political prisoners. Some of these pre-war enemies of Hitler's Reich were still alive in residence; some were merely republicans or democrats who refused to conform; some were old-line, hard and fast Austrian and German Socialists and Communists. Among them were educated professional men who spoke French. Before their keepers got things organized and the various prisoners sorted out, the oldtimers and the newcomers had an instructive talk. Pastor Mahatoto remembered best a Basque school teacher and an Austrian physician, both convinced Socialists, neither of whom had as yet seen the need to change their opinions. To him they were a new breed of white man; they made a great impression on the young Antandröy Protestant pastor, who recalls their good fellowship and their good conversations on the subjects of freedom, the social order, human dignity, and the rights of man, before he lost sight of them. Later in the year, as the hard, northern winter set in, the then Minister of the Colonies in the French state government at Vichy persuaded the Nazis to return the Asian, African, Malagasy, and South Sea prisoners to the milder climate of occupied France, there to work the fields thus to release both French and other forced laborers to work in factories; and already the Africans and Malagasy were dying of pneumonia at an alarming rate.

Pastor Mahatoto was sent to Bordeaux; from there he was ordered further south into Les Landes, a flat and sandy region of pine forests. He was given an axe and put to work chopping down trees to burn as fuel to heat the occupying German headquarters and barracks; apparently he was not kept under close supervision, and not guarded. He got to know the forests well; one day, or one night, he walked off into the trees and escaped into unoccupied France, where he reported to the French Army authorities. They welcomed him and put him to work in various Army offices first in Toulouse, then in Montpellier, and finally in Toulon; he was a loyal French soldier.

As such, he was treated well; he shared whatever food there was to eat—no rice, few potatoes, little bread, but many turnips of the kind usually given to cattle, and a great deal of cabbage. When the Germans occupied the whole of France in 1942, nobody paid any special attention to him; he kept on doing his assigned work in the Vichy French Army.

After the European war ended in May, 1945, Pastor Mahatoto, as a soldier of the French Colonial Army, was sent across to Algeria to work on the edges of the Sahara Desert, where he managed a series of *foyers-du-soldat,* recreation centers for the ordinary troops. All this he much enjoyed. He talked, he listened, he made his observations; he had a great deal of time to think things over. He made up his mind what he was going to do when he got back to Madagascar, where he arrived in October, 1946. He went home to Ampanihy and got to work preaching the words of God and Jesus according to the Protestant Lutherans, and preaching self-determinism according to the new French ideas of speeding up the education of the Malagasy, citizens of Overseas France in the French Union.

Later that same year in the first elections to be held under the new order he was elected deputy in the Provincial Assembly of Tuléar by the voters of the second electoral college made up of *"les citoyens ayant conservé leur statut personel et administrés français,"* the new way of describing the Malagasy of Madagascar. Deputy Mahatoto still was working along with the French of the new order; his goal, which he believed he shared with the French colonists and functionaries, was the freedom of Madagascar as an independent nation. So far, so good. Then, on 29 March 1947, the rebellion broke out.

Pastor Mahatoto had made the mistake of joining the dominant political party of Madagascar, the M.D.R.M.—the Democratic Movement for the Restoration of Madagascar—and the frightened French authorities decided that this nationalistic party had planned the rebellion. Therefore, Pastor Mahatoto, the newly elected provincial deputy to the Tuléar Assembly, was arrested, put in prison in Tuléar, held for two years without specific charges, and then transferred to a cell in Tananarive to await trial after two more years. He was found guilty of inciting the Malagasy to riot, and was sentenced to four years in prison—the four years he had already served—and to ten more years of limited freedom on parole back in Ampanihy, from which town he could not travel without having first obtained specific permission from the French District Commissioner. He had to report regularly to the police; he could not take part in any sort of political organization or action and nor could he indulge in politics. In 1952 came the French general amnesty; Pastor Mahatoto was free to take up where he had left off. As a pastor and a pacifist—and, of course, as a prisoner—he had had nothing to do with the Rebellion of 1947 from beginning to end; he had never been involved. In fact there had been no violence done in his parish. But his personal experiences with French Colonial justice in and after the rebellion, for which he was in no way prepared —for he was innocent—turned him into an ardent nationalist, a man against the French rule. He had found his life work; it was to get the French out fast.

When I asked Pastor Mahatoto what had brought on the rebellion, and who, indeed, had organized it, he spoke out firmly to deny that any Malagasy had plotted to overthrow the government—none of the political parties of Madagascar, not even the handful of Communists in Diégo-Suarez, and certainly not his own party the M.D.R.M, had planned the uprising. Why should they? The Malagasy had everything to gain and nothing to lose under the terms of General de Gaulle's new government; and any man with any intelligence could see that no such native rebellion, lacking in all the necessities of leadership and supply, could have succeeded. It was bound to fail. The whole thing had been the cynical enterprise of the old-fashioned colonists worked out with the enthusiastic help of the French Colonial Army officers and the reactionaries in the government. Their real purpose was to thwart General de Gaulle's Fourth Republic and to smash the liberal ideas and actions of the French Union. They wanted no changes made in the status quo ante bellum. So they let loose the Rebellion of 1947 to flush out the French liberals and the Malagasy nationalists. They meant to break the back of the movement toward freedom in Madagascar before General de Gaulle could lift it off the ground. They wanted to keep the absolute control over Malagasy destiny in their own archaic hands.

I believe that this highly reasonable explanation of the causes of the rebellion has no basis in fact; but it does fit neatly into the aroused French and Malagasy emotions after the Moromanga midnight uprising.

Back in August and October of 1946, not many of the returning veterans had worked out a plan for their life work as had Jean-Albert Mahatoto, then in the prime of Malagasy life. He was thirty years old when he got off the troop transport in Tamatave and stepped onto the soil of his native land after seven years' absence. Most of the others among the returning 15,000 had disembarked and drifted off to their tribal lands and towns to be more or less successfully reabsorbed in the old way of life. Pastor Mahatoto was fortunate in having something clear in mind to do and the emotional drive to do it. The majority, who did nothing, had learned nothing from their experiences in France. But a good-sized minority, perhaps a thousand in all, had learned how to rebel.

At the time of the Fall of France, these young Malagasy soldiers escaped from the Germans, but had not gone back to work for the defeated French Army. They joined the best of the French men and women, and went underground into the Resistance, or up into the hills of the maquis. The French in France have little if any race prejudice; among the intellectuals the quality of the mind alone counts; in the Resistance, the men with black or brown skin, the men who walked silently in the night, the primitives who had not lost their animal-sharp senses—who could flair danger—served best and survived.

The Malagasy were made welcome, they were taken in, trained, and put to work. They learned how to sabotage the complex machinery and communications that hold a civilization and an occupying army together; they learned how to use explosives; they learned how to kill quietly with their hands, with cords, with a single blow or a single flash of a blackened knife. They learned about comradeship, friendship, mutual esteem, and self-respect—shared emotions that bind together men fighting to keep themselves and their ideas alive. In such warfare, even the most civilized of men find an intensity of life—unequated at peace. In the Resistance, these "primitive" and "wild" men found life whole; they also learned how to organize and bring off surprise attacks.

In August, 1946, came the first contingent of returning Malagasy veterans—veterans of the war, the defeat, the Resistance, the Liberation, and of idleness. Packed into the discomfort of a troopship, they had steamed for three weeks or a month through the summer heat of the Mediterranean, through the hot Red Sea, around the Horn of Africa, and down into the cool waters of the Indian Ocean; in Austral mid-winter they spilled ashore in Tamatave. A gang of these released young men, loosed in the shady streets of the quiet port city, went looking for trouble. They found what they were looking for in a mosque full of men and women of the Indian community praying in silence. Domed mosques hold a still and quiet light.

The Malagasy soldiers, trained killers, poured through the gateway, crossed the sunny courtyard, rushed past the fountain of the ablutions under its four trees, ran jumping up the steps onto the columned porch, streamed through the arched and open door, and massacred . . . whoever they were (Ismailis of the Aga Khan's sect in Islam, as a matter of fact). No one knows why. They felt like killing, so they killed. All the authorities agree that, left alone, the Malagasy people are gentle, mild, friendly, and shy; only the highland Merina are described, for good or evil, as aggressive; only the tall, black Sakalava at times go berserk.

I suppose that these assassins were caught; if so, I do not know what their punishment turned out to be. The massacre made no sense to the French in Madagascar, who saw it as a terrible, a horrible, a regrettable, an unheard of, but an isolated incident, trouble between the Malagasy and Indians—part of the price any community must pay for victory or defeat in total war; an aftermath, and not, as in fact it was, a portent.

Madagascar had been through seven lean years. First the outbreak of war in 1939 had stripped the island of the best of the young functionaries, Army and Navy officers, French colonists, and prime Malagasy tribesmen, all called to the colors. Then the Fall of France in June, 1940, stunned the empire. Then Marshal Pétain's decision to collaborate with the Nazis, and General de Gaulle's call to continue the battle, forced a terrible choice upon Frenchmen everywhere—and Madagascar's men in charge, by opting for Pétain and his defeated French state, made the wrong choice. In 1942 came the British invasion first of Diégo-Suarez and then of the whole island, after which the Free French came in to govern, but not necessarily to protect, the island. And all the other French colonies were put through similar upheavals.

An odd and at first an unreasonable historic fact emerged from France's downfall, and that is that an empire's strength is measured in inverse ratio to rapid means of communication. The Malagasy and the French colonials heard all the disastrous current events almost as soon as they took place. They followed the Black African colonies' decision (except for Dakar) to rally to de Gaulle. They heard of the surrender

to the Japanese of the French in Indo-China—as later they followed
Ho Chi-Minh's Communist success. They heard of the Allies' landing
in North Africa in 1942 to liberate Algeria, Morocco, and Tunisia from
the Vichy French authorities. Cut off from France, Madagascar was
thrown open to the world. An empire thrives in ignorance. The Malagasy learned from the outside how badly beaten France had been, and
how helplessly vulnerable they themselves were in their dependence
and their insufficiency. They saw that the French way of life in Madagascar could not support itself without a constant flow of necessities
and implements from France.

The war stripped the French and the tribal people almost quite literally naked; for lack of imported cloth, they went in patchwork and in
rags. All the island's cupboards were bare of medicines, of soap, of
wheat flour, of butter, of wine, of Vichy water, of gasoline, kerosene,
and fuel oil. The hinges, the handles, and the locks of things rusted,
stuck, and broke apart; pots and pans sprung leaks or took on the
value of treasured heirlooms; the big things and the little wore out. In
the towns and in the country, the tried and true tribal ways of doing
things came back to life. The imported French civilization proved itself
to be a fragile and a flimsy shelter, unreliable in time of crisis. To lose
a needle was a major disaster in a household; to read at night, a man
had first to make himself a tallow candle or to float a wick in oil
made from wild nuts gathered in the jungle.

In January, 1944, in Brazzaville, General de Gaulle spoke to representatives of all the French Colonial people; there he outlined his
plan for the French Union and the Fourth Republic, which he created
and put into effect in 1946. From the start, the operative idea was to
set the Colonial peoples free, and to prepare them for eventual self-
government in their own lands. No date was fixed; but the end in view
was freedom inside a French Union held together by the *Présence
Française*. General de Gaulle gave French citizenship to all 70,000,000
French Colonial autochthonous people; to be sure, it was not quite
the same as that of the French citizens of Europe, the 40,000,000
native-born French of Metropolitan France; but it was a start. The
trouble was that, by then, many did not want it. Things got out of hand
in Indo-China, in Tunisia, and later in Algeria. And in France, the
Fourth Republic turned into a politicians' battleground. General de

Gaulle retired from public life to Colombey-les-Deux-Églises in 1953.
Then on 23 June 1956 came the Loi-Cadre, the enabling act to speed
up the education and the preparation of the Colonial peoples to assume
control of their own destinies.

In 1946, for administrative purposes, Madagascar was divided into
five provinces, each named after its capital city: Tananarive in the
central highlands; Tamatave on the northern east coast with its hinterland; Majunga on the northwest shore and inland; Tuléar from coast
to coast at the southern end of the island; and Fianarantsoa from the
south highlands to the south central eastern shore. In 1956, a sixth
province, Diégo-Suarez, was carved out of the north tip of the island
with territory taken from Tamatave and Majunga. Each province had
its own assembly of thirty representatives directly elected in limited
suffrage by the first and the second electoral colleges—that of the
French citizens of metropolitan status, and that of the native-born
Malagasy. These provincial assemblies met in their several capital
cities. Their power was largely restricted to matters of taxation and
finance. However, they did elect from among themselves in all a total
of thirty-six men to sit in the Representative Assembly of Madagascar
that met in Tananarive to assist the Governor-General of the island.
In 1946, the two electoral colleges also elected five deputies—two
French, three Malagasy—to represent the island in the National Assembly in Paris; five senators—two French and three Malagasy;
seven representatives to the High Council of the French Union, in
Versailles; and twenty municipal councils for the big cities of the
island.

The Representative Assembly chose from among its members—or
from private citizens not elected to public office but properly qualified
to hold the position—a High Council of the island, in effect a Cabinet
of Ministers of Finance, Agriculture, Public Health, Commerce, Industry, Equipment (railroads, port facilities, etc.), Civil Service, and
Education and Youth. These ministers were either French or Malagasy.
The Vice-President of the High Council was, however, a Malagasy;
in effect a prime minister, he held the highest directly or indirectly
elected public office in the island. The President of the High Council
was the Governor-General, the French High Commissioner to Madagascar—a career serviceman.

258

The High Commissioner appointed the governors of each province, likewise career service officers from France, as were the heads of the districts into which each province was divided, and the district subdivisions, the administrative posts. Local Malagasy members of the island civil service were named governors, or chiefs of cantons to head the smaller units inside the districts.

The Loi-Cadre of 23 June 1956 came down from Paris; it was a piece of liberal legislation, most probably drawn up and passed in an attempt to keep the Black African and Malagasy territories from breaking out of the French Union, as had the states of Indo-China and North Africa. The two most revolutionary aspects of this Enabling Act were the abolition of the two electoral colleges with the consequent enlargement of universal suffrage—ready or not; and the forming of a truly powerful and responsible executive cabinet of men living in the island. Thus the Representative Assembly, whose members made up this High Council, took on greater importance.

Thus, the island's internal government and system of administration was admirably designed to bring the Malagasy by easy stages into an understanding of the principles and facts of self-rule.

In the elections of 1946, the first under the terms of the French Union of the Fourth Republic, the islanders had not been given universal suffrage, and the two unequal electoral colleges had been established for sound French reasons. With two-thirds of the Malagasy illiterate, the majority of the people did not know what democratic processes were all about. They are foreign concepts in Africa and Madagascar; they are white men's burdens. Therefore the French restricted the suffrage to qualified voters who fulfilled certain educational, residential, financial, and tax-paying property-owning requirements, as well as the expected ones of age, sanity, and habits of life within the law. Out of a total population of roughly 4,100,000, only 883,000 French and Malagasy men and women passed the tests and registered to vote. In those days, the relation between the French citizens of whatever origin in Madagascar and the Malagasy was an equivalent of one in one hundred—an imbalance that, for all its logic, did not result in a working democracy, but instead in an oligarchy working in close sympathy with the Chief Executive, who was (it is to be remembered) a High Commissioner and a Governor-General, a

career civil servant appointed by the French government and sent
down from Paris. As things worked out, this bureaucrat, this functionary was usually more liberal in views and in actions than the
bound-to-be reactionary colonists. Thus in its first form, the French
Union's design for democracy in Madagascar was more of a demonstration than a reality of self-rule. The French felt that the Malagasy
were not yet ready to assume the full responsibilities of guiding their
own destinies. The Malagasy felt otherwise. Nobody fixed a date in
the future to make an end and a beginning.

Even so, 883,000 out of 4,100,000 is a very good number of voters.
Whatever else it shows, it gives evidence of a Malagasy national
characteristic; in or out of the French Presence, they are passionate
about politics. To prepare for the elections of 1946, their first action
was to form, with or without outside help, their own political parties.
The most important was the famous M.D.R.M., the *Mouvement
Démocratique de la Rénovation Malgache*. *Rénovation* can be translated as renewal, restoration, revival, or rehabilitation; none of the
meanings flattered the French. The name of the party in English is
thus the Democratic Movement for the Revival of Madagascar—as an
independent island nation, with self-rule restored. From the first, it
became the party of the great majority.

To offset a surprising and alarming display of anti-French sentiment
in the most popular of the new parties, the authorities in Paris and
Tananarive, with the cooperation of the French colonists and the
French Roman Catholic missionary orders, organized and sponsored a
pro-French political party, designed to split the Malagasy tribes apart
and to group the "coastal" tribes of the seventeen lesser peoples against
the dominant highland Merina. In propaganda fashion, the party was
called the *Parti des Déshérités Malgaches* (the Party of the Dispossessed of Madagascar) or PADESM.

From outside the various parties, the old, the reactionary, the en-
trenched French colonists looked on with jaundiced eyes. No matter
what developed from the French Union's 1946 elections, they knew
they stood to lose. There has always been an antagonism between the
resident French settlers, planters, concessionnaires, and businessmen
and the transient French government functionaries, here today and
gone tomorrow, and good riddance. The two groups rarely met out-

side office hours, and did not mix easily at social gatherings. The old Madécasses French citizens, whether or not they intended to pull up stakes and retire to France when the time came, or to stay in Madagascar for life (as French citizens), later blamed the outbreak of the Rebellion of 1947 on these half-baked elections, and on the soft, as against hard, Colonial policies of General de Gaulle. To these realists, the elections proved one thing and that was the demonstrated fact that the Malagasy were not then (as they are not now) ready for or capable of self-government—no more than are their ancestors, the lemurs in the trees. "The white man is committing hara-kiri." The old hands blamed all the troubles on the new ideas imported from Paris. Without the shouting of the Left Bank intellectuals, Communist, Catholic, or liberal, none of the subsequent events would have boiled over. Let alone, the Malagasy would have been docile and mild. *They* knew what they were talking about; *they* had spent their lives making something of the island; *they* knew the Malagasy as Paris did not. But nobody would listen to *them*.

And, in fact, of course these old hands were right, although in placing the blame they did not go back far enough. All the dangerous ideas, all the radical notions of self-government, self-determinism, and freedom of choice, are foreign importations, as is the concept of government to guarantee the rights of the individual man. In fact, history itself was brought into Madagascar by European white men; once in place, history would not stand still to suit the colonists.

The Rebellion of 1947:
Three Malagasy Martyrs

THE M.D.R.M. party, the Democratic Movement for the Revival of
Madagascar, was organized in February of 1946; the elections took
place in August and in October of that year and, whatever else resulted, three symbolic Malagasy heroes and martyrs of the Rebellion
of 29–30 March 1947 emerged—the three Malagasy of the five
deputies elected to represent Madagascar in the French National
Assembly in Paris. They were, because of their offices, if not the
most powerful, certainly the most distinguished Malagasy in the new
government of the French Union.

The oldest, Joseph Raseta, was the spokesman for the M.D.R.M. in
the 1946 elections. Sixty-one years old in 1947, he was born in 1886,
ten years before Madagascar was annexed by the French as a colony.
An educated man and a doctor of medicine, he is a Merina tribesman
of an old feudal family in the Hova caste of freemen. He was elected
deputy from the Third District on the west coast. These five electoral
districts cut across provincial and tribal boundaries. Dr. Raseta was in
Paris on the night of 29–30 March 1947; he has been involved in
nationalist politics all his life.

The second, likewise a very well known patriot, active all his life in
anti-French politics, is Andrianavalona Ravoahangy, seven years
younger than Dr. Raseta, born in 1893—two years before the French
conquest. Another doctor of medicine and an educated man, he is
also a member of the Merina tribe, and a prince of the royal caste of

Andriana. He, too, is an old revolutionary, elected deputy from the First District in the highlands, where most of the French citizens of all origins live.

The third and youngest of the elected deputies is a poet (in the French language) and a Betsimisaraka—a member of the second largest of the Malagasy tribes. A newcomer to politics, he had earned his living as a favored Malagasy employee of the French Colonial government, and, in fact, spent the war years in France. Aged thirty-six in 1946, Jacques Rabemananjara represented the Second District along the east coast, a country of rich plantations including the vanilla of Antalaha and Andapa, and the island's main port of Tamatave.

Dr. Raseta ("Rah-sate"), Prince Ravoahangy ("Rah-voo-ahng"), and Mr. Rabemananjara ("Rah-beh-mahn-ahn-jahr"), two physicians and a poet, all deputies, two Merina, one of the free caste and one of the royal caste of the former ruling and still dominant tribe, one a peasant intellectual, three small and rather frail men with skin of various intensities of brown, are all three assimilated into, or by, French culture and French civilization. They cut their hair in the French way; they wear French clothes; they use French gestures in a voluntary or involuntary nervous and muscular response to conditioned reflexes; they think French thoughts; they talk like Frenchmen; and they walk like Frenchmen. But they are Malagasy by birth and by choice.

And yet, as properly elected deputies in the National Assembly of France, in Paris, seated in the Palais Bourbon across the bridge across the river from the Place de la Concorde, they were supposed to speak and to vote for France Across the Sea, and not for Madagascar. These three men were revolutionaries.

The two doctors, Raseta and Prince Ravoahangy, were old hands at political action against the French of France. Thirty years earlier, when they were medical students and interns together in Tananarive, they joined a secret political society called Vy Vato Sakelika (V.V.S. for short) which translates as "Iron Stone Scion"; iron and stone had the usual symbolic meanings, and scion referred to the green plant-shoot that springs up from the tenacious root when the *ravenala*, the traveler's tree, is cut down. *Ravenala madagascariensis* of the *Musaceae* order, and a cousin of the banana, is the emblem of Madagascar. The rainwater that collects at the base of its great spreading fan of leaves is supposed to succor thirsting travelers lost in the wilderness; the water is apt to be full of drowned bugs.

Perhaps the medical students were trying to cure the body politics. They prescribed rebellion against the French, but the operation failed. The V.V.S. was suppressed in 1916, and both young doctors, one thirty, the other twenty-three, were arrested, tried and condemned to forced labor for life. Raseta served six years, Ravoahangy four; they were freed and amnestied—and went out to fight again for freedom. Time and again the while they practiced medicine, both men were brought in to face French justice in the Colonial courts. In 1936, when he was fifty, Raseta joined the Malagasy Communist Party—the one repudiated by the French C.P. as being not international but instead feudal. In 1941, the Vichy bureaucrats interned him as a dangerous element; in 1943, the Free French freed him. In 1945, he was the best known of the Malagasy nationalists and patriots; in 1946, a charter member, he helped organize the M.D.R.M.; he was easily elected deputy. But who was he to represent in Paris?

Prince Ravoahangy had a similar history, except for the Communism; instead he had a following of young men who called themselves the Soldiers of Ravoahangy; they fought no battles, but they were ready. The doctor prince earned his living as an employee of the Health Service of the French Colonial government in Madagascar.

Jacques Rabemananjara, the peasant and the poet, might have been a slave in one of the doctors' households, had he been of their generation. Born in 1910, he is a short, thin man of dark-brown skin, by no means a Bohemian in appearance. A devout Roman Catholic, he is not a Communist; he is a conservative in literary taste as well as in politics. A favorite of the French, he was a responsive and a rewarding student in the Malagasy schools. In 1938, his teachers got him a post in the Ministry of Colonial Affairs in Paris—so that he could sample the heady life of the literary cafés, le Dôme, la Coupole, le Flore, les Deux-Magots, and in the Place du Tertre. There he found himself— and he found Madagascar.

He saw France fall; he saw the Germans march in to occupy Paris, and all France. He saw the whole long humiliation, the collaboration, the Resistance, and the Liberation. He saw French friends vanish in the night. His education was not sentimental. So France formed this Malagasy poet and patriot—and martyr.

The Rebellion of 1947: Three Malagasy Martyrs

Back on his own island after the war, he got into politics by way of literature. He started making speeches. Oratory is the whore of the arts; propaganda is a kind of debased poetry. He joined the party of the Democratic Movement for the Revivification of Madagascar, the M.D.R.M.; and he was elected deputy. His speeches then became indeed inflammatory, full of phrases such as "Have you the souls of slaves?" "How can you respect the French?" He called the French colonials that bad word, *embusqués*—shirkers, draft-dodgers, men who prize their skins above their honor. He called them collaborators—he called them swine. He urged the Malagasy tribal people, unlike him, not yet *évolué* and assimilated into French civilization and culture, to massacre the French colonials, to chop them to bits, to pour French blood into the blood-red rivers of Madagascar. Or so his words come out in English from the French translations from the Malagasy—a language said to be mellifluous if not precise in meaning. French concepts, the clarity of French thought, do not suit the Malagasy language, nor yet the Malagasy.

Came the rebellion. Dr. Raseta, the deputy-elect, was in Paris on the midnight of 29–30 March 1947; the prince and the poet were in Tananarive. As soon as Dr. Raseta returned, in April, all three deputies were put under house arrest, and interrogated by the Colonial authorities—whom they were not elected to represent in the National Assembly. All three denied any knowledge of the preparation for, or organization of, the uprising. All three maintained their innocence, and seem to have been genuinely taken aback by the explosion of violence at Moromanga and the close escape of Tananarive. They were, in fact, dismayed—rarely do poets and orators gets such a response to their words. They saw to it at once that the political bureau of their party, the M.D.R.M., issued a proclamation to deny all part of the organizing of the uprising in Moromanga, which they described as "an odious act."

Perhaps they were themselves outraged because, in fact, the rebellion, as they had envisaged it, had slipped in the night from their hands. Instead of a defiance at the barricades such as those the citizens of Paris threw across the old familiar streets in 1588, 1648, 1830, 1848, 1851, 1871, and at the hour of Liberation in 1944, the three deputies' call for action had released the dark forces of the witchdoctors and sorcerers, benighted men whom they themselves knew to be cruel reactionaries, savages, dangerous and wild. The doctors and the poet, being French intellectuals, educated men of orderly, reasonable processes of thought, had surely imagined a revolution *à la française* to prove the Malagasy right to independence, and not this black and bloody horror. For all their hot language used in inflammatory speech, they were revolting toward a new order—not away from enlightenment. They found to their grief that their life work was being swept away, and that the Malagasy then murdering defenseless isolated men and women—Malagasy, Créole, French, and all the rest—were in full regression, and in full power. It was not what they had had in mind.

But the French split no such hairs; in the night of 29–30 March, all the Malagasy were black. In April, 1947, the Colonial authorities rounded up the members of the M.D.R.M.—the doctor, the prince, and the poet along with all the other dangerous elements, cultivated or wild, privileged or down-trodden—and threw them all together into jail, where they can be said to have languished for several months, for a year, for longer. The rebellion still went on outside.

The three deputies—who, of course, lost their jobs—and the other "leaders" held to be responsible for the uprising were brought to trial on 22 July 1948 while the "troubles" were still going on. Thus the trial, conducted according to French law before French justices, took place in a courtroom tense with fear, anger, righteous indignation, and shocked hurt feelings. Some wore mourning. On October 4, the men were all found guilty of treasonable crimes against the state and the French citizens of both European and local status. The two physicians, old offenders, were condemned to death; the poet, a newcomer, to life at hard labor. Two years later, in 1950, the tensions in Madagascar meantime having died down, leaving the French in control, secure and, it may be, somewhat embarrassed by their earlier excesses, the authorities magnanimously commuted the death sentences to life imprisonment.

The French *like* the Malagasy (as much as the French like any other race); and they love all the ways of making politics, of which, after all, rebellion is no more than the major *crime passionnel*. Thus it is thoroughly understandable, after the fact; and it demands tolerance and clemency in fitting a punishment to the crime of rebellion. My guess is that the French, although exasperated by them, were secretly proud of Dr. Raseta, Prince Ravoahangy, and the poet Rabemananjara, who were so very French in refusing to abandon their convictions. Mistaken though, of course, they were, there was something grand and glorious about them.

So, two years later, in 1952, when the lesser criminals—such as Pastor Jean-Albert Mahatoto—were amnestied, the former deputies, who could not be let off Scot-free in Madagascar, were sent into exile for life, not to any Devil's Island—but to France! Dr. Raseta was ordered to live in Grasse, a southern town surrounded by fields of perfume-flowers above the Côte d'Azur. Prince Ravoahangy went to Toulouse in the southwest, a red-brick city of good food. The poet Rabemananjara was exiled to Paris.

In exile, Jacques Rabemananjara went on writing poetry—as he had in prison. He found his audience in a congenial group of literary men and intellectuals, fellow exiles, in Paris although the others all voluntarily left their homes. Some of them, it is true, went to Paris for short stays to indulge their nostalgia, and because life is most attractive for them there. Most of them are also mixed up in politics. All but the Australo-Melanesian-Polynesian-Negro Betsimisaraka tribesman, Jacques Rabemananjara, are Black Africans—although for a short time before his death, the American writer Richard Wright, not himself wholly Negro, and of an alien culture, joined the group; it calls itself the Société de la Culture Africaine.

The Society of African Culture has premises at 42 rue Descartes, a little twisted street named after a great, straight-thinking French philosopher, René Descartes (1596–1650), whose idea has been bent in the street of his name to read "I think, therefore I am . . . French or African." It runs along the slopes rising above the left bank of the Seine on Mont Ste.-Geneviève, named for the patron saint of Paris, who lived from 420 to 512 A.D., and who saved her city from Attila the Hun. Her erstwhile church crowning the hill is now the Panthéon, where (some of) the great dead men of France lie honored in grandeur and glory.

This society to preserve and celebrate African culture has a publishing house and edits a literary revue, both called *La Présence Africaine*. There is a watchword, too: *Négritude*. "Nigritude" means something black—and not white, not French, not European, not of the Western world—found in the Negro soul and spirit. As anyone can see who looks at the "primitive" West African carving in wood and in ivory, or at the Benin and Ife bronzes, or at the Ashanti gold weights; who sees Africans or Malagasy dance; who hears a tom-tom beat or a Negro laugh at night; or listens to spirituals or jazz. Others have recognized it among the Mau Mau and in the Congo. But the Nigritude of the African Presence in the Society of African Culture is as abstract as Pablo Picasso's "Young Ladies of Avignon" of 1907; indeed, more so, for it comes from the inside out, and is not analytical. It is instinctive.

In the beginning, the society was sponsored and financed by Mr. Léonard Sédar Senghor, the first and actual President of the independent Republic of Senegal in the French Community, when he was a senator from Dakar in the French Union. He convinced the Senegalese Assembly to make a grant from the public revenues of what was then the most ancient part of African Overseas France, a fragment of Colbert's and the Sun King's commercial empire. President Senghor is the very type of French intellectual, in himself proof positive of the power and the grace of French civilization. For all his nigritude of skin, he is a witty, cultivated, well formed Frenchman; he speaks remarkably beautiful French; in Africa he is a part of the *Présence Française*—in Paris he is foremost in the *Présence Africaine*. Thus he is—and knows himself to be—a man of two worlds.

It is hard to define the meaning of the *Présence Française* in Africa and Madagascar—for it is both abstract and concrete, generous and niggardly, bodily and spiritual, venal and ideal, methodical and nebulous, emotional and intellectual, good and bad, and so on in the endless perspective of a hall of mirrors—and it is even harder to get a clear idea of the *Présence Africaine* in Paris. Since Freud discovered the dark and forested continent of the Id, and Jung the many mansions of racial memory, who can say for sure why any of us does anything?

One fact seems clear: neither has any meaning without the other. Yet the nigritude of the African presence is more than the reverse of the medallion. It is more than the other side. It is more than the black substance cast by a white shadow; more than the *Présence Française* mirrored in a pool of ink. It must be more than the sum of what it is not. I think it is a search for identity. If ignorance is black, and knowledge is the light, it may well be a cry—"Who am I?"—

from the heart of the educated, detribalized man of whatever birth as he confronts the enormous unknown. In his ignorance he was not alone. The modern man's Ego, of whatever definition, now appears to be.

To more immediate effect, the *Présence Africaine* calls upon the Africans of Africa, the Malagasy of Madagascar, to recognize their own worth, and not to surrender the separate, peculiar, and distinct qualities of their nigritude as modern times—1960, to put an arbitrary date to it—largely a white man's technical and scientific invention, moves down and over them. In effect, the nineteenth and twentieth centuries flowed into Africa and Madagascar like the rivers of a melting glacial age.

It seems clear to me, on surer ground, that the existence of the Society for (the preservation of) African Culture, with its review, the *Présence Africaine,* and its word Nigritude, demonstrates the flaw and the failure built into the French Colonial civilizing mission—as well as its success. For this group of cultivated, educated, displaced *évolués* from Africa, with one from Madagascar, came together in Paris to keep their identity as black men in a white world where they are foreigners, but where one cannot stand up without the other; each brought the other into being.

The nineteenth-century French colonists and conquerors saw themselves as tall men standing in darkness holding aloft the torch of (French) enlightenment. As they illuminated the benighted regions, they took for granted that the grateful Africans and Malagasy, attracted to the light, would join them to live forever and a day at peace. They knew that what they brought with them was of obvious worth. But the hand holding a torch on high casts its own shadow. In this dark island in the light, the *Présence Africaine* lit its own small candle. The civilizing mission was revealed as standing on shaky ground.

The theory and practice of French Colonial policy was based on the assumption that the native is an inferior being who will feel and see no treachery, no act of disloyalty, no breach of faith, in his denial of his own past, the disowning of his way of life, the voluntary abandonment of his language, his line of thought, his customs, his laws, his social structure, his family, and his gods—and of himself—in order to take on the natural superiority of the foreign white man.

To benefit under and from the *Présence Française,* the native first had to feel, understand, recognize, and accept his own inferiority—if not his unworthiness. Then he had to put on the white man's clothing —and walk as a turncoat in the land, a traitor among his own people. After that, as a supreme reward he might, if he passed the trial period and proved himself to be good material, be given French citizenship enabling him to visit or even to live out the rest of his life in France. The *évolué* and the *assimilé* had to be a bad African or a bad Malagasy in order to become a good Frenchman. I wonder what such a man made of Jeremiah's question, "Can the Ethiopian change his skin, or the leopard his spots? then may ye also do good, that are accustomed to do evil." (Chapter 13, verse 23). Even in the United States, a land of voluntary self-exiles, the country of transition to a new world, it takes at least three generations of hard work in residence to make an American like James Baldwin. No good Frenchman would think of doing any such thing, himself. A turncoat is an object of suspicion and of scorn in France, not to be trusted. A Frenchman cannot surrender his identity, it isn't logical, it isn't reasonable, it is not natural.

Yet the foundation of the French Colonial policy with its generous offer of France to all her Colonial peoples was built upon a prerequisite act of self-betrayal. There is nothing crueler than to be taught to despise and to reject the natural self. Out of this nurtured ambivalence arose the Rebellion of 1947—and the little intellectual society of expatriated Africans, and one Malagasy, in Paris. The black man decided not to commit hara-kiri.

The dynamic concept of Nigritude, whatever its origins and meanings may be, that drew these displaced Africans and Malagasy persons together in a social, literary, and intellectual bond in Paris has not noticeably spread—or not in club form. To be sure, the French Communist Party tried to infiltrate the group and take it over for the Comintern, but without notable success. Since independence as of 1960, most of the members of the society have gone back to hard work in Africa—they have gone about their business.

During the last days of the Fourth Republic, the members enjoyed themselves. They had meetings, they organized conferences, they published books, and they gave receptions. At one agreeable soirée, they toasted *la Négritude* in *brut* champagne and made speeches in their common tongue—French. It was a ladies' evening at the club, and all of them were white and some of them were the wives of the married men. There is a shortage of emancipated, cultivated women in Africa; the continent is—as much as any world can be—a man's world. Such is not the case in Madagascar; women have never known inequality on the island.

Back home, the Malagasy agitators would not let the three men alone. By 1959, a collective image of Dr. Raseta, Prince Ravoahangy, and the poet Rabemananjara had been projected onto the Franco-Malagasy political scene. The exiles were being used to make trouble. Over the years, they had become larger than life, their outlines oversimplified, their personalities distorted to fit that of tragic men suffering a martyrdom of heroes.

Politics

AFTER the Malagasy Rebellion of 1947, the Indo-Chinese war of 1945–1954, the North African and Algerian war of 1955–1962, and the Colonels' Rebellion of 1958, General Charles de Gaulle liberated France from the Colonial empire—except for a few islands such as the Overseas departments of Réunion and Martinique, and the territories of the Comoro archipelago—in order to restore the grandeur and glory of his country as the destined leader of civilized Europe.

In Madagascar the decolonization has worked out remarkably well. The successful launching of the island's independence was the work of three men: President Charles de Gaulle of the Fourth and Fifth French Republics and the French Community; Mr. Philibert Tsiranana, first President of the Malagasy Republic; and Mr. André Soucadaux, the last Governor-General and High Commissioner of France in Madagascar from 1954 to 1960. Of President de Gaulle, it becomes clear that the world knows little and understands less, but there is no doubt of his heroic stature as a great Frenchman.

Mr. Soucadaux, chief of the government of the Overseas Territory of Madagascar in the days of the Loi-Cadre of 1956–1958 under the French Union, and representative of the President of the Community in 1959, carried the full weight of France in the island during the revolutionary period of transition when Franco-Malagasy affairs moved very fast indeed, and might well have got out of hand. He had a job to do; he did his job well. A career officer in the Military of the

Colonies and the Ministry of Overseas France, his present address is the Ministry of Foreign Affairs—Quai d'Orsay—where he continues his work under the Secretary of State who heads the Ministry of Cooperation with the African States. As an efficient officer, Mr. Soucadaux is anonymous—careful never to draw attention to himself.

Mr. Philibert Tsiranana ("Philibert" as in French, and the last name "Tsee-rahn"—the final *ana* unvoiced) is a member of the vital and dynamic Tsimihety ("Tsee-mee-ate") tribe Who Do Not Cut Their Hair of the central north section of the island and along the northwest coast in the province of Majunga. The Tsimihety are hard-working cattle-herdsmen and rice growers; they are healthy, prolific, and fairly conservative in guarding a way of life based on the family as a unit. Ethnically of Melano-Polynesian origin and culture, they are not a distinct people like the highland Merina of the south-central Bara. Their ancestors did not all come from the same island at the same time to land on Madagascar in the same place, thereafter to keep together as a social or political entity. Instead, the Tsimihety are thought to be a mixture of the neighboring Malagasy tribal stocks and foreign blood: Merina, Betsimisaraka, Sakalava, and Antakara as a basis, with later infusions from the various Near and Middle Eastern visitors, for the most part the Arab and Zanzibari slavers and traders who visited the northwest harbors over a period of a thousand years, as well as the European and American pirates of the seventeenth and eighteenth centuries—perhaps some are descendants of Misson's Liberi of Libertalia. Whatever the mixture, the combined bloods have produced a short, stocky, strong tribe of people with medium-brown skin and tightly curled, dark brown hair; some of the women more often than the men have light complexions and a notably Arab or Mediterranean cast of features. Perhaps, as with North Americans, the Tsimihety have inherited the dynamic energy of the hybrid.

Mr. Tsiranana is typical in that he is short, robust, barrel-chested, round of head, and brown of skin; he radiates determination and force of character; he gives the impression that he knows what he is doing, will do it, and enjoys doing so. He is self-confident; he is in control.

Mr. Tsiranana's Social-Democrat Party of Madagascar, the P.S.D.M., is, in fact, conservative; it had to be nationalistic and to proclaim its aim to get freedom from the French for the island. But as all the other

273

political parties of Madagascar had an identical plank cut from the same hardwood tree built into their platforms, Mr. Tsiranana had plenty of leeway to move about on his—left or right, to the fore, or to mark time.

In forming his political party, Mr. Tsiranana had the full support and guidance of Mr. Soucadaux, the French High Commissioner. Together they organized the P.S.D.M. so to appeal to the widest range of conservatives, moderates, and liberals in the island, from the educated professional and business men down through the members of the local trade unions, and into the pool of illiterate voters in the *brousse*—the wild tribal men and women. Indeed, the President's opponents said that he and the high commissioner exaggerated in their membership drive before the Referendum of 1958. These two men, one French, one Malagasy, the highest government officials of Madagascar, were said to have brought the weight of their combined prestige and power to bear upon the local Malagasy authorities—small functionaries, school teachers, village and clan headmen—to make use of the soldiers and gendarmes stationed to keep the peace in the backwoods and remote coasts in order to encourage the newly enfranchised voters to register as members of the President's political party. In truth, the two responsible men knew what they were doing; they were protecting the best interests of the islanders, their people, of whom two-thirds were illiterate. And of the literate third, only 13 per cent (217,000, give or take a few) spoke French; still fewer read and wrote the language of emancipation and democracy—and modern times—in Madagascar.

In the Referendum for or against the Fifth Republic and the Community on 28 September, 78 per cent of the Malagasy electorate voted Yes. It is a respectable figure, whether or not the people knew what they were doing. The splendid but yet not exaggerated affirmative (Secou Touré in Guinea ordered and got almost total rejection; Felix Houphouët-Boigny in the Ivory Coast commanded an almost total acceptance) gave Mr. Tsiranana a mandate to go ahead along the lines he had laid down. Whatever else it may have been, it was a vote of confidence in him as the leader of Madagascar for the Malagasy. On 14 October the Representative Assembly, the Cabinet, and the prime minister declared Madagascar to be an independent country inside the French Community, and called it the République Malgache. On 28 April 1959 the Constitution of the Malagasy Republic was adopted in the National Assembly by a vote of 85 out of a possible 86. On 1 May, Mr. Philibert Tsiranana's appointment was announced as one of the Community's delegates to the United Nations.

Mr. Tsiranana is now the foremost man of Madagascar; indeed, he is one of the great names of Africa. He is a world figure.

In his own absolute rule, unlike the other President in the Community (the President of France), although he, too, always knows what is best for his people, Mr. Tsiranana has neither produced a climate of political apathy nor precipitated a murderous, secret opposition. Those Malagasy individuals and parties who do not agree with him and his policies speak up to say so; and some make sense.

If a two-party system tends to limit the electorate to a choice of either for or against (and apparently most Americans vote against the man they dislike), at least both parties carry weight; and the loser remains powerful in defeat. Such is not the case with the multiple-party system, which tends to fragment the franchise, and at times, as in France, to bring chaos into the National Assembly and the Cabinet. The Malagasy Republic is still too new a country for political issues to have taken hard shape. However, the proliferation of parties has produced an active and vocal opposition, both loyal and otherwise.

Miss Gisèle Rabesahala has organized a model apparatus of Marxist workers' and peoples' and intellectuals' and students' and fellow-travelers' and fuzz-heads' parties and groups and committees; some crypto, some wide open, seven in all; some with newspapers, some with banners; and all activists engaged in spreading the classic agitprop. Not a public figure, never standing for elections, Miss Rabesahala is the secretary-general of her Party's political holding company; she sits in the center of her network. So far, she has made little more than a nuisance of herself and of her figureheads—perhaps because she, too, brooks no internal opposition. She holds tight to the real power. Thus no truly popular potential Red dictator has taken shape, either in the image or in the flesh, for the Malagasy Communists to rally round—perhaps because she is both the cardinal and the *éminence rouge,* she inhibits such a growth. Thus although the Province and the Bay of Diégo-Suarez still send her chosen deputies to sit in the island parliament, so far President Tsiranana has been able to exclude all known or suspected Communists from his government.

He has included men of the loyal opposition, as well as others chosen not for their politics but for their proved abilities and special knowledge, one or two of whom are apolitical. Such men may belong to the Malagasy National Rally, which is a gathering of six or seven very minor and amorphous political parties, each with a name and a nature hard to define—as are the nuances of their political beliefs. Some have been gulled in the past by the Communists. All are nationalists with varying intensities of anti-French emotions.

A more interesting group calls itself, somewhat paradoxically, the Union of Independents; it is made up of independent parties and independent men. One such man, a party of one, was elected mayor of Tananarive in 1959: Mr. Stanislas Rakotonirina, an Hova of the Merina, a cultivated man who speaks the French of France. He was outspoken, indeed, in his No to de Gaulle in the Referendum—he advocated a clean break with the Fifth Republic and total independence all at once. He speaks out against the government of President Tsiranana. Yet he does not speak for himself entirely alone.

In 1947, a devout Roman Catholic, a husband, the father of six children (some of whom he sent to France to complete their education), he joined the M.D.R.M.—the Renovation Party of the hero-martyrs— and in the rebellion he suffered the consequences. Mr. Rakotonirina was arrested and interrogated by the then director of the French Sûreté himself. The French officer knocked out two of the civilized Merina's front teeth. The Malagasy as a rule have good teeth; the mayor of Tananarive has never had the gap bridged.

To me the most delightful of the parties in opposition calls itself, openly, the Union of Malagasy Intellectuals and University Graduates! It stands way down in the minority; and, understandably, its most distinguished member has never been elected to high political office. Instead Mr. Alfred Ramangasoavina was appointed by the President to be the Minister of Industry and Economic Planning. He is an Hova of the Merina, a brilliant man, proof of the success of the civilizing mission and of Malagasy worth.

A million and a quarter of the Malagasy people—one-fourth of the total population—are Merina highlanders; the great majority of the educated and intellectual islanders, and certainly the most thoughtful and able public men, are Hovas. Yet partly because the lesser tribal people still suspect their former conquerors of trying to reëstablish their old absolute domination; and partly because of the ancient, but serviceable, imperial policy of Divide and Rule—put back to work by Gallieni to keep the eighteen tribes from uniting against him and his handful of Foreign Legionnaires, and also for lack of a better French Colonial policy, as well as for lack of republican support in men, money, and matériel—the Merina are not, in fact, proportionally represented in the government of the Malagasy Republic.

Before independence, the only strong opposition to Mr. Tsiranana and his P.S.D.M. (Social Democratic Party of Madagascar) came from the Union des Démocrates Sociaux de Madagascar, the U.D.S.M. (in English, the Union of Social Democrats of Madagascar), whose head man was Mr. Nobert Zafimahova ("Zaf-mah-oov"), perhaps a figurehead. The two parties sound very much alike in name; but they are not so in nature. Both are, or were, nationalistic; both came out strongly for freedom and autonomy; both are anti-Communist; each is conservative in policy. But the two parties and the two men were diametrically opposed in their proposals for the Constitution of the Malagasy Republic. Mr. Tsiranana advocated a strong central government—he was a Federalist. Mr. Zafimahova wanted a weak central government and strong provincial government—he stood for States' Rights.

However, both leaders and both parties agreed that independent Madagascar should remain in the French Community and retain the *Présence Française*—in modified form. So Tsiranana, then a deputy in the French National Assembly, and Mr. Zafimahova, then a senator in the Conseil de la République, of France, of the Fourth Republic and the French Union (although in fact neither was functioning during the second de Gaulle interim government), got out the Yes vote in the Referendum. But their alliance turned them into political and personal enemies.

In the contest for power, from October 1958 through April 1959, Mr. Tsiranana outweighed his opponent: he held eight public offices to Mr. Zafimahova's five. The voters of the Province of Majunga had elected Tsiranana to represent them in the Provincial Assembly; his fellow members elected him President of the Provincial Assembly; elected him to the Provincial Council; and sent him to the Representative Assembly of Madagascar. There he was elevated to the High Council of the island; his fellow ministers elected him to be their Vice-President—in effect, the prime minister of Madagascar. When the time came, the Representative Assembly and the High Council chose him to serve as Acting President of the Interim Government, to direct, among the other things, the drawing up of the Constitution of the coming Malagasy Republic.

He thus was a public man; in his private life, besides being head of his family, he was the great man of the Tsimihety, a full professor, and the founder, leader, and boss of his own political party, the P.S.D.M. In office and as himself, the man was a fountainhead of power and a pool of labor.

Mr. Zafimahova was likewise impressive in position: deputy of the Provincial Assembly of Fianarantsoa, member of the Provincial Council, sent to the Representative Assembly in Tananarive—and elected President of the assembly during the interim; and he was a senator in France, as well as head man, but perhaps not the real leader, of his own party, the U.D.S.M. However, Mr. Tsiranana is *masiaka;* Mr. Zafimahova proved to lack that magical authority.

The Constitutional Committee had been instructed to complete its work by 15 March 1959; but by the first of the month, the political situation was so tense, and the outcome of the struggle between Mr. Tsiranana and Mr. Zafimahova as yet so unpredictable (although the early autumn air seemed clear and luminous to me after the summer rains, which had been unusually heavy, and the cyclone season had not ended), that the gossips of Tananarive predicted a delay in the completion of the Constitution. As things stood, if Mr. Zafimahova and his party did not approve it, Mr. Tsiranana's fall from power might well have resulted.

It is quite possible that nature intervened in President Tsiranana's favor. In February and March five tremendous cyclones blew in, bringing torrential downpours to drown the rich eastern escarpment. The highlands were already saturated; dams gave way, canals overflowed, rivers flooded, the terraced hillside rice fields turned into cascades; landslides tore out the roads, cut the railroads, brought houses down, damaged or destroyed plantations. It was the worst natural disaster in the island's modern history. In April the storm damage was estimated in excess of ten billion francs CFA, more than $40,000,000. Two hundred and twenty people were killed; and 2,500 houses in Tananarive destroyed. We do things on a bigger scale in the United States, but those cyclones in Madagascar can be compared to the hurricane that hit New England in 1938 and caused a reported $500,000,000 worth of destruction. Later on, it was found, as usual, that the bad news from Madagascar had been greatly exaggerated.

However, perhaps 250,000 coffee trees were destroyed; and the worst of the cyclones, on 27 March, broke the Tananarive-Tamatave railroad line in six hundred places; some 200,000 cubic meters of rock and earth washed down the cliff to bury the rails. By 30 April the service was back to normal.

The French of President de Gaulle's France responded to the appeal for help—they gave immediately, effectively, and generously. A thousand tons of donated clothing piled up for shipment to the island from the waiting rooms of the disused Gare d'Orsay in Paris. President de Gaulle wrote out a personal check for a million francs (roughly $2,000). Prince Rainier and Princess Grace of Monaco did likewise. By the end of June, France and the French had contributed one billion five hundred thousand francs (not quite $3,000,000) to the relief of the cyclone and flood victims, as well as food, clothing, and equipment worth 500,000,000 francs ($1,000,000). A National Committee for Aid to the Malagasy Disaster Victims took charge, and did great work in France—and in Madagascar.

For what his people had received, President Tsiranana, or rather acting President Tsiranana of the interim government, cabled his country's thanks to General de Gaulle, President of the French Community, saying, "If we had voted No our great island would now be lost." And in another cable, "The Community has now proved its vitality to the world. We thank you for having created it, and we thank it, through your high mediation, for its brotherhood." So the cyclone proved not an ill wind.

In a last galvanic effort, Mr. Zafimahova reached out and seized upon the martyr-heroes still unreasonably in exile in France. Probably he hoped to absorb their still enormous symbolic power, and, thus revivified, to bring down his enemy—and, if necessary, the still shaky structure of the Malagasy government, if not the Republic. In doing so, he turned Dr. Raseta, the Prince Ravoahangy, and the poet Rabemananjara into three red herrings—thereby handing Miss Gisèle Rabesahala the time of her life to make trouble.

It is true that the continuing exile of the martyr-heroes of the Rebellion of 1947, their cause having, in fact, been won, had ceased to make sense of any sort, not in France, nor in Madagascar. All that remained was for the Presidents de Gaulle and Tsiranana to find a face-saving formula by which to bring the exiles honorably home. First things first. In those days, both Presidents had more important work to do, which was to float the Fifth French Republic and the independent Malagasy Republic, along with the other African members of the Community—and to solve Algeria's problems, too.

Seeing his chance on 8 June 1959, Mr. Zafimahova introduced a bill for his fellow members of the Malagasy National Assembly ostensibly to vote total amnesty for the exiles, but actually to show up Tsiranana as a French Quisling. On July 8, the President countered by asking his government and the Malagasy National Assembly to request the French National Assembly to grant a formal amnesty—a technical and legal point necessary to clarify the silly, but historical, situation.

Down in Grasse, Dr. Joseph Raseta jumped the gun. Next day, July 9, the old revolutionary, once a member of the disavowed and suppressed first Malagasy Communist Party, bought himself a one-way airplane ticket to fly home to Tananarive. It is safe to say that the Communists of the French and the Malagasy Parties organized the flight, with or without outside help from the Soviets, the satellites, or China. There is no absolute proof available, to be sure. And it is possible that coincidence and chance alone or together brought on the wildly publicized chain of events. However, it looks very much like a laid-on, correctly timed, and carefully phased propaganda operation. If so, the flight achieved its ends with brilliant success—although the old man did not complete his journey.

He would have got home had he waited a few days, a week or two, a month, no more. Indeed, he might have at the chosen time if his sponsors had put him on an Air France plane that lands to refuel in Nairobi, Kenya, a British colony, and not on the TAI plane scheduled to come down in Djibouti, French Somaliland—where a reception of another sort awaited him. Surely if his backers, who paid the price, had wanted to get him home, they would have avoided French officials in the French territory.

But, whether the witting or unwitting old martyr, aged seventy-three, suffering from a cardiac condition, knew it or not, he had become a vehicle, a medium and not a man. It did not matter to the success of the flight whether he got home to Madagascar safely, or was intercepted and arrested in Djibouti, or died of the excitement in the air or on the ground. No matter what happened to Dr. Raseta, the agitation and the propaganda of his homegoing could not fail to gain its destructive ends. France was to be made ridiculous, or worse, in the eyes of the world.

To this effect, the first step was to get the old man airborne in his right name. His flight was not to be anonymous. Therefore, Dr. Raseta's papers had to be in perfect order, and they had to be authentic— no forgeries, no false names. Only authentic and correct documents could establish Dr. Raseta's right to freedom, thus to point up the monstrous and cruel legalism that had turned this Malagasy patriot into a French criminal—because he had helped achieve the independence of the Malagasy Republic then being celebrated by General de Gaulle.

It is a fact, it is a truth that the old Malagasy went through all the proper procedures in applying for his papers to authorize the trip. And he got his papers back from the French authorities in perfect order, signed and sealed, every one correct. It was a great mistake, no more.

At first glance—we have all learned the hard way to trace such matters after the known facts—it might appear that a French Communist agent had penetrated the Ministries (as a civil servant, a regular employee of the permanent French bureaucracy, not necessarily under cover because the C.P. is legal and open in France), and had thus walked Dr. Raseta's documents through the proper channels. After the success of the Algerian Secret Army's bewildering subversions, any such simple act of treachery seems plausible in France. It jumps to mind.

But such, in fact, was not the case. The conditions of bureaucracy alone betrayed the bureaucrats. July 9 marked the beginning of that year's Bastille Day holiday, a long weekend, and the beginning of the frantic exodus from Paris. General de Gaulle, Prime Minister Michel Debré, and Mr. Jacques Soustelle had already left (they were in Réunion, to promote the coming Referendum); their deputies, the seconds in command, the desk men, the secretaries, the clerks—all fixed securely in tenure—were clearing their desks of routine paperwork, and thinking of other things, such as the traffic on the roads out of Paris.

So, absent-mindedly, somebody in momentary charge signed off on Dr. Raseta's papers put down in front of him at the last moment, perhaps at the bottom of a pile of similar routine requests, not worth the bother of reading through.

At the airport, the police and the immigration authorities must have suspected that something had gone wrong. But nobody could refuse the correctly documented old man the right to buy his TAI ticket, to board his plane, to leave French soil, and to take to the French air. So he left.

Then somebody got on the phone; but the reporters had already sent in their copy. Dr. Raseta was arrested in Djibouti in the name of Premier Debré. In jail in the hot and dusty Red Sea port, he risked his cardiac condition to begin a three-day hunger strike. In Tananarive, his sympathizers called for a day of fasting—and three hundred Malagasy Communists and fellow-travelers obliged, in and around the house of Professor Maurice Rajofera, one of Miss Rabesahala's reliables. The newspapers of the free world and the other world reported the news; some editorialized, some played it straight (which was, perhaps, more effective, and worse).

Back in deserted Paris of the 14th of July, one single woman, a distinguished anthropologist in her own right, the secretary of Mr. Soustelle, set out to walk the dusty corridors of the Ministry, bringing the attention of the skeleton staff to bear to unsnarl the tangle of red tape. She got the work done, but it took away her holiday. Dr. Raseta was flown back to exile, once again, in France.

But not for long. The doctor, the prince, and the poet all eventually got back home. Nobody hears much of them any more; nor of Mr. Nobert Zafimahova.

President Tsiranana formally and historically proclaimed the independence of his island on 26 June 1960. The Malagasy flag has three rectangular compartments; the white is vertical, the red above the green horizontal. The Republic's motto is "Liberty, Country, Progress." The Malagasy Constitution proclaims that the new country "shall be one, indivisible, democratic, and social," in the official state languages, Malagasy and French. The Malagasy Republic is a democracy, but one unlike the United States of America, the Fifth French Republic, or the United Kingdom of Great Britain and Northern Ireland; the written Constitution calls upon the President to be a strong man. So President Tsiranana is.

Although the members of the National Assembly, of the General Councils of the Provinces, and of the rural and municipal "collectivities" are directly elected in universal suffrage by equal and secret ballots, the President, who is his own chief executive without an elected prime minister, is chosen by indirect election. He is voted into office by an electoral college made up of the members of Parliament, of the General Councils of the Provinces (the old Provincial Assemblies have been abolished), and by delegates from the municipal and rural assemblies (the so-called collectivities). He holds office for a seven-year term, and can be reëlected. The President has broad constitutional powers and great personal authority and responsibility. He directs the action of the government; he makes policy. He is empowered to issue regulations, promulgate the laws, and request reconsideration of any law that he does not like. He sees that the laws are carried out of the maintenance of order. He selects and appoints men to the various government offices, including his Council of Ministers, or Cabinet.

Parliament has two chambers. The 107 representatives of the National Assembly are directly elected to office for a term of five years. From among themselves, the representatives choose their President and four Vice-Presidents. As the legislative body, and as the major part of the electoral college to elect the President of the Republic, the National Assembly has great power. But, on the advice of the Senate, and after consultation with the President of the directly elected, representative lower house, the President of the Malagasy Republic can dissolve the National Assembly.

The Senate is composed of 54 members who hold office for six-year

terms, half the body being renewed every three years. Article 28 of
the Constitution states that two-thirds of the senators are elected in
equal number from each of the six provinces by the directly elected
representatives of the High Councils of the Provinces, and the municipal and rural collectivities—six senators from each province. The
remaining one-third or eighteen senators are designated and appointed
by the government (in short, by President Tsiranana) from among the
"forces économiques sociales, et culturelles" of the island—the business,
social, and cultural communities—to be chosen in part from the most
representative members of such overlapping groups, and in part from
among individual men and women who have demonstrated special
competence in any field. The Malagasy Senate is thus unique among
democracies.

The Constitution provides for a kind of Supreme Court called the
Conseil Supérieur des Institutions and made up of five members, of
whom three at least must be chosen for their juridical competence.
They hold office for terms of seven years, which are not renewable.
Two of the "personalities" of this Conseil Supérieur—a designation
used to make clear that both men and women may hold office—are
appointed by the President of the Republic, two by the President of
the National Assembly, and one by the President of the Senate. This
Board of Review takes action only upon request; only the President of
the Republic and the members of the National Assembly and the Senate
can initiate action. The five members of the Superior Council of the
branches of the government, the Institutions, are responsible, when
called upon to do so, for determining whether or not the laws and
regulations are constitutional.

Firmly inside the French Community, the Malagasy Republic has
decided to share certain portions of its government with the other
member nations, and in particular with France, whose President is
likewise the President of the French Community. Therefore, General
de Gaulle, as over-all chief executive, decides and directs for the entire
Community and specifically for Madagascar, its foreign policy, its
defense, its currency, its common economic and financial policies, and
all strategic matters. France, in the office and the person of its President, also controls the Community's over-all laws, law courts, and
legal justice; the institutions of higher learning and the standards of

education; and generally directs the organization of means of transportation among the members of the Community, and between the Community as a whole and the other nations of the world, as well as the communications by telephone, post, telegraph, and radio.

In effect, the Malagasy Republic is largely autonomous in all matters of internal administration; it regulates its own revenues and manages its own finances (inside the French franc zone); to be sure, the island is not yet economically able to support itself—nor has it ever been since 1895. To maintain the peace of the republic, French police officers remained after independence to work with the Malagasy police department. French Army, Navy, and Air Force personnel are stationed in Madagascar to defend the Malagasy Republic in case of attack— and to maintain the naval base of Diégo-Suarez. The island's foreign relations are handled by French diplomatic and consular representatives throughout the world, except for a few Malagasy ambassadors to the great powers. In Paris, La Délégation de Madagascar is housed in a modest former *hôtel particulier* at 1 Boulevard Suchet, an elegant address in the XVI arrondissement. Any of the Malagasy internal affairs that have a bearing on the welfare of France or of the other member states of the Community are handled by the Minister of State for the African states, Quai d'Orsay. It is to be understood that the old Ministry of the Colonies that became the Ministry of Overseas France for the French Union no longer exists; its functions have been absorbed by the other appropriate Ministries, and by President de Gaulle himself.

It still costs the French of France an enormous sum of money each year to maintain their freedom from their former colonies—and to guarantee the independence of the new countries. In 1962, President de Gaulle's Ministry of Cooperation with the African States (and Madagascar) spent the equivalent of $554,000,000 to support the *Présence Française* and to continue the *mission civilisatrice* begun so casually so many years ago. The former colonies cannot yet pay their own way in the world.

People and Places

MANAKARA is a steaming little port; the center of the town is French with proper houses; the outskirts are Malagasy with woven and thatched native huts that seem, indeed, cooler, cleaner, and more livable in that climate than the permanent importations. Above high tide, the straight sandy beach is planted with *filao*—casuarina trees—in a pretty grove whispering in the hot, wet breeze. The sea is full of sharks. The main avenue, planted with royal palms, has great dignity. On Sunday mornings, the Frenchmen play bowls. I spent my short stay there wet with sweat.

One evening on the porch of the C.C.B. (Compagnie Commerciale de Betsiléo) Hotel, I was invited to sit down and drink beer with two young, brown Malagasy men dressed in proper European jackets, trousers, white shirts, and knotted ties. They did not seem to mind the heat, although they sweat grievances at every pore. The lighter-skinned young man told me that he was a clerk in the customs house; the taller, darker man worked in the local Air France office. I think he must have been paid less well, for his spotless shirt was badly frayed at the cuffs and collar.

I was the first French-speaking American that they had met. Having heard I was in town, they had come to the hotel to meet me, and had chosen their table next to the front door of the bar in order to invite me to join them if I passed by. The lighter man spoke better French; he seemed surer of himself. I noticed that the right lens of his horn-rimmed glasses was cracked across. The darker, with wooly hair and a less aquiline caste of features, wore round steel-rimmed spectacles that kept sliding down his flat nose. The other, whose broken glasses stayed in place, soon told me proudly that he was descended from noble Arabs and indeed he looked like a trim and high-nosed Semite. He belonged to the Antaimoro people, of whom there were some 178,215 tribesmen that year. "Shore People," they live along the coast north of Manakara. The other was an Antandröy from the far south (Pastor Mahatoto's wild tribe). Each young man had cultivated a Mandarin length of little fingernail on his left hand. The Antaimoro owned a small motorcycle on which they had come to the hotel, and on which, after a good deal of kicking to get the engine going, and several loud explosions, they later went off, only a bit drunk.

At first we were correct and polite; but as we sat and drank, the talk came easily. The Antaimoro told me bitterly that he hated the French. "You can see for yourself," he said, "under what a heavy yoke we live." It was good literary French. I asked him to tell me about himself. He said that he was twenty-six years old, and again proclaimed his Arab ancestry. From there he jumped to North Africa and the Algerian war, which pleased him. He was delighted by the French setbacks. Syria, Lebanon, Morocco, Tunisia, and soon Algeria all would be completely free of the French yoke. And then it would be Madagascar's turn. He talked louder and louder; I knew that a French police commissioner sat inside the hotel at the bar, within earshot. I got him back on the safer subject of his own life.

Five or six years earlier, after he had graduated from the special school that trained him for a government post, he had gone to work as a forester in Nosy-Bé, far from home. There in the woods of that enchanting tropical island, he had met and married a Créole school-teacher. But things had not worked out. They had separated, although they were not formally divorced. Perhaps the male dominance of the Arab had conflicted with the matriarchal independence of the Polynesian in their mixed backgrounds; in any case, theirs was a civilized defeat.

I ordered a round of beer—Dutch, imported from Holland; the liter bottle cost 160 francs CFA, or about 75 cents U.S.A., plus 10 per cent tip. Served very cold, it came out of the hotel's big Electrolux, a kerosene-burning refrigerator behind the bar, imported from Sweden at I do not know what cost. The Antaimoro hadn't a good word to say for the French. Everything wrong in Madagascar was their fault. He was enthusiastically negative and destructive. He was a bit drunk.

The Antandröy decided that the time had come to shut his friend up. He wished for an intellectual exchange between civilized men able to hold a conversation in a mutually foreign language. The problem was to find a fitting subject. We dropped a few safe words about good books; we admired the Malagasy landscape; we agreed that Tananarive was a charming city. We soon dried up. He seemed relieved when I began to ask him personal questions.

He was twenty-five years old, and he, too, had been married—and his marriage also had failed. His wife was a country girl of his own tribe, a simple girl, not an *évoluée*. They had not been able to communicate, he said, speaking carefully, sitting upright in the hard wooden chair at the square wooden table, his head turned to look at me as we talked. Automatically his hand went up to push his glasses back along his nose. With quiet dignity he explained to me that he had tried to educate his wife, but that she had not wanted to change her ways. She did not like her nice new house; nothing about it was familiar. She did not know what to do at any moment of the day or the night. It was all very hard for her. "I had to send her home," he said.

In the little silence following the end of these careful phrases of textbook French, a young Malagasy matron came walking along the road into the bright light from the high porch of the hotel. She wore a length of dirt-colored cotton cloth wrapped around her, a dress that can be described as a strapless sheath in the sack style, underneath which it was evident she had on no sort of foundation garment and no radio. On her head she wore a square straw hat like a strawberry box. She had magnificent arms and shoulders. On her back, she carried her fat brown baby slung in her *lamba*, spread-eagled, riding her comfortable buttocks. As she passed beneath us, she slid the baby round to straddle one hip, so to give him her full and pointed breast, which he opened his mouth to receive. They walked along happily,

288

the baby pulling away at his source of life, his black and white eyes round and happy in his uncontaminated head.

The young Antandröy courteously asked me if it would please me to describe New York to him. I began with the skyscrapers.

THE CONCESSION

ON my next trip in my hired Ariane, I drove south from Fianarantsoa in January, 1959, carrying a letter of introduction from the handsome Créole wife of a Corsican French judge in Ambositra, to her brother, a vintner, in a concession on the Ambavaloa plain, 130 miles away. Lunch was late that day. The judge, a thin and active man in his fifties, had been delayed at the scene of a crime out in the hills. A young Betsileo villager, a bachelor, had been murdered, apparently because a Betsileo widow in her forties, after having tried out several other men, some older, some younger, had made of him her final choice as a permanent lover. One morning his body was found dead in an irrigation ditch in the rice fields. Alive, he had fought hard to defend himself; that much was at once to be seen. The autopsy revealed the marks of several hands and different weapons: a blow on the head (searchers found the bloodied stone); water in the lungs; and the fact that he had been mutilated and castrated before he drowned. Such evidence led the judge to think that the discarded, and thus publicly humiliated, lovers had ganged up to punish him for pleasing the sophisticated widow, it may be, as they had not. Perhaps he had teased them?

The judge knew that all the villagers knew all about the murder. Yet nobody would talk; all professed innocence and ignorance of what had been a noisy act of violence nearby. I had been told that the Malagasy were tolerant and understanding about sex and consequences. The husbands who go off for periods of a year or more as contract laborers, for example, in the northern sugar-cane fields, take for granted that their wives left behind will find lovers. On their return, some men find new babies—whom they casually accept and adopt as their own.

I asked the Corsican judge why this independent widow's multiple love-affair had climaxed in murder. The judge shrugged and, speaking in the off-hand French tone of voice that suggests it is best not to try to understand, said, "Oh, for some unexplained, inexplicable, insufficient reasons. Nobody knows, not even the murderers. It is a Malagasy *crime passionnel*. One cannot hope to unravel it. One can arrive only at the demonstrable facts, and judge accordingly."

Before independence, the judges, the attorneys general, and the court officials in Madagascar were French from France—permanent employees of the French Ministry of Justice, not dependent upon nor paid by the Colonial or Overseas Franc-Malagasy government. Thus when the Fourth Republic fell, for a short time the courts ceased to function in the island, and the processes of law and order, trial and punishment, were suspended. Yet no crime wave arose. To be sure, the Army and the police-force went on working. I am told that there are few thefts in Tananarive. One of the most charming buildings in that high city is a little Greco-Roman temple of sixteen Ionic columns, open to the wide view and the winds. It is the royal Praetorium, the Queen's Palace of Justice; judging from its dimensions, there could not have been much crime—or not many trials. The judge's wife gave me a very good meal *à la française*. I drove off.

South of Fianarantsoa, the highlands dry out; the landscape changes to isolated hills of smooth rock (one is called "the Brioche") in red and green plains set about with termite castles of a melted Gothic, Gaudi-like architecture; they are as hard as concrete. Among them here and there a tombstone marks the grave of a tribal chieftain—a T-shaped cross of two rectified monoliths, the upright eight or ten feet high, the balanced transverse held in place by gravity. Sometimes a solitary tamarind tree casts its black shade. The termite castles, the Tau crosses of St. Anthony, and the tamarinds mark the emptiness of the wide and luminous space, through which I drove alone on the road.

I came to a small river flowing between banked rice fields. Here I found men at work. It was the day to let in the water to flood the sun-baked fallow earth for the new crop—one of three a year, depending on the region. The Betsileo grow rice as they have for two or three thousand years, unchanged except for the spreading on of French-introduced fertilizers and manures. I stopped the car to watch. I had all the stages of the culture going on all at once in the various dyked fields of the alluvial valley (except for the harvest), as in an illuminated manuscript.

In the background on a hill stood the town; the villagers had sorted themselves out according to age and sex and the appropriate division of labor. Each member of the community knew what he and she had to do. Rice appears to be a cooperative crop; these were individual holdings collectively worked. In the broad valley, the fields were big and level, rectangles of an acre or two, separated by low dykes—much easier to work than the stepped and narrow fields on the terraced hillsides. First the old men and the boys spread fertilizer on the parched soil. Then the hydraulic engineers opened the sluices so that water from the reservoir higher upstream flooded in over the grey earth, which turned black, and then to liquid mud, and then into a mirror, its surface reflecting the clouds in the sky.

Next came the hard work of disking and ploughing. But never having got around to inventing the harrow or the plough, the farmers called in the herdsmen and their humped cattle to trample and tread the flooded earth with their cloven hoofs. These were the strong young men; four or five of them brought in twenty or two dozen young cows and bulls, chosen, it may be, for their good tempers and team spirit. It looked like sport; dark-brown men stripped to breechclouts, and black, or black and white, or grey young zebus, milling in a round. The men began to shout and now and again to slap one of the cattle on the neck or flank with a flat and flexible stick. They ran around in circles, the men laughing and waving their arms, the zebus kicking up their heels, tossing their lyre-horned heads, waving their stiff tails, and now and again bellowing. They seemed to be having a very good time splashing up the churned mud until all of them were uniformly black and glistening.

I stripped off my shoes and stockings, picked up my cameras, waded the shallow river, and went to join the fun. One of the herdsmen left the team and came running along the levees to pose for his picture in the hot sunlight. Covered with mud, he looked like a roughed-out Adam; as such, the finished man promised to be well made. The mud began to bake dry and to flake from his head and shoulders. He spoke; he laughed; his teeth were sound and white. Out of his mouth came the language of Pascal and La Fontaine to wish me well on my journey and to say good day, before he turned to run back laughing to join the rollicking herd.

In the still waters of the fields flooded and trampled the day earlier, the women were busy transplanting the tender shoots brought down in foot-long green bundles from the seedbeds. Each woman hiked up her skirts and tied them; she then took up a supply of seedlings in her left hand, and waded out to take her place, one after another in line. Up to their knees in water, they bend their backs and get to work. Each woman takes a seedling in her right hand, and plunges in above the elbow to root the plant in the rich black mud. Each one seems to strike and grow; in its straight row the rice shoots up, thickens, turns from pale green to emerald, sends up its bearded spike, ripens, and turns to pale gold—but not all in a day. Men reap the grain with a saw-toothed knife; they offer the first sheaf to the gods. Women help with the winnowing.

I recrossed the river, got out a towel, sat down on a rock, and dried my bare feet carefully. I took no chances; for, despite the magnificent health of the Betsileo in their rice fields under the *Présence Française*, there might have been the tremetodes of the liver fluke—bilharziasis —in the water. With my shoes and socks back on, I drove off to do my errand for the Corsican judge's Créole wife. She had sketched a road map and had told me the landmarks to look for; soon I found the turning-off place, and left the highway to take a dirt lane. It ended at the brother's concession.

The family, now in its third generation in Madagascar, began with one of Gallieni's French troopers, who, having spread his spot of oil, decided to stay on for life. He married a Créole from Réunion. Their children were the judge's wife, as pale as a southern French woman; the brother, darker as befits a man; and another sister, unhappily much darker, for she got so many of the Malagasy-slave ancestress's genes that her choice of husband was restricted to a prescribed circle.

The brother's wife, a small dynamic woman, is a Créole, too; but fair of skin. So are their children, a strongly built son of twenty, home from his garage in Antsirabé to recuperate from infectious jaundice hepatitis; and an eighteen-year-old daughter, as pretty as a flower—an exotic bloom. The judge's wife was most annoyed with her niece for having refused, in marriage, a young Frenchman, going home at the completion of his military service to his farm in the north of France. He had hoped to take her as his bride, to bear a dozen children and to work in the fields and the cow barn in wooden shoes—an orchid transplanted to the blood-soaked mud and cold dawns of Flanders. She chose to stay at home in Madagascar.

The judge's wife had told me that, after the war, her brother and his young family had settled down on their pioneering father's coffee plantation, well established on the fertile ground of the escarpment halfway down the railroad line from Fianarantsoa. But in the Rebellion of 1947, the Tanala tribesmen, wild jungle people ruled by their sorcerers and witch-doctors, had come in by night to put fire to the house and the coffee trees. They took the family prisoner, and might have killed them had not neighbors seen the flames and come to the rescue.

They moved up to Fianarantsoa; and having been wiped out, the father got a salaried job in the administration. His wife did dressmaking at home. They saved money. Ten years after the rebellion, they had enough to try once again. This time they took over an abandoned concession on the Ambavaloa plain. The land is fertile, but dry; whatever grows must be irrigated. It is a safe place to live. Fifty years earlier, a Corsican had originally worked the virgin land. Things had gone wrong; his wife died. If he had any children, they grew up and left him. He lived alone with several dogs. Soon he became eccentric, then downright peculiar; finally he went out of his mind. He barricaded his gates, and he turned his savage dogs on any chance caller. He took to sitting up at night with a loaded shotgun in his hands to repel . . . I'm not sure whom, or what, and nor was he or anybody else. Perhaps the rebellion finished him; perhaps he confused the uprising with some classic vendetta that caused him to leave Corsica when he was young. Certainly nothing on his concession was worth stealing. The authorities finally had to trick him to call off his dogs, lay aside his weapon, and come out to be put into an asylum. They sent him back to Corsica; the dogs had to be put down.

The concession reverted to the government, who were pleased to hand it over to the Créole family. The house was a primitive structure of one story, with few windows in the adobe walls. It looked as though it had begun with a single room and had accumulated others as needs be in natural growth. The atmosphere seemed very strange.

I delivered my envelope; and after the note had passed from hand to hand, I caught the members of the family eying me. The very pretty girl, as shy as a fawn, excused herself; she went back to her sewing machine in a dark room, and took up once again her work of making a skirt of bright cotton cloth. The son recuperating from jaundice looked gloomy. He walked away to lie down on a porch.

The father showed me his winepress housed in a room full of vats built onto the homestead. This was the moment of the vendange and a pleasant odor of fermentation filled the air. He wore stained workclothes, and after he had told me that he expected a yield of twenty-thousand liters that year, and that it was an honest wine, not, to be sure, like a wine of France—it had a taste of raspberries—and that people came all the way from Tananarive to buy it, all of it having been sold, he fell silent, excused himself, and went about his business. It was potable, he said over his shoulder.

The wife then took charge of me. It was clear that she was the dynamo and the executive of the family. A quick and a vivid little woman, active, interested, she was the only member of the family who seemed to be perfectly at ease. She wore a very brief pair of white shorts and a sleeveless cotton blouse, orange in color, with sandals on her small feet. She led me out into the bright sunlight on a tour of the property.

To the right of the main building was an open space of hard red earth, a kind of farmyard edged by a crescent of outbuildings—the garage and sheds, the storehouses, the chicken run and hen coop, the dove cote, the quarters for the Malagasy hands and their wives and families. I recall no sheep or cows, but perhaps there were some out in the fields. I do remember a truck, its body piled high with the purple grape pomace emptied from the winevats, waiting, I guessed, to be carted into town to a distiller.

From the dry side, we walked into the gardens and orchards planted in reach of the water running in a clear and rapid stream from a spring on a distant hillside, a work of canalization that must have taken months of back-breaking labor. Here in no special order grew—let's see—peaches, plums, apples, pears, oranges, lemons, roses, coffee trees, artichokes, string beans, carrots, lettuces, chili and bell peppers, eggplants, tomatoes, cucumbers, squash, watermelons, cosmos and zinneas, sunflowers, and, of course, the grapevines, although most of the vineyards lay further up the irrigation canal on the slopes. I sampled the fruit as I went along, and had a great time among the grapes.

My hostess handed me a pair of scissors, and showed me how to choose the ripe green grapes by looking for the drying, woody, brown stems. We filled a basket for her sister-in-law, the judge's wife, and we made conversation of a noncommittal kind—a recognizably polite social noise reserved for strangers. I wondered if I had arrived on a taboo day. I was made welcome, but not encouraged to linger. So I took the grapes, made my farewells, and left.

TWO GERMANS

I DROVE on through more empty, barren land, saturated in sunlight; and I came to Ihosy—"Ee-oosh"—a red-brick arbitrary town built in the past century by the Merina and the French for administrative convenience. Its name sounds like a gusty sigh; I don't know what it means.

I stopped at the only hotel in town, an agreeable place of two brick buildings, one housing the public rooms and kitchens, the other the bedrooms giving off a wide wooden verandah; there I slept well, but only until dawn when the crowing cocks, cackling hens, quacking ducks, hissing geese, gobbling turkeys, and rusty-screeching guinea fowl woke me up. The hotel proprietress was a pink and white French woman, a widow who must have been well into her seventies. She wore a clean and pretty dress of cotton—it seemed always to be fresh —and she carried about with her, as she supervised her hotel rooms, her bar, her kitchens, her restaurant, her general store, her filling station and garage, and, of course, her poultry yard, that peculiar authority of the French woman; it amounts to a national characteristic.

She went about her work in an aura of matter-of-fact efficiency; smiling and knowledgeable, she seemed to make sense of the human condition. She was a reassuring sort of woman. She looked as though never for a moment in her life had anything she touched got out of hand. As she walked with the sure, light step of the well fleshed, it was clear that the purpose of the ground under her feet was to support her. She put sense to things.

Two years later on the Red Sea I learned that in her earlier full maturity she got to be known all over the Great Island as *"la panthère de l'Isalo,"* the pantheress of the Isalo. The "Ee-shall" is the wild, empty, rocky desert region above and beyond Ihosy, to the south. The lady panther was, I suppose, *Vénus toute entière à sa proie attachée,* Venus clawed into the flesh. When I knew her, she had sheathed her claws as befits the keeper of a poultry yard. I understand that she has sold her hotel and returned to France.

In her bar, I met a truly displaced person, a German of about thirty-five, short and muscular, with yellow hair and a medieval sort of face, as ugly and as full of character as the soldiers around the saints in Albrecht Durer's wood engravings. He had an entrancing daughter eight years old, flaxen-haired, blue-eyed, a happy little girl, dressed in a clean and frilly edifying manner. She loved her father, he loved her; they took me swimming in the somewhat scummy municipal pool, spring-fed on the edge of town, a rectified oasis, in concrete, with a wide and luminous view of bare hills, red and purple in the sunset.

He was, he told me, an engineer, the manager of the French-owned piezo-electric quartz company; ordinarily he spent his days driving in a jeep all over the countryside collecting limpid blocks of this special rock crystal used in all sorts of electronic equipment, including radar. With coming independence, business had fallen off; and then abruptly he had been confined to the town limits of Ihosy, and not allowed to drive about among the Bara tribal people. These were the artists, the sculptors, the dancers of the Malagasy tribes, a nomadic, uncivilized people famous for cattle rustling. Many are athletes, some are handsome; they are lean and dark of skin. In 1959 there were 215,026 of them. They do not mind at all whether the piezo-electric business thrives or fails. Their refusal to work regular hours had driven several of the mining engineers to quit and go back to France; that is how the German got his job—no Frenchman wanted it. Back at the judge's house later on I learned that he was thought to be a spy. I asked him how he got to Madagascar.

At the swimming pool in Ihosy, he pulled down his swimming trunks to show me a jagged scar across his belly—aged nineteen he had been bayoneted on the Russian front. It had been a patrol action in a winter forest, and he had been left behind to die. But he had not wanted to die, so with one hand holding the wound closed, he had crawled across the thick-crusted snow until he came upon some other Germans, who got him to a doctor. I forget the sequence, but in 1945 he ended up as prisoner of the English.

He should not have been on the Russian front at all, for he was not a soldier, he was a sailor, a ship's engineer, in the Germany Navy; but before he was twenty, he had three ships sunk under him. Therefore, according to the Nazi ruling, he had automatically been transferred to the infantry, whether as punishment for having survived, or for fear that he was a Jonah, I cannot say. After the war, he got a job as engineer on a British freighter; on the way to Liverpool from Karachi, he came down with malaria. He was put ashore at Tamatave, and cured. Once on his feet, he looked around for work—and ended up in the piezo-electric quartz crystal business in Ihosy. Therefore, the French decided he must be a secret agent. In the swimming pool of Ihosy, while he helped his daughter climb up on his shoulders to dive off, he laughed and said the time had come for him to move along, and did I know of a job for him in the United States? I did not. I do not know what the end of his unlikely story has been, or will be.

The year before I had come across another German, a long resident in Madagascar, in Ampanihy ("a Plethora of Bats"), a man in his late fifties, dressed in khaki shirt and shorts, his weathered face lined and grooved with character, his hair white; he likewise was a mining engineer, and he also had been called a spy. He dug garnets, most of them to be exported to England, ground up as abrasives, and made into fine sand paper for cabinet makers. Others were used as "rubies" in Swiss watches; the best were cut and polished as jewels.

One day he drove me out of town into the thorny desert to see the mining process. Garnets, hexagonal crystals of silicates of iron and aluminum, occur in mica schist and gneiss in veins crushed between the upheaved and upended strata of ancient rock. To get them out is a digging process; some lodes go down deep, too deep for economic mining. Others lie close beneath the ground, and break the surface. Almost naked wild brown men worked with pick and shovel in the open trenches, and loaded the unimpressive red-brown dirt into handtrucks of a small railroad to be pushed along the inclines up to the surface. There women sitting in the dense shade of a tamarind tree, their children playing about them, dumped the gravel into troughs made by cutting an empty oil drum lengthwise in half; they poured water on the mixture of earth and broken pebbles, and rocked the iron cradle for a time, then, having washed the crystals, they culled the big stones and put them aside from the lesser stuff.

Back in town at the factory beside a stream, the roughly graded garnets are once again washed and sorted in a series of cement troughs made for the purpose around a well-head—the stream is liable to fail in very dry years. The bulk, now a coarse, sharp sand, is shoveled into sacks, loaded into trucks, and sent off to Tuléar for freighters to pick up. Garnets are cheap and plentiful; it is a steady, small commerce. Down at the southern tip of the island, there is a beach of garnet sand on the banks of the Menarandra River as it flows into the Indian Ocean; it is the color of dry blood.

This German also dealt in green and yellow jasper that comes in great striped chunks; the various silicates of beryllium and aluminum —no emeralds, but fine aquamarines as well as the best of the Malagasy gems, a pale pink beryl of great hardness, clarity, and brilliance; the tourmalines, complex silicates of boron, aluminum, and other minerals—the one he gave me was black, the commonest variety; red-brown corundum, a very hard variety of aluminum oxide—the limpid or starred crystals, which do not occur in Madagascar, are rubies and sapphires; water sapphires, greyish-blue in color, transparent silicates of magnesium, aluminum, and iron, also called iolite or cordierite; yellow quartz called citrine; a violet quartz called amethyst; and rose quartz.

He lived in a good modern house of his own design and construction; recognizably in the tradition of the Bauhaus, it had the only complete bathroom in town, made functional with running water and electricity from the storage batteries of a wind-driven generator. He had shelves of books in German and in French, and alongside his good radio-phonograph an international collection of recorded Bach, Beethoven, Brahms, Mozart, and other classic and contemporary composers.

On the verandah, a family of weaver birds had chosen to hang their nest; the small, grey, social bird has untidy habits. The German thoughtfully had placed a square of cardboard on the tile floor underneath the woven nest, but the birds do not aim carefully. He told me that he did not like to chase them away for they bring good luck to the household they elect to live with.

His household consisted of a middle-aged Mahafaly *ramatoa*, a homebody, cook, housekeeper, and (so gossip had it) faithful friend; and a middle-aged man, likewise of the Mahafaly tribe, who still wore the classic Malagasy loin cloth and *lamba* of handspun, handwoven, wild cotton, bordered and fringed at the ends—a magnificent figure. The German introduced them to me with pride as well as obvious appreciation and affection. "His" people had known him and worked with him for thirty years. They had followed him from Ampanihy when, after his release from prison, he was exiled to Marovoay ("Rich in Crocodiles") in a rich, swampy region of deep earth on the Betsiboka River, inland from Majunga, where not even the mails can get through during the rainy season. It has the hottest climate in Madagascar. The German had been transported there from prison; the Mahafaly man and woman had walked from home—a matter of some 900 miles by road, although they had gone across country; therefore, for them it may have been less, 750 miles or so. They all had prospered raising alien rice of the best export quality; it grows six feet tall in the rich soil. Madagascar exports between 35 and 50 thousand tons of such rice annually. But when his ten years of enforced residence were over, he had gone back to Ampanihy in the thorny desert.

The Great Red Island

He had surrounded his house with specimen trees and plants of the region—the tamarinds, the baobabs, the pachypodiums, the *Didiereae,* the euphorbias, and the aloes. He had lined the driveway with sisal agaves (from Yucatan); that year, their last, each of the great rosettes had sent up a branching tree of waxy white flowers against the blue sky. He had built his terrace of jasper, rose quartz, and rock crystal, and strewn his paths with a gravel of garnet, of amethyst, and of beryl.

This German had come to Madagascar when he was was twenty-seven, a violinist in a symphony orchestra. Before his generation, the men of his family had alternated between theology and medicine; his eponymous ancestor had been a fellow monk with Martin Luther and an original Protestant of the Reformation. The man in Madagascar had kept his German citizenship; he saw to it that, whatever form of government at home, his papers always were in good order.

Thus as an enemy alien in 1939, he had automatically been sent off to prison. In 1940, after the Fall of France, that unfortunate collaborator, Governor-General Armand Annet, had released him. In 1942, the conquering British had left him free to live in his own house. But in 1943, the Free French had arrested him once again—because his neighbors in Ampanihy had made up their minds that, by day, he was signalling across the forty or fifty miles of rough terrain with a heliograph, and, by night, with his homemade electricity, to the Germans or Italians or Japanese in their submarines on the surface of the Mozambique Channel and the Indian Ocean.

So he spent the last two years of the war in a highland prison camp in company with ten or a dozen Italians, some central Europeans, and a Japanese, guarded by Senegalese who were not intentionally cruel. He told me that when he had been arrested, quite naturally the French authorities had sequestrated all his property, but after the war they had, most scrupulously, returned it to him intact, in good order.

On the banks of the stream running through his garden, he had planted a lemon tree twenty-five years earlier. And for twenty years, above ground, it had done little; below the surface, the roots had slowly thrust themselves down and down until they had reached the water seeping from the river bed. Then suddenly the tree shot up, put out thick branches dense with glossy green leaves. It spread, it took shape. When I saw it, the lemon tree was thirty feet tall, flourishing, heavy with yellow fruit. It seemed to me to be all that a lemon tree should be.

FORT DAUPHIN

ALTHOUGH I did not realize it until much later, I, too, was taken to be a spy when I arrived via Air France in Fort Dauphin, a stray American, unannounced, unexpected, unbooked, and unknown—and, indeed, unaware. Fort Dauphin on the southeast shore is a beautiful place, its coast almost as lovely as the Attic shore. It is the oldest of the French settlements; founded in 1643, it has failed and failed again and again. I arrived in April, 1958, in the midst of its latest failure, although at the time, the French there thought that they had at least come into their own with a bonanza in the thorianite mines of the hinterland and in the dark-brown dunes and beaches of monazite sand. I came down out of the blue sky, then, into the thick atmosphere of a boom town; the clear golden air was compact and solid with suspicion, in which the French held still like flies in amber regarding me with hard, fixed faces out of multi-faceted eyes. Spies in Ambler. Alas for Madagascar, in France the French have found close to home in the Massif Central great deposits of uranium ores, enough and to spare for their small entry fee into the thermonuclear club, and to pay the mounting annual dues. So the French Atomic Energy Commission stopped its subsidies to the miners of Fort Dauphin and suspended operations.

If Fort Dauphin were not so far away from everywhere—even in Madagascar it is remote, lying at the end of a rough road 682½ miles from Tananarive on a bay too shallow for modern ships—it could become a Côte d'Azur. The beaches are splendid, the shallow bays and coves (usually) free of sharks; the sky is blue, the sea is blue, the air is pure. The climate today is mild and healthy; the arid land beyond the pretty hills that run down into the ocean is grown with plants that exist nowhere else on earth. One of them, a liana of the *Euphorbiaceae*, the *intasy*, produced the first rubber used to make the first Michelin tires; but it would not take to culture like the *Hevea* trees of Brazil, and in its wild state was almost wiped out. In the winter of dry July, the xerophytic forests drop their curious leaves; in dormant August, their coralline growth of twigs and branches turn ashen white, like bones. Then the slanting rays of the setting sun glitter and sparkle in the crystal sand, and the flakes of mica refract a dazzle of broken rainbows.

Fort Dauphin was named for the Sun King, then a child. The first French East India Company, the Société de l'Orient, sent out a ship, the *Saint Louis,* in March of 1642, when Louis XIII was on the throne, when Cardinal Richelieu ruled France, and when the dauphin was three years old. The cardinal died on 4 December of that year; the king died on 14 May of the next; but the colonists had yet to hear the news when they built their fort in December, 1643. Thus the first French colony in Madagascar was named by mistake.

Louis XIV reigned in all for seventy-two years; he ruled France as absolute monarch ("I am the state.") for the last fifty-four of them. He died of gangrene. He might have made of France the richest and the strongest nation of history had he bothered to support Fort Dauphin and the rest of Colbert's businesslike mercantile Colonial empire; but he confused his own Bourbon grandeur and glory with the grandeur and glory of France.

So, in 1671, on the advice of Michel Le Tellier, Marquis de Louvois, the minister of war, he broke Jean-Baptiste Colbert, an indefatigable, clear, cold man, founder of the French Navy and merchant marine, one of the greatest of Frenchmen, who Mme. de Sévigné called "the North Wind." In choosing to pursue his history and French destiny on the battlefields of Europe, Louis XIV turned his back on his burgeoning colonies. Out of the radiance of his regard, the empire withered; but for a few years, Fort Dauphin in Madagascar glittered and sparkled with a dazzle of great French names back in Versailles.

302

The colonists themselves had no good name; neither puritans nor sober pioneers like their contemporaries of the *Mayflower* in the Massachusetts Bay Company, the Frenchmen were strapping roisterers, adventurers, younger sons and riffraff. They had little in common to hold them together. They had no cause for thanksgiving—they found no gold, no cinnamon, no ivory, no diamonds. They lived in neglect; they died of fever; and they made trouble with the Antanosy tribesmen over girls. They were never a big company; and yet 1,400 men died in Fort Dauphin between 1643 and 1675, some slaughtered by the Malagasy, "the People of the Islands," wild and naked dark-brown men. In 1959, there were 148,132 of the Antanosy; however few there were in 1643, they outnumbered the handful of undisciplined white colonists, tough young men.

Sent out by Richelieu and Louis XIII, neglected by Cardinal Mazarin and Anne of Austria during the Frondes of 1648 and 1653 under the Regency, Fort Dauphin caught the eye of that great but extravagant man, Nicolas Fouquet, the Superintendent of Finances. When he reached for it, Fort Dauphin brought on his downfall. Already he had tactlessly built himself the greatest house in France; the chateau of Vaux-le-Vicompte, grander and more magnificent than the palace of the king. So Louis XIV broke him and put Colbert in his place; then Fort Dauphin had its moment of prosperity.

A good man tried to make a go of things. His name was the Chevalier Étienne de Flacourt. He was an educated gentleman of the late Renaissance, an intellectual man of action, a scientist with the mind of a humanist. In his day, and for a century to come, it was still possible for one man to learn and to absorb all there was to know about the world he lived in. Flacourt enlarged that sum of knowledge by adding Madagascar to the known.

A director of the first East Indian Company, he went down to find out what was wrong. As a leader of the colony, he saw that he had to establish order. To do so, first he gained the confidence of the colonists by showing them that he was open-minded, flexible, just—and tough. Then he came to terms with the Antanosy tribe. Next, he got the Frenchmen free of the exasperating confinement inside the stockade by sending them out in groups to explore and to forage up and down the coast, and inland. Whenever he could, he went along; he wrote down notes of what he found of the island's geography, of the tribes and their way of life and legends, of the language (later he compiled a dictionary), of the mineral wealth and poverty, of the plants and of the animals.

Intrigue among his enemies back in France almost defeated him— not Couillard, the bad man of the colonists, whom he had to exile to Réunion with his gang (and with a few female slaves; so started the Créole breed); nor the hard climate; nor the hostile Malagasy. Flacourt was recalled, and dismissed. The Chevalier got to work to found his own commercial enterprise, the Company of the Island of Madagascar; it took him five years to find backers and to select a group of adequately prepared colonists. Meantime, he wrote a book, *The History of the Great Island of Madagascar*, published in Paris in 1658. It is still an essential reference, accurate and reliable. In 1660, he set sail in his own merchant ship, equipped and manned properly in the light of his own experience.

Corsairs attacked him off the Barbary Coast; the Chevalier's ship blew up and sank. Étienne de Flacourt drowned three hundred years ago. His memorial is a living order of Malagasy trees that he identified and described, the *Flacourtiacea*. Of the seven genera and twenty-five species, two occur nowhere else on earth. *Tisonia* is a tall deciduous tree with a great flowering of pink bloom in spring. *Lamoty,* the Madagascar plum, is good to eat. *Aphloia theaeformis* provides a cure like quinine from its leaves.

Nothing could save the colony of Fort Dauphin, certainly not the shipload of brides sent down to settle the young men then working under the new management of Colbert and the king himself. The French East India Company had been reorganized, with royal letters patent on 26 May 1664. Louis XIV bought one-third of the stock for five million livres; gave cannon, powder, and ball to re-equip the fort, and lent a fleet of the Royal Navy to police the seas and escort the merchantmen.

The first cargo of well-brought-up orphan brides of good family, twenty in all, aged from fifteen to seventeen, and all, both charming and healthy, set sail, chaperoned by a nun, in the *Dunkerquoise*, whose captain received strict order to guard them well. The voyage took eleven months. The *Dunkerquoise* proved to be a bad ship, the captain to be a brutal man. By the end of October, 1672, when he put into the pretty bay of Fort Dauphin, six of the girls and their chaperone, the nun, had died. Of the surviving fourteen, six jumped ashore and fled from the captain and his crew into the thorny forests of man-eating trees (*Cycas thouarsii*; the Malagasy brew a strong drink from the sap).

There was no lack of volunteers among the young colonists to catch the fleeing orphans, pick them up, and carry them, kicking and screaming, inside the stockade, where all fourteen of the orphans quickly found husbands, and, it may well have been, tenderness and love. The trees are not, in fact, carnivorous. The men all had Malagasy wives. Divorce is easy in Madagascar, or so it was then. The husband returns the wife to her father and he says, "Thank you for this woman." It is hard to believe that the *ramatoa* went willingly; but off they went with whatever light-skinned children they had, back to the Antanosy tribe. Their fathers and brothers received them.

Two months later the massacre took place on a fragrant moonlit summer midnight—Christmas of 1672—in the candlelit church outside the walls, where the fourteen brides, their fourteen husbands, the priest, and the bachelors were celebrating Mass. Only one of the orphans escaped the spears, although her groom did not.

Her maiden name was Françoise de Clossy; her husband, a clerk in the East India Company, was named Lelièvre de Sauval. She was born in Paris either in 1658 or in 1659, and widowed for the first time aged about fifteen. The Antanosy besieged her and the surviving men inside the fort for eighteen months; no Frenchman outside the stockade escaped—the tribesmen hunted them down and killed them. Then, on either 27 August or 8 September 1674, a company ship, the *White Pigeon*, sailed in and dropped anchor. They took the thirty young men and the widow across to Réunion. Six months later another ship reported that nothing was left of Fort Dauphin but its ashes.

When Louis XIV heard the news, he decided to abandon the colony named after him; his decision cost the stockholders ten million livres. Twenty-four livres equalled one louis d'or, or twenty gold francs. The Palace of Versailles took twenty-one years to build and cost 66,000,000 livres, "a staggering sum." It was ready in 1682. Four years later, on

June 4, the Sun King made a ceremony of taking possession of Madagascar—the whole island, where not a Frenchman was left alive. He changed its name to Oriental France and called the great red island the brightest jewel in his crown.

Françoise de Clossy, Mme. Lelièvre de Sauval, married a second time aboard the *White Pigeon* on the way to Réunion, where she lived for the rest of her long life. He was a gentleman from Provence, Michel Esparon d'Acutéas, allied to the House of Savoy; he died young. Her third husband was a Lieutenant Commander in the Royal Navy, Jacques de Talhouet. When he died, she married again; and then again. In all she bore her five husbands seventeen children. Thus Fort Dauphin cannot be written off as a total loss.

THE CACTUS

A CENTURY later, in September, 1766, another Frenchman, Count Dolisie de Maudave, an officer in the French Navy, was sent over from Mauritius to establish an outpost. He did so; the Malagasy liked the count; he prospered in a modest way. But the Royal Navy had no right to found a successful colony on Madagascar; Maudave infringed upon the French East India Company's concession in abeyance, but not invalid, except in fact. Once again intrigue in Versailles defeated the French empire.

In 1769, the year before he left, Maudave introduced a cactus from Mexico, the prickly pear or Barbary fig, the nopal, *Opuntia stricta* or *O. vulgaris*. It thrived. In the next century, this rambunctious plant had spread across fifty or sixty thousand square miles of the arid south to make a most astonishing landscape. The opuntia begins with a single "article," ping-pong-paddle-shaped (perhaps more oval, less round), its tough green skin formidably armed with hairlike spines. One end of the article takes root; the other edges sprout more articles, until, in its logical if helter-skelter manner, it thickens and grows eight or ten feet tall. In spring, rows of waxy, creamy flowers bloom along the uppermost edges; fruit shaped like miniature barrels, likewise prickly, replace the flowers.

This repetitious cactus jungle turned out to be a blessing to the arid land; as ground cover, it raised the water table so that the wells, the springs, and even the rivers flowed all the year round. Then the Antandröy and the Mahafaly tribes could plant their fields and gardens and count on a harvest even in the driest years. The vanishing land tortoises, the lemurs, and the half-wild herds of cattle found food and shelter under the opuntias. The cactus thus supported the economy of the desert tribes, until 1925.

In that year a French colonist near Tuléar introduced the cochineal to his estate. This scale insect, *Dactylopius coccus*, likewise from Mexico, lives on the various opuntia cactuses. In Mexico, it has its own natural enemies; not so in Madagascar. To most of the genus it is deadly; only one species, *Nopalea coccinellifera*, withstands its attack. From the dried bodies of the female cochineals, a fine red dye is made. Perhaps the experimental colonist thought to benefit the Malagasy and to introduce an industry. Perhaps, instead, he wanted to clear his arable land of the interlocking cactus mazes and labyrinths in order to plant commercial crops like cotton, lima beans, and peanuts. In either case, the cochineals multiplied prodigiously. In the season, swarms and clouds of the flying males choked and blinded travelers. In two years, all of Maudave's benign opuntias withered, collapsed, and died. The water table fell. The springs and wells dried up; the rivers ran dry. The desert returned.

Nobody knows how many thousands of head of cattle died of thirst and starvation, nor how many Antandröy and Mahafaly died in the sudden famine; the dessicated bodies of the very young and the very old lay alongside the paths where they had stopped for the night but had not got up in the morning to go on trekking to the north. Since 1925, drought and famine have returned four times—in 1930–31, in 1936–37, in 1943–44, and in 1957–58. The government sends down food; and French agronomists have introduced a sophisticated variety of opuntia, a fodder plant without the spines, distasteful to the cochineal—a creation of Luther Burbank. It does not seed itself; the articles have to be set out by hand.

Count Dolisie de Maudave left Madagascar in October, 1770. He resigned his commission in the Royal Navy and went into the service of the Great Mogul. There he died in India.

The Thorny South

EVEN without the tumultuous prickly pears, the trip in Holy Week of 1958 from Fort Dauphin going west across the south took me through an hallucinating landscape of surrealist clichés. It began with an unfinished highway, and that started out as good as a French road can be (very good indeed)—excellently engineered and constructed, traced in curves and straightaways appropriate both to the topography and to man's needs. Then while I marveled once again at the peculiarly humanistic genius of the French, their splendid highway came to an abrupt end in midcareer; a bumpy, dusty, unaccommodating dirt road took over. The road builders had come to the end of their "credits." When the allotted funds had run out, they stopped work.

The foremen then ranged the first-rate road building machinery—bulldozers, earth movers, Diesel road rollers, cranes, and excavators, all well washed and well greased—in neat family groups alongside the unfinished thoroughfare, parked on level places, and called upon the local men to erect palm-frond- and banana-leaf-thatched shelters over them.

Twisting and turning and bouncing up and down, I rode along in a red jeep station wagon and saw off to one side some complete and specimen bridges, models of engineering art carrying nothing from one side to the other of nowhere across dry ravines and gulches, detached, disassociated, arbitrary, and curiously disturbing—perhaps because they were not ruined, each was perfect and intact. One such great, high-arching steel suspension bridge had in 1958 thus stood for eight years spanning a wide river bed on the way to the as yet and still unexploited coal-fields between Betioky and Tuléar. Who knows how many million tons of not very good coal lie in that bed? To get it out would mean not only finishing the bridge, but also building the road system and a railroad, and a port, and a town at the mine-head with streets, houses, sewage system, finding a source of water, erecting schools, hospitals, government buildings, offices, shops, and all the rest, the while someone else found workmen from among the wild tribes, and trained them to get out the coal. Others would have to find investors, and find customers to buy the not very good grade of coal. The great bridge—leading nowhere—hangs suspended in the desert air.

I drove along the dusty rough dirt road—which climbed a hill. There I found the black, hard road again! It took me fast into a dazzling, white and sun-bleached landscape, past the town of Amboasary, and up and across a functioning bridge across the Mandrare River, to come down onto a handmade lane, the first road put through (perhaps by Gallieni). It was built by naked tribesmen working out their taxes by gathering water-smoothed pebbles as big as goose eggs and laying them in a neat mosaic in a straight line all the way across the south.

In this rolling arid country once again the reality improves upon those fast and flat, ruled and surreal perspectives fanning out of the foreground into infinity. On either side of the highway, sisal plantations of dusty green agaves in seemingly endless spiky rows of limp and twisted spears and blades arranged in set-piece bouquets grow one after another in military order out of flat red earth. The sisal industry is underwritten by the French Navy to assure a supply of hawsers and ropes, which could be purchased at less expense from Kenya, or from the original home of the fiber plant, Yucatan.

Now and again, as we drove by, we passed an Antandröy road maintenance man, dark brown and splendid, a primitive but whole being, dressed in a strip of handwoven wild cotton cloth, with a brimless straw hat like a small beehive on his head. One young man took a look at us, turned, and ran out of sight into the bush.

I was sharing the ride with a lanky blond Norwegian-American by no means alarming. He was a Lutheran missionary about thirty years old, named, as like as not, Piers Pettersen; with us was his tow-headed son, Petter, a four-year-old. The red Willys station wagon belonged to Piers. I had got the ride by chance. In Fort Dauphin, I tried to hire a car without success, partly, I suspect, because the authorities did not want a stray foreigner driving about the fissionable south, and partly because the roads were bad. Cars cost a lot. In 1957, a 1956 Ford station wagon imported from the U.S.A. had cost one Indian merchant 840,000 francs CFA, plus 100,000 francs CFA for insurance, plus a tax of 60,000 francs CFA on every horsepower above the maximum fifteen allowed in free, plus 4,000 francs CFA in local taxes—or the equivalent of $5,737.00 (at the then rate of 175 francs CFA to the $1.00). So I had decided to give up and take the morning plane, when, at noon one day, I was caught up in a bright blond cataract—a river of school children in assorted sizes from kindergarten through junior high, spilling through the open door of what I recognized immediately to be a white-painted clapboard schoolhouse from the midwestern plains.

Carried along I was cast up at a birthday party—a slice of homemade cake from a packaged mix, a dish of ditto ice cream, and a cup of Nescafé—and soon I was fixed up with the ride across the south. Piers Pettersen, the missionary pastor of Ampanihy, was leaving the next morning to get back to his parish for Easter.

The ride of about 190 miles took all day and went on into the night because we stopped to visit with the other missionaries along the route in their isolated parsonages. Fort Dauphin is the headquarters of the Norwegian-American Lutheran Missionary Society. In the twenty-two mission outposts scattered across the thorny land, there live and work some twenty-five or thirty families—all of them, I think, from Minnesota, and all prolific. The children are sent to the community school in Fort Dauphin. From grandfather to father to son, married to neighboring grandmother, mother, and daughter, the Norwegian-Americans have worked steadily in the south of Madagascar for three generations, since the original pastor, J. P. Hogstad, arrived in 1868. Since then the Lutheran mission has been going strong.

When we drove into the compounds and stopped, we were invited to come in for lunch, for lemonade and ice cream, for coffee, for dinner, for a visit to pass along the accumulating news—how were the children getting on at school? when was the baby expected? what was the news from home? when were the Gerd Gerdsens arriving?—and to introduce me, a random American at large in Madagascar. At first I thought it was an imposition to stay for the noonday meal; but such was not the case. There are no party lines in Madagascar. And although there are old movies, novels to read, and now and again a dance, in the French towns, these entertainments are denied the American missionary families. Therefore, I suppose I can classify myself as a source of innocent amusement, if not merriment. I do not know what they thought of me, but I found them all astonishing—American Gothic figures cut from their frame of reference and imposed upon a surrealist landscape, a collage of hospitable unselfconsciousness upon a background of outrageously sophisticated trees.

So we progressed from parsonage to parsonage, from lunch with the Anders Andersens in Ambovombe ("Ahm-boo-voom-bay"), to lemonade with the Jan Jansens of Tsihombe ("Tsee-oom-bay"), to dinner with the Ole Olsens of Beloha ("Bay-loo")—mashed potatoes, meat and gravy, corn on the cob—middle-western oases in a strange dry land.

In the slanting golden light of late afternoon on a level stretch, the road twisted and turned through a congregation of tremendous individual trees. Usually a vegetable does not startle me, but these did; I gawped and burst out laughing. Piers stepped on the brake and stopped the car—he was an amiable, accommodating man, who had made a pact with God in Korea to devote his life to His service if He spared his life. Piers took things seriously, and anyhow he was used to these bloated malvaceous bombacaceous baobabs, the endemic *Adansonia madagascariensis*.

The baobab of Madagascar *ought not to be like that*! It is an evil growth, it is an outrage against nature, self-indulgent, a shocking tree, monstrous. At its bloated base, the trunk is forty feet around—forty-five! And what is worse the baobab has a nasty habit of growth. It bears no branches except on top, way up at the blunt end of the tapering bole, leaving all that smooth grey corpulence unconcealed—and then the branches and twigs are allowed to grow in wild confusion, untidily. The naked bark is stretched tight over soft and fibrous tissue; it looks like an unhealthy skin pitted and pocked as from old suppurating wounds, or the eruptions of a dread disease. It is not right.

I *like* trees! I put my mind to work and remembered that the Malagasy call this baobab *raine-ala*, "the mother of the forest," or *betroka*, "the big-bellied tree." Slowly as I looked—for this immensity fills the eye and holds the attention—I saw that the baobab of Madagascar has great character; it has its own integrity; and it has courage. There came to mind the image of a misshapen old woman, bloated, dropsical, perhaps tumorous, hiding under that distended sheath a pair of limbs afflicted with elephantiasis, an old lady used by life for life's own purposes, distorted, worn out, discarded—the big-bellied mother of the forest, so she is. I looked and caught a glimpse of a slim girl as lovely as a dryad embedded in the grotesque flesh of a fat and helpless old woman, crying at times—perhaps at night?—to be set free, to be released, to get out of the cage of ugly old age and the flesh.

The baobab of Madagascar is a mortally useless growth, although some of the Malagasy cut into the trunk and hollow out a living tomb for their dead. Shallow rooted, it is harmless but, standing, it covers a lot of ground. It falls easily. The tractor pulls, the bulldozer gives a push, and down goes the baobab. There, lying full length, it takes but a season for the uprooted mother of the forest to collapse. Its spongy, fibrous, cellular tissue, achieved to soak up and store moisture, dries out; the thick skin crumples, the tumid tree disintegrates. So the government agronomists clear the rich alluvial soil along the Mangoky River to plant commercial crops like cotton. There is too much cotton grown today everywhere, but not enough comedy.

I got back into the red jeep station wagon; Piers drove off. I kept on looking back at the congregation of great baobabs, their ponderous curves lit up by the level rays of the setting sun. The young ones are just as fat as the old ladies; it is inherited. They cast broad shadows on the ground.

At dusk we came to a water hole, its marshy borders circled with a grove of trees, ordinary trees, their branches entangled with rope-like lianas. We had the luck to come upon a tribe of ring-tailed lemurs awake after their long day's sleep in the treetops. They had come down for a drink of water, fifteen or twenty of them of all ages. The *Lemur catta* family looked at me. I looked at them. I cannot say what they thought of me, but I found them delightful. Fox-faced, big-eyed, these soft grey-furred primates have arms and legs, hands and feet, and splended tails—ringed black and white, and as long as they are. I found them much more comfortable to look at than the monkeys and the apes, perhaps because they are our most distant living cousins, and thus the *Lemuroideae*, who branched off from the family tree as long as thirty or forty million years ago, in the Eocene, do not resemble me, of the *Homines;* at least, not much. The best I can do is to trace my genealogy to the Pleistocene, 500,000 or 1,000,000 years ago; and that takes stretching. Five hundred thousand to 100,000 is more like it.

Madagascar has almost a monopoly in lemurs: ten genera, twenty-two species, and thirty or so varieties. The Malagasy claim them as ancestors; and, indeed, Madagascar is all that is left of an ancient, sunken, conjectured continent called Lemuria. Nocturnal, haunting, ghostly beings, they take their family name from the Lemures of the Romans. If so, they have changed in character, for the Roman Lemures were malevolent spirits to be placated at midnight of the 9th, the 11th, and the 13th of May, with offerings. The lemurs of Madagascar are gentle and beguiling creatures, possessed by an insatiable curiosity.

The big ones by the water hole were no more than two and a half feet tall; when an old male stood up straight to get a good look at me from a thick branch, I saw that his body was short, but his legs were long, that his arms were short, but his tail was long. He had a black nose in a white face, and sharp-pointed ears. The lemurs have no malice in them. They have alarmingly small brains, and so it follows that they are very stupid animals. To catch one for a pet, all a man need do is find a stout hollow gourd with a narrow bottleneck, tie it securely to the branch of a likely tree, and bait it with a nut or two, a hard fruit, or a boiled bird's egg dropped to the bottom of the gourd. Then comes the lemur in the night to investigate this new thing in the tree. He sniffs, he spies the tidbit at the bottom; he inserts his narrow hand and grasps the handy prize—and having made a fist around it, he cannot withdraw; it does not occur to him to let go. So there he is, caught in his refusal to figure out the link between cause and effect. In the morning, still held fast, still holding on, trapped in his own limitations, comes the man, who carries him away into an alien environment, into captivity, to make of him a lemur *évolué*, a soft, furred, small, remote reflection of himself. *Homo sapiens,* the unique, such as he is, thus once again demonstrates that he is the king of the primates, in whose hands now lies the future of the going world.

314

As pets, the lemurs are not sly as are the monkeys, although they, too, like to take things apart to see what is inside, and they like to tear up paper for the fun of it. Therefore, they cannot be allowed the run of the house. My friend, the ring-tailed *Lemur catta* makes the best pet. Although nobody yet has been known to toilet-train one of them, they take to home life and learn to like the society of man. They persist in sleeping throughout the day, but they come down for the cocktail hour; they prefer a sweet vermouth.

Once the appetite has been opened, they choose for the main meal some boiled rice garnished with birds' eggs or insect larvae, with a few carrots, turnips, beetroots, or potatoes. They enjoy a salad of tender green shoots. For dessert, a ripe guava will do; but to make friends with a lemur, give him a banana. He sits down, picks up the golden fruit, savors it and smiles. Then he gets a firm grip on one end of it, and carefully peels it, strip by strip, and tosses the skin aside. Then like a true gourmet, he eats up every bit in dainty bites, slowly, making the pleasure last. The family I met by the roadside pool at dusk in the south did not wait long enough for me to offer them a drink, and I had no bananas. So they went away. I cannot remember hearing them make any sort of sound as they left the dark water, crossed the red dirt road, and hand over hand climbed the lianas, or, in great acrobatic leaps, took to the trees, all of them, the patriarch, the grandmothers, the fathers, the mothers and the babies and the young, stopping now and again to look back over their shoulders—at me. Some of the lemurs, I am told, cry out in piercing tones. "Ka-ka-ka-ka!" they comment. As we drove on in the red jeep, I turned and caught sight of a big fellow—perhaps the rear guard?—standing in the middle of the empty road, looking back at me.

Night fell. The full moon rose. We drove through a deserted landscape in the black and white light and came to the end of our journey, the town called Ampanihy, in English, "a Plethora of Bats." There are no lunatic asylums, although there are three belfries on the two churches, one on the Protestants', two on the Roman Catholics'. The bats referred to are fruit bats, flying foxes, big animals said to be good to eat, and why not? They feed on ripe fruit. There are twenty-six sorts of bat in Madagascar. These of Ampanihy, *Pteropus rufus* of the *Pteropodidae*, of the *Megachiroptera*, of the *Chiroptera*, have a five-foot wing-spread and a thick reddish fur, for which no use has yet been discovered. The Chevalier Étienne de Flacourt dined upon them in the seventeenth century, but I did not in the twentieth. He found their flesh to be good. In Madagascar I was told that if you pierce the membrane of the alae even with a pinprick puncture, the mammal can no longer fly; I did not try it out.

As we drove into Ampanihy, a few bats flew and a few dogs barked, but none of the two to three thousand human inhabitants stirred the white dust of the moonstruck market town, the administrative center of the Mahafaly tribal lands. "The Tabooers" are strong and independent people, dark of skin, wild and peaceful of countenance; they are primitive. They see no cause or reason to change their ancient ways. The Mahafaly like things as they are, ringed about with interlocked taboos, closed circles.

Through this black and white taboo town we drove in moonlight past the flimsy basket-woven thatched huts, the rough stone houses, the white-plastered two-storied villas, the Indian and Chinese shops—human habitations and workrooms, still and withdrawn in a mortal silence. The night should have been calm and serene, but instead it seemed to be drenched in withheld violence. Something should have stirred. Bats and dogs hear sounds that the human ear cannot.

We drove into and out of the inky shade of tamarind trees, went through an open gate, followed along a curving drive, and we drew up. Piers pulled on the hand brake; we were there, parked in the sheltering angle of the parsonage ell. "Lady wants to sell her ell," I muttered, quoting. "Hm?" asked Piers. "Nothing," I said, "not a thing." I got out slowly and straightened up my aching back, once more bottomlessly grateful to the anonymous lady of Damariscotta, Maine, for her classified advertisement in the summer of . . . I don't know, it was a prewar summer at home. She made a published statement that adapts itself to any sort of mood or frame of mind and nervous state. It is as comforting to me as an incantation or a poultice, and it has served me well—as it did that night of the long jeep ride over the rough road to Ampanihy in the thorny, much-tabooed, Malagasy south. I dared not swear among the missionaries at Piers' parsonage.

We stood a moment in the dry stillness of the moonlit night outside the shuttered house—every one of its openings had been closed with locks and bolts, hooks and bars. I wondered then what this big, four-square, stone-built farmhouse, brought with its porches and flat roof from the Minnesota plains, was barricaded to withstand.

Then the silent night air shuddered. A tomtom drumbeat broke the quiet moonlit stillness. A knowledgeable dark hand out of sight thumped the drumhead once again, and then again, and another time, and once more. Soon the dry black and white night throbbed with tomtoms drumming at a pace just above the beat of the heart. I had been weary; I was not. I turned to Piers and found Petter clinging to him.

"Witch-doctors," said the missionary pastor in flat middle-western tones; and just in time I stopped myself from asking if we might not follow up the drumbeats to the source to join in the goings-on. Then from inside the house another hand slid the iron bolts, turned the keys in the locks, swung the solid wooden front-door open, and reached out to unhook the screen door. It belonged to a young and smiling woman in her early thirties, unmistakably American. She came out to greet us in a fresh cotton housedress, a scarf tied around her head to hide the curlers in her hair; she wore no rings on her fingers, no wedding band.

This was Anna, Piers' missionary assistant, who did a hundred things about the parish—organized the Sunday school, arranged the church sociables and bazaars, ran the charities, spurred on the ladies' auxiliaries, saw to the young peoples' picnics, baked bread, demonstrated needlework, visited the pregnant or the disconsolate, and kept her finger on the pulse of the community, as well as her ear to the ground. She was, in truth, Piers' connection with the outside world. I came to wonder if anything escaped her in the town, in the community—indeed, in the south. Certainly nothing did in the parsonage. She managed the servants, too, and doled out their wages to keep the men from splurging it on payday for unnecessary luxuries—such as bicycles for themselves, and nylons for the wife—for otherwise they would go hungry at the end of the month. She donated milk powder to the young. Anna was expecting us—Piers had sent a telegram from Fort Dauphin, and what is more it had come through in time. Having satisfied herself that we had dined, and that all was as well as could be expected with Piers' pregnant wife in the mission hospital, back near Fort Dauphin, we said good night and went separately to bed. I listened to the tomtoms until they faltered; then I went to sleep.

In the morning of the Saturday before Easter, seated at the breakfast table Piers said grace: "Come, Lord Jesus, be our guest. And let these gifts to us be blest." And after boiled rice and canned Swiss evaporated milk, homemade bread and that seasonal rarity, home churned butter, topped by a real luxury, homemade peanut butter, he said, "Thanks, Lord Jesus, Thou art good. And Thy mercy endureth forever."

Piers then went off to his dark office to clear his desk of the work that had piled up on it in his absence; I stayed behind to drink another cup of Nescafé and to talk, which is to say to listen to Anna. Anna was a natural-born talker, wide awake in the mornings, as am I. I found her to be a pleasant, comfortable, courageous woman, large in her sound views of practical reality if, to be sure, arbitrary in such professional matters as dancing (only for married couples) and religion (none but the Lutheran faith was fit for Christians). She had a sense of style in conversation and in dress, and she enjoyed herself in company. By no means narrow or intolerant, she looked at the world and liked what she saw—although people, being people, sometimes *would* behave foolishly. There was nothing sour in her outlook. Indeed, she had a sweet tooth, and was devoted to candy and cake. She smiled easily. All her teeth were false—"Yankee Clippers," she called her uppers and her lowers. The diet of the missionaries in the south is perforce unbalanced. No fresh European or American fruit or leaf or root vegetables will grow in that dry heat; and anyhow the limited water supply will not cover the irrigation of garden patches. Canned goods are way beyond the missionary means. (They are paid less than servants are at home. But the Lord sends compensations, and the Church takes care of them for life.) So Anna had offered up all her own teeth on the altar of her faith. There are no dentists in the south, none closer than Tananarive. Anna was not a gossip, but she missed, I think, above all things the chance to talk, to talk freely and easily, to sit down over a second cup of coffee and chat—to forget all, or nearly all, the occupational restrictions and let go.

And she had a wry sense of humor of that rarest of kinds—she was able to let a good laugh reveal her own relation to the outside world in which she worked. She knew what she was up against as a missionary. To illustrate the absurd aspects of her job, she told me that the Malagasy of the town—Catholic, pagan, and Protestant, too—called her among themselves Madame Tournée. The Malagasy are humorous people, enormously perceptive, unspoiled by intellectual discipline, unable to imagine any but their own taboos, and they believe their own eyes. A *tournée* is a pastoral trip around among the several churches of the mission district. Piers conscientiously made several *tournées* each year to encourage the Malagasy pastors of the hinterland, and to talk things over. His wife, housebound by woman's work, stayed at home in the parsonage. But Anna went along to help out in the Sunday schools, to visit the troubled, the faltering, and the halt. She had a soothing way with her. And she enjoyed the ride, although there were no roads at all and, after the rains, no tracks through the wilderness. The longest *tournée* took the better part of a week to complete. Thus it was, to the Malagasy, obvious that Piers had made a sensible arrangement in practical polygamy. He had two wives, one for the house, and one for the road: Mme. Maison, and Mme. Tournée—and how the French loved the joke! Anna had to laugh. There was nothing else she could do; if she gave up the *tournées* (and she did not want to, they gave her real opportunities to do the work of God), the Malagasy would only think that she was . . . well, they would think the worst. No, she corrected herself, the worst thing that can happen to a Malagasy woman is to live a barren, childless, empty life.

Anna seemed to me to be a total, but intact, young woman. By no means an old maid, she was very feminine. I had a hunch she was waiting for Mr. Right Rightsen to happen by to ask her hand and her whole heart in Christian marriage. His arrival I thought unlikely in the arid, thorny south, but I was wrong. Three months before my own unexpected arrival, a legendary sailor at liberty—the second officer on a Norwegian freighter loading peanuts in Tuléar, a handsome Lutheran —had come down out of the blue, walked up to the parsonage, knocked, and gone in. Anna lived in a barricaded house lacking electricity, without running water, with old copies of the *Reader's Digest* in the privy, alone in a walled compound among aliens, but not without hope. The sailor had said that he would come back for a longer stay if all went well on the next voyage and if there were enough dried lima beans or peanuts in Tuléar to fill the holds of the cargo. While Anna went on talking, it crossed my mind to wonder how to phrase a prayer for a bumper peanut crop.

I listened and I learned that Ampanihy was in turmoil. The troubles had begun with a crime wave. A gang of nationalistic, anti-foreign, patriotic bandits, all of them young Malagasy men, was terrorizing the town, although now that the moon was full, things had calmed down. They struck at night. In the dark of the moon, just before bedtime, they crept up to the front door of their selected victims, the prosperous householders, the Europeans, Asians, Créoles, and Merina, and knocked on the front door. When it was opened, they rushed in, laid hands on all portable valuables, stripped the house, cleared out fast, and vanished. They killed one man who resisted, and wounded several others. The police concluded that they had many willing helpers among the average citizens; but none came forward to offer information or to claim rewards. Only the silence deepened at night.

Sometimes the young xenophobes—or another gang—waited in the shadows of the by-roads off the main street of the town until the cinema let out and the hotel bar had closed and the foreign bachelors and errant husbands had been entertained. Then, having observed their victim's pattern of action on her way home from work, they stalked her. She was always a woman alone, one of the *métisses* or detached Malagasy girls, the pretty ones who had broken free of the Mahafaly taboos—not necessarily for pay or gifts. When she arrived at the chosen crossroads, deserted and dark, the hunting pack closed in on her, threw her down, stripped the gold rings from her ears, her wrists, her fingers, broke the chains from her neck, and ripped away her pins. Never did they rape her, or kill her. They slashed her cheeks with razor blades to spoil her pretty face. And although they usually stole her fat purse, these vigilantes were not robbers, they were censors, punishing the light young woman for betraying the nationalistic cause and the Malagasy way of life. By day these young patriots went about their ordinary business; all the town knew who they were, but none dared speak up to identify them.

Then one morning, the auditors from Tananarive came unannounced in their usual way to look at the books of the local government; and suddenly in the night one of the district commissioner's subordinates, an assimilated Malagasy in the Civil Service, the local paymaster, had hanged himself; he had an ambitious wife and he had borrowed all the petty cash. In their position it was incumbent upon them to keep up with the Ampanihy Joneses; the man had planned to put the money back on next payday; but the auditors had come down without warning.

"It is really very sad," said Anna. "They cannot bring themselves to work out a proper budget and live within their means. They just do not understand money. If I pay the servants their full wages at one time, they spend it all on things they do not need; they splurge. Then the whole family goes hungry at the end of the month. I must say, they don't seem to mind, they think it is all perfectly natural. They are like the grasshoppers in the story." She smiled. "You know, the Malagasy eat grasshoppers. That is to say, they are not really grasshoppers, they are locusts, they come in plagues like the ones in the Bible. Clouds of them. They settle down and eat up anything that is green. Now the French have pretty well got them under control, but I believe back in the early days a plague of locusts settled on the rice fields around Fort Dauphin and ate up all the crops. It was a famine year. So the Malagasy attacked the fort and drove the French away. Perhaps it was punishment for their sins." She stopped to reflect. "I don't know what they taste like—the grasshoppers, I mean. The Malagasy fry them. They sound crunchy."

The Chef-de-Poste had hanged himself in the night. His wife—that is to say, his widow—found him. He had strung himself up in the office on the ground floor, below their living quarters up above. She had locked all the doors and had refused to open up to the auditors. It took the district commissioner himself, called from his office to talk to her across her barricades, to get her to surrender the keys. She threw them out through a small high window, and when they got the front door open, they found that she had fled out the back way, leaving her new high-heeled shoes behind her as she ran away. It took the fleetest men in town to catch her; they brought her back scratching and struggling, wide-eyed and silent.

Then, on Palm Sunday, my friend Pastor Jean-Albert Mahatoto, the ardent nationalist, the veteran of the Second World War and the Malagasy Rebellion of 1947, that grizzled, solid man, stood up in church in the morning, and preached a forbidden political sermon to his captive audience, seated upon hard wooden benches. He filled the quiet air of the whitewashed Protestant church with themes of liberty, equality, freedom of choice and of action. Nothing would have happened had not some enemy betrayed him to the authorities. Pastor

Mahatoto still lived under the old injunction to confine his sermons to heavenly concerns, and never to point his finger at the French.

He could not help himself; and soon none but the District Commissioner could handle the uproar. *"Du calme! Du calme!"* the harassed man pronounced, using all his authority to smooth things down. For the Roman Catholic community was riven by a scandal of its own.

It happened that the free-thinking and free-living hotelkeeper, a full-blooded, easy-going Frenchman of about fifty—a good man—had chosen that moment to marry the French woman to whom he was devoted, and with whom he had lived in well worn and comfortable irregularity for long enough to have four charming small daughters— the last of whom, indeed, had just been born, out of wedlock, it may be, but in fidelity to one another. Years back, he had come down to Madagascar as a young gendarme with a legal bride; the climate did not suit her, and nor, apparently, did her husband; so she went home.

Then he had met the young wife of a not-so-young French Colonial career officer in the government—in Majunga. They had come down with a bad case of the *grande passion,* and they had run off together. Forced to quit the police force, other official circles closed to keep him out of other jobs. Finally the pair had settled down in adultery to hotel-keeping in Ampanihy. It was an uncomfortable hotel, the only one in town; but it was a contented management—except for one flaw. They were never invited to the official fête of the 14th of July.

Before long, the man's wife back in France found someone else to marry; she had decently and quietly divorced the former gendarme. However, the hotel proprietress's husband, the injured party of the first part, had refused to cooperate in an arranged divorce. He was not vindictive; he couldn't be bothered. So time passed and the babies came; the years went by. Then, just the month before, word had arrived from Africa, by way of Paris and Tananarive, through bureaucratic channels to the district commissioner's office, that the long-deserted functionary husband in the pursuit of his official duties had caught an obscure tropical disease (in the Upper Volta), and had quietly died of it. He had never changed his will, and so his widow had come into a pleasant bequest. She now was free to remarry.

For years, she had felt left out of things in Ampanihy. She wanted to be invited to the garden party at the residence of the district com-

missioner on Bastille Day. But the wives always said no! Discreetly un-
faithful couples were often asked to dine; but the hotelkeepers, known
to be faithful to one another in their life of sin, were never *never*
NEVER issued an invitation to attend the 14th of July festivities, with
fireworks, although every other French citizen in Ampanihy automatically got one.

The hotelkeeper, in his quiet way, was a free-thinker; but he never
forced his opinions on any customer in his bar. However, he loved his
bride-to-be, and so he had agreed to her reasonable and natural request that they be married not only legally, but also openly in church.
To do so, first he had to renounce free-thinking and then to return to
the bosom he had so long ago left. Both had to confess and to be
absolved of their reiterated one and only sin, and to promise to go forth
and sin no more. As they planned to be married before nightfall, that
would not have been difficult. But, they also had to baptize their four
girls.

The hotelkeeper took a stand. It was his one and only gesture of
defiance against the society that patronized his bar but excluded his
belovèd from the fête of the 14th of July. He was stubborn. All the
hotelkeeper demanded was to get the churchings over with once and
for all, all at once. Therefore, he had asked the Roman Catholic parish
priest to baptize the pretty girls and to marry the parents at the same
time; that is to say, one after the other in turn. His was not an unreasonable request; he had no one to tend the bar while both he and his
wife were seeing to the christenings and being married; the servants
were the wedding guests.

The parish priest called the proposed mass ceremony unseemly, and
he questioned the spirituality and sincerity of the motivation. The
hotelkeeper then had begun to get red in the face. He had wanted
no fuss; all he wanted was to regularize his household, to get it over
with. A big man physically, he rarely lost his temper; but when his
nervous wife-to-be began to weep, he suddenly shouted that the
parish priest was not a one to talk, and went on to name the precise
number of the old priest's grown-up half-breed and wholly irregular
children (five as I recall) born to his faithful housekeeper and
ramatoa, a smiling and delightful old Mahafaly woman, long since
comfortably past childbirth. He was immediately sorry, he could have

bitten out his tongue; for the old priest had suddenly sat down. He fumbled for his cross, and stared through the burly hotelkeeper as though he were a window.

It was a true, and an ancient story, well known; but the good Father had nurtured the delusion that none but his *ramatoa*, his God, his confessor, and he, himself, had been fully cognizant of his mortal sins— and often he had suspected that the mother of his bastard boys and girls, in her heart of hearts, saw no sin in loving him. So he had failed to come to terms with the flesh until age had cleared his mind and spirit. He looked out at the thorny desert; he looked into his own soul.

In a faltering voice, the old priest asked for a drink of water. The wife ran to the kitchen of the rectory; the hotelkeeper ran across the square to fetch a bottle of brandy; the four girls, the baby in the arms of the eldest, sat still and watched with interest; they had never seen their father or their mother so upset. They were kindly people, although hardened sinners, and did not like to give pain or cause trouble. Back with Rémy Martin in one hand and a *petit verre* in the other, the hotelkeeper begged the priest to take a drop; and when the old man smiled and accepted the offered cognac, the big man grinned, kissed his wife and all four girls, and would have kissed the priest had he not seen that the old man was lost in thought. Then the priest put down the empty liqueur glass and stood up. In a firm voice, he thanked the hotelkeeper and said, "I cannot marry you. I cannot christen your daughters. I am unworthy."

So the district commissioner had been forced to intervene. He pointed out that the priest could not refuse—he had no choice in the matter. Tactfully he arranged for the children to be baptized and the hotelkeepers to be married, but on successive days. He proposed himself as general godfather, and he gave the bride away. His wedding present to her was a perpetual and permanent engraved invitation to all the Bastille Day garden parties from then on.

In his way, the district commissioner was a secular saint. He served France in Madagascar. He served the Malagasy on their tribal lands, not from headquarters. In the field, none could surpass him. The Malagasy trusted him.

Therefore, at the end of his career, he had been reassigned to the District of the Tabooers in the Thorny South; it had been his first, as it was to be his last, post. His wife, who had heard about the hard-

ships of the Ampanihy Residence from the wives of other functionaries, had refused to join her husband there. She elected to remain
in France to prepare her own house for retirement. The district commissioner thus lived alone as he worked alone in the dry climate. His
solitude gave him freedom and considerable scope. His superiors in
Tananarive asked of him only not to bother them while they worked
on the grand scale to withdraw in dignity from Madagascar, the while
they paved the way for the future of the independent Malagasy Republic inside the French Community. The petty problems of Ampanihy
were his alone to handle.

The district commissioner had his hands full, what with the breaking up of the gang of robbers and the punishment of the patriotic assassins; the cutting down and covering up of the embezzling Malagasy
functionary suicide, and the reassimilation of his detribalized widow;
the smothering of the flames lit by the political parson in his Protestant
pulpit; the marrying of the town's well tempered sinners, the christen-
ing of their charming daughters, and the fortifying of the tormented
priest. Meanwhile, he had been visited with a truly appalling run of
bad luck in the construction of *his* well and fountain.

The district commissioner had few illusions left about himself; but
what man does not want to leave evidences of his passage behind him?
He thought of France; he thought of what the civilizing mission meant
to him. He considered the Mahafaly in their arid tribal sands of time.
It came to him to build an ever-flowing fountain of pure water in the
market place, a great dusty square in the center of Ampanihy. He got
down to work.

First he deepened and enlarged the existing well and lined it with
dressed stone. Then, having studied the catalogues, he bought a
gasoline-powered motor pump, the best he could obtain. It was American; some of his own dollars went to pay the price. It was a great
relief for him to see it installed according to his own ideas, bolted to a
system of steel girders set inside the well, above the reach of the
water, but below the ground level.

He tested the machine. It worked. The water flowed. His masons
then built a wellhead and capped it with a dome. To be sure, the commissioner had thought to provide an unobtrusive trap door so that the
mechanics could get down to look after the pump.

The fountain-reservoir itself, he placed in the center of the square.

On a stepped platform of masonry, he built a hollow cube of dressed fieldstone roofed with wide overhanging eaves to provide shade and a resting place for the women as they came to fill their empty petrol tins and plastic buckets. It distressed the commissioner to see them put aside their beautiful and functional water jars to take up the ugliest of the products and by-products of the machine age; but he could no nothing about that. However, he saw to it that the bronze spigots, each set in a niche above an oval basin on the four sides of the fountain, were beautiful, as well as solid and well made. As he watched his plans take shape, he thought this would be a pleasant place for the women to gather and to talk as they drew water.

To adorn the corners of the fountain-reservoir, he had hoped to find a Mahafaly sculptor to carve a pattern of traditional designs into the stone. But the tribal artists work in wood. In the end, he brought down a French stonecutter from Tananarive; under the commissioner's supervision, the man did very well with motifs taken from the tomb posts of the Mahafaly kings, low reliefs of the circles and squares, the back-to-back crescents, the hexagons, octagons, and diamonds, and the various crosses piled up one above the other—all of which have meanings (so he had read) as old as the mind and the soul of man.

The result pleased him. To be sure, the fountain was not perfect—nothing is, nothing man can achieve ever is. But it worked, the water flowed! Because, after all the delays, the fountain had not been completed until Holy Week, the district commissioner decided to forgo a ceremony, and simply to turn on the pump, fill up the reservoir, and let the water pour. He did so. The whole town seemed to share his pleasure. The two young Mahafaly mechanics, into whose specially trained hands he had put the full responsibility of the pump machinery, walked about in their overalls with the sober dignity of kings; they took it as a personal affront when the automatic cut-off, perhaps damaged in the long voyage, balked and refused to stop the pump when the cistern was full.

So early in the morning with the pump going, they went through the small door of the wellhead pumphouse, climbed down the steel ladder, and perched on the girders supporting the machinery above the well water. No one had thought to provide the imported American gasoline-powered pump engine with an exhaust pipe to carry off the carbon monoxide fumes. On his way to work, later in the morning, the district commissioner passed by. He saw the overflowing fountain, saw the open door in the wellhead, heard the pump engine, and went over to investigate. When his eyes got used to the darkness, he saw floating on the round surface of the quiet water the two bodies of the young mechanics, one face up, one face down. He shouted an alarm before he climbed through the small door and went down the ladder to turn off the pump. The chief of police, who had had the foresight to grab up a gas mask left over from the war, and to put it on before he went into the wellhead, found the district commissioner unconscious, dangling on the rungs of the steel ladder.

They had to demolish the stone masonry to get the bodies of the young mechanics out. One was Catholic, the other Protestant; they were buried at the district commissioner's expense. He had a proper exhaust pipe installed and a temporary thatched roof put over the well. He had the well pumped dry and the fresh water tested for purity. But the Mahafaly men and women refused to go near the fountain—they walked out into the country or went down to the dirty river for their water—not because they believed the well to be contaminated by germs from the young bodies, but because the witch-doctor had put a taboo on the district commissioner's fountain.

The district commissioner knew the witch-doctor to be a cynical man, greedy for the absolute power that his ancestors once wielded over the tribe. The man claimed that the impious *vazaha,* the white foreigners, had enraged the water spirit in the well, and in revenge had reached up and pulled down the two young apostates, the *évolués,* the Roman Catholic and Protestant Mahafaly mechanics, to drown them in punishment for breaking the taboos of their ancestors. Having made his position clear, the witch-doctor then allowed the district commissioner to know that he was ready to treat with him on equal terms, and to do business in a bargain for the souls—and the money— of the Mahafaly people of Ampanihy. He demanded recognition as a third force in the community, and he would not remove the taboo put upon the fountain unless the French authorities and the Christian missionaries allowed him to practice his ancestral profession, and be paid for his services.

He got his way. The witch-doctor agreed to lift the taboo on the night of the full moon—on Good Friday—in a traditional ceremony, the rites to be followed in the usual way with an orgy. Those were the drums I had heard tomtoming in the full moonlight on the night of my arrival at the barricaded parsonage.

When I left Ampanihy, Anna and I exchanged gifts. I had been allowed to pay Piers for the gasoline and the use of his jeep, but I dared not suggest payment for his hospitality. So I offered him an almost new wash-and-wear summer suit, and found a raw silk shirt that Anna could make over for herself. She gave me an inscribed copy of John Bunyan's *The Pilgrim's Progress from This World to That Which Is to Come.*

Out of the Taboo Forest; Onto the Plateau of Learning

THE taboo forest of the tombs of the Mahafaly kings, a thorny en-
tanglement of trees and vines, is a quiet place of the dry dead. In
it, even the air holds still; no breeze blows through the untouched
stand of endemic trees. None of the sweet smell of forest humus
arises from underfoot; the earth is dry as dust. No birds sing because
there are no birds to sing perched in the branches. No small animals
rustle the undergrowth because none lives there and no bush sur-
vives under the unique and specialized, xerophytic trees, which are
both prehistoric and definitive in shape and in nature. No great
spotted or striped cats stalk these woods; there are no pachyderms
among the pachypodiums. There are no looped constrictors hanging
among the rubbery lianas, and no venomous snakes. The trees have
taken over the defenses of the other kingdom here; they are tusked,
fanged, saw-toothed, clawed, and armed. The *Didiereaceae* grow tall,
their tentacle branches upraised like inert octopodes or giant squids.
The pachypodiums and baobabs have grown smooth bark like thick
skin; the acacias scratch the unaware; the aloes grow like trophies
of spearheads and bloom like a brand. The *Euphorbia oncoclada* have
got rid of whatever leaves they might have had to grow like dead
dry colonies of branching corals. They have evolved a multitude of
dull-green, smooth-skinned shoots and sticks; break one and the wound
oozes a thick, milk-white sap that is poisonous. It blinds the eye.

The taboo forest casts crisscrossing shadows but gives no shade.

329

Nothing there escapes the light of day, or of the moon and stars. It offers no repose; there is no refuge in it. There is no comfort to be had, and no shelter. Intact, untouchable, the taboo forest stands in wait for another death.

The last great ceremonial interment took place two generations back—there are no kings at work ruling among the Mahafaly clans today, although some of the lesser royalties now hire out as gardeners for the white communities. They prefer to work for the Norwegian-American missionaries, because these *vazaha*, whose concern is the immortal soul, do not remind the cousins of the kings of their lost powers, nor impatiently require them to touch unclean, tabooed tasks like gutting fowl or cleaning filth. The living will not serve as guides to the royal graves.

Pastor Jean-Albert Mahatoto, by then my friend, agreed to go along to help me find the distant forest of the tombs. He is an alien Antandröy, and thus the taboos do not hold good for him, except in courtesy. We set off in the red jeep with a picnic lunch that Anna packed for us. It was the Saturday before Easter. Christ lies dead that day; therefore, the pastor was free to go. He wore clean khaki pants and a checked sport shirt with his topee on his grizzled head. He told me about his life during the war in France, and of his discoveries in the prison camps and the Occupation, and later in the Rebellion of 1947. So we drove along.

Once off the main highway, the track to the south toward the forest frays out like the strands of an unraveled rope discarded on the ground. Once we got into the forest, we might have missed the place of burial had we not overtaken a man and wife walking single file along the road, he first, wearing the twisted loin cloth and carrying a *sagai* spear, a hat of woven fiber on his head, she following after, wrapped in a covering of dirt-tan cotton cloth, a heavy bag on her back slung from a strap across her forehead. She walked bent forward against the weight, her hands free to carry, in one, an upside-down, red-brown bunch of chickens, their heads turned right side up at the ends of their necks to peer from eye to eye at us and squawk, and in the other a can of kerosene. Pastor Mahatoto asked the way. The man looked at us in sober astonishment, the wife in fear. Then he pointed with his spear, and told us to go along until we reached a certain baobab; we did so. There I parked and locked the borrowed car although there was no other living soul in sight. We walked into the trees.

I stopped to look up at the virgin grove of *Didiereaceae;* elsewhere they are vanishing. Their punky wood can be put to use as planks to make boxes and chests. There are two varieties, *Alluaudia procera* and the other, I forget its name. One is more compact in growth with a dense, coarse, green, fur-like foliage all over it, the blade-like leaves sprouting directly from the skin to hide the thorns. The second is much worse; it has leaves like small, succulent green butterflies perched all over it, as though a swarm had settled in spirals along the trunk up and out around the upthrust, terrible, tapering branches bristling with three-inch thorns. Some of the *Lepidoptera* feed on the slime of unspeakable corruption.

These are trees especially suited to taboo; there is no wonder that such trees were mistaken for man-eating vegetable growths. As I stood well within their reach, looking up at the thirty-foot monsters, I felt the myth begin to work in me. I could—it was not hard at all— see the butterflies fly up in a green cloud as the branches writhed and twisted and came looping down to wrap me in a mortal embrace, punctured and pierced by the blood-letting thorns. The green butterflies, I supposed, would settle back in place once I began to rot; but why in spirals?

On the other hand, the pachypodiums are comical; these trees have silly shapes, not frightening at all. They stand about like ill-considered giant bud-vases, twelve or fifteen feet tall, an objectionable bouquet of branches jammed tight in the bottleneck, everlasting funeral flowers, it might be. Then I saw the tombs among the trees.

None but the very old now alive attended the last great royal funeral; and they were then too young to have gorged, got drunk, danced, laughed aloud, and stood up, humping to it, or thrown themselves down lollopping upon the ground. Round-eyed, these oldsters, who were then fat-bellied brown babies and gangling youngsters, looked on and learned; if the wake went on long enough—as much as six months or more for the very great—perhaps a few went into adolescence and took part. I have done my homework, so I know that, when the king died, his body, washed, the eyelids closed, the jaws tied shut, was wrapped first in fine mats of woven fibers and then in

331

the royal *lambamena*, that universal covering—emblem, shawl, blanket, and shroud—loomed of wild silk, sometimes of spiders' filaments, a tough, heavy, lumpy fabric dyed dark red-brown, bordered with metal beads in a pattern and edged with looped fringe. They are longer than the standing man's measurements, and wide enough to wrap around laid out. The enshrouded body is then put aside in an especially built and—I suppose—airy woven reed and thatch hut to decompose and dry out.

All the while professional mourners, women reclining on one elbow in attitudes of grief upon the ground around the bier wail, moan, cry noisily, and lament the death of the great king. They are paid to do so. Meantime, the clans of the tribe have gathered. The masons go to the quarries and dress the stone blocks; the sculptors fell the tallest trees to get out thirty-foot timbers for the *aloalo* tomb-post soul-perches. The herdsmen round up the handsomest of the lyre-horned, fat-humped bulls to be slaughtered in hecatombs for the funeral meats. In the late decadent days, Indian and Chinese merchants moved in, set up stalls, and sold red wine and rum by the hogshead, imported novelties, and who knows what necessities, specialties, and souvenirs?

A great death called forth all the culture of the tribe in ceremony. The musicians played their stringed instruments, drums and reed flutes; the singers sang songs; the dancers, solo or in rank, danced bird dances, war dances, and dances that they felt like dancing. The athletes ran, wrestled, and played games. Almost naked, well adorned, the young men and women must have been handsome and beautiful, well muscled, lean, straight-backed, the virgin girls famous for their breasts, their black hair plaited in tight braids and annointed with melted rancid zebu suet, their smooth dark-brown skin gleaming with sweat in the sun or in the firelight.

The mourning family and clan members, the tribal men and women, ate and drank enormously by day; night was devoted to a ritual orgy. Perhaps the taboos of incest were not so complex as those of other Polynesian societies. The idea was to get children; they did so in the presence of death, itself a strong stimulus. The dead man, in body and in hovering spirit, encouraged the living the while he lay rotting alone in his hut.

Only after his skin and bones were dry were they given burial.

The enshrouded skeleton was put into the grave; the blood of sacrificed bulls was then poured over it, replacing the earlier blood of slaves. Over the filled grave in the center of a cleared ground, the masons built the king's tomb, a great, dressed stone, dry platform, a solid rectangular parallelepipedon in shape, from thirty-five to fifty feet to a side, rising from three to four feet above the surface of the level ground. The lesser chieftains and the queens (who were buried adorned with all their jewels and ornaments) had smaller tombs.

Then came the placing of the *aloalo*—the tomb posts, the soul perches—twenty or so feet tall, set in order on the grave platform, as many as two or three dozen for the greatest kings, each one of them cryptic and biographical in sculpture. Next came the piling up of the horned skulls of the cattle slaughtered to feed the mourners. The greater the number of bucranes, the greater the evident wealth, the power, the status, and the prestige of the dead man in the nomadic Mahafaly cattle cult. Finally, the utensils of the king—his dishes, his drinking mugs, his pots and pans, his kettles—were arranged on the tomb platform for the use of his living spirit, not yet ready to quit the earth, so that he could have food prepared and served him (I suppose by the working spirits of the slaughtered slaves in the original practice) to nourish him in after-life. On the tombs I looked at, this *batterie de cuisine* and cutlery were French made—blue enamel plates and mugs and cast-iron kettles, each one carefully punctured to spoil it for the use of any but the living dead, thus to reënforce the taboos in the onslaught of enlightened decadence.

Pastor Jean-Albert Mahatoto and I walked among the tombs of the taboo forest, which alone of all things there seems to renew itself. I cannot say how many platforms there may be—a very great many, one after the other among the shadeless trees; their walls begin to tumble, the corners fall, the sides crumble and collapse. The tomb posts slant as tombstones do; some have broken; all have weathered. One or two serve now as standards for climbing growths.

The *aloalo* are works of art. "Al-oo-al" they are pronounced. They are full of meaning and, of course, taboo. Carved in a style at once representational and abstract, each post is full of information about the life of the dead, as well as of the tribe. Conventional, recognizably all alike, each one is different from the others. I could not make out the whole code, but it reads from the bottom up. Level with the surface of the stone platform, as though upright on its own two feet, stands a representational figure in the round, a naked man or woman, not a portrait, but a sort of informant. The position of the arms and hands tells the onlooker in the know a circumstance of the entombed man's death. For instance, if the figure has a hand upon his mouth, he signals to the living that the manner of death was lamentable. Or if the figure is a woman, as is the dead, and she has her hand on her belly, the queen died in childbirth; if both are male, the man died of a disease. And so on.

Balancing on the head of the conventional, but representational, human figure arises a piling-up of flat but thick squares, diamonds, hexagons, octagons, swastikas, crescents back to back, and circles, sometimes filled in with the X-shaped cross of St. Andrew, or the plus mark of the Greek cross, each figure pierced through the wood—*à jour,* as the French say of holes cut through solid mass to let in the light of day—their flat surfaces incised with shallow designs, perhaps to catch the play of light and shadow. Clearly these plane figures are schematic as well as mystic. I asked, but I could find no one who would—or could—tell me their significance; I suspect that no man can, for they are symbols, variations on that most ancient and universal design, the mandala—the wheel of life, the closed and completed round, the squared circle, all the crosses, and all the stars. Dr. Jung informs us that they represent the state of perfection that every man and all mankind aspires to achieve, or, it may be, to impose on imperfect nature. Perhaps on the *aloalo* soul perch, they represent rungs in the ladder to the after-life. Stepping stones across a shallower Styx. No one has returned to earth from that journey, neither a Mahafaly of the Malagasy, nor a classic Greek of Humanism, nor a Catholic of the Middle Ages, nor the universal man of the Renaissance, nor an Encyclopedist of the Age of Reason, nor a Rationalist of the past century, nor a statistical man of today (except, perhaps, as ghosts); and so I was a fool to ask my question.

On top of the *aloalo* post stand recognizable carvings in the round— a zebu with a mighty hump and a tremendous spread of horns, the sign of Malagasy grandeur and glory; or a pair of birds, perhaps doves, the symbol of sexual potency and pleasure. On one I saw a more recent

334

finial status symbol—an airplane. It looked all right and, as a sort of Rosetta stone, provides a key to the older reassuring shapes of the essential, the absolute, the ultimate value of man's life on earth, proofs of his worth, in an everlasting scale of things.

There is another sort of *aloalo*, this one much more explicit, carved with obvious biographical scenes of the great moments in the life of the dead man, like ten or a dozen Rogers Groups, without the moralizing sentimentality, piled one on top of the other; or like glimpses of family life seen through the picture windows of a skyscraper apartment-house. Such a storied *aloalo* begins with the standing figure, but leaves out the mandala symbols, replacing them with the crises in the life of the dead man: his encounter with a crocodile on a river bank, his arm or leg held in the jaws of the grinning reptilian—a close escape from death; or his intervention in a battle between great-horned bulls; or a journey in a piragua in a stormy sea; or it may be a schoolroom scene in which he learns his ABCs; or the moment of crisis in an illness with either the witch-doctor or the French doctor caught in the act of driving out the evil spirit of the malady; or a carving in miniature of a fine dinner with friends seated at a table eating and drinking; or a time of lovemaking in great detail; or an obvious battle between the sexes—the woman never the inferior, nor the superior—the equal; or the carving might show the man at work as a soldier in the French Colonial Army, or as a postman making his rounds. Such *aloalo* have as finials either an old-fashioned status symbol, or an official portrait of the man—for instance, a noncommissioned officer in tropical uniform, a peaked cap on his head. I saw one elaborate and sophisticated tombsculpture, not an *aloalo*, of a modish Christian woman carved in the round, not quite life size, dressed in her best—high-heeled shoes, fashionable short-skirted frock, her hair neatly arranged, a handbag in her hand, a gold cross on a chain about her neck.

Thus perhaps the Mahafaly and the other "primitive" tribal sculptors can survive the arid transition out of the past and into the future; but perhaps not. There used to be carvings literally to burn—the French hacked them up for firewood. Pastor Mahatoto told me that the tax collector is stamping out the art by forcing the young men into permanent and more lucrative employment; the carving of funeral monuments to order is an uncertain trade; it requires a long apprenticeship. Death comes but once to the great; taxes now fall regularly in ordinary lives.

The best of the Malagasy work comes from the dark Bara ("Bar") tribe. No one knows the meaning of their name, but their sculpture in wood lies wholly within the instrument; it is achieved. To be sure, none of the Malagasy tribes has produced anything to equal the Ife portrait heads, the Benin bronzes and ivories, the Senufo masks, the Bamako antelopes, and the various African fetishes. Who knows why? I suspect it has to do with Madagascar's nature, an island apart, preserved under its bell jar, intact (or almost intact) in its *vase clos*, as the French like to say, removed from all the "regions" of the globe. But the Bara work is curious and whole.

This tribe of handsome, melanic nomads, among whom a young man, to prove and demonstrate his virility to his bride before he marries, must steal a head or two of cattle, live in the great spaces of the dry southern highlands. They are the athletes, the dancers, and the artists of the eighteen tribes. Their carvings are small and representational—individual figurines cut out of hardwood and stained with earth and vegetable dyes. The sculptor carves what he sees: he sees his neighbors; he sees himself. He peoples his world with solitaries, fighting men, athletes, dancers; farmers and herdsmen; the sorcerers, the witch-doctors; the women at their women's work; the old, the middle-aged, the young. I remember seeing no unearthly images, no idols, no totems, no fetishes, not a single anthropomorphic deity, and nothing at all abstract.

I bought several, as many as I could. They are hard today to lay hands on, for they make handy souvenirs and curios for the retiring functionaries. As a rule, there is nothing disturbing about them, nothing outrageous, nothing enormous, not a thing bewildering. The comfortable past-Pantheress of the Isalo, in her hotel in Ihosy, very kindly let me have the one I like best; it came from Iakora ("Ya-koor"), the center of the Bara land, and it was carved in the wet winter season when all the roads in the red country of rock crystal are cut by washouts and flash floods. Eight inches, perhaps ten inches over-all, it is the seated figure of a young man, knees drawn up, arms folded, wrapped up in his spotted dull red *lamba* out of which only his head emerges. His eyes are inlaid black and white, and his eyelashes are real hair set into the wood—the unique characteristic of Bara art. He looks pensive. He sits still looking out but looking in—into some sober happening remembered; the effect is of thought.

It is a real—that is to say, spontaneous—work of art, carved out of a block of wood because the sculptor felt like it, working for himself and others like him, even for strangers. It has a life of its own, a curiously still, quiet, and stoic life in which dignity is a consideration, but protest is not. Those long-lashed, inlaid, black and white eyes are wide open upon an enormous world. His own small, gathered-together dimensions place him in a huge and empty time and space over which he can exert little or no control, except, it may be, to cover up and keep warm in the bad weather, and sit it out—hang on until the climate changes.

Bara life long ago reached its high and dry plateau, and has, since then, gone on and on, essentially unchanged, each life a link in an endless chain; so his inlaid eyes are turned in upon himself. I think his thought must move in images; I know his tongue makes use of figures of speech; the Bara have no written words, no alphabet, and no history. They are inarticulate—they are the dancers, the athletes, the artists; and so I guess they receive the meaning of whatever world they live in through their senses. As English seems to lack a good, strong word to define the opposite of decadent, so we lack a way to define the present state of culture of this still intact tribe. It is not primitive, it is not classic, it is not sophisticated, yet something of all three meanings obtains. *Decadent* is one of those damned words, having its existence in the emotions of the beholder; it is a point of view. Who among us dares use it today? And what was Plato? What is Picasso? If vitality is implicit in the meaning, the Bara are on the increase; they are healthy. There is a fateful stillness in their sculpture: the inlaid eyes, the inset real-hair eyelashes are tricky, distracting, even trivial; but they look out contemplating what appears to me to be the inevitable.

I found a puzzling Bara sculpture in Tananarive, in the villa of an agèd, agèd man, a M. Pommier, an old Colonial French functionary well over eighty—he must have been ninety—returned to his belovèd island to end his days. He had tried retirement in his native France, but finding he could not do without Madagascar, after his wife had died, he returned to his mouldering house built into the rock of the

337

Tananarive high town in hanging gardens fronting an enormous view of the rice-grown plain and the purple hills with the bloom of plums upon them and those stupendous highland sunsets—the western sky ablaze over Mozambique. I had been invited to view his collection; my purpose was to buy, but his prices were too high. On a littered shelf I found a dusty Bara carving of two figures. I took them to be athletes wrestling, but they were not. These two naked young Bara men were sexually engaged.

"Ce sont des pédérastes," quavered the thin, the ancient, the skeletal, white-headed, far-retired Mr. Appletree, well covered up from tight-hooked round collar to his high laced boots in old-fashioned tan drill Colonial functionary summer uniform, tailored for a fuller man. *"C'est connu."* He had the male ghost of a disembodied voice, but he was mistaken. The two young Bara men carved in the round were full grown, of an age—the age, it is called, of discretion. They were in the act of exerting as much free choice and free will as any similarly occupied young men, poles apart.

A well washed, well looked-after, very clean old man, in his youth and in his prime—all of fifty years ago—old Mr. Appletree had collected everything that caught his eye, and had retained it. Now he was, himself, the masterpiece of his own collection. His house of life and of retirement was kept by his daughter, an old maiden lady, as well as she could with the help of old retainers; for they obviously had been ordered to keep their hands off the dusty, mellowing collection, disordered and discoloring on the shelves, on the tables—on top of everything, spun together by spiderwebs and by the old man's then inquiring mind. He had picked up something of whatever took his eye: *sagai* spears, knives, old blunderbuses and pistols, shields, basket-woven traps and snares, beaded talismans, crocodile-tooth amulets, musical instruments, tools and utensils, wrought-iron branching candlesticks and lamp holders, pots and vessels, carved and stained boxes and basins, raffia mats, all the tribal woven hats, carved Merina bed-boards, Mahafaly *aloalo* funeral posts, the Bara figurines (many more than the pair), Sakalava and Vezo sculptures, silver jewelry and adornments—many of those silver bangles, not quite closed circles, made from melted-down Second Empire and Third Republic five franc coins, and worn by the young men as, I gather, signs of virility.

He had shelves and shelves of mouldering cardboard filing boxes for documents. The walls of his house were mildewed, the stained paper hung loose in blisters and in tatters; perhaps he had built his house on a vein of water or a welling hillside spring.

In his collection, I came upon some of the figures carved to top the corner fenceposts on the graves of the Vezo kings, inland from Morondava ("Moo-roon-dav"), a shallow port in the middle of the dry west coast on the Mozambique Channel. The Vezo ("Vehz," the word means "Row!") are fishermen; they are tall, cheerful black men, big and muscular members of a distinct clan of the southern Sakalava tribe. I do not know how many Vezo there are, but not many. The Malagasy as a rule are not seafarers today, although it is surmised that there was a commerce between the island and the African east coast two hundred and fifty or so miles away—one way of accounting for the Negro blood and the Bantu words in the language of the Sakalava and the other coastal tribes, which is clearly Polynesian. There is, by the way, an excellent hotel in Morondava, clean, comfortable, and hospitable despite the lack of water, with first-rate French food, despite the fact that the road to Tananarive, by way of Antsirabé is cut and thus impassable for six months of the year in the bad season. Therefore, the lettuces and all fresh vegetables come in by air; it is too hot and dry for them to grow along the coast.

I went to Morondava on the advice of a blond, red-blooded Burgundian, who had begun his Colonial career in Madagascar as a tobacco planter for the *Régie française* on the Tsiribihina ("Tsee-ree-bean") River not far away. The Burgundian told me not to miss the carvings on the Vezo kings' tombs, but he did not describe them to me; nor did he tell me why he failed to make a go of the tobacco plantation. There is a connection; the connection is sexual. He had absented himself (so an old Irish-American priest allowed me to know) too often from his fields to make a personal study of the Malagasy girls of the various tribes—all eighteen, and their clans. He himself told me (and it surprised me) that the women of Madagascar as a general rule are dull in bed, even puritanical. To practice birth control upon them is an insult, it is an outrage, it is unspeakable; it is an unnatural, unthinkable abomination, nasty and sacrilegious, too.

I arrived in Morondava in time for lunch. I told the hotelkeeper—a thin and nervous Frenchman, a retired sergeant-major with stomach ulcers—that I hoped to hire a car to visit the Vezo kings' tombs, which I understood to lie at some distance inland, out of town. He was used to foreigners—the American and French geologists and oil prospectors often stopped at his hotel. They have not as of today discovered deposits of petroleum in any commercial quantities, although there are pitch springs in the neighborhood. But it struck me that there was something odd in the way he looked at me, for a space of a minute, perhaps two, before he answered by saying that I should require a jeep.

Then a sophisticated and distinguished Frenchman, grey-haired, humorous, and immaculate in bush jacket and shorts, sitting within earshot at the bar (I never saw him before or afterwards), spoke to ask in civilized and educated tones (he had a particle to his long name, and, as I later learned, was a successful tobacco planter living in a great house with his wife and eight children), if I had come all the way to Morondava just to see the Vezo tombs. I had just been through the spies-in-Ambler atmosphere once again, this time not in the frontier-bonanza uranium boom of Fort Dauphin, but in the stickier, murkier suspicion of Tuléar, the center of the petroleum prospectors. So I said yes, I had; and once again I turned into a curious specimen. I decided that there must be something peculiar about those Vezo tombs.

So there is. In the morning I scouted the town—a main street with regular side roads like a fish skeleton—and at last arranged with an Indian merchant to hire his Land Rover, with driver (a Malagasy). The Indian's twenty-five-year-old son decided to go along—he had never seen the tombs; he spoke excellent French. I bought a couple of bottles of Contrexéville mineral water, but did not take along a picnic hamper—that proved to be a mistake. We picked up a young Malagasy to act as guide; he had never seen the tombs, but he knew the general direction. We drove out of town, across the rough airfield, onto dusty woodroads, and through the scrubby brush as far as we could go. We parked under a mango tree in a native village of thatched huts on a river bank. We learned that we had a long way still to go; the Indian, a sophisticated, elegant young man, then gave up his plan to accompany me—but then changed his mind after he had talked to the villagers to ask the way. I did not ask him why. I was in a hurry to get going; it was already late in the morning and the sun was hot.

It got hotter. We waded two shallow rivers and covered a great deal of back country before we got there. The *brousse* here is a low growth of not very interesting trees, just high enough to shut out any view and to block whatever breeze was blowing off the Mozambique Channel; the dry, sandy, winding paths made every step a pulling up of one foot, and a sinking in of the other—hard work. But at last we got there.

From a distance, at first sight, the tombs were flimsy and trivial affairs, weathered, ill-kept enclosures, fenced in with wooden palings, plunked down on a great sand dune rising above the coastal plain. I was pleased to see that a few big trees grew out of the sand among the graves; I wanted to sit down, take off my shoes and rest my feet in the black shade. What was all the mystery about? We walked closer and got a closer look.

Each of the fence posts—some of which were sadly dilapidated and broken—terminated in a representational statuette carved in the round, detailed, distorted only in exaggeration, and sometimes painted. Most of the colors had faded, but one young man had bright blue balls, and the end of his erect penis (a third as long as he was tall) was red. He wore a *poilu's* uniform, unbuttoned, to be sure, but he was unmistakably a Malagasy. His virile member was ringed around with scar tissue, to add, the guide informed me, by way of the young Indian, to the friction and the pleasure—they don't do it nowadays, he said.

On other finials, two-figure groups, male and female, coupled variously. So it goes. Some were not human representations, but instead long-legged, long-beaked, wading birds—storks, maybe? All of the images were carved with great exuberance, joyously, from an attitude of observant, humorous approval. The eye and the hand of the woodcarver gave these wooden images of men a somewhat startled, yet wholly preoccupied expression; I found it understandable.

The wooden women, on the other hand, were totally given over to the primary sexual attribute of the female of the species—the breasts, it seemed, were devoted to the babies, not to grown men; and, there being no infants, no children, and no preadolescents anywhere in evidence on the Vezo fence posts, the mammary apparatus was not emphasized, although it was necessarily alluded to. The women waited ready to receive in attitudes of concentrated high seriousness, stark naked, no fooling. Only the men, one felt somehow, took the whole thing . . . how to say it? Standing up? They did not appear to abandon themselves to it, especially the more recent images of men who'd kept on their uniforms. To them it was a part of life, not all of life and death.

Not great works of plastic art, the sculptures on the tombs of the Vezo kings are remarkable. The word for them, in English, is obscene; it is hard to keep their description from being pornographic. I turned from them more puzzled than enlightened. What's going on in this folk art and this folklore? I thought of marble angels, draped urns, broken columns, and I got nowhere at all.

The Land Rover bogged down in a marshy place on the return journey, but after a late lunch I cleaned up and went to pay a visit to the Roman Catholic bishop of Morondava, an American French-Canadian from Providence, Rhode Island, and of the missionary order of Our Lady of La Salette. An authoritative and talkative man in his early sixties, he asked me what I was doing in that part of the world, and I heard myself ask him what the Vezo tomb sculpture was all about. Why not? If any man knew, he should have, for they fell in his parish, and death as well as burial lay in his province. His life work was to save souls, such as those of the Vezo; he should have known. The bishop did not answer me directly. He told me of an even more curious cemetery further up the coast near a town named Seven Trees; he suggested that I go see it, and told me how to get there.

I was to go that evening after dinner down to the beach to hire a dug-out, out-rigger canoe and two oarsmen (well, they used paddles, and the canoe had a sort of sail), to leave early the next morning. I did so. I saw a tall, dark-brown young man, an official—a guard or a patrolman, I gathered, for he had on a uniform, a dark blue shirt with a shoulder patch, and shorts. So I went up to him to ask for directions, and read—according to the lettering on his insignia—that he was a traffic policeman of Nassau County, New York. However, he could speak neither English nor French, so I must have been mistaken, or his old shirt lied.

Out of the Taboo Forest; Onto the Plateau of Learning

An old man came up to translate; and thus I hired the improbable cop's canoe, which turned out to be the real thing, a scooped-out log pointed at each end. I sat in the middle and was by no means comfortable. The bishop had assured me that I would be back well in time for lunch. I had had the foresight to buy a two-meter length of red and white striped awning cloth—I couldn't find a beach towel—and to take along another bottle of Contrexéville water. I wore swimming pants. The cop had stripped to a G-string, which is what the other oarsman wore. We spent eight hours—four going up the coast, four coming back. I never did get to see the graveyard or the carvings— they were another four hours up an estuary, or so we were told by the villagers along the coast. I came back red as a lobster, wrapped up in my striped awning. But the trip had been worthwhile—or so I told the bishop firmly. From time to time the traffic cop had put down his paddle and taken up his harpoon to catch a sea turtle swimming by (he missed); and a few sharks passed us, their fins cutting through the flat sea—one came back to investigate, not a very big shark so far as I could see.

That evening when I limped in (my feet were sunburned) to report to the bishop, he said that he was very sorry, he was much concerned, or so he declared. He said as much, but he never did make clear the significance of the sexually excited or copulating tomb fence-post finials. He did not have to explain the meaning of the wild goose chase.

It took me a great deal of digging in the books of the Bibliothèque Nationale, the British Museum, and the Library of Congress, and then a lot of lucky thinking about the nature of ancestral worship, to hit upon the obvious "explanation." Maybe the Malagasy erect "obscene" memorials to their dead because they want to. But most likely they do so to encourage procreation. In a land of people often sterilized by malaria and syphilis, killed off by plagues and conquests, with a low birth rate and a high incidence of infant mortality, a dying man's (or a dead man's, if you like) first thought must be to insure the comfort, the repose, and above all the continuity of his spiritual existence in the afterlife of the afterworld. A childless man has no future; if his line dies out, so does he, and so do all his forefathers along with him in a mass obliteration. For if life on earth is aimed at eternity, eternity is

343

anchored in life on earth. Therefore, it is prudent in the cult of the worship of ancestors to encourage the living to make love while they may. Little things like right and wrong, good and evil—all that morality—are subsidiary to the main idea; and that is to survive.

I bought none of these religious images, these icons in the round, these idols—call them fetishes—from Mr. Appletree's mildewed and cobwebby collection because I knew I would encounter trouble getting them through the customs of *les autres pays*, including my own. I am very sorry now that I did not do my best to smuggle in one (*"Il est bien monté,"* remarked the agèd man, the ghost of a chuckle in his frail and quavering voice), or two, a few, to serve as models now. For God's sake let us erect a phallic monument in the town square beside the war memorial to encourage us in our best efforts to stay alive on earth.

Back in the Taboo Forest, the Reverend Mr. Jean-Albert Mahatoto and I turned our backs on the tombs of the Mahafaly kings, into the side elevations of which great platforms had been set, in patterns of lighter and darker stones, squashed crosses, not the Christian kind. The transverse is longer than the upright; such crosses are not suitable for crucifixions, but they are crosses just the same. We walked away into the obdurate mazes of thorny, shadeless trees. I turned my head to get a last look through the tangle of branches and creepers; for the *aloalo* still puzzled me. "Soul perches"—what can they be? Perhaps the great, squared tomb platform is a sort of launching pad.

So musing, I did not watch where I was going and ran into a baobab. Farewell, my fat and comic friend, the Mother of the Forest of taboos. There was an old lady who lived in a comfortable old shoe; and she found herself in the familiar maternal predicament. What an astonishing message that nursery rhyme conveys.

We found the car untouched; I unlocked it, we got in; we drove back to Ampanihy. I often wish real people and real places had noncommital names. "A Plethora of Bats," indeed. On the way we passed a woven and thatched town labeled Gogogogo. I refuse to know its other meaning. I'll bet it is pronounced "Goo-goo-goog," but perhaps merely "Goo-goo," or even "Goog." A man ran out with his hat full of small hen's-eggs to give the pastor. He accepted them in the spirit with which they were offered—white magic, I guess, replacing black.

344

The eggs were eggshell white, marked by their passage through the all-purpose canal.

"Taboo is a taboo is a taboo," said I aloud.

"I beg pardon?" Pastor Jean-Albert Mahatoto stated courteously.

At last I found myself on the Horombé ("Oor-oom-bay"), a high plain south of Ihosy ("Ee-oosh" of the gusty sigh), but above the Thorny South of the Taboo Forest, and, ultimately, Tuléar at the end of the road. It is a high and blinding plain, a great level expanse, a waste in all directions as far as the eye can see, empty and luminous under the impenetrable dome of a glass-blue sky, as wide, as flat, as endless, as still, and as bleak as a plateau of learning. "So this is where I've got to," I said to myself. (It was O.K. to talk to myself, nobody else was nigh to call me crazy, unless I chose to do so myself.) I stopped the hired Ariane in that perfect late summer day at the end of January, and got out to stand upright on the highroad—a line as straight as a die, ruled in red pencil from there to here to there; it was the diameter of my circle, and I stood in the dead center of . . . elsewhere, on the spot. I know that the surface of the earth is curved, not flat at all; and I am told that the sky is not a dome, it is immaterial. But that's what the earth and the sky, all I'll ever know of them, looked like.

The Horombé is a high, dry, red and green desert at that season. The earth is as red and, underfoot, as hard as brick. Yet individual grass plants have separately got their roots down into it to grow at equidistant intervals together and apart. Each stands up straight, eight to ten inches tall; each is an entity, an individual close by; but in the distance, the grass plants merge to become collective grass. Well, we did it to ourselves by overindulgence in mass production; soon there will not be enough food for thought, let alone room to turn about in. I looked around me on the spot, and I realized that I had never before been alone in time and in space. So this is what it feels like to be a specimen of the American variety of a subdivision of the sole surviving species, *Homo sapiens,* of the once brave *Hominideae,* born by chance in New England (in other words, I felt alone and lonely); a sample among the *Gramineae* (there are now growing all over the earth more than 3,500 species of the grass family, including timothy, rye, sugar cane, and bamboo), I didn't have a blade of grass to hide behind. "Incommunicado," I said to myself, and walked carefully back to the car; well, I have a weak ankle left over from the war. I'd better watch my step; mankind is endemic to things as they are, not as they ought to be, on earth, his only natural habitat.

Suddenly, I wanted somebody to talk to—not necessarily to hold a conversation. But instead I read a book: in geological fact, the Horombé is a peneplain eroded by the violent shifting winds and rains of an earlier atmosphere, in which the action of the heat of the day and the chill of the night broke the crust of the earliest rocks on earth in explosions that no man heard. (Can a virus hear? No.) Apparently, in its first form, this high, dry, flat land was a rippled surface of narrow parallel crests and grooves; it is still zebraed and tiger-striped with cipoline, quartzites, and the various sorts of metamorphic gneiss banded in garnet, in hornblends, in asbestos, in graphite, and in mica. Over the years, these rocks have covered over with deposits of skeletal-lateric soil; it is red but not fertile. Just so.

I got out of the car to take another look around; I looked down at my feet and saw my shadow set at high noon. My belly informed me that it was time to eat. So I got back into the Ariane, started up, and set off to go thataway.

I am credulous enough to believe maps, but I have never read a guide book in my life that told me where I was going, or that prepared me for what I was going to find when I got there. Then it came to me like a bolt out of the blue (reference to Zeus, maybe?) that *all my life I have lived under a bell jar*, protected from reality by my own built-in limitations, and by the encircling taboos of my ancestors and of—damn the phrase!—my environmental conditioning. Upon that thought, I stuck my head out of the rolled-down window of the self-propelled—by an internal-combustion engine—Ariane (Who the hell was *she?* At this moment, I consult the encyclopedia and see that it is not a she but an ancient Persian province from which comes our much-abused word Aryan; and possibly so do I; means "noble" in Sanscrit, a dead language) to take another look at the great circular plateau on which I was served forth under a clear and luminous sky, as hard as a bell jar. So I ran off the road; but that did not matter, for off and on were just about the same. But the road is a surveyed and beaten track, and the rest is not; so I got back on it in line again, and was soon rewarded by arriving at Ranohiro ("Rah-noo-ear").

It is an important market town and an administrative post, but a very small village. It is dazzling to come upon because the plastered houses are painted white. At the central crossroads is a signpost pointing in the several directions, naming the various destinations, and adding the distances in kilometers. Tananarive is 708 k., or, according to that platinum meter bar kept in a vacuum in Paris, France, and my best calculations, 439.92996 miles away. That is as far as I had gone.

Ranohiro has one restaurant; so that was my choice of a place to eat. I was the only guest that day for lunch. The restaurateurs are a Frenchman and a French woman, colonists, man and wife in or past middle-age, with, as they informed me, grown sons—one in Tuléar in the trucking business, the other in his military service. The couple had come down to Madagascar on their honeymoon in 1924, and to stay to live. In the end, they settled for this place to eat. The wife set about preparing me a meal, while the husband sat and drank some more, and entertained me—and possibly himself. Yes, it was a lonely place, but they had their cats for company—Siamese cats, a family of three generations, seal points, clearly pedigreed, beautiful, regally independent, but, because of their isolation, dangerously inbred, ten or a dozen of them in three sizes. They looked at me coldly out of round blue eyes. One yawned most delicately, curling its pale pink tongue between its sharp white teeth; one yowled. A kitten abruptly lay down and died.

The wife remained behind her kitchen counter, busy with her hands, arranging the hors d'oeuvres. I remember my lunch in Ranohiro as an excellent meal, well chosen, well balanced, well cooked, well served on the plates, with a perfectly good rosé table-wine to drink. It was a French *déjeuner* at *midi*. But I forget just what it was I ate because of the husband's lamentations as he mourned his dead Siamese kitten. He made considerable commotion, although the Siamese cats did not— they behaved with the indifference that, I suppose, passes for dignity and self control. The thing that emerged from the man's grief was his abject failure as a man. It was so close to total that his wife had got used to it; at least, she paid him no mind. The dead kitten lay on the floor; the man slumped in his chair, all his virtue draining out of him. He poured himself a drink from the bottle of Calvados handy on the red-and-white checked tablecloth; it was a slug, not an aperient. I have never seen a man with so poor an opinion of himself.

He told me in a dismal tone of voice that Siamese cats are very difficult to raise; they have no stamina at all, they sicken easily—a draught will carry them off. He had sat up night after night nursing the last litter of consanguineous kittens, but they were dropping, one by one. It was not his fault, he had done his best. I have no doubt that he had; I am sure he had. I began to feel vaguely guilty, as though I'd brought in the fatal draught, or added the last straw to the overburdened nervous system stretched to breaking point. So I ate my good French food with all due respect, but did not linger. I paid for it, got up, and left. I was headed for the Isalo ("Ee-shall").

And what is this? The Isalo is a soft sandstone, sedimentary, and ill-cemented massif that transgresses the further Gondwanaland karoo; it stands on the edge of the Horombé peneplain. Its eroded peaks rise up to 4,000 or more feet above sea level, with declivities of six and seven hundred feet among the heights. Petrified trees lie where they fell in the Triassic forests where they grew in the Age of Reptiles— toppled, maybe, by an itchy dinosaur scratching in the secondary geological, or Mesozoic, period—and that was from 220,000,000 to 70,000,000 years ago. By now the wood has been replaced by agate, jasper, the various quartzes, and the other silicas and silicons.

But I am taking liberties again, and being fanciful, for none of the bones of the great reptiles has been found on Madagascar, none left footprints behind. Therefore, it is believed that the great island detached itself from what are now Africa and the Deccan before Triassic times. Thus forewarned, I took notice of a great deal of geology around me as I drove along. In fact, there was nothing but geology all over, much too much of it, to be seen to be believed. The Isalo is a landscape of total waste, an extravagance of nothing, a silent turbulence of jagged, red-brown, soft (as rocks go) stone mountains, concentrated, much reduced. There was no need to get out and kick a rock to refute Dr. Johnson; the Isalo exists only as a wild imagining.

The French, being nothing if not civilized, took a good look at this eroded massif, and described the separate bits and pieces altogether as *ruiniforme*—they have given the Isalo the shape of ruins, ruined castles, keeps, donjons, redoubts, fortresses, walled cities, and so on—but all ruined, man-made and man-razed. The French today are themselves much concerned with bastions and walls, and the ruins of the same. They see what they look to see, as who does not?

I saw a landscape such as Noah may have seen from his stranded arc; but I cannot say whether I looked on in hindsight or in foresight.

If, indeed, *"Après moi, le déluge!"* is not so much the cynical utterance of a Bourbon king riding the wave of the past to its breaking point, but is, instead, the last heartfelt cry against death and the *dernier cri* torn from the throat of each of us as we—or most of us—go down to die, there in the Isalo I saw what the idiotic and romantic protest means: no more than the epitaph for an age.

I parked and got out of the car to walk into the scenery. It was the obvious thing to do. I left the road and followed along through a sort of cleft in the rocks, and I came upon an oasis, a small one. There, growing in the pockets and patches of earth, I found a vegetable buffoon, a bloated, thorny pachypodium, not a foot tall, a shallow-rooted, prickly dwarf with a few skinny and misshapen branches twisting and writhing out of the top of it. Why were glandular human runts and genetic sports once considered to be comical and kept as pets by inbred Spanish kings and heavenly Chinese emperors? Velasquez painted them—kings, infantas, dwarf buffoons—for all time as no man ever will again paint anything anywhere. With his magnificent generosity and courtesy, he gave them humanity—it was his own, not theirs. He gave them dignity which they lacked, having only arrogance and touchiness. The Spanish Hapsburgs had removed themselves so far from the commonality that these royalties were confined to marrying among themselves, cousin to cousin, uncle to niece, but not brother to sister—that was taboo—until Charles II, a cousin germain to his mother, his father's great-nephew, and his own first cousin once removed, found that he was impotent and sterile, at the dead-end of the line.

The poor in China, calculating to assure the future of their boys and girls, made use of the environmental factor to put the soft-boned infants into porcelain moulds, where they grew into grotesque and fantastic shapes, thus to catch the emperor's eye, with or without new clothes. The freak and unique pachypodiums of the Isalo looked perfectly content to be themselves. So I walked back through the encroaching landscape, which only *looked* violent, and got into the untroubled automobile. I started up again.

I drove along until, ahead of me, I thought I saw the abrupt end of the road; it seemed to rise a bit between an up-and-down cliff and a jagged peak, and then to gather itself together in a straightaway for a leap off into empty space. The space was luminous. I went cautiously along, and found, as usual, that I had been mistaken; the narrow road turned to the right and twisted along a descending slope. But I stopped.

"Thus far and no further," I said aloud, and got out to walk up to the apparent end to see what I could see. I saw the Thorny South stretched out below me in a hazy prospect of shimmering dust and heat, a glaucous grey in color from the endemic flora that has grown in the same uniform shape and color out of the Dark Ages into the Light Years. This dry land was not wine-dark; it was not Homer's and Odysseus' scrotum-tightening sea; I backed away from the edge of the cliff. There was too much space under me. Homer was blind, if, indeed, Homer lived in the ninth century B.C. For a moment as I stood there, I knew what it was to be sightless. There was too much light, much too much. I looked into a coruscating emptiness ahead of me. A shudder rose up from where I stood, ran up my spine, and shook me. I looked away. I have not got the slightest notion of what will happen next in Madagascar, or elsewhere. But as I looked down at the earth under my feet, I saw growing in a drift of white sand beside the red road at the base of the abrupt rock cliff, on a shelf, on the edge of the declivity, in full sunlight, with no evidence of water anywhere, a solitary plant in full bloom, a small shrub growing flat out to the dirt. The stem is woody; the leaves are neat, dark, oval, glossy, and, I think, evergreen; the flowers are flat, round, single, and a shocking pink. It seemed to have a thrifty habit of growth on the 21st of January, 1959. I looked to find another, but did not. *Catharanthus lochnera* is its moniker in the Linnaean nomenclature *d'après* Karl von Linné, Swedish botanist.

Heureux qui comme Ulysse a fait un beau voyage.

BIBLIOGRAPHY

ALFRED GRANDIDIER (1836–1921), the French explorer and naturalist, is the authority on Madagascar. Together with his son, Guillaume, he compiled twenty-two volumes of the *Histoire naturelle, physique et politique de Madagascar;* nine volumes of a *Collection des ouvrages anciens concernant Madagascar* (both series published in the first twenty years of the twentieth century in Paris by the Imprimerie Nationale); as well as four volumes of *Ethnographie de Madagascar* (Paris: Société d'Éditions Géographique, Maritimes et Coloniales, 1908–1929); and more. It is a formidable life work.

I hunted for an adequate study of French Colonial policy and a history of the nineteenth-century French Colonial Empire, but found neither—a lack that is surprising and may be significant. Surely the *Mission Civilisatrice* and the *Présence Française* are worth close examination.

There seems to be no point in naming the standard references in English and in French, except the *Encyclopaedia Britannica,* and the encyclopedic dictionary for everybody and everything, the *Petit Larousse.* Nor can I cite all the newspapers of Madagascar, of France, of England, and of the United States in which I read the current events of the years from 1958 to 1962, except to say that I took the word of *The New York Times* and *Le Monde,* of Paris, as factual reporting. When I was twelve or so, which means, nearly forty years ago, I remember vividly reading about the man-eating trees of Madagascar in a Hearst paper Sunday supplement, illustrated by Nell Brinkley. I have not looked up the article. The victim feeding the tentacled tree was a nearly nude Ziegfeld-Follies-type beauty. I cannot imagine how she got there.

Bibliography

Sometimes, to be sure, I cannot or will not cite my sources for much of the political gossip and interpretation that I got for myself in Madagascar and in France. For example, the story of the bureaucratic confusion that enabled Dr. Joseph Raseta to leave France on his flight for home from exile came from an unquestionable authority, encountered by sheer chance in Normandy, on a stroll in the wet, green countryside. So I come to be an "authority" on Madagascar, too. As I wrote—this book is a piece of writing—I did what I chose with my facts, or conclusions, or beliefs, or educated guesses.

Among the periodicals, I used the *Bulletin de Madagascar, Publication Mensuelle du Service Général de l'Information du Haut Commissariat,* in Tananarive, as a primary source; and although its statistics sometimes vary in detail from month to month, the information contained in its pages is authoritative. The articles cover all phases of life in Madagascar.

Most, but not all, the facts about vanilla came from an article *"Une des grandes richesses de Madagascar, La Vanille";* the author, an *Ingénieur des Industries Agricoles de Douai et des Services Agricoles aux Colonies,* signed his last name only Josselin. The piece appeared in a short-lived glossy publication, *Entreprises et Produits de Madagascar, Revue trimestrielle, #9, Octobre, Novembre, Décembre, 1951;* Tananarive, Éditions *Tana-Journal.*

The information about the Rebellion of 1947, and Dr. Joseph Raseta, Prince Ravoahangy, and the poet Jacques Rabemananjara, in part, came from an article, *"Je Reviens de Madagascar,"* by Pierre de Chevigné, a former high commissioner of France in Madagascar, in *Les Annales—Conferencia—Revue Mensuelle des Lettres Françaises,* for February, 1951, of Paris.

The facts of Jean Laborde's life came from an article by J. Chauvin, *"Jean Laborde 1805–1878,"* in *Mémoires de l'Académie Malgache, fondée le 23 Janvier 1902 à Tananarive par M. le Gouverneur-Général Gallieni, Fasicule XXIX;* Tananarive: 1939.

William A. Hance, Associate Professor of Economic Geography, of Columbia University, is the author of a brief and factual study of the island, "Madagascar," in *Focus,* a publication of the American Geographical Society, Vol. VIII, No. 9; New York: May, 1958.

The Ambassade de France, Service de Press et d'Information, 972

Fifth Avenue, New York, N.Y., published in September, 1960, an admirable pamphlet, *The Malagasy Republic, hour of independence.*

There seems to be little use in citing interesting, but on the whole peripheral, articles and books, such as Baron Albert-François-Ildefonse D'Anthouard's *"L'Expédition de Madagascar, Journaux de route"; Revue de l'histoire des colonies françaises,* Paris: 1930; although it describes the French Community's exodus from Tananarive in 1895, just before the invasion. Nor do I include books like Thomas Cubbin's *Wreck of the Serica, the Wonderful Adventures of a Manxman;* London: Simpkin Marshall & Co., 1870. It is the account of a shipwreck on the shores of Madagascar during the time of the Merina monarchy, but all it contributed was atmosphere. Nor do I list the dubious journal of Robert Drury, *The Adventures of Robert Drury during Fifteen Years of Captivity in the Island of Madagascar,* first published in London in 1729, republished, London: T. Fisher Unwin, 1890. Robert Drury was a real man and an actual captive of the Sakalava tribe, but his journal may well have been ghost-written by Daniel Defoe.

The only proper guidebook to the island is *Le Guide Bleu: Madagascar, Comores, Réunion, Ile Maurice;* Paris: Hachette, 1955; it is, of course, out of date, but it is admirable.

ANNET, ARMAND, *Aux Heures Troublées de l'Afrique Française, 1939–1943;* Paris: Éditions du Conquistador, 1952.

BOITEAU, PIERRE, *Madagascar, Contribution à l'Histoire de la Nation Malgache;* Paris: Éditions Sociales, 1958.

BURGESS, ANDREW, *Zanahary in South Madagascar;* Minneapolis: The Board of Foreign Mission, 1932.

BURLEIGH, BENNET, *Two Campaigns, Madagascar and Ashantee;* London: T. Fisher Unwin, 1896.

COUSINS, W. E., *Madagascar of Today;* London: The Religious Tract Society, 1895.

CROFT-COOKE, RUPERT, *The Blood-Red Island;* London & New York: Staples Press, 1953.

DANDOUAU, A., and MANICACCI, M. JEAN, *Manuel de Géographie de Madagascar, à l'usage des écoles du territoire;* Paris: Éditions Larose, 1958.

DECARY, RAYMOND, *La Faune Malgache;* Paris: Payot, 1950.

———, *Moeurs et Coutumes des Malgaches;* Paris: Payot, 1951.

Bibliography

DESCHAMPS, HUBERT, *Madagascar, Comores, Terres Australes*; Paris: Éditions Berger-Levrault, 1951.

DuTOIT, ALEX. L., *Our Wandering Continents;* London & Edinburgh: Oliver & Boyd, 1937.

ELLIS, WILLIAM, *Three Visits to Madagascar during the Years 1853–1854–1856;* London: John Murray, 1858.

———, *Madagascar Revisited, describing the Events of a New Reign and the Revolution which Followed*; London: John Murray, 1867.

FLACOURT, ÉTIENNE DE, *Histoire de la Grande Ile de Madagascar*; Paris: 1658.

FOURY, B., *Maudave et la Colonisation de Madagascar;* Paris: Société de l'Histoire des Colonies et Librairie Larose, 1956.

GALLIENI, JOSEPH-SIMON, *Lettres de Madagascar, 1896–1905;* Paris: Société d'Éditions Géographiques, Maritimes et Coloniales, 1928.

———, *Gallieni Pacificateur*, edited with an Introduction by Hubert Deschamps and Paul Chauvet; Paris: Presses Universitaires de France, 1949.

GANDAR DOWER, K. C., *Into Madagascar;* London & New York: Penguin Books, 1943.

GHEUSI, P.-B., *Gallieni, 1849–1916*; Paris: Charpentier, 1922.

GOSSET, PIERRE ET RENÉE, *L'Afrique, les Africains*; Paris: Julliard, 1959.

GRANDIDIER, GUILLAUME, *Gallieni*; Paris: Plon, 1931.

HARDYMAN, J. T., *Madagascar on the Move;* London: The Livingstone Press, 1950.

HARRY, MYRIAM, *Routes Malgaches, le Sud de Madagascar;* Paris: Plon, 1943.

HOWE, SONIA E., *The Drama of Madagascar*; London: Methuen & Co., Ltd., 1938.

LENTONNET, LT. COL. JEAN LOUIS, *Carnet de Campagne, Expédition de Madagascar*; Paris: Plon, 1897.

LINTON, RALPH, *The Tree of Culture*; New York: Alfred A. Knopf, 1955.

LUETHY, HERBERT, *France Against Herself*; New York: Frederick A. Praeger, 1955.

MALOTET, ARTHUR, *Étienne de Flacourt ou Les Origines de la Colonisation Française à Madagascar*, Doctoral thesis; Paris: Ernest Leroux, 1898.

MALZAC, P., *Histoire du Royaume Hova depuis ses Origines jusqu'à la Fin*; Tananarive: 1912.

MANNONI, O., *Prospero and Caliban, the Psychology of Colonization*; New York: Frederick A. Praeger, 1956.

MOLET, LOUIS, *Le Bain Royal a Madagascar*; Tananarive: 1956.

PERRIER DE LA BATHIE, H., *Biogéographie des Plantes de Madagascar*; Paris: Éditions Géographiques, Maritimes et Coloniales, 1936.

PFEIFFER, IDA, *The Last Travels*; London: Routledge, 1861.

POLO, MARCO, *The Adventures of Marco Polo*, edited by Richard J. Walsh; New York: The John Day Company, 1948.

RABEMANANJARA, JACQUES, *Antsa*; Paris: Présence Africaine, 1956.

———, *Lamba*; Paris: Présence Africaine, 1956.

———, *Les Boutriers de l'Aurore*; Paris: Présence Africaine, 1957.

———, *Rites Millenaires*; Paris: Présence Africaine, 1955.

———, *Témoignage Malgache et Colonialisme*; Paris: Présence Africaine, 1956.

RABEMANANJARA, RAYMOND W., *Madagascar sous la Renovation Malgache*; Paris: 1953.

RAZAFY-ANDRIAMIHAINGO, MME. PIERRE, *Le "Rova" de Tananarive et le Palais de la Reine*; Tananarive: 1958.

ROBEQUAIN, CHARLES, *Madagascar et les Bases Dispersées de l'Union Française*; Paris: Presses Universitaires de France, 1958.

ROMIER, LUCIEN, *A History of France,* translated and completed by A. L. Rowse; New York: St Martin's Press, 1953.

SMITH, J. L. B., *The Search Beneath the Sea, the Story of the Coelacanth;* New York: Henry Holt & Co., 1956.

WILLIAMS, PHILIP, *Politics in Post-War France, Parties and the Constitution of the Fourth Republic;* New York: Longmans, Green & Co., 1955.

INDEX

Index

Index

Index

Index

Tiger shark, 60
Togo, West Africa, 135
Tombs, 329
  forest of, 329-336
  Vezo kings, 341-342
Touré, Sekou, 92
Tourmalines, 298
Tournée, Anna, 317-319, 321, 328
Trepangs, 119
Trial by ordeal, 173-180
Tsarantanana (mountain), 79
Tsiavondahy caste, 130
Tsimihety tribe, 85-86, 242, 273
Tsiomeko (Queen of Sakalava tribe),
  112, 113, 136
Tsiranana, Philibert, 86, 110, 272-
  273, 274-280
Tuléar, 258, 298

U.D.S.M.: *see* Union of Social Demo-
  crats of Madagascar (U.D.S.M.)
Uganda, 113, 135
Union des Démocrates Sociaux de
  Madagascar: *see* Union of Social
  Democrats of Madagascar
  (U.D.S.M.)
Union of Malagasy Intellectuals and
  University Graduates, 276
Union of Social Democrats of Mada-
  gascar (U.D.S.M.), 277, 278

Vanilla, 5-7, 44
  in Antalaha market, 33, 35-39
  Aztecs and, 7
  bean currency, 31
  Bourbon: *see* Bourbon vanilla
  development of, 7-8
  false orders for, 37-38
  history of, 66
  House of Palimore and, 60-66
  S. V. Mukra & Son and, 33, 36-37

Vanilla (*Continued*)
  1947-48 price war of, 57
  1957-58 price of, 55-56
  Ogilvy & Company and, 35-37
  planters and, 8-10
  production of, 8-9
  profit in, 8-9
  PTT and, 56, 58
  See also: Bourbon vanilla
Vanilla planifolia orchids, 7
Vazaha, 95
Vazimba tribe, 2-3, 127, 130
Vetiver, 51
Victoria (Queen of England), 198,
  199
Vilers, Charles–Marie Le Myre de,
  136, 142
Vorondolo (fetish), 173
V.V.S.: *see* Vy Vato Sakelika
  (V.V.S.)
Vy Vato Sakelika (V.V.S.), 263-264

Wake Island, 74
Weber, Father, 197
West Africa, 135
White Pigeon (ship), 305
White shark, 60
World War II, 71
  British and, 77-79, 80
  French bureaucrats during, 71-75
  Japanese and, 74-75, 256-257
  Madagascar and, 71-75, 77-79, 80,
    252-255
  Malagasy prisoners of, 251-252
Wright, Richard, 267

Zafimahova, Nobert, 277, 278, 279,
  280, 282
Zanahary, 172
Zanzibar, 135
Zaza-Hova caste, 130
Zebu beef, 17

368

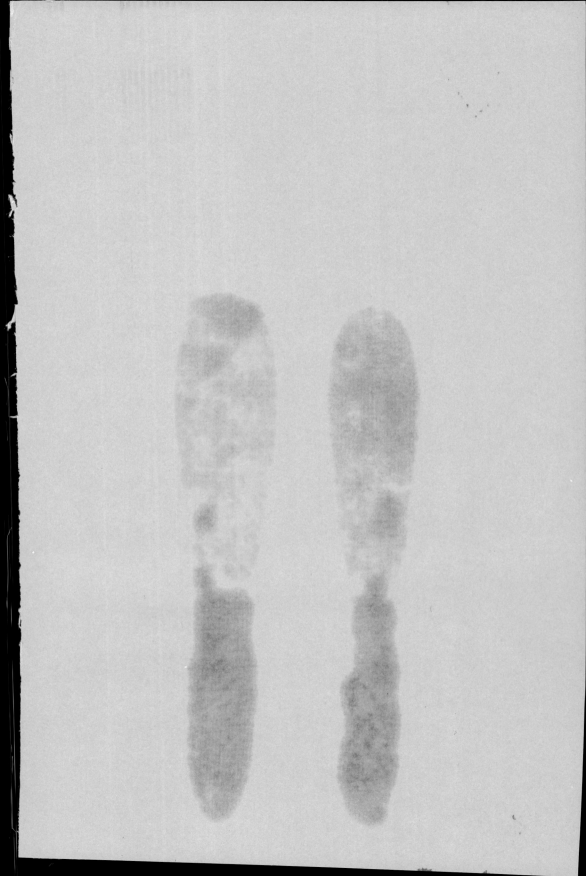